CW01671774

SUCCESSION OF THE PROPHET (PBUH)

Author
Aneela Sultan

First Self-published in the United Kindom 2007
Re-Edited in the United Kingdom 2010
Self-published Revised Second Edition 2014

Book Cover Design: Ruqayyah Nur Sultan

Printed and bound in UK by:
Think Ink
11-13 Philip Road
Ipswich
Suffolk
IP2 8BH

ISBN: 978-0-9556575-5-9

For any further details contact:
authentic_teachings@hotmail.com

بسم الله الرحمن الرحيم

IN THE NAME OF ALLAH
THE BENEFICENT, THE MERCIFUL

DEDICATION

I dedicate this book to my mother, my father, my siblings and all the mu'mineen that have helped me towards accomplishing it.

Contents

Succession of the Prophet (PBUH)

Foreword

Sayyid Fadhel Hosseini Milani

For centuries Muslims have discussed the succession of the Prophet Muḥammad (pbuh & hf).

Profoundly aware of the corrosive effect internecine discord over leadership would reek on the nascent Muslim *Ummah* after Muḥammad (pbuh & hf), Shī'ah Muslims believe Allāh guided the Prophet Muḥammad to appoint Imām Alī (AS) his successor. In order to stress that this was so, he announced it on many occasions in a variety of circumstances. However, there are some who believe that the Prophet left this matter for the debate and resolution of the people themselves.

Unbiased academic research of many scholars has led to hundreds of volumes being written on this subject. The arguments and debates between Shī'ah scholar Shaykh al-Mufīd (d.413 A.H) and contemporary Sunni scholars were amongst the first documented works on this subject. Later, protracted discussions between al-Allāmah al-Hillī (d.726 A.H) and Shaykh al-Islām ibn Ibn Taymīyyah, were recorded in the former's *Minhaj al-Karama* and the latter's *Minhaj al-Sunnah*.

Roughly a century ago the Lebanese Shī'ah scholar, Sayyid 'Abdul Ḥusayn Sharaf al-Din's discussions on this subject – with Sunni Shaykh al-Azhar – Salīm al-Bishri, were recorded in The Right Path – al-Muraja'āt. Although some questioned the credibility and authenticity of the sources listed in the work, published research has confirmed the discussions and verified the quoted references.

Ms Aneela Sultan's unbiased contemporary examination of sources of the Holy Prophet's (pbuh & hf) *Aḥadīth,* concludes that Imām Alī (AS) was the only qualified companion to have been appointed to succeed the Prophet Muḥammad. It follows that to follow the true teaching of Qur'ān and *Sunnah*; the interpretations of Imām Alī and the "Error-Free" Imāms (AS) have to be adopted.

This work was not undertaken to sow disunity amongst the Muslim *Ummah* but with the intention to create deeper awareness and understanding.

> Say: "This is my way, guided by inner-sight; I summon to Allāh all those who follow me." Qur'ān 12:108

Sayyid Fadhel Hosseini Milani
Head of Department of Jurisprudence
Islamic College for Advanced Studies
London
2005

Foreword

Shaykh Arif Abdul Hussein

This book is a study of the early texts concerned with the issue of succession following the demise of the blessed Prophet (pbuh & hf). Ms. Aneela Sultan born into a Sunni household takes her readers through her own deliberation around the matter, which ultimately resulted in her conversion to Shī'ah Islām.

The author in a very simple logical manner has arranged the chapters of this book in a way that the whole theme, which at first glance appears extremely complex, becomes manageable.

The references quoted within the book are largely from leading and mostly undisputed Sunni sources which the author herself had recourse to during her own years of research into the subject.

By far the most valuable feature of this work is in its simple rational analysis and interpretation of the historical texts within context of the texts themselves and through cross reference and comparison with other equally authoritative historical texts.

Reading through the work we find that Ms. Sultan has remained objective without an element of bias throughout her deliberations. She does not impose her own views or understanding upon the reader but simply quotes her arguments as were perceived by her during her own search for the truth. This is especially important since the book has been written with an aim to assist others in a similar position of seeking clarity with regard to the issue of succession. I feel this work given the richness of the references that the author has painstakingly provided together with her own insights clarifying certain ambiguities within the references, will equally be useful to students of early Islamic history and theology in general.

Ms. Aneela Sultan has been a part-time student at the al-Mahdi Institute and it gives us great pride to see her contributing in the way of learning. May Allāh be pleased with her and bless her! Amin!

Shaykh Arif Abdul Hussein
Al-Mahdi Institute
Birmingham

2007

Succession of the Prophet (PBUH)

Introduction.

I have grown up in a Sunni household, and followed the teachings of Islām given by my parents whom both are native to the north of Pakistan. They taught me Islām, taught me how to pray, and sent me to the mosque after school to learn the Qur'ān. My brother, three sisters and I use to sit with my father, and listen to his talks about the various prophets mentioned in the Qur'ān. We as children would always try to read some Qur'ān before we started school in the morning, and at that time I had no idea about the four Imāms of the Ahl al-Sunnah wa al-Jammāh (Imām Abū Ḥanīfah, Imām Mālik, Imām Shāfī' and Imām Aḥmad ibn Ḥanbal). I had heard of such companions of the Prophet (pbuh & hf) as Abū Bakr, Khālid ibn Walīd, 'Umar, 'Uthmān, Imām 'Alī (AS), the wife of the Prophet 'Ā'isha. If I had heard of the four Imāms, I would have discovered that they were considered very important authorities to follow and adhere to in regards to the teachings of the Qur'ān and the *Sunnah*, (the Prophet's words, his actions, and his silence) this being something, which came to my knowledge very much later on.

The environment I live in is not really multi-cultured, and the primary school I was taught in mainly consisted of western children; racism was always a problem for the very few Asian children who were within my school. As my father taught us Islām, our minds were very focused on the environment around us, my friends who were all English were much interested in the religion itself, they would come around to my house and learn how to perform ablution (how a Muslim washes his or herself before commencing prayer) and learn the Arabic alphabet, as this is what I was learning at that time. I remember telling them about Īsa (AS) (Jesus) and his recognition as a prophet amongst the Muslims in the same way my father taught. The teachings of the Qur'ān in regards to the prophets were what I only really knew about whilst growing up. As stated, I knew of such companions like Abū Bakr, 'Umar, 'Uthmān and Imām 'Alī (AS) only because of the brief reference my father would give in regards to them. I also had and still have small booklets on each one of them, which I never really took any interest in. Never in those days did I see any kind of problems within the Muslim community and the word Sunni or Shī'ah did not mean a great deal.

Introduction

I really did not know what the difference was between a Sunni or Shī'ah even up until my University years. I was very much focused on my study of Chemistry and Biology, which later helped me to understand Science and Islām and how Islām correlates with the scientific discoveries of today. Still within this moment in time, this subject is of high interest to me and will carry on being a subject, which I will further study and grasp, as knowledge is the key to answer those questions, which many of us want answered.

However, as I stated, the word Sunni or Shī'ah did not really signify a difference to me and that the various divisions, which had occurred within the Muslims corresponded with either of these words. My mind was always at ease with the religion as a whole. Nowadays such division has become more apparent and youngsters are constantly being reminded through the media of their Muslim identity, be they Sunni or Shī'ah, and both these words are mentioned a great deal more than when I was growing up. It has become a topic of discussion in many peoples lives be they Muslim or non-Muslim. However, in my own life, it became a topic of discussion more than a few years ago, at a time when my days were passing by with much contemplation on my religion. I felt that I needed to gain more knowledge in order that I could further progress in my understanding of Islām. I began to read further about the companions of the Prophet (pbuh & hf), and many of them started to take a great place in my heart because of their love for the religion and zeal for spreading the truth no matter what they faced. *Fadhāil e A'māl* (virtuous actions) was one of the books that gave me insight into many of the events that occurred within the lifetime of the Prophet.

As I have great respect for my father, I would speak to him about narrations in regards to the companions. I would state many things in regards to Abū Bakr such as, he was the first *Khalīfah* (caliph), he freed Bilāl, the slave, who later became the one who calls people to prayer, he pushed away Uqba ibn Mu'īt, who was about to strangle the Prophet (pbuh & hf) with a piece of cloth whilst he was praying, calling out "Would you kill a man for saying Allāh is my Lord?" he gave away all his possessions on the expedition to Tabūk.

My days were passing trying my best to uphold a righteous character from what lessons I was learning about those who came before our time. At that time, I had never heard of the words Ahl al-Bayt, and that they referred to the People of the House of the Prophet (pbuh & hf), and it was not even brought to my attention through what I was reading. This House, whom the Shī'ahs were acquainted with, was not projected to me at all.

It was when I had access to the World Wide Web that the Ahl al-Bayt came into my life. It was quite strange, because, although I had heard of Imām 'Alī (AS) and Sayyedah Sayyedah Fāṭimah (AS), I never had heard that they were of the Ahl al-Bayt. Whilst growing up, both Imām 'Alī and Fāṭima were seen in my eyes as children and that was the end of their story. Again, Fāṭimah being an individual who I had hardly heard anything about. All I knew about her was that she was the daughter of the Prophet (pbuh & hf).

It all started when I logged into a discussion forum and clicked onto a topic being discussed in regards to the succession of the Prophet (pbuh & hf). My mind was focused on Abū Bakr and many matters had been mentioned in regards to events, which had occurred upon the Prophet's demise. Such matters were not known to me and were never spoken of by anyone I knew. I read that division had occurred the very day the Prophet had passed away and prior to his demise, after the farewell pilgrimage, he had made a declaration towards the issue of succession in regards to Imām 'Alī (AS). I had never heard of such a declaration, which occurred at a place called al-Ghadīr, but only knew of a sermon that was given by the Prophet at Arafat. Such occurrences made me wander in regards to this subject. There was no possibility that I could ignore this matter and continue on with my life without investigating into it; because, I am the type of person who does not stop searching until I find an answer.

This led me to converse with both Sunnis and Shī'ahs. The Sunnis I conversed with were religious friends of the family. I was sent a book written by Ehsān ilahī Zahīr called al-Shī'ah wa al-Sunnah. I noticed that the book was full of things I had never come across against the Shī'ah and it really did not provide any intellectual reasoning towards the issue of succession as this was the issue I was focusing on. In that book and also what I heard from the Sunnis I was conversing with, was that the Shī'ahs lie, they have their own Qur'ān, which contains the verse of Wilāyah containing Imām 'Alī's (AS) name, they have their own books, which are not true, because they follow a Jew called 'Abdullāh ibn Sa'ba, and the references to Sunni books are not true. I was informed by Sunnis that the Prophet did not declare Imām 'Alī (AS) as his successor but Abū Bakr, he was the companion in the cave, he led the prayers before the Prophet passed away, and was made the *Amīr* (leader) on the recitation of *Sūrah* al-Tawbah (Chapter of Repentance). I was already acquainted with the event in regards to the companion in the cave, but was not familiar with his leading of the prayers and being made the *Amīr*. All these words did not satisfy me for the reason that the declaration at al-Ghadir continued to play on my mind, hence, I contacted a Shī'ah bookshop and enquired to them about this issue, and as a result, they sent me a few books to read.

The very first book I read in regards to this topic was al-Muraja'āt by Sayyid 'Abdul Ḥusayn Sharaf al-Din al-Mūsawi, which was a compilation of all the letters that were written due to discourses, which took place in 1913 between two scholars, one whom was Sharaf al-Din al-Mūsawi and the other Shaykh Salīm al-Bishri. Shaykh Salīm al-Bishri was the head of al-Azhar University in Egypt at that time, and he was a Sunni. This book was written with good etiquette and I did not at all feel that I should dissociate from it and wished to continue reading it.

It was the discussion of these two scholars that gave me further insight into the declaration at al-Ghadir and the differences, which had occurred within the *Ummah* (Muslim nation). Various narrations in regards to the Ahl al-Bayt also became known to me. However, I wished to look into the Sunni reference books myself, make it clear within my own mind, that what was being stated was a reality. I searched within books such as *Ṣaḥīḥ* al-Bukhārī, *Ṣaḥīḥ* Muslim, Sunan Abū Dawūd and Nasā'ī, *Jāmi' al-Ṣaḥīḥ* al-Tirmidhī, *Muwaṭṭā'* Imām Mālik, al-Tabarī's *Tārīkh*. I purchased Allāmah Shiblī Nu'manī's book, Umar al-Farūq and Imām Abū Ḥanīfah, Life and Works was given to me by my father, which is written by the same author. I found so many things being illuminated that Sharaf al-Din al-Mūsawi had stated, and thus many questions started to arise within my mind. Such questions as, how do I decipher, which *Aḥadīth* (plural - sayings of the Prophet) are teaching me the true words of the Prophet? How was it possible for the Muslims who were around the Prophet to have caused such a commotion and divide amongst one another, when what I had read in regards to them was so beautiful? Why were the Shī'ahs, who followed the Ahl al-Bayt, given such bad publicity? My mind, as one may say, was jumping cart-wheels. I prayed that I may receive guidance from Allāh for what was going through my mind. I then undertook extensive research on the topic, rationally looking at the references on this issue and using reason to elucidate the truth. Over a year had passed and Alhamdulillah, I accepted the authority of the Ahl al-Bayt, those to whom the Shī'ah Ithna 'Asheri adhere to, as they are regarded by them as the leaders of the *Ummah*.

Once my change came out into the open, it was very difficult for me to be able to address the issue of succession to my family and friends in the way I had experienced it. I wished for them to know the reason behind my change, but I was just not able to properly convey what I wished.

At the time of my change, I started working for a chemical company where the people were always intrigued about Islām and my passion for the religion as a whole. At that time, people had not really heard of the word Sunni and Shī'ah as is evident at this moment in time. I remember conversing with them about theology, about the divisions in religion and that even amongst the Christians such splits had occurred due to the reason of authority. Although the people were believers in God, if a prophet or a man of God came in succession of another, they rejected this authority, which left them to interpret the divine Book in the way they pleased, also causing them to split up amongst one another in regards to it. The Muslims were no different, divisions had occurred due to the reason of authority, the one who was to succeed being called the *Khalīfah* (caliph). It was actually at work in my dinner hour that I began to note things down on paper for my family; I would come home after work and type them up. These notes progressed into small articles and as time passed became more and more detailed, until I decided on writing a book. Time passed and my book began to progress even further. I began to get to know other Shī'ahs living within other areas of England, because, as I stated that my home town is not really multi-cultural, there was not really any Shī'ahs living close by to converse with.

My family, although at that time were shocked in my change, observed an increase in my devotion to the religion. My father, as like any father would be, was worried about what I believed in and would speak to me in regards to Imām Abū Ḥanīfah and the followers of the Ahl al-Sunnah. Maulana 'Ala Maududī being one follower whom my father holds in high esteem, whose books *Khilāfat Mulukīyat*, and *Tafhīm al-Qur'ān* (Towards Understanding the Qur'ān) he has.

The book I was given in regards to Imām Abū Ḥanīfah mentioned areas of Islamic law as taught by the four Imāms of Ahl al-Sunnah such as *Zakāt* (Islamic Tax), divorce, which the Sunni scholars now adhere to and teach, these teachings coming from the study of the texts that were narrated by various companions of the Prophet (pbuh & hf). I also read that Imām Aḥmad ibn Ḥanbal spoke against both Imām Abū Ḥanīfah and Imām Mālik because of acting upon opinion (*Ra'y*) rather than what was narrated. I thought of the Imāms of Ahl al-Bayt, their knowledge, wisdom and their close connection with one another and those that taught their knowledge to others, i.e. the Shī'ah scholars who studied the texts in relation to the Imāms. I did not agree that the followers of the Ahl al-Bayt had left the path of the Prophet and they were the ones who followed the path of dissension as the word *firqa* (division) was always directed to them. I understood that those who did not recognise the authority of the Ahl al-Bayt became known as Ahl al-Sunnah and those who did, Shī'ah, and so the word *firqa* could not have been placed only upon the Shī'ah.

I am aware that there are brothers and sisters at this moment in time who can relate to this and my sentiments go out to them, and I feel that this book will also provide support to them. I can understand how they may be feeling; because at the beginning of my change, I felt emotional towards those I love not being in reach of what I knew. This did use to lead me to cry due to my frustration of not being able to tell them everything in the way I wished, and asking for patience from Allāh, because I knew my family were only worried about me and loved me and still love me to this very day regardless, love being a word which we all should use most highly in connection with Allāh.

It is very important for us to remain close to our families and help them however much we can, as this is part of Islām, and it is through this goodness that we remain close to one another. I have always been close to my family, and I still am, and I firmly believe, because of this close attachment, they have grown to respect my devotion to the teachings of the Ahl al-Bayt. When observing what duas (supplications) I read, they have learnt that these duas have been taught by the Imāms, which truly amaze them. Alhamdulillah, my sisters take interest in the supplications, Dua e Tawassul and Dua e

Kumayl. On the *Mīlād* (birth date) and *Wafāt* (death date) of the Imāms of Ahl al-Bayt, they also wish to recite the *Ziārahs* (salutations sent upon beloved ones of Allāh) in connection to the Imāms just as I do, something that they have grown to understand through what I have stated to them in regards to the *Durūd/Salawāt*, which is the sending of peace and blessings upon the Prophet (pbuh &hf) and his *Āli* (family). Sunnis also recite a certain *Durūd* on special occasions called *Durūd Tūnajjīna,* one such occasion being when a new house is purchased. Allāh recognises that individuals wish blessings to be sent upon the Prophet and his family through their reciting of *Durūd*; and through this, also wish for their needs to be fulfilled. We do not realise, that when we are reciting the *Durūd*, we are automatically proving the close connection of these people with Allāh, and what I mean by this is their love and devotion to Him. I have realised that there cannot be any other persons whom I know to be closer to Allāh than them (Prophet and his *Āli*) and understand now the importance of it in our daily prayers and why it is beneficial to recite *Durūd* before any dua. This dua could be for us or anyone else.

In my household, the names of the Imāms of Ahl al-Bayt are mentioned now, something that never would have come into fruition, if I had remained the way I was. There is an awareness of, for example, Imām Ja'far as-Sādiq's (AS) scientific knowledge, Imām Ali's (AS) wisdom, and Imām Zayn al-Abidīns (AS) worship.

It would be beneficial to mention that there is a book that has remained in the hands of the Shī'ah called Sahīfah Sajjadīyyah, which is a collection of duas recited by Imām Zayn al-Abidīn (AS), the fourth Imām of the Ahl al-Bayt. This is a book of such eloquence that it cannot be deserted; there is ample proof in it, that such words could not have been narrated by ordinary scholars. This book also provides an insight into how much truth actually lies in the hands of the Shī'ah that many Muslims are being denied access to, due to the widely spread misconceptions against them. I state this because it is sad, that even though we are Muslims, we are accepting statements that are being propagated without truly investigating into them first. It is very important for us to first look into matters before taking them on board.

Moving onto the books structure, it has been written in an easy and simple manner in order that any individual will find ease in reading it.

Introduction

What one will notice is that I have not referred to myself as "I" throughout the book, but my speaking is revealed through the logical viewpoints and questions, which I address to the reader. What the reader will notice is that I may have stated points within a certain section of the book that later on will relate with another section. Also, one will find that the abbreviated words "pbuh & hf" have been restricted in a single paragraph throughout the course of the book to denote "Peace be upon him and his Family". The same applies to (AS) which denotes Alayhi-s-Salām in Arabic meaning "Upon whom be Peace". The reference of "pbuh & hf" is only made to Prophet Muḥammad whereas (AS) has been referred to the other prophets of God and the Ahl al-Bayt.

Finally, I believe that I am not a harsh person and when writing this book I had no intention of addressing matters in a harsh or aggressive way. But if I have upset or offended any of my Muslim brothers or sisters in any way, I seek forgiveness from Almighty Allāh, as this was not my intention when writing this book. I am an individual who gets along with most people, who loves to talk to people from all walks of life, be they Muslim or non-Muslim. I do not wish to spread disunity amongst the masses; I love my Muslim brothers and sisters and I was once a follower of those whom the majority adhere to also. Never in my life have I hated other Muslims in such a way as to clog up inside and force myself to keep away from them. This is irrational behaviour, which we have not even adopted amongst the non-Muslims we live amongst, who do not believe in the Prophet-hood of Muḥammad (pbuh & hf); because we as Muslims know that this is unacceptable behaviour.

My relations with the Sunni community and my family will always remain. May we all continue to develop good relations with one another and try our utmost to bring out the authentic teachings of Islām on every issue, as this is an important duty for us all.

I pray that matters, which I have had difficulty in addressing, are made sense of, and I pray that this book truly helps in understanding the reasons why the Shī'ah Ithna 'Asheri adhere to the Ahl al-Bayt.

Amin

Succession of the Prophet (PBUH)

Note - Sources of Reference.

Although what I will mention in this book has been reported within Shī'ah sources of reference, I have strictly taken the references from Sunni sources, as this is what I had looked into. In places I have referred to Shī'ah references in order that the reader is able to observe what the Shī'ahs read in regards to the teachings of the Imāms.

One may be an individual who expects all references to have been taken from *Ṣaḥīḥ al-Bukhārī*, as many of us have taken the notion, that if it is not stated in this book, we do not need to know about it, a concept, which I also had stamped in my mind. This book contains references not only from al-Bukhārī, but also from many other Sunni scholars of *Ḥadīth* such as Imām al-Ḥākim al-Naysābūri, Imām Muslim, Tirmidhī, Nasā'ī, Ibn Mājah, Imām Aḥmad ibn Ḥanbal, Ibn Qutaybah, al-Ṭabarī, Ibn Ḥajar al-'Asqalānī, Ibn Ḥajar al-Haythamī, Ibn al-Athīr, Ṭabarānī, and others. I have received various emails on various issues, which contain narrations from these very people but yet when the subject of succession is raised, narrations from these very *Ḥadīth* (singular - saying of the Prophet (pbuh & hf) scholars are refuted. This is totally unreasonable, and has no basis to claim for disapproval. My approach on this matter is based on logical and rational analysis, and it is this that provides the reader with the reasons of my acceptance of the Ahl al-Bayt.

Succession of the Prophet (PBUH)

Section 1

The law of Allāh and the want of Man.

Every human being has been given a free will; it is the choice of every individual to either follow a law as it has been prescribed or to follow whatever one wishes.

As Muslims, we believe that Allāh created the Heavens and the Earth sent His laws to the prophets by way of divine revelation to convey it to the people. The prophets taught mankind the correct way in order to live life in accordance to the law.

> "Lo! We have shown man the way be he grateful or ungrateful." Qur'ān 76:3

We wish to live in accordance with the dictates of Islām and understand that such a law has been developed and instituted from the very beginning of creation through the creator. Its progress within this day and age being understood by various people who accept that Allāh's method can never be inferior to the human beings as He is above all creation. His order perfectly established and His wisdom being far beyond the human beings.

Many of us will agree that a management that is primarily focused on the gaining of capital will not totally base its principles on traits that elevate the inner consciousness. Dishonesty, squandering of wealth, being acquisitive predominating in such spheres as opposed to honesty, generosity and selflessness needed within a just and moral society. We could state that this mind set of a continuum of richness and pleasure is deteriorating it from gaining spiritual knowledge and thinking about the meaning of existence and the hereafter.

We are observing that society is becoming increasingly engrossed in this power hungry manner, deteriorating true ethics, which is very much needed by it, something of which the law of Allāh calls one to, calls man to the true nature of his existence. We are far too involved in being power hungry to realise our inner being and that one day we will meet our end leaving behind all that we have accumulated.

The law of Allāh and the want of Man.

It would be beneficial to state here the following words of the Prophet (pbuh & hf).

> Narrated 'Abdullāh ibn Mas'ūd, the Prophet of Allāh said: "'Islām began as something strange, and it will revert to it being strange as it was at the beginning, so good tidings for the strangers.' Someone asked: 'Who are the strangers?' He said: 'The ones who break away from their people (literally tribes) for the sake of Islām.'"[2]

We may state we follow Islām as a way of life but we have to accept that our minds are being diverted away. When we use the word freedom, yes, we are free to follow whatever we wish, but no matter what we follow, if we break a law, even it is the law of the land, we could be penalised for it and could also end up in prison. Hence as Charles Kingsley states (1819-1875):

> "There are two freedoms - the false, where a man is free to do what he likes; the true, where he is free to do what he ought."[1]

As Muslims, we believe in Allāh's system of government, which allows us comfort; it allows one to be content in life as Allāh wants the best for His faithful servants. He wishes us to earn and live happily within our communities, He wishes us to live lawfully, marry and live in peace and harmony, but He does not favour those who start to behave in a way which is destructive towards themselves and others. Those whose minds become solely focused only on their life in this world and on material gain, those who become greedy and selfish, those who cause oppression, those who start to treat people unreasonably and differentiate between people unjustly, favouring the rich over the poor, the young over the old, the Whiteman over the Blackman.

Prophets who came to warn and teach people were commanded to judge matters with truth and justice.

> "O David! Verily We have placed you as a vicegerent on the earth, so judge between men with truth and

> justice, and follow not your desires, for they will mislead you from the path of Allāh." Qur'ān 38:26

Hence the law of Allāh was not brought to harm mankind, it was brought to protect, to discipline, to teach righteousness. We understand that it was not conveyed to be ignored and if one was to follow other than it, it would be tantamount to rejecting the prophets of God and rejecting what they followed and adhered to.

It is accepted by many that past records indicate that people rejected the prophets who were sent to them and those who would come after them. Many of these people marked as being of the elite and from the ones in authority. If we take Pharaoh as an example, do we understand why Pharaoh rejected Mūsa (AS)? Was it not due to his power and glory, which he could never denounce? Was it not due to his position as the leader, his want of continuing to do whatever he wished, his want of keeping his own dominion alive? This made him resist what Mūsa had addressed to him.

As Muslims we must recognise that religious governance began from the very onset of creation. When our prophets came with the word of God, they were opposed and rejected; they were ridiculed and mercilessly tortured. They faced the toughest of tests but they continued with their struggle in propagating the message of the oneness of God and His existence. Their opposition and rejection from the people never caused them to denounce what they were informed to convey. We are taught this throughout history; we are taught that there have always been people who have always wished to adhere to the law of Allāh and accept His decree, and there have always been those who have stood in opposition to it.

Succession of the Prophet (PBUH)

Section 2

Al-Qadar (Allāh's Decree).

Although the subject of *al-Qadar* is a fundamental aspect of our religion, it has been briefly touched upon in order to relate it towards the discussion on the succession of the Prophet (pbuh & hf).

As Shī'ahs recognise succession to be a matter of divine instruction, they state that it can be understood through understanding Allāh's attributes, which hopefully will come to light through the proceeding words within this section.

However, we first need to touch upon whether or not a decree of Allāh can be disputed. Most Muslims are aware that when Allāh has decreed something we cannot dispute it, it's His choice and this decree whether accepted or not can never alter it. For example, prophets who were given this position by Allāh regardless of whether or not human beings had accepted them remained as His prophets. Shī'ahs state that the successors of the Prophet (pbuh & hf) have also been decreed by Allāh and regardless of whether or not a human being accepts them; they will remain as His appointed successors.

Speaking on the topic of succession and its discussion, what we find is that because of the differences, which occurred within the Muslims after the demise of the Prophet (pbuh & hf), some people tend to state that throughout Islamic history what wrong occurred there is no point in discussing it now. Some imply that this is what Allāh decreed and are attributing the actions of the human being to come from Allāh. The seventh Imām of the Ahl al-Bayt, Mūsa al-Kāzim (AS) refutes such a claim in the following way. He states that there are three possibilities:

Either Allāh forces man to do his actions.
Or, both Allāh and man are responsible.
Or, man does them alone, out of his own free will.

The Imām explains:

If the first is true then man should not be judged on the Day of Judgement and sent to Heaven or Hell, because he would not deserve that. He had not been responsible for his actions. This is not the case.

If the second is true that both Allāh and man should be judged on the Day of Judgement. This also does not make sense.

This leaves only one possibility. The true position is the third one, because man has been given a free will after receiving guidance about what is right and wrong.

Imām 'Alī (AS) stated:

> "Woe to you. You take it as a final and unavoidable destiny (according to which we are bound to act). If it were so, there would have been no question of reward or chastisement and there would have been no sense in Allāh's promises or warnings. (On the other hand) Allāh, the Glorified, has ordered His people to act by free will and has cautioned them and refrained them (from evil). He has placed easy obligations on them and has not put heavy obligations. He gives them much (reward) in return for little (action). He is disobeyed, not because He is overpowered. He is obeyed but not under force. He did not send down prophets just for fun. He did not send down the Book for the people without purpose. He did not create the skies, the earth and all that is in between them in vain. That is the imagination of those who disbelieve; then woe unto those who disbelieve — because of the fire."[3] (Qur'ān 38:27)

Hence to claim that what took place in the history of Islām, in regards to the succession of the Holy Prophet (pbuh & hf) was decreed by Allāh is exactly to hold Him responsible for the actions of others consciously and unconsciously and to deem Him to be unjust against His creation.

Succession of the Prophet (PBUH)

The Divine *Lutf* (Grace) of Allāh.

Again, the divine *lutf* of Allāh has been briefly touched upon in order for us to be able to understand it in relation to the subject of succession.

Sh'iahs recognise that Allāh has provided His creation with everything, which is required to guide the individual to the right cause. Without this provision, Allāh's servants will not be able to fully fulfil their duty towards Him, and it will cause them to lag behind. Allāh cannot execute injustice upon His creation and not provide mankind with all the things necessary in order to be able to carry out everything correctly in obedience to Him. As this attribute of justice is what we know Allāh as, His order works towards this justice and provides the necessary pathway to prevent wrong.

We as Muslims should be able to comprehend that Allāh does not wish for His creation to go through difficulty in deciphering His words, hence He provides mankind with chosen representatives in order that they are not swerved away from the true cause; this is His mercy, His *lutf* on His creation, no man has an excuse not to be able to follow His word and follow that which will keep him aright when Allāh has provided him with all things essential for this, and it is man himself who then chooses which path he wishes to take and Allāh in no way leads His creation astray.

When man does wrong and Allāh punishes man for it, it is not Allāh who caused the wrong to occur, because through His mercy He has already provided us with its route to prevention.

When Allāh is all Merciful, His mercy is greater than all of mankind, when Allāh is all Just, His justice far outspreads the justice of the human being, the human being can never over ride His Creator. An individual's need is provided through the fruits of the Creator, the Creator knows what is of benefit for His creation and what is destructive for it. It is mans choice to adhere to that provision or take a route other than it and this is where His creation becomes divided and disobedient, far away from Allāh's grace sending man into harm and sedition. No doubt Allāh gives grace to His creation and it is man himself who does not recognise it.

The Divine *Lutf* (Grace) of Allāh

We need to reflect and consider that on the demise of the Prophet (pbuh and hf), did the issue of succession need to be looked after in order that the Muslims remained on the one right path? Was this issue looked after by Allāh as a divine *lutf* upon His servants in order that they would not become divided?

Succession of the Prophet (PBUH)

Section 3

The *Khalīfah* of Allāh.

Allāh has used the word *Khalīfah* (representative, vicegerent, caliph) for the very first creation of mankind, which we can find in the Qur'ān.

> "Behold thy Lord said to the angels: 'I will create a *Khalīfah* on earth.' They said: 'Wilt thou place therein one who will make mischief therein and shed blood? Whilst we do celebrate Thy praises and glorify Thy Holy (name)?' He said: 'I know what ye know not.'" Qur'ān 2:30

The above verse references Ādam (AS) who is addressed by Allāh to the angels as a *Khalīfah* who will be placed on earth, although we all primarily recognise him as a prophet.

It has been explained in both Shī'ah and Sunni *Tafasīr* (commentaries) of the Qur'ān, that the angels had doubts about this creation, which Allāh was going to fashion, the various traits and disposition this creation would have, it not being free from want of matter, it not being free from emotion and desire, it being a creature of the earth, which would have to face varying hardships and calamities within its terrain, causing it to lose its good sense and foresight of existence and the law of Allāh. The angels who had no desire or want, who beforehand followed their Lord and glorified His name, could not understand why this earthly creature, which was capable of such mishaps, would be given the vicegerency on earth.

'Abdullāh Yūsuf 'Alī, in his *Tafsīr* (commentary) of the Qur'ān, stated in regards to the angels response to Allāh:

> "It would seem that the angels, though holy and pure, and endued with power from God, yet represented only one side of creation. We may imagine them without passion or emotion, of which the highest flower is love. If man was to be endued with emotions, those emotions would lead him to the highest and drag him to the lowest. The power of

> will or choosing would have to go with them, in order that man might steer his own bark. This power of will (when used aright) gave him to some extent mastery over his own fortunes and over nature, thus bringing him nearer to the God-like nature, which has supreme mastery and will. We may suppose the angels had no independent wills of their own; their perfection in other ways reflected God's perfection but could not raise them to the dignity of vicegerency. The perfect vicegerent is he who has the power of initiative himself, but whose independent action always reflects perfectly the will of his principal. The distinction is expressed by Shakespeare (Sonnet 94) in those fine lines: 'They are the lords and owners of their faces. Others but stewards of their excellence.' The angels in their one-sidedness saw only the mischief consequent on the misuse of the emotional nature by man; perhaps they also, being without emotions, did not understand the whole of God's nature, which gives and asks for love."

Allāmah Tabataba'ī who is a Shī'ah scholar renowned for his work on *Tafsīr* stated:

> "The angels heard the announcement: 'I am going to make in the earth a vicegerent', and at once arrived at the conclusion that the would-be vicegerent would make mischief in the earth and shed blood. Apparently they understood the ultimate behaviour of the said vicegerent from the words, 'in the earth.' A vicegerent appointed in the earth would certainly be created from material components; he would necessarily be bestowed with two basic traits of desire and anger; the earth is a place of unceasing struggle and constant confrontation; its resources are limited, its opportunities finite; but the proposed vicegerent's desire would be unlimited, infinite. The condition of the earth and earthly things was hardly reassuring. Its creatures were subjected to ever-continuing deterioration and disintegration; its good

was always turning into bad; it was a place where an individual could not live without a group having similar characteristics and traits. Keeping all this in view, the angels at once understood that what Allah intended to create was not only an individual, but a species. The members of that species would have to live together, cooperating with one another; that is to say, they would have to establish a society, a social order. And with a venture like this, they were bound to cause mischief and to shed blood.

On the other hand, they knew that vicegerency - setting one thing in place of another - was unthinkable unless the vicegerent was a true copy of his predecessor in all the characteristics, traits and intrinsic abilities. The proposed earthly creature was to be made vicegerent of Allāh in the earth. Allāh has got for Himself the best names, the sublime attributes; His mercy and power are beyond the comprehension of His creatures; He, in His person, is untouched by any defect; and, in His actions is free from all kinds of evil and disorder. How could an earthly vicegerent, with all his defects and deficiencies, represent the majesty and splendour of Allāh in the earth? Well, could a lowly creature of earth be a mirror of divine beauty and sublimity?

This was their question - and it was no more than a question. It was not a protest, not an objection; they actually wanted to know the truth. They later asserted their belief that Allāh was the Knowing, the Wise. They believed that what Allāh intended to do was based on knowledge and wisdom; and their question was put in order to learn the underlying wisdom of the decision of Allāh."[4]

Man would be given all these traits but controlling them within the limits set by Allāh, was something of a great task, which would place him on a high rank with His Lord. A representative of this type was very different to the angels who obeyed every command, who were not in want of anything. They then understood that it is Allāh who had the supreme knowledge in regards to His divine decree; this can be observed within the proceeding verses of the Qur'ān, which are not part of the discussion at hand. Should one wish to pursue the topic of the proceeding verses, one can do so at ones own pace.

Allāh is greatest in wisdom and places whom He wills as His representatives on earth as He is acquainted with what others are not. Certainly the knowledge which was given to Ādam (AS) was not given to the angels, this knowledge gave him the distinction as the vicegerant of Allāh, who would not dampen the word of Allāh but extol it, praise it and keep His word in tact, as would those who were to come after him. All the different traits of the human being would be within them, but because of their knowledge and closeness to Allāh, it would keep them aloof from the mischief, which the angels were addressing.

> "O David! We indeed make thee a *Khalīfah* on the earth, **so judge thou between men in truth (and justice), nor follow thou the lusts (of thy heart),** for those who wander astray from the path of Allāh is a penalty grievous for that they forget the day of account." Qur'ān 38:26

If an individual was to follow the lusts of his heart and break the boundaries set within the religious code of conduct, he would swerve away from the truth and such an individual could not be given the title *Khalīfah* as the Qur' ān clearly teaches.

No Muslim denies the word *Khalīfah*, and if the word was stated in this day and age, it would automatically be recognised as a word connected to the leadership of one or another person, and especially recognised towards those who took up leadership positions after the demise of the Prophet (pbuh & hf).

It is the Prophet (pbuh & hf) who taught us that there would be *Khulafah* (caliphs) after him, and if we were to understand this word through the teachings of the Qur'ān, in regards to the men of God, we could state that those the Prophet spoke of also could not represent anything contrary to truth and justice. This can also be illustrated and brought to our attention through a *Ḥadīth* of the Prophet in regards to our final leader Imām Mahdī (AS).

> It was narrated that Abdullah said: "While we were with the Messenger of Allāh some youngsters from Banū Hāshim came along, when the Prophet saw them, his eyes filled with tears and his colour changed. I said: 'We still see something in your face that we do not like (to see).' He said: 'We are members of a Household for whom Allāh has chosen the Hereafter over this world. The people of my Household (*Ahla Baytī*) will face calamity, expulsion and exile after I am gone, until some people will come from the east carrying black banners. They will ask for something good but will not be given it. Then they will fight and will be victorious, then they will be given what they wanted, but they wil not accept it until they pass it to a man from my Household (*Ahlī Baytī)* to fill the earth with justice as it has been filled with injustice. So whoever lives to see that ought to come to them even if he has to crawl over snow.'"

> It was narrated from Thawban that the Messenger of Allāh said: "Three will fight one another for your treasure, each one of them the son of a caliph, but none of them will gain it. Then the black banners will come from the east, and they will kill you in an unprecedented manner." Then he mentioned something that I do not remember, then he said: "When you see him, then pledge your allegiance to him even if you have to crawl over the snow, for that is the *Khalīfatullāh* al-Mahdi."[5]

What can also be brought to our attention through the stated narration is that a *Khalīfah* does not necessarily have to be a prophet.

It is stated in the Qur'ān:

> "**Allāh has promised those of you** who believe and work righteous deeds that He will surely make them

> *Khalīfah* in the earth as He made *Khalīfah* of those before them." Qur'ān 24:55

Plus, in *Ṣaḥīḥ* al-Bukhārī, it is stated in the Book of Judgements, *Ahkām*, Vol. 9, Book 89, Number 306:

> Narrated Abū Sa'īd al-Khudrī, the Prophet said: "Alllāh never sends a prophet or **gives the caliphate to a caliph** but that he (the prophet or the caliph) has two groups of advisors. A group advising him to do good and exhorts him to do it, and the other group advising him to do evil and exhorts him to do it. But the protected person (against such evil advisors) is the one protected by Allāh."

We are taught both through the Qur'ān and *Aḥadīth* that those who came before were given the position of *Khalīfah* through Allāh and Allāh promised that those who showed faith in Him and worked towards righteousness would be granted the same.

The Prophet (pbuh & hf) stated:

> It has been narrated on the authority of Jābir ibn Samūra who said: "I joined the company of the Holy Prophet with my father and I heard him say: 'This caliphate will not end until there have been ***Ithna 'Ashara*** **(twelve)** ***Khalīfatan*** **(caliphs)** among them.' The narrator said: 'Then he (the Holy Prophet) said something that I could not follow.' I said to my father: 'What did he say?' He said: 'He has said all of them will be from the Quraysh.'"[6]

> It has been narrated on the authority of Jābir ibn Samūra who said: "I heard the Messenger of Allāh say: 'Islām will continue to be triumphant until there have been ***Ithna 'Ashara*** **caliphs**.' Then the Holy Prophet said something, which I could not understand. I asked my father, 'What did he say?' He said: 'He has said that all of them (twelve caliphs) will be from the Quraysh.'"[7]

> Awn quotes his father Abu Juhayfah as saying: "My uncle and I were with the Holy Prophet when he said: 'The affairs of my nation passes until ***Ithna 'Ashara* caliphs** come.' The he lowered his voice. I asked my uncle who was sitting in the front about what the Prophet had said. He answered: 'O my son! The Prophet said that they would all be from Quraysh.'"[8]
>
> Jābir is quoted as saying: "My father and I were before the Messenger of Allāh when he said: 'There will be ***Ithna 'Ashara* caliphs** after me.' Then he lowered his voice. I asked my father what the Prophet had said softly. He replied: 'The Prophet said, 'All of them are from Banī Ḥāshim (the Ḥāshimites).'"[9]
>
> Narrated Jābir ibn Samūra: "I heard the Prophet saying: 'There will be ***Ithna 'Ashara Amīran*** (Muslim rulers) (who will rule all the Islamic world).' He then said a sentence, which I did not hear. My father said: 'All of them (those rulers) will be from Quraysh.'"[10]
>
> Narrated Anas ibn Mālik: "Allāh's messenger said, 'The **Imāms are from Quraysh**, if they ruled they would set justice, if they promised they would fulfil it, if they were asked for pardon they would be merciful."[11]

These twelve leaders would have to possess the characteristics, which verse 24:55 directs us to. The above mentioned tradition can be observed in abundance in the Sunni sources of *Ḥadīth* and Ibn Ḥājar al-Haythamī, who is a famous Sunni commentator and scholar admits to the validity of this tradition. In his own book *al-Sawā'iq al-Muhriqah* p.11, Ibn Ḥājar speaks of the leadership of the first three recognised caliphs for the Sunnis, whilst marking his rejection of what the Shī'ahs state, but then refers to the tradition in regards to the twelve leaders and declares:

> "All Sunni scholars accept the validity of this tradition."

What we find within the narrations are three terms stated in relation to the leaders from the Quraysh, (*Khalīfatan*, *Amīran*, Imāms) and these terms are not contradictory to one another in respect to what subject the Prophet (pbuh & hf) was speaking of. If we state that we are happy, we are content, we are merry in life, we exemplify that we are at ease with ourselves, we are feeling good, we may use all these terms, providing others with the surety and definiteness of this state we are in. As we may state within the English language, words, which under a given context relate to one and the same thing, the same can be stated for the Arabic language. If the Prophet spoke of matters using different terms, it would not be difficult to comprehend what was being directed by him when relating it to the context.

If we observe the following two narrations, they can further clarify our understanding that these terms used under such a context do indeed reference towards the leader of the Islamic state. Quoted in *Ṣaḥīḥ* al-Bukhārī, Vol. 3, Book 46, The Manumission of Slaves:

> Nāfi'ī from 'Abdullāh, Allāh's Apostle said: "Everyone of you is a guardian and is responsible for his charges. **The *Amīr* who has authority over people**, is a guardian and is responsible for them, a man is a guardian of his family and is responsible for them; a woman is a guardian of her husband's house and children and is responsible for them; a slave ('Abū) is a guardian of his master's property and is responsible for it; so all of you are guardians and are responsible for your charges."

> Sālim ibn Abdullāh from 'Abdullāh ibn 'Umar said that he heard Allāh's Apostle saying: " 'Everyone of you is a guardian and is responsible for his charge; **the Imām is a guardian and is responsible for his subjects (the people)**; the man is a guardian in his family and responsible for his charges; a woman is a guardian of her husband's house and responsible for her charges; and the servant is a guardian of his

> master's property and is responsible for his charge.' I definitely heard the above from the Prophet and think that the Prophet also said: 'A man is a guardian of his father's property and responsible for his charges; so everyone of you is a guardian and responsible for his charges.' "

Nevertheless, Shī'ahs state that these twelve leaders cannot be individuals **nominated** for this responsibility. They illuminate the actions of the Muslim masses as observed within the narrative, which have led to this thinking that this position (caliph, *Amīr*, Imām) was left within the hands of the people to choose whereas the Qur'ān does not depict to us that **successors/vicigerants of prophets** (AS) have ever been **nominated** by the people. There is a difference when the Qur'ān refers to successors of nations or tribes; it demonstrates to us that certain groups of people or tribes were replaced by others who are then referred to as successors (of the previous people or tribe). This can be observed for e.g. in the story of prophet Ḥud (AS) when he states to his people:

> "I but fulfil towards you the duties of my Lord's mission; I am to you a sincere and trustworthy adviser." Qur'ān 7:68

> "Do ye wonder that there hath come to you a message from your Lord through a man of your own people, to warn you? Call in remembrance that He made you ***khulafah*** after the people of Noah, and gave you a stature tall among the nations. Call in remembrance the benefits (ye have received) from Allāh that so ye may prosper." Qur'ān 7:69

It is very important to keep in mind that matters always need to be understood in accordance to their context.

Shias illuminate that successors of prophets (AS) including the final Prophet (pbuh &hf) were divinely appointed and the first rightful *Khalīfah* in the Islamic *Ummah* was Imām 'Alī (AS) whose truthfulness and justice could not have been placed below others. His place in leadership being directed by the Prophet (pbuh & hf), and after him remaining within the chosen Imāms of the Ahl al-Bayt.

The *Khalīfah* of Allāh

Sunnis state that their first *Khalīfah* was Abū Bakr, some stating he was chosen by the Prophet (pbuh & hf) and others that he was nominated. It is also stated that after Abū Bakr, 'Umar was to be followed, and after him, 'Uthmān. It is also stated that 'Uthmān was nominated through a consultative (*shūra*) council of six people set up by 'Umar.

This projects to us that there can be varying comments given by the Sunnis in regards to the issue of succession, and this is due to what has been recorded. It would be beneficial to re-iterate these comments as:

(1) Abū Bakr was the only one chosen by the Prophet (pbuh & hf) and then the rest were nominated. This can be projected using a narration, which states that a woman enquired from the Prophet who she should refer to if she did not find him, and he informed her to refer to Abū Bakr. This can be found in *Ṣaḥīḥ* al-Bukhārī Vol 9. Book 89, Number 327

(2) Abū Bakr was given leadership then 'Umar and then 'Uthmān because they were regarded as the best, and after them no distinction can be made amongst the companions, therefore any of them can be nominated. This comment can be related to a narration found in *Ṣaḥīḥ* al-Bukhārī Vol. 5, Book 57, Number 7

> Narrated Ibn 'Umar: "We used to compare the people as to who was better during the lifetime of Allāh's Apostle. We used to regard Abu Bakr as the best, then 'Umar, and then 'Uthmān."

(3) Abū Bakr was chosen by the Prophet (pbuh & hf), 'Umar by Abū Bakr and 'Uthmān through a council of six people chosen by 'Umar before he passed away. This council consisted of 'Uthmān, Abd al-Raḥmān ibn Awf, Talḥa ibn Ubaydullah, Zubayr ibn Awwām, Imām 'Alī (AS) and Sa'd ibn Abī Waqqās. These six people have been mentioned in *Ṣaḥīḥ* al-Bukhārī Vol.5, Book 57, Number 50.

> "...The people said (to 'Umar), 'O chief of the believers! Appoint a successor.' 'Umar said: 'I do not find anyone more suitable for the job than the

> following persons or group whom Allāh's Apostle had been pleased with before he died.' Then 'Umar mentioned 'Alī, 'Uthmān, Az-Zubayr, Talḥa, Sa'd and Abd al-Raḥmān (ibn Awf) and said: ''Abdullāh ibn 'Umar will be a witness to you, but he will have no share in the rule. His being a witness will compensate him for not sharing the right of ruling. If Sa'd becomes the ruler, it will be alright; otherwise, whoever becomes the ruler should seek his help, as I have not dismissed him because of disability or dishonesty...'"

Also, it has been quoted by Ibn Sa'd in his Tabaqāt, Vol. 3, p.342, within a long narration that 'Umar said:

> "...He told them: 'If five out of the six agree and one disagrees, kill him. If four agree and two disagree, kill the two. If they are divided equally, have 'Abdullāh ibn 'Umar as an arbiter. If they do not accept his arbitration you should side with the party of Abd al-Raḥmān (ibn Awf) and kill the rest if they do not agree with what the people agree upon.'"

(4) None of them were referred to in the issue of leadership by the Prophet (pbuh & hf), all were considered through nomination.

We find that 'Umar stated:

> Narrated 'Abdullāh ibn 'Umar: "It was said to 'Umar: 'Will you appoint your successor?' 'Umar said: '**If I appoint a caliph (as my successor) it is true that somebody who was better than I (i.e., Abū Bakr) did so, and if I leave the matter undecided, it is true that somebody who was better than I (i.e., Allāh's Apostle) did so.'** On this, the people praised him. 'Umar said: 'People are of two kinds; either one who is keen to take over the caliphate or one who is afraid of assuming such a responsibility. I wish I could be free from its responsibility in that I would receive neither reward

> nor retribution I won't bear the burden of the caliphate in my death as I do in my life.'"

The above narration can be found in *Ṣaḥīḥ* al-Bukhārī, Vol. 9, Book 89, Number 325.

It needs to be addressed here that it is odd that we find no reference to Imām 'Alī (AS) in any such statements, except that he was placed within a consultative committee devised by 'Umar, when in fact he was a great companion of the Prophet (pbuh & hf). There is also a report narrated by Marwān ibn al-Ḥakam, which can be found again in *Ṣaḥīḥ* al-Bukhārī Vol.5, Book 57, Number 64, that states:

> "While I was with 'Uthmān, a man came to him and said: 'Appoint your successor.' 'Uthmān said: 'Has such successor been named?' He replied: 'Yes, az-Zubayr.' 'Uthmān said thrice: 'By Allāh! Indeed you know that he is the best of you.'"

'Abdullāh ibn Umar directs our thinking towards the first three being superior to others and makes no distinction between Imām 'Alī (AS) and any other companion. 'Uthmān in the above narration places az-Zubayr above the rest on the issue of his succession.

We also observe that 'Umar makes his own statement in regards to the issue of succession, which differs with the statements given that suggest the Prophet (pbuh & hf) directed the Muslims to follow Abū Bakr, and prior to 'Umar's own demise, he placed 'Uthmān for nomination in a council of six people, which if looked into with an open eye, is very dim and baffling. We need to contemplate, and also question, where are we taught that it is appropriate to devise a method, which allows the killing of those who are placed within a committee, who are all nominees for the issue of leadership?

Are we to believe that such perplexity points towards definiteness?

It can be stated that the idea of nominating a *Khalīfah* is accepted by the majority of people without any real contemplation.

Nevertheless, the Sunnis state that they have *Khulafah Rāshidūn* (the rightly guided caliphs) and others who are classed only as *Khulafah* (caliphs). This brings countless people into the picture. An example of an individual who is classed as amongst the *Khulafah* and not *Khulafah Rāshidūn,* is Yazīd, who ordered the killing of the grandson of the Prophet (pbuh & hf), Imām al-Ḥusayn (AS). We need to understand that does the Qur'ān carry such a concept? Would Allāh accept the splitting of the *Khulafah* who are to represent the Islamic state and religion of Islām into those who were rightly guided and those who were not, because this is what we would be implying by splitting the leaders into *Khulafah and Khulafah Rāshidūn*? The Prophet was the leader of the Islamic state and his whole life was spent teaching the people the religion of Islām, because he represented it. Would not all *Khulafah* have to emanate the same, hence, be rightly guided, or, could they have ruled as they pleased? Again, Shī'ahs do not give such a title to anyone and do not feel obligated to accept those who plainly have been nominated into power.

We find that Sunni scholars of the past have had difficulty in deciding from amongst those they recognised as caliphs, which ones were intended in the stated *Ḥadīth* in regards to the twelve leaders. Jalāl al-Dīn al-Suyūtī in his *Tārīkh al-Khulafah* (History of the Caliphs) stated:

> "We see that from the twelve, four are the *Khulafah Rāshidūn* (Righteous Caliphs), then Ḥasan, then Mu'āwīya, then Ibn Zubayr, and finally 'Umar ibn 'Abd al-'Azīz. They are eight. Four of them remain. Maybe Mahdī, the Abbasid could be included as he is an Abbasid like 'Umar ibn 'Abd al-'Azīz was an Umayyad and Tāhir 'Abbasi will also be included because he was a just ruler. Thus two more are yet to come. One of them is Mahdi, because he is from the Ahl al-Bayt."

Also, Ibn al-'Arabī states in his *Sharh Sunan al-Tirmidhī* (commentary on Jāmī al-Tirmidhī) Vol. 9, pp. 68-69:

> "We have counted the *Amīrs* after the Holy Prophet as twelve. We found them as follows: Abū Bakr,

> 'Umar, 'Uthmān, 'Alī, Ḥasan, Mu'āwīya, Yazīd, Mu'āwīya ibn Yazīd, Marwān, 'Abd al-Malik ibn Marwān, Yazīd ibn 'Abd al-Malik, Marwān ibn Muḥammad ibn Marwān, As-Saffah... After this there were twenty-seven caliphs from the Bani Abbās. Now if we consider twelve of them we can reach only till Sulaymān. If we take the literal meaning we have only five of them and to these we add the four Righteous Caliphs, and 'Umar ibn 'Abd al-'Azīz...I cannot understand the meaning of this *Ḥadīth*."

Shī'ahs do not accept such statements and demonstrate that the twelve leaders have been chosen by Allāh and not through nomination as a divine grace, these being the twelve Imāms of Ahl al-Bayt, and not separating the words *Khalīfah, Amīrs,* Imāms from them.

The Imāmah in the Qur'ān.

The term Imām has been expressed by Allāh in the Qur'ān and its meaning can only be fully understood through it.

> "And remember that Abraḥam was tried by his Lord with certain commands which he fulfilled. He said: 'I will make thee an Imām for mankind.' He pleaded: 'And also (Imāms) from my offspring!' He answered: 'But my covenant is not within the reach of the *dhālimīn* (unjust).'" Qur'ān 2:124

If we read the beginning of verse 2:124, it teaches us that Ibrāhīm (AS) underwent many trials and tests.

> "And remember that Abraham was tried by his Lord with certain commands..."

One of the very first trials of Ibrāhīm (AS) involved addressing his people in denouncing the idols they worshipped and submitting to the one true God. He observed much hostility for speaking the truth and bore it with patience and constancy and as is very well known, king Nimrūd tried to burn him alive. Migrating from his home in Syria, he witnessed the same from other people who were worshipping the stars. He would speak to them about the following of the one true Lord, and he would speak of His Might, just as he had done so with the people whom he had left behind. These trials were given to him in order to test his faith and through them such characteristics as his patience, sincerity, submission, truthfulness, and piety became illuminated.

What needs to be brought to our attention is that Ibrāhīm (AS) was a prophet from the very beginning of all these trials.

> "Also mention in the Book (the story of) Abraham; he was a man of truth, a prophet. When he said unto his father; O my father! Why worshippest thou that which heareth not nor seeth, nor can in aught avail thee?" Qur' ān 19:41-42

What also needs to be brought to our attention is that Ibrāhīm (AS) had no offspring at that time and Allāh granted them to him when he had become very much older in age.

> "Praise be to Allāh who hath granted unto me in old age Ishmael and Isaac; for truly my Lord is He the Hearer of Prayer!" Qur'ān 14:39

Al-Ya'qūbī in his book of *Tārīkh* (History)[12] states that Ibrāhīm (AS) was 86 years old when Ismaīl (AS) was born.

If we come back to all the trials Ibrāhīm (AS) went through, the command to sacrifice Ismaīl (AS), his first son, was one of the greatest:

> "Then when (the son) reached (the age of) (serious) work with him he said: 'O my son! I see in vision that I offer thee in sacrifice; now see what is thy view!' (The son) said: 'O my father! Do as thou art commanded; thou will find me if Allāh so wills one practicing patience and constancy!'" Qur'ān 37.102

What we can comprehend is that only after going through all such trials, did Allāh make him an Imām.

The Imāmah in the Qur'ān

"I will make thee an **Imām for mankind**."

We find that Allāh specifically used the word Imām and not *Nabī* (prophet) or *Rasūl* (messenger) in order for us to understand another post depicting something other than the prophet-hood or the messenger-ship that we all know Allāh has spoken of in the Qur'ān. Allāh did not state:

> "I will make thee a prophet or a messenger for mankind..."

Rather, Allāh set a separate post, the post of Imāmate, which laid no boundary that it was only confined to the prophets or messengers, and signified to us its existence and meaning through Ibrāhīm (AS), which he addressed as wanting to remain within his offspring. This made him the pinnacle to which mankind was to turn to for the right direction, no matter which vicinity they were residing in marking both his spirituality and stature above that of others.

Evidently the sons of Ibrahīm (AS) were already in existence on the revelation of this verse, for there would have been no sense in Ibrahīm asking for this Imāmate to remain within his offspring if he did not have any. Hence the reason it was previously stated that this Imāmate was given to him when he had become very much older in age. A time after he had gone through so many different stages of spiritual training and uplifting, raising him to a certain rank in the eyes of his Creator.

One point needs to be addressed before moving on is that past and present day Sunni scholars tend to state that this Imāmate, which was given to the offspring of Ibrahīm (AS), meant the prophet-hood. This is in clear contradiction to the beginning of the verse in question. Ibrahīm was already a prophet before he received news of becoming an Imām. If it were true that the meaning of Imām in the verse was intended to direct us to prophet-hood, then this means that Allāh put Ibrahīm through all those trials only in order to re issue the prophet-hood to him.

Also, it is beyond reason to use one meaning for the beginning part of the verse and then a different meaning for the second part when the verse speaks **under one context** towards Ibrahīm's (AS) Imāmate.

We find Ibn Kathīr states in his book of *Tafsīr* under verse 2:124:

> "Allāh is informing us of the honour of Ibrahīm *al-khalīl* (friend), who He **made an Imām** for the people, and a model to be imitated; because of the way he conducted himself and adhered to *tawhīd* (oneness of Allāh). **This honour was given to prophet** Ibrahīm when he adhered to Allāh's decisions and prohibitions."

Ibn Kathīr recognised that Ibrahīm (AS) was a prophet on the revelation of this verse and then was made an Imām, but when speaking in terms of the offspring of Ibrahīm he reverted to the prophet-hood.

> "The proof that Ibrahīm's supplication to Allāh was accepted is that Allāh said in *Sūrah al-Ankabūt* (Chapter of the Spider, 29:27): 'And We ordained among his offspring prophet-hood and the Book). Hence, every prophet whom Allāh sent after Ibrahīm was from among his offspring, and every Book that Allāh revealed was to them.

When it is understood through the beginning of the verse (2:124) that the subject of prophet-hood was not being addressed to Ibrahīm (AS) then why did Ibn Kathīr revert to it in the next part of the verse quoting another verse of the Qur'an, which speaks in regards to prophet-hood? It is very well known that the prophet-hood and the Books would be sent in the line of Ibrahīm and this is not disagreed upon, but, what also was made known is that the Imāmate would also be bestowed within that same lineage. Verse 29:27 Ibn Kathīr stated is not denied, but what is denied by the Shiahs is his idea that it was the prophet-hood that was being addressed for the offspring of Ibrahīm in verse 2:124.

Ibrahīm (AS) as a prophet of God had requested Allāh in his old age to continue this same Imāmate in his own progeny. We find that the Qur'ān also states:

> "And We bestowed on him Isaac and as an additional gift (a grandson) Jacob and We made righteous men of every one (of them). And **We made them Imāms guiding (men) by Our Command**..." Qur'ān 21:72-73

Through such verses we are provided with certain knowledge, that Allāh did not confine His chosen ones only to the prophet-hood and that the Imāmate, a separate post, was very much apparent. But, Ibn Kathīr quoted the verse contained in *Sūrah al-Ankabūt* to concord with his own thinking and forgot about the above stated words of Allāh.

The same can be addressed if we were to state that the Imām intended in the verse (2:124) was directing us to the post of messenger-ship. The Qur'ān teaches us that Ibrahīm (AS) was a messenger in his youth a long time before he was made an Imām, as we know this Imāmate was given to him at a later age. The Qur'ān teaches:

> "They said: 'We heard a **youth** (*fatan*) talk of them; he is called Abraham. They said: 'Then bring him before the eyes of the people, that they may bear witness.' They said: 'Art thou the one that did this with our gods, O Abraham?' He said: 'Nay, this was done by - this is their biggest one! Ask them, if they can speak intelligently!'" Qur'ān 21:60-63

> "And (We also saved) Abraham, behold, he said to his people: 'Serve Allāh and fear Him; that will be best for you, if ye understand! For ye do worship idols besides Allāh, and ye invent falsehood, the things that ye worship besides Allāh have no power to give you sustenance; then seek ye sustenance from Allāh, serve Him, and be grateful to Him; to Him will be your return. And if ye reject (the Message), so did

> generations before you; and the duty of **the apostle** (*al-Rasūli*) is only to preach publicly (and clearly).'" Qur'ān 29:16-18

It is observed through the teachings of the Qur'ān that Ibrahīm (AS) from the very beginning of his mission spoke of idol worship, continued to do so whilst in his youth. He called his people to serve Allāh and shun idol worship and the Qur'ān also provides us with the knowledge of his messenger-ship at this time. He was not old in age when such occurrences took place. Therefore it would not be reasonable to take recourse to the messenger-ship and state that Ibrahīm was given this post rather than the prophet-hood at a later age.

Another point, which needs to be addressed, is that the Qur'ān teaches us that the Imām guide's mankind through divine command, therefore their guidance does not come from the people. Any individual whose guidance comes from others cannot be from amongst those who fit this position. If we read the following verses the same can be observed:

> "We verily gave Moses the Scripture; so be not ye in doubt of his receiving it; and We appointed it a guidance for the Children of Israel. **And We appointed from among them Imāms giving guidance under Our command** so long as they persevered with patience and continued to have faith in Our Signs." Qur'ān 32:23-24

Again, the Imāms who were chosen from among the Children of Israel were to give guidance through divine command and Allāh does not specify who these people were, and whether they were from the prophets or not. We find that Allāh stated their Imāmate, it being due to their patience and certainty in the signs of their Creator. We do not need to be acquainted with who they are, in order to understand why they were made Imāms; we can learn what their nature must have been like through what we understand in regards to Ibrahīm (AS) whom we know faced so many trials with humility and patience. If Allāh had not put Ibrahīm through such trials, his patience, his submissiveness, his firmness in faith, would never have been illuminated. It is through such spiritual uplifting that the position of

Imāmate is understood. The Qur'an teaches us through Ibrahīm that this Imāmate had a spiritual dimension that could only be attained by those who were in control of their inner selves, which would bring us to the crucial condition laid on this Imāmate:

> "But my covenant is not within the reach of the *dhālimīn* (the wrong doers)."

The Arabic word *dhālimīn* comes from the root word *dhalama*, which means to harm, to do wrong or evil, to treat unjustly, hence one can deduce from which class these people would come from. We could split these classes of people into four types as al-Qadhī Nūrullāh Shustari in his *Ihqāq al-haqq* has stated:

1. Individuals who remain unjust throughout their lives.
2. Individuals who have never been unjust in any period of their lives.
3. Individuals who have been unjust at the beginning of their lives but become just later on.
4. Indiviuals who have never been unjust at the beginning of their lives but then becomes unjust later on.

We would be right in stating that any type of injustice committed by an individual regardless of how big or small it is, as the word *dhālimīn* would encompass all of that, would not be eligible for this position. Therefore individuals, who have committed injustices whether in the past or present, cannot fit this role, it only being worthy for those who have never been unjust in **any** part of their lives.

Concluding this, we should understand from the clause:

> "But my covenant is not within the reach of the *dhālimīn*..."

Imāmate was not general to all people, that this covenant could not reach any individual, even if a person was observed as being one whom we could state Allāh is pleased with. The people who would take this position as verse 2:124 clearly illustrates, would be from those who were divinely appointed. There could be no likeness to this role with an individual who we class as an Imām whom leads the people in prayer. The position of an Imām in a mosque is not specifically recognised, anyone after qualifying from certain studies can attain this position. Ibrahīm (AS) when asking Allāh in regards to his progeny received an answer that portrayed that only Allāh chooses for Himself those eligible to become His appointed Imāms. Not all of Ibrahīm's progeny would be able to attain such a position, a position that can also be illustrated through the following verses of the Qur'ān:

> "And those who pray: 'Our Lord! Grant unto us wives and offspring who will be the comfort of our eyes and make us Imāms of the pious.' Those are the ones who will be rewarded with the highest place in Heaven because of their patient constancy; therein shall they be met with salutations and peace." Qur'ān 25:73-74

Although we do not know from the verses stated those who are reciting such a prayer, we do know that Allāh grants it to a people who will be given the highest place in Heaven. By merely reciting such a prayer, a person cannot be given such a high place. We can comprehend that such a rank can only be given to an individual who illuminates certain characteristics, patience being one spoken so highly of by Allāh, as the one who is patient is not hasty in his affairs, and as we know haste can cause wrong doing and harm to others. Now if we were to think of Ibrahīm (AS) and his prayer in verse 2:124, the prayer is accepted, this acceptance being specific to certain people within his progeny who would have these characteristics.

Furthermore, we need to contemplate on whether this specific Imāmate was necessary to continue after the Prophet (pbuh & hf), contemplate on whether or not the Qur'ān or that very verse (2:124) indicates a limitation of it as well as the *Aḥadīth* of the Prophet.

No Muslim denies that finality of prophet-hood came on the demise of Prophet Muḥammad (pbuh & hf) and there would be no new revelation in regards to the religion after him, but what we need to consider is whether or not people needed the correct guidance in regards to it after he departed. If we admit that the correct guidance of mankind was essential in order to fulfil religious obligations, this guidance could not have come from anybody who was simply chosen by others, as there would be no surety in what one was being taught, to be secure from error, and Allāh's grace does not allow such insecurity upon His faithful servants. A pinnacle, a leading figure was required in order for the right cause to remain as one.

Also, we observe in the Qur'ān:

> "Or do they envy mankind for what Allāh has given them of His bounty? Yet we had already given the family of (Abraham) the Book, and the Wisdom and we gave them a mighty kingdom (sovereignty)." Qur'ān 4:54
>
> 'Alī ibn Ibrāhīm has narrated from his father from Muḥammad ibn Abū 'Umayr from 'Umar ibn Udhayna from Burayd al-'Ijlī from Abū Ja'far as-Sādiq who has said the following about the words of Allāh, the Most Holy: "We have given to the family of Abraham the Book, Wisdom, and a great Kingdom." (Qur'ān 4:54)
>
> "Great kingdom means that He set Imāmate in the descendants of Abraham, whoever would obey them he has obeyed Allāh and whoever would disobey them has disobeyed Allāh and thus is the great kingdom."[13]

Here would be a good place to state something in regards to Imām Mahdī (AS), because at the time of his re-appearance it will be obligatory on all who live to see him to abide by his guidance and not deny his lead. As stated, he is the final representative of Allāh, a *Khalīfatullāh*, and as we know, the Prophet (pbuh & hf) stated that the *Khilāfate* (caliphate) will remain within the Quraysh, and will do so even if two people are left on earth. This has been reported by Imām Muslim in his Book on Government (*Kitāb al-Imāra*) and is also well documented within the books the Shī'ahs possess. Denying the Imām's lead would in fact be denying the teachings of the Qur'ān and the *Sunnah* because Imām Mahdī (AS) will administer everything in accordance to it and will not swerve from it. He will come with this knowledge deeply bestowed within himself as a guidance and grace from Allāh. But how many will in fact follow his lead when he will correct many changes, which have occurred within the *Ummah*. It is very well known by most Muslims that Īsa (AS) will descend after the Imām appears:

> Narrated Abū Ḥurayra, the Prophet said: "*Kayfa antum idhā nazala abna Maryama fīkum wa imāmukum minkum* (How will you be when the Son of Mary (i.e. Jesus) descends upon you and your **Imām is among you**)?"[14]

From the above tradition as well as many others, it is known that at the time of the descent of Isā (AS), Imām Mahdi (AS) will be present amongst the people, and it is well known through the books of the *Ṣaḥīḥ Sittah* (the six authentic books) that Īsā (AS) will pray behind the Imām. Imām Mahdi (AS) is of the Ahl al-Bayt; he is from Banī Ḥāshim, a Qurayshī, and a direct descendant of the Prophet hence also a descendant of Ibrahīm (AS). No one with a sound mind can deny the validity of his Imāmate and no one can deny his ancestry, plus knowing this, automatically proves that the Imāmate has not been brought to a halt at Prophet Muḥammad (pbuh & hf). It also demonstrates that the Imāmate is set apart from prophet-hood and messenger-ship and is not only confined to prophets and is a divine covenant.

Another point worth mentioning is that if we look deeply into the Qur'ān and take lessons from this great book, we find that Allāh also uses the word Imām for those who lead people into the Hell-Fire, the wrong doers. Those who have led others astray in this world will be made to represent exactly that on the Day of Judgement.

> "And We **made them (but) *A'imma* (Imām in plural i.e. Imāms) inviting to the Fire**; and on the Day of Judgment no help shall they find." Qur'ān 28:41

Although the stated verse signifies those whom rejected every command of Allāh, an individual who rejects even one command of Allāh is not in reach of the Imāmate spoken of in verse 2:124. They are not amongst the wrong doers, they hold firm to the hand of justice, they follow the command of Allāh and give the same guidance to others, they can never lead one into the Hell-Fire when truly followed and hence knowing them is of high importance to us all.

The Importance in Recognising Our Imāms.

We read in the Qur'ān:

> "One day We shall call together all human beings with their (respective) Imāms; those who are given their record in their right hand will read it (with pleasure) and they will not be dealt with unjustly in the least. But those who were blind in this world will be blind in the Hereafter and most astray from the Path." Qur'ān 17:71-72

Allāh instructs that all people will be gathered together with their Imām. What we find is that there are many opinions that people have considered in respect to the word Imām in the above verse. This needs to be addressed and explained in order for us to be able to contemplate on what is the true reality and significance of this verse.

The first most commonly prescribed opinion is that Allāh is addressing the prophets and everybody will be raised up with their prophet, but this explanation shows discrepancy when looking into the context of the verse. Allāh teaches us that all human beings will be gathered together on the Day of Judgement, not only those who followed the prophets of God but all people will be gathered together with a certain someone. The term Imām within the verse could not have been used to only mark the prophets, for if this was the case, then it would mean that the unbelievers will also be raised up alongside them. We know that cannot be the case and Allāh teaches us about the Imāms who lead people into the Hell-Fire, (Qur'ān 28.41) they are the Imāms of unbelief, who believe in no prophet of God and are opposed to the believers.

The Qur'ān teaches us that on the Day of Judgement Pharaoh will lead those who followed him into the Hell-Fire.

> "He (Pharaoh) will go before his people on the Day of Judgement and lead them into the Fire (as cattle are led to water); but woeful indeed will be this leading (and) the place led to!" Qur'ān 11:98

As it is clear, all people will not be raised with the prophets and the word Imām cannot have been used to signify this in the verse under discussion.

It is also necessary to re-iterate that Allāh has specifically used the word Imām in the aforementioned verse and not *Nabī* or *Rasūl*.

It is crucial to realise that all human beings within every age, believers and disbelievers will be placed in their respective groups and brought together on the Day of Judgement with those they followed in life, those whose precepts they took and utilised.

As previously explained, Allāh's decree and the choice of the people are not the same; the verse is very much based upon whom the people have taken as their Imāms. If we read the verse again, we do not read the words of Allāh as:

> "One day We shall call together all human beings with **our** (respective) Imāms..."

BUT

> "One day We shall call together all human beings with **their** (respective) Imāms..."

We have been left to make our own decisions, our own choices and we will surely be resurrected and brought together with those whose lead we have considered and taken in life, those whom have been addressed by Allāh as Imāms.

Allāmah Tabataba'ī has given extensive explanations towards this verse under discussion and one can learn a great deal from him when reading his book *al-Mizān*, which we will find being touched upon, not as extensively as he has done so, but enough for us to make sense of the verse.

Moving on to the second explanation, which we find being propagated in regards to this verse is that, the word Imām refers to the Heavenly Books, that every individual will be called with its Heavenly Book. What may lead us to declare that the Imāms referred to in the verse under discussion are the Heavenly Books, are certain verses that are present in the Qur'ān, that refer the word Imām to the protected tablet, what we call *al-Lawh al-Mahfouz,* or, the Books revealed.

> "And of all things have We taken account in a clear Book (of evidence) (*Imāmim mubīn).*" Qur'ān 36:12

> "Can they be (like) those who accept a Clear (Sign) from their Lord and whom a witness from Himself doth teach, as did **the Book** of Moses before it, a guide and a mercy (*Imāman wa Raḥma)*?" Qur'ān 11:17

The first verse (36:12) is speaking of the preserved tablet, which is 'One' and we do not separate it apart, as all the Books have been preserved within this fixed tablet. It does not make sense that all people will be placed in one group under one tablet, this is not appropriate to the verse in question, if we remind ourselves of the beginning of the verse again:

> "One day We shall call together all human beings with their (respective) Imāms..."

There is no indication in the verse that all human beings will be raised as one and again whatever man may have followed in life does not necessarily mean it what was correct. Again, taking the word Imām in its context is fundamentally important.

The second verse (11:17) speaks of the Book of Mūsa (AS), it being the source of guidance and bringing mercy upon those at that time who followed it through the divine instruction of prophet Mūsa. This can also be observed through other verses explaining exactly this.

> "We did reveal to Moses **the Book** after We had destroyed the earlier generations (to give) insight to men a guidance and mercy (*Hūdaw wa Raḥmata*) that they might receive admonition." Qur'ān 28:43

> "We verily gave Moses **the Book**, so be not in doubt of his receiving it, and We appointed it a guidance *(Hūdan)* for the children of Israel." Qur'ān 32:23

There is no contradiction here of the above verses with 11:17, also the Qur'ān, the final testament, which came after all the Books that preceded the advent of Muḥammad (pbuh & hf) is referred to in the same way. It being a source of guidance and bringing mercy for those whom were alive at that time and for all time.

> "And We have sent down to thee the Book explaining all things, a guide and a mercy (*Hūdaw wa Raḥma*) and glad tidings to Muslims." Qur'ān 16:89

Allāh expresses the word Imām or *Hūda* for the guidance, and what one must always remember is that when we look into the Qur'ān and look at it's remarkable language, we cannot state plainly just for the reason that a certain word is used in a verse, it's context is fixed and it provides the sole explanation for the various other verses in the Qur'ān that contain that very word. This methodology is becoming somewhat prominent within certain people. We always have to bear in mind that Qur'ānic verses have to be looked at within their context and clearly the language is unique.

The Qur'ān or any of the previous Books for that matter did not come into existence without the receivers of it, the knowledge they contained being taught by those great in wisdom and understanding. No Book within its age could have been left on its own. The Books of previous prophets of course were the source of guidance but this wisdom needed to be taught. Without those in authority over the Book, there could not be its true following. Such teaching is expressed in the Qur'ān quite beautifully through verses already mentioned (32:23 & 32:24).

For everyone within every age that has passed there has been a divine Book for them to be followed, but we know that not all people within every age followed it and not all believed in it. Can the unbelievers within every age be placed in the same category as the ones who believe, and be gathered together alongside them with the divine Book? If the word Imām represents the divine Books, then what is it that will represent the unbelievers, who also will be gathered together? Is it not clearly understandable that the word Imām represents individuals whose lead people within every age have taken in life, be it those decreed by Allāh or not?

The third explanation we find mentioned in regards to the word Imām under the verse of discussion is that people will be called with their book of deeds as either:

> "O companions of the righteous deeds book"

OR

> "O companions of the evil deeds book."

What we find in regards to such an explanation is the mis-understanding of what the book of deeds actually is. The book of deeds is an account of all our deeds whether they are good or bad of which the description of them will be brought to light on the Day of Judgement. There is no righteous deeds book and there is no evil deeds book, there is only one book, which will either be given in our right or left hand, which is separate to the Imām being discussed in verse 17:71.

> "Then he that will be given his record in his right hand will say: 'Ah here! Read ye my record!'" Qur'ān 69:19

> "And he that will be given his record in his left hand will say: 'Ah! Would that my record had not been given to me!'" Qur'ān 69:25

No record of deeds has been addressed as an Imām in the divine Book; it does not make sense that a book of deeds ascribes to such.

We find immediately after Allāh addresses the Imām in the verse under discussion (17:71), the book of deeds, which will be give to those in the right hand is addressed, if the word Imām amounted to the same, the change in address to the book of deeds or record would not have been needed and we would have read the verse as:

> "One day We shall call together all human beings with their (respective) Imāms; those who are given their Imām in their right hand will read it (with pleasure) ..."

As it is plain to see, those who are astray follow a lead, which sends them into darkness, that which is contrary to the people of the right hand, who follow a lead which sends them into the light, a lead that teaches the path of truth, and without this light, there is only blindness.

> "But those who were blind in this world will be blind in the Hereafter and most astray from the Path."

The fourth explanation, which is sometimes given in regards to the verse under discussion, is that on the Day of Judgement people will be called with their mother's name. Such people who state this suggest that the word for mother *al-Umm* is from the same root as the word Imām hence people will be called with the name of their mother:

"O son of so and so mother!"

"O daughter of so and so mother!"

Addressing an individual with the name of their mother when the mother herself will also be addressed as a daughter of so and so mother and again this mother will be addressed as the daughter of another mother and so forth and so forth, is far-fetched and illogical. There is no significance in this address; it is rather irrelevant to the texts of the Qur'ān and neither here nor there in the Arabic language.

What should be coming into ones knowledge is that all people within every age, which also includes the age after the demise of the Prophet (pbuh & hf) and also this day and age, will be represented by those they considered as their lead, what Allāh refers to as **"their Imām"** and Imām 'Alī (AS) has stated, as observed in al-Qurtubī's *Tafsīr*:

> "**Their Imām** in the honourable verse means Imām of their age."[15]

One individual who lives within the same age of another individual may not consider the same lead as them, thus **"their Imām"** will be different. Again, this is something, which not only needs to be understood in regards to the lead before the Prophet (pbuh and hf) but also is of high importance after his demise. It would be beneficial to read the following *Ḥadīth*:

> The Prophet said: "In every generation of my followers there are going to be just and righteous members of my Ahl al-Bayt to counteract the alterations and corruptions which the misguided people will try to make in my religion, to remove the false allegations of the untruthful and contradict the misinterpretations of the ignorant. Be aware! Your Imām shall be your representative before Allāh, so be careful whom you adopt as your representative."[16]

If we move on to a well-known *Ḥadīth*, which has been expressed by the Prophet (pbuh & hf), and is acknowledged by both Shī'ahs and Sunnis:

> Narrated 'Abdullāh ibn 'Umar: "It has been reported on the authority of Nāfi', that 'Abdullāh ibn 'Umar paid a visit to 'Abdullāh ibn Mutī' in the days (when atrocities were perpetrated on the People of Medīna) at Harra in the time of Yazīd ibn Mu'āwīya. Ibn Mutī' said: 'Place a pillow for Abū 'Abd al-Raḥmān (family name of 'Abdullāh ibn 'Umar)'. But the latter said: 'I have not come to sit with you. I have come to you to tell you a tradition I heard from the Messenger of Allāh, I heard him say: **'One who withdraws his band from obedience (to the *Amīr*) will find no argument (in his defence) when he stands before Allāh on the Day of Judgment, and one who dies without having bound himself by an oath of allegiance (to an *Amīr*) will die the death of one belonging to the days of *jahilīyyah* (ignorance).'"**[17]

We find that 'Abdullāh ibn 'Umar recognising this address of the Prophet (pbuh & hf) re-iterated it at a time when the people were taking their oath of allegiance to Yazīd ibn Mu'āwīya, he himself having taken the same.

> Narrated Nāfi': "When the people of Medina dethroned Yazīd ibn Mu'āwīya, Ibn 'Umar gathered his special friends and children and said, 'I heard the Prophet saying, 'A flag will be fixed for every betrayer on the Day of Resurrection,' and we have given the oath of allegiance to this person (Yazīd) in accordance with the conditions enjoined by Allāh and His Apostle and I do not know of anything more faithless than fighting a person who has been given the oath of allegiance in accordance with the conditions enjoined by Allāh and His Apostle, and if ever I learn that any person among you has agreed to dethrone Yazīd, by giving the oath of allegiance (to somebody else) then there will be separation between him and me.'"[18]

It is known that Imām al-Ḥusayn (AS) spoke against Yazīd and did not wish to attach himself to such a person, and if we look into the words:

> "...one who dies without having bound himself by an oath of allegiance (to an *Amīr*) will die the death of one belonging to the days of *jahilīyyah* (ignorance)."

We would have to understand the eligibility of those to whom allegiance needed to be taken.

Within the Shī'ah sources of reference, we find that Imām al-Bāqir (AS) stated:

> "One who dies without having (accepted) the Imām, it is as if he died in the *jahilīyyah*, and people are not exempted from recognising their Imām."[19]

Here we find that the Imām's words are in no way different to what is stated in the Sunni books, and there is no obscurity in what the Prophet (pbuh & hf) wanted to make clear.

Also, the above *Ḥadīth* in no way contradicts the verse of the Qur'ān (17:71), which has been discussed, but very much compliments it and teaches us that the Muslims are also not exempt from this.

If we read the first narration, indeed 'Abdullāh ibn 'Umar recognised that it was necessary to bind oneself to an *Amīr*, from what the Prophet (pbuh & hf) had taught. However, he did not substantiate the legality of the term *Amīr* in the way the Prophet had expressed it on such a person like Yazīd, whose allegiance people were taking at the time of the above narration, whose lead was never accepted by Imām al-Ḥusayn (AS), the grandson of the Prophet. A few questions need to be addressed in regards to this. Was Yazīd a representative leader whose adherence would guarantee us the receiving of our book in the right hand and would prevent us from blindness, which we can call *jahilīyyah*? Was Yazid one of the *Amīrs* as prescribed by the Holy Prophet to whom allegiance was binding in order that we did not die in *jahilīyyah*? If so, then such a personality as Imām al-Ḥusayn disobeyed his own grandfather when not accepting the ruler of that time who was one prone to misdeeds and the one who ordered his killing. Ibn Kathir has mentioned in his *al-Bidāyah wa an-Nihāyah* (the beginning and the end) Vol. 8, Yazid's misdeeds and his order to kill the grandson of the Prophet, hence this can be looked into as a separate issue and at one's own pace should one wish to do so.

Anyhow, the following narration attributed to 'Abdullāh ibn 'Abbās states:

> The Prophet said: "**If somebody sees his Muslim ruler doing something he disapproves of, he should be patient,** for whoever becomes separate from the Muslim group even for a span and then dies, he will die as those who died in the Pre-Islamic period of ignorance (as rebellious sinners)."[20]

Imām al-Ḥusayn (AS) separated from the ruler, whose ruling he disapproved of and was martyred in the process. Can we believe, God forbid that because of this reason the Imām died in ignorance? Also, those within the age of Imām al-Ḥusayn (AS) who were firm in their stand with him never accepted such a representative as Yazīd. Who was it that they acknowledged as their lead, i.e. **"their Imām"**?

It is very important to realise that the above narration earns no credence for the Shī'ahs. Shī'ahs do not negate the saying of the Prophet (pbuh & hf) about binding oneself to the *Amīr* but negate those classed as the *Khalīfah* or the *Amīr* by the people. Shī'ahs also cannot accept that the Prophet stated to his followers **that it is obligatory** to remain bound to a person **who is committing acts of disobedience**. It could never have been obligatory, for surely if it was, then Imām al-Ḥusayn (AS) defied it, and so died in a state other than Islām (God forbid!).

We read in the Qur'ān:

> "O ye who believe! Fear Allāh as He should be feared and die not except in a state of Islām." Qur'ān 3:102

And the Prophet (pbuh & hf) teaches us that:

> "One who dies without having bound himself by an oath of allegiance (to an *Amīr*) will die the death of one belonging to the days of *jāhilīyyah* (ignorance)."

Meaning that if we do not bind ourselves to the *Amīr* we will die in a state other than Islām, we will die in a state, which resembles those whose actions portray ignorance. By the Prophet (pbuh & hf) stating that we are to bind ourselves to the *Amīr*, it would mean that if we were to separate ourselves from him, we would be depriving ourselves of the guidance we need to remain on the path of Islām. We would not be provided with the nurturing we need to be able to carry out our religious obligations, which would cause us to wander and become lost causing ourselves to die in a state of not knowing our religion.

> But those who were blind in this world will be blind in the Hereafter and most astray from the Path.

The real sense of the word *Amīr* in the stated *Ḥadīth* in every way relates to guidance.

Also, there would be no sense in the Prophet teaching us to bind ourselves to the *Amīr* just to conform with everyone else, again, we acknowledge the *Ḥadīth* of the Prophet, but are we to believe that all those who were classed and labelled as the *Amīr* to be those whom the Prophet intended in his words in the stated *Ḥadīth*? It is through such narrations that some Sunnis state that the *Khalīfah* even if he commits acts of disobedience is to be adhered to, as it is not permitted to withdraw oneself from them. Such narrations are the reasoning behind the acceptance of those who were classed as the *Khalīfah* or *Amīr* at that time, even when they speak very much against what Allāh teaches in the Qur'ān, and again, the Shī'āhs cannot accept this.

But can we seriously believe that a leader who represents disobedience is a true representative of Allāh and is one whom we would love to be placed together with on the Day of Judgement? What we must also contemplate on is could one whose deeds represented disobedience to God provide the nurturing and guidance to prevent the people from dieing in a state of *jāhilīyyah*? Could one who was prone to misdeeds set the example for the one who was in need of reform and direction? If a leader himself shows the signs of *jāhilīyyah*, can his *jāhilīyyah* wipe out for the one who is bound to him, marks of *jahilīyyah*, which they may also possess? What would be the importance of such a labelled *Amīr*? Does it seem plausible to follow such a person? This is something, which Shī'ahs will never do and again cannot accept.

The true *Amīr* is not one who performs misdeeds but is the driving force for his people to keep them aloof from mischief and the non-Islamic practices, providing the Muslims with the means to act in accordance to the teachings of their Lord and not oppose them.

Also a main body in Islām does not literally denote that the majority of people represent it, even one truthful person could represent it, and we find that Allāh addresses prophet Ibrahim (AS) as an *Ummah*.

> "Abraham was indeed an *Ummatan* (nation) devoutly obedient to Allāh (and) true in faith and he joined not gods with Allāh." Qur'ān 16:120

If one person represents the truth, while there may be many who are opposed to that one person, in the eyes of Allāh he is seen as the greater. This person is seen as the main body to which one should turn to, for his representation portrays the greatest model of Islām. Allāh never states that we are to remain with a body, a model, whose actions portray something other than what the religion teaches, and we are to remain with it and Imām al-Ḥusayn (AS) beautifully demonstrated this.

Section 4

The Twelve Imāms of the Ahl al-Bayt (People of the House) of the Prophet (pbuh & hf).

Shī'ahs recognise that the custodians of the Qur'ān are twelve in number, whom they address as the twelve Imāms, the twelve successors of the Prophet (pbuh & hf) who are absolutely necessary to follow. These Imāms being from the progeny of the Prophet, the mighty descendants of Ibrahīm (AS) from his son Ismaīl (AS); and Shī'ahs state that it is they who have been bestowed with the teachings of the religion and are to be adhered to.

Al-Juwaynī al-Shāfi'ī reports:

> 'Abdullāh ibn 'Abbās remarked that the Messenger of Allāh said: "I am the chief of the prophets and 'Alī ibn Abī Tālib is the chief of successors, and after me my successors shall be twelve, the first of them being 'Alī ibn Abī Tālib and the last of them being al-Mahdī."[21]

Al-Dhaḥabi states in *Tadhkirāt al-Huffaz,* [22] that Sadruddīn Ibrahīm ibn Muḥammad ibn al-Hamawayh al-Juwaynī al-Shāfi'ī was a great scholar of *Ḥadīth,* also in his biographical notes he mentions the same, which has been recorded in Ibn Ḥajar al-'Asqalānī's *al-Durar al-Kāminah.*[23]

Al-Juwaynī has also quoted another tradition from Ibn 'Abbās:

> "'Certainly my caliphs and my legatees and the proofs of Allāh upon his creatures after me are twelve. The first of them is my brother and the last of them is my (grand) son.' He was asked: 'O Prophet, who is your brother?' He said: ''Alī ibn Abī Tālib.' Then they asked: 'And who is your son?' The Prophet replied: 'Al-Mahdī, the one who will fill the earth with justice and equity like it would be brimming with injustice and tyranny. And by the One Who has raised me as a warner and a giver of good tidings, even if a day remains for the life of this world, the Almighty Allāh will prolong this day to an extent till he sends my son Mahdī, then he will make Rūhullah Īsa ibn Maryam to

> descend and pray behind him. And the earth will be illuminated by his radiance. And his power will reach to the east and the west.'"[24]

He further quotes:

> "I and 'Alī and al-Ḥasan and al-Ḥusayn and nine of the descendants of al-Ḥusayn are the purified ones and the infallible."[25]

The Ḥanafī author Sheikh Sulaymān ibn Ibrahīm al-Qandūzī quotes the following in his book *Yanabī' al-Mawaddah* from the Prophet (pbuh & hf) in regards to Imām al-Ḥusayn (AS):

> "You are a chief, brother of a chief; you are an Imām, son of an Imām, brother of an Imām; you are *Ḥujjah*-Proof (of Allāh), son of a Proof (of Allāh), brother of a Proof (of Allāh), and father of nine Proofs (of Allāh), the ninth of whom will be al-Mahdī."[26]

Another tradition, which is worthy of reading, has been narrated by Imām Ja'far as-Sādiq (AS) in the book "Lantern of the Path".

> It is related with a sound chain of authority from Salmān al-Farsī: "I visited the Messenger of Allāh who looked at me and said: 'O Salmān, Allāh does not send a Holy Prophet or messenger unless there are with him twelve chiefs'. 'O Messenger of Allāh, I know this from the people of the two books'. 'O Salmān, do you know my twelve chiefs, whom Allāh has chosen to be leaders after me?' 'Allāh and His Messenger know best.'
>
> 'O Salmān, Allāh created me from the quintessence of light, and called me, so I obeyed Him. Then He created 'Alī from my light, and called him, and he obeyed. From my light and the light of 'Alī He created Sayyedah Sayyedah Fāṭimah (AS); He called her and she obeyed. From me, 'Alī and Fāṭimah, He

created al-Ḥasan and al-Ḥusayn. He called them and they obeyed Him. Allāh has named us with five of His names; Allāh is al-Maḥmūd (the Praised) and I am Muḥammad (worthy of praise); Allah is al-'Alī (the High), and this is 'Alī (the one of high rank); Allāh is al-Fātir (Creator out of nothing), and this is Fāṭimah; Allāh is the One with al-Ḥasan (beneficence), and this is al-Ḥasan; Allāh is al-Muḥassin (the Beautiful), and this is Ḥusayn. He created nine Imāms from the light of al-Ḥusayn and called them and they obeyed Him, before Allāh created either Heaven on high, the out-stretched earth, the air, the angels or man, we were lights who glorified Him, listened to Him and obeyed Him.'

'O Messenger of Allāh, may my father and mother be your ransom! What is there for the person who recognises these men as they should be recognised?' 'O Salmān, whoever recognises them as they should be recognised, and follows their example, befriends them and is free of their enemies, by Allāh! He is one of us. He will return to where we will return, and he will be where we are!'

'O Messenger of Allāh, is there belief without knowing their names and lineage?' 'No, Salmān.' 'Messenger of Allāh, where will I find them?' 'You already know al-Ḥusayn then there will be the master of the worshippers, 'Alī ibn al-Ḥusayn (Zayn al-'Abidīn); then his son Muḥammad ibn 'Alī, the piercer of the knowledge of the early and the later Holy Prophet and messengers (al-Bāqir); then Ja'far ibn Muḥammad, the truthful tongue of Allāh (as-Sādiq); then Mūsa ibn Ja'far, the one who kept his rage silent through patience in Allāh (al-Kāzim); then 'Alī ibn Mūsa, pleased with the secret of Allāh (al-Ridha); then Muḥammad ibn 'Alī, the chosen one from the creatures of Allāh (al-Mukatar); then 'Alī ibn Muḥammad, the guide to Allāh (al-Hādī); then al-Ḥasan, son of 'Alī, the silent, trustworthy guardian over the secret of Allāh (al-'Askarī); then *mīm ha' mīm dāl* (Muḥammad), called Ibn al-Ḥasan, the announcer who establishes the right of Allāh.'

Salmān said: 'I wept. Then I continued: 'O Messenger of Allāh let my life be deferred until their time!' He said: 'O Salmān, recite this, When the promise for the first of the two came, We sent over you our servants of mighty prowess, so they went to and from among the houses, and it was a promise to be accomplished. Then We gave you back the turn to prevail against them, and aided you with wealth and children and made you a numerous band.' (Qur'ān 17.5-6)

'I wept a lot, said Salmān, and my yearning became intense. I said: 'O Messenger of Allāh, is it a pledge from you?' 'Yes, by the One Who sent me and entrusted me with the Message; it is a pledge from me and from 'Alī, Fāṭimah, al-Ḥasan, al-Ḥusayn, and the nine Imāms descended from the children of al-Ḥusayn, to you and those who are with us, and those of us who are wronged. Whoever is truly sincere in his belief, then, by Allāh, Salmān, let Iblis and his armies come. Whoever has pure disbelief will be punished by retaliation, torture and inheritance (i.e. by others rather than them). Your Lord will not wrong anyone. It is we who are indicated in this verse: 'We desired to bestow a favour upon those who were deemed weak in the land, and to make them the Imāms, and to make them the heirs, and to grant them power in the land, and to make Pharoah, Haman and their armies see from what they feared.' (Qur'ān 28:5-6)

'Salmān said: 'I took leave of the Messenger of Allāh, completely unconcerned as to how Salmān would meet death, or how death would meet him.'''[27]

These are the twelve Imāms that the Shī'ahs adhere to, the Ahl al-Bayt of the Prophet (pbuh & hf).

Another narration, which is also worthy of reading is stated in *Usūl al-Kāfī*, a book that was written by Sheikh Kulayni, one of the most prominent Shia *Ḥadīth* scholars.

> Muḥammad ibn Ismaīl has narrated from al-Fadhl ibn Shadhan from Safwan ibn Yaḥyā from Mansūr ibn Hāzim who has the following. "I asked Imām Abū 'Abdullāh (Imām Ja'far as-Sādiq): 'Allāh is the Most Holy, the Most High to be recognised through His creatures. In fact, it is the creatures who are recognised through Allāh.' The Imām said: 'What you have is very true.' I then said: 'One who knows that he has a Creator he must also know that his Creator becomes pleased with certain things and displeased with certain other things. That the only way to know what it is that pleases the Creator and what displeases Him is through divine revelation or messengers. One who does not receive divine revelation must find the messenger and when one finds the messengers, one would learn that they are the divine authorities and obedience to them is obligatory.' I say it to people: 'Do you not acknowledge that obedience to the Holy Prophet possessed divine authority from Allāh over His creatures?' They say: 'Yes, it is true.' I then say to them: 'When the Holy Prophet left this world who possessed divine authority over the people?' They say: 'The Holy Qur'ān.' I then looked in the Holy Qur'ān and I found out that all kinds of people consider this Holy Qur'ān as the basis for their beliefs. The group called al-Murjī'a, consider it as the basis for whatever their belief. Those who believe in predestination also consider this Holy Book as the basis for whatever they believe in. Even the atheists who do not even believe in it at all refer to this Holy Book to defeat the others. This proves that the Holy Qur'ān cannot be considered a divine authority without a guardian whose words about the Qur'ān

would be the true ones. I then ask them: 'Who is the guardian of the Qur'ān?' They reply: 'Ibn Mas'ūd knew the Qur'ān. 'Umar knew the Qur'ān. Ḥudhayfah knew the Qur'ān.' I then ask them: 'Did these people know all of the Qur'ān?' They say: 'No, they did not know all of the Qur'ān.' 'I do not find anyone who would say that he knows all of the Qur'ān. The only one who says that he knows all of the Qur'ān is 'Alī, may Allāh's peace and blessings be upon him. If any question would arise in these people, that one would say that he did not know. The other one would say that he did not know and so on except 'Alī that would say that he did know. That gives enough proof to say that 'Alī was the guardian of the Qur'ān. Obedience to 'Alī was obligatory by the command of Allāh and he possessed divine authority over the people after the Holy Prophet. Whatever 'Alī said about the Holy Qur'ān is true.' The Imām said: 'May Allāh's blessings be with you.' I then said: "Alī did not leave this world without introducing the person who possessed divine authority over the people after him just as the Holy Prophet had done. The person who possessed divine authority over the people after 'Alī was al-Ḥasan. I testify that al-Ḥasan also did not leave this world without introducing the person who would possess divine authority over the people after him just as his father and grandfather had done. The person who after al-Ḥasan possessed divine authority over the people was al-Ḥusayn. Obedience to him was obligatory by the command of Allāh.' The Imām said: 'May Allāh's blessings be with you.' I then kissed his head and said: 'I testify that al-Ḥusayn did not leave this world without introducing the person who would possess divine authority over the people after him. That person was 'Alī ibn al-Ḥusayn obedience to whom was obligatory by the command of Allāh.' The Imām said: 'May Allāh's blessings be with you.' I then kissed his head and said: 'I testify that 'Alī ibn al-Ḥusayn did not leave this world without introducing the person who would possess divine authority over the people after him. That person was Abū Ja'far, Muḥammad ibn 'Alī, obedience to whom was obligatory by the command of Allāh.' The Imām said: 'May Allāh's blessings be with you.' I then said: 'Please let me kiss your head again.' The Imām smiled. I then said: 'May Allah grant you success. I know that your holy father did not leave this world without introducing the person who would possess divine authority over the people after him just as his father had done. I testify that you are the person who possesses divine authority over the people after your holy father and that obedience to you is obligatory by the command of Allāh.' The Imām said: 'It is true enough.' The Imām said: 'May Allah's blessings be with you.' I then asked for his permission to kiss his head and the Imām smiled. I kissed his head. The Imām then said: 'Ask whatever you want. I, from this day on, will never deny you anything.'"[28]

Recognition of the last Imām from the Ahl al-Bayt of the Prophet (pub & hf).

The last Imām which almost every Muslim knows of and the majority of Muslims accept, is Imām Mahdī (AS), who is the living Imām of this age, who is in *Ghaybat* (Occultation) and will re-appear at a time when also Isā (AS) will descend, of-course Shī'ahs and also some Sunnis are acquainted with the Imām's *Ghaybat*.

> The Prophet said: "al-Mahdī is one of us, the members of the Household (Ahl al-Bayt)."[29]
>
> Narrated Umm Salama (the wife of the Prophet) that the Prophet said: "The Mahdī will be of my family, of the descendants of Fāṭimah (the Prophet's daughter)."[30]
>
> The Prophet said: "Allāh will bring out from concealment al-Mahdī from my family and just before the Day of Judgement; even if only one day were to

remain in the life of the world and he will spread on this earth justice and equity and will eradicate tyranny and oppression."[31]

Narrated Abū Sa'id al-Khudrī: "The Prophet said: 'The Mahdī will be of my stock, and will have a broad forehead a prominent nose. He will fill the earth with equity and justice as it was filled with oppression and tyranny, and he will rule for seven years.'"[32]

Many Sunnis only recognise Imām Mahdī's (AS) lead and not the lead of those who preceded him.

If we learn that the Prophet (pbuh & hf) mentioned the name of his last *Khalīfah* Imām Mahdī (AS), that the number of *Khalīfah* would be twelve and also stated their line of descendancy (Quraysh); we could arrive at this question:

Why is it that we automatically are led to believe that the names of the first eleven *Khalīfah* were kept secret by the Prophet (pbuh & hf)?

We find it incomprehensible that the Prophet (pbuh & hf) could have informed the Muslims about the names of all his successors and do not find it as such when he mentioned the name of the very last one who would come centuries upon centuries later.

We should think, if we had heard from the Prophet (pbuh & hf), that there would be twelve *Khalīfah* and the last one would be Imām Mahdī (AS), would not have even one person questioned the Prophet in regards to the other eleven? Any individual present even from this day and age would most certainly have felt curious in regards to the other eleven leaders. Do we firmly believe that not even one individual may have asked the Prophet anything in regards to this?

There is no narration to the effect that the Prophet (pbuh & hf) stated that he did not know who the other leaders would be and only knew the name of Imām Mahdī (AS), however narrations have been reported as mentioned, indicating otherwise, that the Prophet had clarified their names.

Succession of the Prophet (PBUH)

A Teaching from the time of Mūsa (AS).

When Mūsa (AS) took the children of Israel from Egypt, twelve chieftains were appointed for them, placing them into their twelve distinct groups.

> "Allāh did a foretime take a covenant from the children of Israel and We appointed twelve (*Ithna 'Ashara*) captains among them and Allāh said: 'I am with you if ye (but) establish regular prayers, practice regular charity believe in My apostles honour and assist them and loan to Allāh a beautiful loan verily I will wipe out from you your evils and admit you to gardens with rivers flowing beneath; but if any of you after this resisteth faith he hath truly wandered from the path of rectitude.'" Qur'ān 5:12
>
> Masrūq said: "We were sitting with 'Abdullāh ibn Mas'ūd learning Qur'ān from him. Someone asked him: 'Did you ask the Prophet how many caliphs would rule this nation?' Ibn Mas'ūd replied: 'We surely asked the Messenger of Allāh this question and he replied: '*Ithna 'Ashara* (Twelve), like the number of the Israelite chieftains.'"[33]

Allāh took a covenant from each of the children of Israel under each chieftain to follow the practices of prayer, charity, belief in the prophets, in order to receive the good bounty from Allāh. There was no difference in lead to any one of the twelve chieftains, as they all would not be dissimilar but adhering to the same practices as prescribed within the divine law. These chieftains were chosen for the benefit of the people, they were chosen not to cause them to falter in their duty towards Allāh, but in order for them to keep with their duty and prosper. This in itself was a bounty prescribed for them, to keep them safe from dispersing themselves into insurrection and bad rebellion. No doubt Mūsa (AS) gave this direction through the divine instruction of Allāh and placed the people in good hands as prophets do not place their people in the hands of men who carry out turmoil and oppression, who are not concerned of the divine law, who do not practice it and act ignorantly.

A Teaching from the time of Mūsa (AS)

Those who follow the earlier scriptures also are aware of these twelve chieftains and acknowledge them; but what we also find within these scriptures is that there is a reference to another twelve leaders from the descendants of Ismaīl (AS).

> "I have heard your prayer for Ismaīl. I have blessed him and will make him fruitful. I will multiply his descendants; he shall be the father of twelve Princes and I will raise a great nation from him." Genesis: 17-18:20.

As we Muslims already know, Ibrahīm (AS) had two sons, Īsāc (AS) and Ismaīl (AS), and in the line of Īsāc (AS) came such prophets as Ya'qūb (AS), Musā (AS), Hārūn (AS), Yahyā (AS) and of-course Īsa (AS). In the line of Ismaīl (AS) came Muhammad (pbuh & hf) whose chosen descendants after him as the Shī'aīhs recognise, would also be the springs of wisdom to quench the thirsty ones in need of guidance with their knowledge and keep them in one direction, as it was bestowed within them as a divine grace from Allāh.

> "Do they envy the people for the bounty that Allāh has given them by His Grace? Yet we gave the family of (Abraham) the Book, and the Wisdom and we gave them a mighty kingdom (sovereignty)." Qur'ān 4:54

Ibn Kathīr stated in regards to the above verses, which are extent in the Torah:

> "In the Torah of the Scriptures, there is material implying that God, the Almighty, gave good tidings to Ibrahīm over Ismaīl's birth and that He will raise Ismaīl and increase his children and select twelve persons from his generation, great in status."

Then Ibn Kathīr added:

> "Our master Allāmah, Ibn Taymīyyah says: 'These twelve are the same persons about whom Jābir (Ibn Samūra) gave good tidings in his tradition. It is established that they are spread in the nation and the

Resurrection Day will not come unless all those twelve appear. A great number of Jews embracing Islām has made mistake and thought that these twelve people are those who the heretic (Rafidī) group (i.e. the Shī'ah) call on the nation to follow! Hence, they followed the Shī'ah.'"[34]

Whether the verses in Genesis relate to the twelve leaders after the Prophet (pbuh and his family) or not, Ibn Taymīyyah, of course very well known by the majority of Muslims, claimed that what was stated in the Torah related to what is found narrated from Jābir ibn Samūra. Although we have no surety of such a link, the comments he made marked his awareness of the twelve leaders of the Prophet. However, he provided no specification of whom the Prophet had spoken in regards to, and without reference to anything, construed that those who converted from the Jews and followed the twelve Imāms of the Shī'ah made a mistake.

Ibn Taymīyyah had his own set of beliefs; hence it is not surprising that he wrote this. However, what is interesting is that he admitted that Banī Ḥāshim was the best of clans:

> "Banī Ḥāshim (the Prophet's clan) are the best of Quraysh (his tribe) and Quraysh is the best of all the Arabs. An authentic saying of the Prophet confirms this: 'Allāh chose Banī Ismaīl, and chose Kinanah from Banī Ismaīl, and chose Quraysh from Kinanah, and chose Banī Ḥāshim from Quraysh."[35]

Although Ibn Taymīyyah was well acquainted in regards to the Hashimītes being placed above any other clan of the Quraysh, he still did not query those people from other clans who were placed above them.

Also, Imām 'Alī (AS) in one of his sermons in *Nahj al-Balāghah* stated:

> "Surely Imāms will be from the Quraysh, they have been planted in this line through Ḥāshim. It would not suit others nor would others be suitable as heads of affairs." [36]

A Teaching from the time of Mūsa (AS)

Sheikh Sulaymān ibn Ibrahīm al-Qundūzī al-Ḥanafī stated in his book *Yanabī' al-Mawaddah*:

> "Some of the scholars have said that: 'The Tradition, which mentions the rule of the caliphs after the Prophet are twelve people is famous and it has been recorded in many places. That which we can surmise is that, after the passing of time, what the Prophet was referring to was twelve successors from the Ahl al-Bayt and his family because it is not possible that this tradition refers to the first caliphs because they are only four people and it does not conform to the Umayyads because they were more than twelve people and all of them, other than 'Umar ibn 'Abd al-'Azīz were oppressors and also, they were not from the Banī Ḥāshim and the Holy Prophet said: 'All twelve are from the Banī Ḥāshim.' When 'Abdul Mālik ibn 'Umar records from Jābir ibn Samūra and how the Prophet quietly said who they were from, he bore witness to what he said because some people were not happy about the caliphate of the Banī Ḥāshim and the tradition does not conform to the Bāni 'Abbās either, because they were more than twelve people and beyond this, they did not conform to the verse: 'No reward do I ask of you except the love of those near of kin...' (42:23) Thus, the tradition only can relate to the twelve Imāms of the Ahl al-Bayt and the family of the Prophet. It refers to those whose knowledge is higher than that of any others, whose piety is unquestioned and from all points of view, is more knowledgeable and who gained their knowledge from the Prophet. That which confirms this view is the tradition of *thaqalayn* and many other traditions, which have come from the Prophet."[37]

Discussion in regards to the tradition of *thaqalayn* (tradition of the two weighty things) and the verse of the Qur'ān (42.23) will be observed within the course of the book, as these have not been touched upon as yet. But what we observe is that al-Qandūzī's al-Ḥanafī's words expressed his awareness of such teachings of the

Prophet (pbuh & hf), their veracity and their credence, his reasoning on the subject of the twelve leaders beautifully explained to the knowledge seeker.

Section 5

Ul il Amr (Those charged with authority).

> Allāh teaches: "Oh ye who believe! Obey Allāh; obey the Messenger and those charged with authority amongst you. If you differ in anything amongst yourselves, refer it to Allāh and His Messenger, if you do believe in Allāh and the Last Day that is best and most suitable for final determination." Qur'ān 4:59

The verse stated not only signifies obedience to Allāh and His Apostle but also obedience to those charged with authority.

> Narrated Abū Ḥurayra: "Allāh's Apostle said: 'Whoever obeys me, obeys Allāh, and whoever disobeys me, disobeys Allāh, and whoever obeys the *Amīrī* (ruler I appoint), obeys me, and whoever disobeys him, disobeys me.'"[38]

Those charged with authority are not prophets but people who take lead in the affairs of the *Ummah*, who are from amongst the *Ummah* and Allāh has instructed us to obey the Messenger and *ul il amr*.

> "Obey Allāh, obey the Messenger and *ul il amr*..."

NOT

> "Obey Allah, obey the Messenger, obey *ul il amr*..."

Allāh has placed the *ul il amr* in conjunction with the Prophet (pbuh & hf) not setting them apart from him, establishing their authority in close attachment to the Prophet's. Thus, automatically when obeying the *ul il amr,* we would indeed be obeying the Prophet, and when disobeying them we would automatically be disobeying the Prophet. When this specific attachment is understood we can never believe that their teachings would ever be dissimilar and contrary to the Prophet's.

However, as Allāmah Tabataba'ī states in his al-Mizān, there are arguments given by others, which state that the leaders who manage the affairs of the people, although they are to be obeyed in this verse, if they give an order dissimilar to the Qur'ān and the *Sunnah*, they cannot be obeyed. It is stated that if these leaders were to make a mistake, which was very clear and known, then it would have be changed to conform to what the Qur'ān and *Sunnah* states, and if such a mistake was not clear then the order would be carried out like no mistake has occurred. Allāmah Tabataba'ī counteracts such a statement and argues that the verse strictly portrays obedience to the Messenger and *ul il amr* without any condition being laid upon the *ul il amr*, and should such a condition have been placed upon them, it surely would have been mentioned within the verse. Allāmah Tabataba'ī solidifies his argument through a verse from the Qur'ān in relation to the parents.

> "We have enjoined on man kindness to parents; but if they strive to make thee join with Me that of which thou hast no knowledge, **then obey them not.** Unto Me is your return and I shall tell you what ye used to do." Qur'ān 29:8

Allāmah Tabataba'ī's words depict that if the *ul il amr* could misrepresent the teachings of the Qur'ān and the *Sunnah*, then a restriction should have been placed alongside them as is the case with parents.

Allāmah Tabataba'ī states that the clause, which proceeds the obeying of *ul il amr*:

> "If you differ in anything amongst yourselves, refer it to Allāh and His Messenger."

It is a referral to Allāh and His Messenger for the reason of revelation, meaning the Qur'ān and *Sunnah*. Ibn Kathīr in his *Tafsir* states in regards to this clause:

> "(And) if you differ in anything amongst yourselves, refer it to Allāh and His Messenger). Mujāhid and several others among the Salaf said that the verse means: '(Refer) to the Book of Allāh and the *Sunnah* of His Messenger.' This is a command from Allāh that

> whatever areas the people dispute about, whether major or minor areas of the religion, they are required to refer to the Qur'ān and *Sunnah* for judgment concerning these disputes. In another verse, Allāh said: 'And in whatsoever you differ, the decision thereof is with Allāh).' Therefore whatever the Book and *Sunnah* decide and testify to the truth of; then it is the plain truth. What is beyond truth, save falsehood? This is why Allāh said: '(If you believe in Allāh and in the Last Day.)' meaning, refer the disputes and conflicts that arise between you to the Book of Allāh and the *Sunnah* of His Messenger for judgment. Allāh's statement indicates that those who do not refer to the Book and *Sunnah* for judgment in their disputes are not believers in Allāh or the Last Day."

We can comprehend that the *ul il amr* also emanate the teachings of the Qur'ān and the *Sunnah* through the clause in regards to the people of dispute, because, we can observe that there is a separation of the *ul il amr* from them.

> "O ye who believe"

> "If you differ in anything amongst yourselves."

Allāh does not connect the *ul il amr* with the people of dispute, although they are also from amongst the believers, they are marked as being separate from them. The following verse can also help us to understand what is being cited.

> "When there comes to them some matter touching (public) safety or fear they divulge it. If they had only referred it to the Apostle **or** to those charged with authority among them the proper investigators would have tested it from them (direct). Were it not for the Grace and Mercy of Allāh unto you all but a few of you would have fallen into the clutches of Satan." Qur'ān 4:83

Ul il Amr (Those charged with authority)

If the Muslims hear of a certain matter and circulate it amongst one another, there could be falsehood in such a statement. Allāh teaches that if such matters were referred to His Messenger or those charged with authority, the truth would be brought to light, as they are the appropriate people to enquire from. Allāh would not teach us to refer to the Messenger or the *ul il amr* if the decisions of the *ul il amr* were contrary to the teachings of the Qur'ān and the *Sunnah*. We can infer through such teachings, that these people can never be from amongst those who may speak against the truth and they can never be disobedient.

The renowned Sunni scholar of *Tafsīr* Imām Fakhr al-Dīn al-Rāzī, states in his *Tafsīr al-Kabīr* in regards to verse (4:49):

> This verse proves that *ul il amr* must be *ma'sūm* (do not commit sin). He argues that Allāh has commanded the people to obey *ul il amr* unconditionally; therefore, it is essential for the *ul il amr* to be *ma'sūm* because if there is any possibility of their committing sin (and sin is forbidden), it will mean that one has to obey them and also disobey them in that very action. And this is contradictory and therefore impossible![39]

Imām Fakhr al-Dīn al-Rāzī explains in his *Tafsīr al-Kabīr* and very much brings to light that those who are *ul il amr* cannot be of the disobedient. He also states that those whom Sh'īahs believe to be *ma'sūm*, we do not know them, and because we do not know them, we do not accept them. As Imām Fakhr al-Dīn al-Rāzī gives such a comment, this does not mean that the one who has no knowledge of such personalities cannot become acquainted with them. Although understanding the position of *ul il amr*, he further states that on a consensus the Muslim *Ummah* is *ma'sūm*. We could state that Imām Fakhr al-Dīn al-Rāzī has taken such a standing through his own interpolation of a *Ḥadīth* of the Prophet, which teaches that the Muslims will never agree to wrong, and due to this, he then feels that anyone is eligible to take up the position of *ul il amr*. We already know that not all believers can be *ul il amr* and that the *ul il amr* have been separated from the general population of the believers in verse 4:59. But if we come back to the statement depicting that the *Ummah* will never agree to wrong, this does not at all portray that the whole of the Muslim population will always decide rightly upon something, rather, it teaches us that if wrong was to occur, the whole of the Muslim population will never unite and agree to it, there will always be a band of people opposed to it, hence, also teaching us that **amongst** the Muslims, there are knowledgeable and just people. Nowhere does the verse assert that those who are in conjunction with the Prophet are the whole of the Muslims, as this is what we are led to believe, if we were to follow the notion Imām Fakhr al-Dīn al-Rāzī carries.

Shī'ahs comprehend that such specific authority after the Prophet (pbuh & hf) belongs to the Imām, who cannot be chosen freely from the whole of the Muslim *Ummah* as not everyone within the Muslim *Ummah* is an idyllic model for society. Allāh teaches us in the Qur'ān (4:59) that those left in authority are from **amongst** the Muslim *Ummah*. Allāh uses the word *minkum* in the verse, which means from among you. Clearly from this we learn that not everyone is eligible for this authority, which also directly opposes the thinking of Imām Fakhr al-Dīn al-Rāzī.

The Choosing of those in Authority.

We should ponder over these questions:

Did Allāh and His Messenger leave the Islamic state to the hands of the public in order that they differed and did as they pleased with it?

Can we believe as Muslims that the issue of authority after the Prophet (pbuh & hf) was something that was of no interest to him? It is accepted without thought that Allāh's Messenger did not inform his *Ummah* in regards to the people of authority, did not secure the people with those who would guide them towards the law revealed and take care of the Islamic state after him.

However, we read:

> Muḥammad ibn Muslim az-Zuhrī relates: "When the Most Noble Messenger went to the Banī 'Āmir to invite them to Islām, a man by the name of Bayharah said: 'By God, if this young man allies himself with me, with his help I can conquer all the Arabs.' Then he turned

> to the Prophet and asked: 'If we accept all your commands and you conquer your enemies with our help, do you promise that after your death rule will pass to us?' The Most Noble Messenger answered: 'The matter of government belongs to God; **He will appoint to rule whomsoever He wills**.' The man replied: 'Are we to endanger ourselves defending you against your enemies only to see rule passing to others?'"[40]

The Prophet (pbuh & hf) would explain such matters as the beneficial way to sleep, the recommended way to take food and water, he informed his *Ummah* that a time will come when there will be much wine drunk, that female singers will become prominent, that women will begin to wear clothes, which will be likened to a second skin due to the way the clothes will cling to the body. The Prophet foretold many things, which were to happen up until the Day of Judgment, which many of us may think of as being minute and insignificant.

When the Prophet (pbuh & hf) took time in explaining such matters, would he not have mentioned anything in regards to the safeguarding of the religious teachings and the Islamic state? Would he not have mentioned anything at all in regards to the authority after him? Was it that the people were more concerned about who was to take charge of affairs? If this matter was of interest to the Muslims and they found it a matter of great concern and of high significance, then no doubt the Prophet's concern was even greater. Never would the Prophet have wanted the established Islamic state to be taken into the hands of the wrong people.

Allāh warned the Prophet (pbuh & hf) that there were hypocrites amongst the people.

> "When the Hypocrites come to thee they say: 'We bear witness that thou art indeed the Apostle of Allāh.' Yea Allāh knoweth that thou art indeed His Apostle and Allāh beareth witness that the hypocrites are indeed liars. They have made their oaths a screen (for their misdeeds); thus they obstruct (men)

> from the Path of Allāh: truly evil are their deeds." Qur'ān 63:1-2

The newly established Islamic state had to have been safeguarded from not allowing the above type of individuals to take lead in affairs, something of which was a danger and a threat to the Islamic state if a system based upon the choice of the people, was to be brought in after the demise of the Prophet (pbuh & hf), for not even the most intelligent of the Muslims would have known every hypocrite. If this type of individual became the one in authority through this type of choice system, their legitimacy in leadership would stand even if one opposed it. How can one declare that this type of system was taught by the Prophet? How can one declare that this type of system would have ensured the safety of the Islamic state and the teachings of the Qur'ān and the *Sunnah*, when this would have paved a path for any individual to become the one in authority after the Prophet (pbuh & hf)? In this sort of system the Qur'ān could have been taken in the hands of any individual who would administer its teachings how they pleased, and as they saw it fit, thus endangering and jeopardising it teachings.

> "...but those in whose hearts is perversity follow the part thereof that is allegorical seeking discord and searching for its hidden meanings but no one knows its hidden meanings except Allāh and those who are firmly grounded in knowledge..." Qur'ān 3:7

The *ul il amr* are excluded from such discord as they have been detached from those who may dispute amongst one another in regards to the Qur'ān and the *Sunnah*.

It can be concluded that after the demise of the Prophet (pbuh & hf) the Qur'ān needed a custodian, a protector of its teachings, and an individual in authority who had a clear understanding of it, in order to be able to implement its teachings and guide the people. Shī'ahs acknowledge that an individual of this calibre was chosen by Allāh, one who is recognised as the first in the line of authority to obey.

Succession of the Prophet (PBUH)

Section 6

The Proclamation of Imam 'Alī's (AS) Authority/Master-ship.

(1) An Event known as *da'wat dhu 'l-'ashīra'* (Calling upon the family).

Allāh called upon His Prophet to first declare his mission to his nearest of kin. This event took place three years after the Prophet (pbuh & hf) had been commissioned with prophet-hood, at a time when he had not openly declared his mission. The Prophet called all his family to his place of residence, food was prepared and served, and then he addressed them with certain words detailed in the narration below:

> When the Almighty revealed unto him the verse "And warn thy nearest kin." Qur'ān 26:214. "The Prophet invited his relatives to the house of Abī Tālib. There were about forty men gathered. Among them were his uncles Abī Tālib, Ḥamzah, al-'Abbās, and Abū Lahab. The Prophet said: 'O descendants of 'Abd al-Muṭṭalib! I swear by God that I know no youth among the Arabs who has brought his people something better than what I have brought you. I have brought you the best of this life and the life to come, and God has commanded me to call you towards Him. Therefore, who among you shall support me in this matter and be my brother, the executor of my will, and my successor?' Everyone listened, they all kept silent, but 'Alī the youngest of the group answered the Prophet: 'I, O Messenger of Allāh, am willing to be your vizier in this matter.' The Messenger of Allāh then took 'Alī by the neck and said: **'Verily, this is my brother, my successor, and my caliph amongst you; therefore, listen to him and obey him.'** Those who were present heard this laughed and looked at Abī Tālib saying: 'Allāh has commanded you to listen to your son and to obey him.'"[41]

Those present laughed at the idea of Imām 'Alī (AS) having been given such a responsibility, as he was only thirteen years old at the time, but the Prophet (pbuh & hf) not once expressed any weakness in him. He placed his hand on Imām 'Alī's neck and said:

> "*Inna hādha akhhī wa wasiyy wa khalīfatī fīkum, fasma'ū lahū wa atī'ū* (Verily this is my brother, my executor, and my *Khalīfah* amongst you; therefore, listen to him and obey).

These words illustrate to us that the Prophet's (pbuh & hf) approval of Imām 'Alī (AS) came from none other than Allāh, as the Prophet could never have approved of something, which his own Lord disapproved of.

It is noted that al-Ṭabarī the famous Sunni historian quoted the stated narration in his book of *Tārikh* and also quoted the same narration in his work on the commentary of the Qur'ān, however, we find the following words in place of the above words of the Prophet (pbuh & hf):

> "*Inna hādha akhhī wa kadha wa kadha* (my brother, and so-and-so, and so-and-so)"[42]

Although the full words are still extent in al-Tabarī's *Tārīkh*, one must contemplate on the reasons behind why such words have become missing in the text contained in his commentary.

Unequivocally this is the first of all evidences in regards to the successor of the Prophet (pbuh & hf) as these words were declared at the beginning of the Prophetic mission.

(2) The Verse revealed to the Prophet (pbuh & hf) at Ghadir Khumm.

The Prophet (pbuh & hf) almost towards the end of his mission performed the *Ḥajj* (pilgrimage to Mecca in the Islamic month of *Dhu'l- Ḥijjah*); this is the last pilgrimage he performed before his demise.

On the 18th *Dhu'l- Ḥijjah* when returning home after completion of the *Ḥajj*, the Prophet (pbuh & hf) ordered everyone who was with him to stop and make arrangements for a small camp at a place called

Ghadir Khumm, whereupon he delivered a speech in front of them proclaiming the authority of Imām 'Alī (AS). It is in this place that the Shī'ahs recognise a verse was revealed in connection with the Imām's authority. However, many Sunni commentators of the Qur'ān have quoted narrations indicating that this verse was revealed at Ghadir Khumm, regardless of whether they believed in them or not:

> "O Apostle! Proclaim the (message), which hath been sent to thee from thy Lord. If thou didst not thou wouldst not have fulfilled and proclaimed His Message, and Allāh will protect thee from mankind, for Allāh guideth not those who reject faith." Qur'ān 5:67[43]

If we were to acknowledge that this verse was revealed at Ghadir Khumm then we would become acquainted with the speech delivered by the Prophet (pbuh & hf) at this place where Imām 'Alī's (AS) authority was announced.

Allāmah Tabataba'ī has delved into this verse in his *al-Mizān*, giving us a great insight and understanding towards it, which will be touched upon in the words of the proceeding paragraphs but not as extensively as he has done so.

It may be stated that the verse is connected with the previous and proceeding verses, which speak of those who preceded the Muslims, the *Ahl al-Kitāb* (People of the Book), but the context of verse 67 rejects such a notion. If we read the two verses, which are directly above and below this verse:

> "If they had observed the Torah and the Gospel and that which was revealed unto them from their Lord, they would surely have been nourished from above them and from beneath their feet..."

> "Say: 'O People of the Book! Ye have naught of guidance till ye observe the Torah and the Gospel and all the revelation that has come to you from your Lord.'"

The Proclamation of Imam 'Alī's (AS) Authority/Master-ship

We can observe that these two verses follow on from one another and speak in context to one another, both are speaking about the lack of adherence of the People of the Book to the previous scriptures and what the Prophet (pbuh & hf) came with, whereas verse 67, the way it is addressed, is demanding something to be revealed by the Prophet, an announcement of something, which is part of the prophetic mission.

If we think of the People of the Book, many of them continued opposing what the Prophet revealed and regardless of how many revelations were being sent upon him, they continued rejecting his call.

We also read within the verse:

> "...and Allāh will protect thee from mankind."

We must contemplate and think when it is stated that the verse refers to the People of the Book, was it really them the Prophet (pbuh & hf) needed protection from? We find that the verse states Allāh will protect the Prophet from mankind (*al-nās)*; we do not observe the words *Ahl al-Kitāb*, we will later further touch upon on this when citing the clause, which proceeds it. Nevertheless, can we state that the Prophet was not aware that Allāh is His protector when as we know, he faced opposition from various people throughout his entire mission?

> "But Allāh hath full knowledge of your enemies, Allāh is enough for a protector and Allāh is enough for a Helper." Qur'ān 4:45

If we can understand that whatever the Prophet (pbuh & hf) was instructed to inform throughout his mission did not need the statement; "Allāh will protect thee from the people" added to it, then why in this instance did Allāh attach such a statement? It is clear that those the Prophet needed to inform almost certainly were holding reservations towards this matter, which needed revealing, otherwise there was no need to state such protection to the Prophet when he was already acquainted with it.

Even so, if we were to state that the Prophet (pbuh & hf) needed protection from the People of the Book, declaring that the verse under discussion speaks of them, we must realise that prior to the revelation of *Sūrah al-Maidah,* (Chapter of the Table Spread) in which this verse was revealed, the Prophet had already entered into many peace treaties with them and they were paying the *jizyah* (the tax given by non-Muslims who have entered peace treaties living in an Islamic state). Any threats he may have faced would not have remained as strong as they were prior to the establishment of such treaties. It would be beneficial here to state that narrations are found, which point out to us that *Sūrah al-Maidah* was one of the last revealed chapters of the Holy Qur'ān, signifying that this verse was revealed not at the beginning or the middle as some people may state, but towards the end of the completion of the Holy Qur'ān when peace treaties were existent.

> Allāmah Jalāl al-Dīn al-Suyūtī has reported a narration from Muḥammed ibn Ka'b who has narrated from Abī Ubayd that *Sūrah al-Maidah* was revealed during *Ḥajj al-Wida* (the final pilgrimage) between Mecca and Madīnah.[44]

Also,

> Ibn Kathīr has reported from 'Abdullāh ibn 'Umar that *Sūrah al-Maidah* and *Sūrah al-Fath* (Chapter 48-The Victory) are the last chapters revealed. He has also stated that Imām Nasā'ī, Imām al-Ḥākim and Imām Aḥmad ibn Ḥanbal have reported from 'Ā'isha her statement that *Sūrah al-Maidah* is the last chapter revealed.[45]

If we come back to the thought of those from whom Allāh addressed protection, and think of the polytheists, they were far more violent and had caused more harm to the Prophet (pbuh & hf) than the People of the Book. They also were among those who rejected the Prophet's words, were the ones the Prophet mainly had to fight defensive battles with and the Muslims were far more persecuted and tortured through them than the People of the Book. Yet we know the Prophet continued in his mission no matter what he also faced from them. Stating the People of the Book and leaving the polytheists out when both were involved in varying degrees in harming the Prophet means we do not realise that the Prophet was handling this throughout his prophetic mission. Their antagonism was not the trouble that could begin on delivering such a message and was something the Prophet really needed to think in regards to, when it was already there to begin with.

If we next think of the hypocrites amongst the Muslims who also wanted to harm Islām and create hindrances and difficulties for the Prophet (pbuh & hf), who were conspirators aiding in the opposition that the Prophet faced, and many were living within the Muslim quarters, whose aims and ambitions were not known of by everyone, and we know their mentality has been spoken much of in the Qur'ān, we would come to realise and be able to answer the question of whether or not it was only the People of the Book that were the mischief makers and whom the Prophet was wary of.

We should be able to comprehend that such a verse was revealed on its own through divine command and although having no relation to the People of the Book was placed in between such verses that relate with one another.

What tends to be stated by some people is that the verse speaks in regards to the Message of Islām and if we translate the verse as such, we would find it would read something like this:

> "O Apostle! Proclaim the Message of Islām, which hath been sent to thee from thy Lord. If thou didst not thou wouldst not have fulfilled and proclaimed the Message of Islām..."

We need to contemplate, the Prophet (pbuh & hf) had been preaching Islām for a period of 23 years and it was not something revealed in an instant but in stages, in which such belief and practices as *Tawhīd* (Monotheism), *Nabūwat* (Prophet-hood), *Sawm* (fasting) etc had already been conveyed. The Prophet was not called upon to reveal everything and if he did not then it is as though he had not revealed everything as this is what we are led to believe with such an interpretation. Even if one was to then state that the verse was revealed at the beginning of the prophetic mission, although there are narrations stating otherwise, it would not seem plausible that Allāh would state to His Prophet, you have not proclaimed the Message of Islām, when it is obvious that other revelations indicating further commands such as the laws of inheritance, divorce, *Ḥajj* etc were still to be revealed:

Also, it would not be fitting to state that the verse implies:

> "O Apostle! Proclaim the message, which hath been sent to thee from thy Lord. If thou didst not thou wouldst not have fulfilled and proclaimed this message."

This statement sounds altogether erroneous, imagine we stated:

> I informed my brother: "Deliver the message to our cousin and if you do not do it, you have not delivered the message."

If we were to state such a thing to one of our loved ones in such a manner, would this not sound condescending? Would not the Prophet (pbuh & hf) have known that if he did not state what he had been informed to, he would not have stated it? We all should know that Allāh is outside of all such expressions.

The real sense of the verse is that Allāh informed the Prophet to deliver a certain message to the people and if he did not do it, it would be likened to not delivering the Message of Islām at all.

Hence, the Prophet was called upon to reveal something of a final nature, something that the religion depended on. A declaration that had to be addressed; regardless of what the people would do and regardless of what reservations they may have had in regards to it. As already stated the verse uses the word mankind and the clause, which follows it mentions:

> "For Allāh guideth not those who reject faith."

The word mankind is general to all people, men and women but the next clause stated above then limits people into rejecters and what one must contemplate on is whether or not this clause is referring to those who totally reject faith or those who will reject what the

Prophet (pbuh & hf) was commanded to declare on the revelation of this verse. When Allāh states that He will protect His Prophet from the people and then states under the same context that He does not guide the rejecting people, there is an implication that one has to have faith in this announcement. We as Muslims are obligated to believe in all the commands, which were revealed to the Prophet, and if we were to reject even one of them, it would throw us out of belief as a rejection would mark us as not being wholly true to it. We could understand the clause through another verse in the Qur'ān:

> "In it are signs manifest; (for example) the Station of Abraham; whoever enters it attains security; pilgrimage thereto **is a duty unto Allāh for man-kind**; for those who can afford the journey; **but if any reject faith** Allāh stands not in need of any of his creatures." Qur'ān 3:97

We can observe that the whole of Islām is not the subject of both verses (5:67 and 3:97) and the rejection spoken of in such a context is not marking the rejection of the whole of it but a part of it. We find the word *al-nās* is also used in verse 3:97 when speaking of the *Ḥajj*. Those who do not follow Islām do not practice the *Ḥajj* and already are in rejection to this act, along with all other acts, which mark ones faith in it. No non-Muslim enters Mecca to practice the pilgrimage, the verse becomes restricted to a certain set of people, and if anyone was to reject such a practice, it will do no harm to Allāh in the least, but rather it will harm the Muslims themselves. To reject even one command of Allāh's would throw us into disbelief as already mentioned above.

(3) The Prophet's (pbuh & hf) Proclamation at Ghadir Khumm.

As stated, Shī'ahs recognise that on the 18th *Dhu'l- Ḥijjah* the Prophet (pbuh & hf) stopped at a place called Ghadir Khumm whereupon verse 5:67 was revealed and a speech was delivered by him to the Muslims present.

It was around the time of midday when the heat had intensified, many of the pilgrims had moved ahead and so the Prophet (pbuh &

hf) commanded that they be called back, and those who had not yet reached al-Ghadir, to hasten towards it.[46]

This means that the Prophet must have sent messengers in both directions (in the direction of Makkah and Madīnah) to inform them to hurry to al-Ghadir, as something was about to take place, something, that was separate to the *Ḥajj*, which they had fulfilled in Makkah.

The Prophet (pbuh & hf) immediately ordered the clearing of the ground under a few trees providing for him a small camp where he could deliver what it was he was summoned to deliver, and as already stated, it is here where the authority of Imām 'Alī (AS) was announced.

Narrations indicating this event have been recorded in many books recognised by distinguished scholars of the Sunni school of thought, which clarify to us what happened at Ghadir Khumm.

The following narration in connection with this incident has been mentioned by Ṭabarānī in his *Mu'jam al-Kabīr*:

> Narrated Ḥudhayfah ibn Usayd: "The Messenger of Allāh once delivered a sermon at Ghadir Khumm under the shade of a few trees saying: 'O people! It seems to me that soon I will be called upon and will respond to the call. I have my responsibility and you have yours; so, what do you say?' They said: 'We bear witness that you have conveyed the Message, struggled and advised the nation; therefore, may Allāh reward you with the best of His rewards.' He asked them: 'Do not you also bear witness that there is no god but Allāh and that Muḥammad is His Servant and Messenger, that His Paradise is just and that His Fire is just, that death is just, that the life after death is just, that the Hour will undoubtedly approach, and that Allāh shall bring the dead to life from their graves?' They said: 'Yes, indeed, we do bear witness to all of that.' He said: 'O Mighty Lord! Bear witness that they have.' Then he said: **'O people! Allāh is my Master, and I am the *mawla* (master) of the believers. I have more**

> **authority over their lives then they themselves have; therefore, to whomsoever I have been a *mawla*, this ('Alī) is his *mawla*;** O Lord! Befriend whoever befriends him, and be an enemy of whoever sets himself as his enemy.' Then he said: 'O people! I am to precede you, and you shall join me, at the Pool (of Kawthār) which is wider than the distance from Basra to San'a; it contains as many silver cups as the stars; and I shall ask you when you join me about the two weighty things, how you shall succeed me in faring with them; the Greatest Weighty Thing is the Book of Allāh, the Omniscient, the Sublime, one end of which is in Allāh's hand and the other in yours; so, uphold it so that you may not go astray, and your faith shall not suffer any alteration; and the other are my Ahl al-Bayt, for the most Gracious and Knowing has informed me that they both shall never part from each other till they join me at the Pool.'"[47]

Imām al-Nasā'ī has reported the following tradition in his *Khasā'is al-'Alawiyya* found in his Sunan al-Kubra:

> Narrated from Muḥammad ibn al Muthannā, he from Yaḥyā ibn Ḥammād, from Abū 'Uwwanāh, from Sulaymān, from Ḥabīb ibn Abī Thābit, from Abū al-Tufayl, from Zayd ibn Arqam, who said: "When the Messenger of Allāh returned from the last *Ḥajj* and came down at Ghadir Khumm he ordered the ground under a few huge trees to be swept clean. Then he declared: 'I am about to answer the call (of death). Verily, I have left **two weighty things (*thaqalayn*)** amongst you, one of which is greater than the other, the Book of God and my *'itrah*, my Ahl al-Bayt. So watch out how you succeed me (*takhlūfūnī*) in faring with them (the two weighty things), for indeed, they will never separate until they return to me by the side of the Pond.' Then he said: 'Verily, God is my *mawlaya* (master) and I am the *walī* (master) of every believer.' Then he took 'Alī's hand and declared: 'To whomever I am his *walī*, this one is also his *walī*. May God befriend whoever befriends him and

> be hostile to whoever is hostile to him.' Abū al-Tufayl says, I said to Zayd: 'Did you hear it from the Prophet?' He replied: 'There was no one in the caravan who did not see it with his eyes and hear it with his ears.'"[48]

Ibn Kathīr has recorded the same above tradition from Imām Nasā'ī where he quotes the latter's statement that this narration is *Ṣaḥīḥ* (authentic).[49] Although Imām al-Nasā'ī deemed this tradition authentic on the basis of his own conditions, he left it in his Sunan al-Kubra when being informed by the Abbasid governate of his time to compile another Sunan only comprising of authentic traditions. The reasons behind such an occurrence no doubt the inquisitive researcher will find. The Abbasid governate asking Imām al-Nasā'ī to compile a book of only *Ṣaḥīḥ* traditions has been stated in Muḥammad Ḥāshim al-Kamāli's book – A textbook of Ḥadīth Studies p.41.

Imām al-Nasā'ī also reports in his *Khasā'is al-'Alawiyya* found in Sunan al-Kubra:

> Narrated al-Barā' ibn Āzib: "I was travelling with the Holy Prophet, we reached al-Ghadir. The Holy Prophet announced: 'Assemble for prayers.' **It was customary when something serious was about to happen that the Holy Prophet ordered the people to assemble for prayers.** When the people had assembled and prayers had been offered, the Prophet used to preach a sermon. A special place was provided for the Holy Prophet between two trees. After the performance of the prayers the Holy Prophet, raising the hand of 'Alī's above his head, spoke to the crowd: 'Do you not know that I am the master of the believers and have more rights over them than they over their own selves?' All of them said: 'Yes, we know that.' He again said: 'Do you know that I have greater rights over every believer than he has over his own self?' All of them answered: 'Yes, we know it.' Thereafter the Holy Prophet said: 'Of whomsoever I am *mawlā* this 'Alī is also his *mawlā*.' Then he prayed to Allah: 'Oh Allah! Be a friend of him who is friend of him (i.e. 'Alī) and

> be an enemy of him who is an enemy of him.' Immediately following this, 'Umar ibn al-Khaṭṭāb met 'Alī and said: 'Congratulations to you, Oh son of Abū Tālib! You have now become *mawlā* of all believing men and women.'"[50]

Imām al-Ḥākim reports in his al-Mustadrak.

> Narrated to us Abū Bakr ibn Isḥāq and Da'laj ibn Aḥmad al-Sijzī, both of them from Muḥammad ibn Ayyūb, from al-'Azraq ibn 'Alī, from Ḥasan ibn Ibrāhīm al-Kirmānī, from Muḥammad ibn Salamah ibn Kuhayl, from his father, from Abū al-Tufayl, from Ibn Wāthilah that he heard Zayd ibn Arqam say: "The Messenger of Allāh came down at a place between Makkah and Madīnah near the trees with five big shades and the people swept the ground under the trees. Then the Messenger of Allāh began to perform the evening prayer. After the prayer he began to address the people.
>
> He praised God and extolled Him, preaching and reminding (us), and said what God wanted him to say. Then he said: 'O people! Verily, I am leaving behind two *amrayn* (matters) among you if you **follow them (the two) *(attaba'tūmūhuma)* you will never go astray (*lan tadillū)*. These two (*huma*)** are, the Book of God and my Ahl al-Bayt, my *'itrah* (family members).' Then he said thrice: ***'Innī awlā bi al-Mu'minīn min anfūsihim* (Do you know that I have more right over the believers than they over themselves)**?' The people said: 'Yes.' Then the Messenger of Allāh said: 'Of whoever I am his *mawlā* 'Alī also is his *mawlā*.'"[51]

This tradition has also been reported from other scholars of *Ḥadīth* such as al-Tirmidhī, Imām Aḥmad ibn Ḥanbal and Ibn Mājah.

We also find narrated through such companions as Abū Sa'īd al-Khudrī, Abū Qudāmah, 'Āmir ibn Dhumrah, al-Arānī, and Ḥudhayfah ibn Usayd in Imām Aḥmed's Musnad and Ibn Mājah's Sunan:

> "We came with the Messenger of God in his farewell pilgrimage, and he stopped at the road and called for congregational prayer. Then he took the hand of 'Alī and said: 'Am I not guardian who has more right over the believers than they have over themselves?' They said: 'Yes.' He said: 'Do I not have more authority over every believer than he has over himself?' They said: 'Yes.' He said: 'This is the *mawlā* of whomever I am his *mawlā*. God love whoever loves him and be hostile to whoever is hostile to him.'"[52]

Imām Muslim has also reported a tradition containing the incident of al-Ghadir in his *Ṣaḥīḥ*.

> Zuḥayr ibn Ḥarb and Shujā ibn Makhlad narrated to me from 'Ulayyah that he said, Zuḥayr said, narrated to us Ismā'īl ibn Ibrāhīm, from Abū Ḥayyān, from Yazīd ibn Ḥayyān, who said, I, Ḥusayn ibn Sabrah and 'Umar ibn Muslim went to see Zayd ibn Arqam, who narrated: "...One day the Messenger of Allāh addressed us near a pond called Khumm between Makkah and Madīnah. He praised God and extolled Him and preached and reminded (us). Then he said: 'Lo, O people, I am only a human being and I am about to respond to the messenger of my Lord (i.e. the call of death).
>
> **I am leaving behind two *thaqalayn* among you**. The **first of the two is the Book of Allāh**. In it is guidance and light. So get hold of the Book of Allāh and adhere to it.' Then he urged and motivated (us) regarding the Book of Allāh. Then he said: '**And my Ahl al-Bayt,** I remind you by God in regards my Ahl al-Bayt. I remind you by God in regards my Ahl al-Bayt. I remind you by God in regards my Ahl al-Bayt....'" [53]

Allāh is greatest in authority, and appoints whom He pleases as the authority and guide for the people. Shī'ahs recognise that this is the position the Prophet (pbuh & hf) first spoke of, he reminded the people about Allāh and His mastery, then he spoke of his own position amongst the believers:

> "*Innī awlā bī al-Mu'minīn* (Do you know that I have more right over the believers) than they over themselves)?"

This very much correlates with the verse of the Qur'ān:

> "*An nabīyyū awlā bī al-Mu'minīn* (The Prophet has greater right over the believers) than their own selves..." Qur'ān 33:6

All Muslims scholars, both Sunni and Shī'ah, are acquainted with what the above verse implies. For the Prophet (pbuh & hf) to state *awla bī al-Mu'minin* would mean that we would have to place the Prophet before ourselves or anyone else and it is this that would make us true believers. We cannot be classed as one of the truly faithful if we were against this. We need to understand that something fundamentally important is being addressed here. Allāh and His Prophet are teaching that those who recognise the Prophet's closeness, who truly acknowledge his right over them are the *Mu'minīn*, they would have to remain attached to this until the day they die.

If we were to use the term love then love would not be absent from this as we know the Qur'ān teaches:

> "Say: 'If you love Allāh then follow me and Allāh will love you and forgive you your sins for Allāh is Oft Forgiving Most Merciful.'" Qur'ān 3:31

Showing ones love towards the Prophet (pbuh & hf) would in fact mean to follow him, such an attachment would portray ones acknowledgement of his authority.

The Qur'ān teaches in regards to the *Mu'min*:

> "The desert Arabs say, 'We believe (*āmanna*).' Say, 'Ye have no faith; but ye (only) say, 'We have submitted (*aslamna*) our wills to God,' for not yet has faith entered your hearts. But if ye obey God and His

Apostle, He will not belittle aught of your deeds; for God is Oft-Forgiving, Most Merciful." Qur'ān 49:14

The word *Āmanna* i.e. we believe, comes from the root word *Amuna*, from which also the word *Mu'minīn* is derived. The word *Aslamna* i.e. we submit comes from the root word *Salama*, which means to submit, and we know that both the words Islām and Muslim are derived from this word. Although Islām can mean peace, everyone agrees that the meaning in accordance to the Muslim is submission, or a person who submits. When the desert Arabs would state that they are *Mu'mins*, the Prophet (pbuh & hf) was taught that they were not so, as although they were Muslim, there was something missing in their hearts. We could state that the real following and conviction of the Prophet having greater right (*awla*) over them was not being portrayed.

It makes sense that the Prophet (pbuh & hf) is closer to those people who have truly taken him in authority, who follow what he brought, they are the ones who do not wander away from him and it these people who have the right to be called *Mu'minīn*. We can also state that guidance protrudes to us all, but it is the *Mu'minīn* who grasp this guidance and adhere to it, taking precedence of it above self-opinion, be it their own or anyone else's, again, needing to remain like this until the day they die.

The Prophet (pbuh & hf) beautifully addressed those who were present with such words, in order for them to understand what it was he was expressing towards Imām 'Alī (AS). The Prophet made it clear to the people with such wordings the position of the Imām, its significance immensely understood by us when first understanding it in relation to the Prophet.

If we come to what many Muslims express, or should we state scholars when reading the tradition of al-Ghadir, we find that they by-pass the words *innī awlā bi al-Mu'minīn*, and directly delve into the word *mawla* stating it represents a friend, brother or a helper. Merely taking a part of the narration and mentioning it, then bringing in a different context, is not correct. When we can observe the context it cannot be ignored. Even Shī'ahs understand that the word *mawla* has many meanings but we seriously have to think, did the Prophet (pbuh & hf) really mean to say: "To whomsoever I have been friend, brother or helper, 'Alī is a friend, brother or helper?" The Arabic word specifically for brother is *akhi,* for friend, *khalīl* and for helper *nasīr,* if this is specifically what the Prophet had intended to state, he would have clearly used these words to prevent any misinterpretation from occurring. What also must be addressed is that some Muslims state that the words spoken at al-Ghadir relate with an incident, which took place when certain individuals were speaking against Imām 'Alī (AS) when the Prophet had dispatched him to Yemen (this can be observed in section twelve of the book in a report in regards to a complaint being made against the Imām). This led the Prophet to state:

> "'Alī is from me and I am from him and he is the *walī* of every believer after me."

It is stated by many Muslims that the Prophet (pbuh & hf) informed those who were complaining against the Imām (AS) to show friendship towards him, and therefore the same was stated at al-Ghadir because there were people still holding ill feeling towards him.

The tradition documented at al-Ghadir irrespectively, beautifully clarifies to us the position of the Imām (AS) after the Prophet (pbuh & hf) and it is this position that was **also** being directed towards those who had spoken against the Imām when they came to complain about him. Why are we so certain of this? When studying this event that took place at al-Ghadir, we observe that the Prophet addressed words to everyone marking the authority of Allāh, and then his own, and then he related something, which flowed on from this. It has to be noted that the Prophet did not only address those who may have been holding ill-feeling against the Imām, but **everyone** who had gathered, with a very clear direction that **related to all** of them and was **necessary to follow after his departure**. It needs to be re-iterated that the ones begrudging the Imam (AS) were not the **only** people being addressed. Again, every matter needs to be looked at in regards to its context to understand what is being implied, friendship, brotherhood, helper do not come to mind when looking at the Prophet's words. Imām 'Alī (AS) was already the Islamic brother, a friend, a helper regardless of whether certain people were holding ill feeling towards him or not. This address specifically to Imām 'Alī and no other companion in front of the *Ḥajjies* (those who complete the Prophet's final pilgrimage in the Islamic month of *Dhu'l- Ḥijjah*) who had gathered together to hear it carried a great significance from the

Prophet, which can be deeply understood through the mode of address given by him.

Imām 'Alī's (AS) authority was addressed and recognising this 'Umar, who was present, congratulated his position and status over the believers, as he had become the master, the guardian, the leader of all believing men and women as it would be these people who would follow him.

> "Congratulations to you, Oh son of Abū Tālib! You have now become *mawlā* of all believing men and women."

There is no sense in the congratulating of the Imām for becoming the friend, brother or the helper and neither did 'Umar say it as a joke or a jest to him. The statement of the Prophet (pbuh & hf) at al-Ghadir was expressed in such a way that it gave such a response of congratulations from 'Umar, which teaches us that it was something **other than** what had already been solidly established by the Prophet, it was something that was dissimilar to what is ascribed by others, as the words: "You have now **become** *mawla* of all believing men and women," evidently express this awareness and this coming from a companion of the Prophet.

The whole idea of the Prophet (pbuh & hf) stopping at such a place in the blistering midday heat, ordering the sweeping up of an area in order to make place for prayer and a pulpit and then delivering a speech, under such a context, **clearly** directs one to something important.

We should also contemplate on the words expressed by the Prophet (pbuh & hf) in relation to his Ahl al-Bayt to understand what he was directing. If we were to state that "we are informed to love Ahl al-Bayt", although there is a separate verse in relation to this, which will be observed in section ten, we need to understand that the Prophet did not **only** mention the Ahl al-Bayt but **both** the Qur'ān and Ahl al-Bayt and that they both were weighty things. Even if we were to attach the word love to what the Prophet was directing, the word love is a synonym of the word devotion; to devote oneself to something would in fact be to show ones attachment to it, to follow it. If we were to state, "we are informed to love the Qur'ān" in the same way the sentence in regards to the Ahl al-Bayt is targeted, it is blatantly obvious what the Prophet was directing one to for **both** the Qur'ān and the Ahl al-Bayt.

The words as stated in *Ṣaḥīḥ* Muslim are **enough** to illuminate to us this reality.

> Prophet said: "I am leaving behind **two thaqalayn** among you. The **first of the two** is the **Book of Allāh**. In it is guidance and light. So get hold of the Book of Allāh and adhere to it."
>
> Then he urged and motivated (us) regarding the Book of Allāh.) **NOTE:** These are **NOT** the words of the Prophet (pbuh & hf).
>
> Then he (Prophet) said: "**AND my Ahl al-Bayt (*Wa Ahlū Baytī*)**..."

The narrations, which exist in relation to the two weighty things corroborate with each other and provide us with the full picture, they have enough contextual evidence within them that relay to us the authority of the Ahl al-Bayt. Placing the Qur'ān alongside the Ahl al-Bayt was not something trivial, as these two authorities could never have been ignored and left separate from one another, and the Prophet (pbuh & hf) stated that they would never separate from one another up until the Day of Judgement, for the obvious reason that both of them were essential to keep one on the right path i.e. to keep one from being led astray.

Also, the Prophet (pbuh & hf) stopping all of a sudden at such a place and speaking at that very point in front of everyone present, is enough to teach us that this address was not through his own choice but that it was a commandment from Allāh.

We need to understand that when we only comment on part of the tradition of al-Ghadir we are actually shying away from the actuality of it.

Succession of the Prophet (PBUH)

Ḥasan ibn Thābit a companion of the Prophet (pbuh & hf) asked permission to orate a few couplets in regards to the address at al-Ghadir providing us with a further insight into the tradition:

> Muḥammad ibn Aḥmad ibn 'Alī ibn Mukhallad (d. about 357 A.H) narrated to us, he said that Muḥammad ibn 'Uthmān ibn Abī Shaybah narrated to us, he said: Yaḥya al-Himmanī narrated to me, he said; Qays ibn al-Rabi` narrated to me from Abī Harūn al-'Abdī from Abū Sa'īd al-Khudrī, may Allāh be pleased with him:
>
> "The Prophet, blessings and salutations of Allāh on him, summoned people to 'Alī in Ghadir Khumm. He gave instructions about the thorns under the tree and they were swept up. That was a Thursday. He called 'Alī and took him by his upper arms and raised them up until the people saw the whiteness of the armpits of the Messenger of Allāh. They did not disperse until this verse was revealed: 'Today I have perfected for you your religion...' (5:3).
>
> The Messenger of Allāh, blessings and salutations of Allāh on him, said: 'Allāh is most great at the perfection of religion and the completion of blessings, and the Lord's acceptance of my mission and the *wilāya* (mastership) of 'Alī, after me.'
>
> Then he said: 'Of whomsoever I am *mawla*, 'Alī is his *mawla*. O Allāh, befriend one who befriends him and be at enmity with one who is hostile to him; help the one who helps him and forsake the one who forsakes him.'
>
> Ḥasan said: 'Permit me, O Messenger of Allāh, to recite some verses on 'Alī for you to hear.' He said: 'Recite, with the blessing of Allāh.'
>
> So Ḥasan rose and said: 'O elders of Quraysh, I follow it with my profession of the testimony of the Messenger of Allāh concerning the *wilāya* that is

> decreed.' Then he recited: 'On the day of al-Ghadir their Prophet calls to them at Khumm, so listen to the Messenger calling; He says: 'Who is your master and your guardian?' They said, without displaying blindness there: 'Your God is our Master and you are our guardian, and you will not find among us anyone disobedient concerning the *wilāya*. He said to him: 'Rise, O 'Alī, for I approve of you as Imām and guide after me; of whomsoever I am *mawla*, then this is his guardian; be to him followers of truth, adhering. Thereupon he called out: 'O Allah befriend his friend and to him who opposes 'Alī, be at enmity.'"[54]

The Prophet (pbuh & hf) did not object to the words of Ḥasan ibn Thābit because he was not wrong to state them as the word *mawla* in every way pointed towards the authority of Imām 'Alī (AS). We could state that in later times, the meaning of the word *mawla* in the prophetic tradition was diluted to mean something other than what it was understood and expressed as by the Prophet and the companions at that time.

If we use the example of the word gay and we know that in earlier times the word gay was used by people to mean happy, content, merry and in this present day the word has completely been given a new meaning, the gist of what is trying to be expressed should come to light. Regardless of what the meaning of the word *mawla* is classed as by others in this day and age, it does not altar the meaning of the word within the tradition, which was expressed by those within that time and understood from the context of the words of the Prophet (pbuh & hf).

(4) *Ḥādīth* al-Ghadir is a *Ṣaḥīḥ* (authentic) Tradition.

Ḥadīth al-Ghadir has not only been narrated widely within the Shī'ah sources, it has also received recognition from the Sunni scholars of *Ḥadīth*. They have either narrated the proclamation of Imām 'Alī's (AS) leadership on the one hand or *Ḥadīth al-Thaqalayn* (the tradition of the two weighty things) on the other, or a lengthier tradition expressing both.

Imām Tirmidhī has reported the tradition from the companions[55] through various chains of transmission, his collection being one of the six authenticated books within the Sunni school of thought. He wrote in regards to the tradition:

> "This is an acceptable *Ḥasan* (sound) and *Ṣaḥīḥ* tradition."[56]

Imām Aḥmed, the fourth Imām of the Ahl al-Sunnah wa al-Jammāh, has recorded it from various chains of narrators, which he has reported in volume 1, 4, and 5 of his Musnad.[57]

Imām al-Ḥākim commented in regards to the tradition:

> "This tradition is *Ṣaḥīḥ* according to the criteria of the two Shaykhs, al-Bukhārī and Muslim."[58]

Ḥadīth al-Ghadir is a recognised *Mutwātir* (continuous) tradition; it has been reported from various companions of the Prophet (pbuh & hf) through various chains of transmission. A *Mutwātir* tradition being as Allāmah Shiblī Nu'manī points out in his book entitled Imām Abū Ḥanīfah's Life and Works:

> "A tradition whose narrators at every stage of it's transmission were too numerous for any room being left for the possibility that a lie became established by continual repetition; or in other words, a tradition initially heard from the Prophet by innumerable persons and transmitted by a succession of innumerable persons down to the last narrator."[59]

The famous Sunni scholar, Nawwāb Siddīq Ḥasan Khan of Bhopal, who also recognises the tradition of al-Ghadir, is reported to have said:

> "Ḥākim Abū Sa'īd says that the traditions of 'two precious things' and 'whose master I am, 'Alī is his master' are *Mutawatir* because a great number of companions of the Prophet have narrated them, so much so that Muḥammad ibn Jarīr has written these two traditions by seventy-five different chains of narrators (*asānid*)."[60]

The Proclamation of Imam 'Alī's (AS) Authority/Master-ship

It would be worth mentioning that Muḥammad ibn Jarīr has extensively documented these traditions in his book *Kitāb al-Wilāyah*, which have been touched upon by Ayatullāh al-Aminī in his book al-Ghadir.

It is very sad that almost every Muslim has heard of the sermon at Arafat on the 9th of *Dhu'l- Ḥijjah*, but is unaware of the most widely reported event, the sermon at Ghadir Khumm, which took place a few days later, on the 18th. Why this unawareness? Imām Aḥmad ibn Ḥanbal said as stated by Abū Bakr al-Khallāl, in his *as-Sunnah*, Vol. 2, p346 (Researcher: Dr Attiyah al-Zahrānī):

> Aba Tālib said: I asked Aba Abdullāh (Imām Aḥmad ibn Ḥanbal) about the Prophet's saying to 'Alī: "To whoever I am master then 'Alī is his master" what does it mean? He said: "Don't talk about this, leave the *Ḥadīth* as it came." The chain of this *Ḥadīth* is authentic.

A question needs to be posed here, if the sermon only directed the masses who were present towards the friendship of Imām 'Alī (AS), why was there this need to remain silent? If the whole event only had the meaning of friendship attached to it, why shouldn't individuals have mentioned it, why shouldn't it have been spoken about? This trend remained and is currently present in this modern era also.

(5) The Proclamation at Ghadir Khumm Perfects the Religion.

It is widely known amongst Shī'ahs that immediately after the Prophet (pbuh & hf) had finished his speech, the following verse of the Holy Qur'ān was revealed:

> "Today I have perfected your religion and completed my favour upon you, and I was satisfied that Islām be your religion."[61] Qur'ān 5:3

However, again, many Sunni commentators of the Qur'ān have quoted certain traditions, which indicate to us that this verse was revealed at Ghadir Khumm irrespective of whether they believed in them or not.

Before we state some of them, it would be beneficial to mention certain statements that could be made on the verse alone without reference to anything. Again, Allāmah Tabataba'ī has dealt with this in great detail in his book *al-Mizān*, which will be touched upon through the proceeding sentences.

Looking at where this clause is placed, we would find that it has been placed in between words that explain matters, which can also be found in other *Sūrahs* of the Qur'an. The verse commences as:

> "Forbidden to you (for food) are dead meat, blood, the flesh of swine and that on which hath been invoked the name of other than Allāh, that which hath been killed by strangling or by a violent blow or by a headlong fall or by being gored to death; that which hath been (partly) eaten by a wild animal; unless ye are able to slaughter it (in due form); that which is sacrificed on stone (altars); (forbidden) also is the division (of meat) by raffling with arrows, that is impiety."

Then we observe the **middle clause**:

> "This day, are those who disbelieve in despair of your religion; so fear them not but fear Me. This day have I perfected your religion for you completed my favour upon you and have chosen for you Islām as your religion."

Finally ending with the clause:

> "But if any forced by hunger with no inclination to transgression Allāh is indeed Oft-Forgiving Most Merciful."

If we add the first and third clauses together, we find that the words follow on from one another and are in context. The **middle clause** is not in context with the rest of the verse, this will be discussed shortly.

However, if we come back to the first and third clauses, we find that other verses of the Qur'ān have also touched upon this subject in

Chapters such as *al-Baqarah* (the Cow), *al-Anām* (the Cattle) and *al-Naḥl* (the Bee).

The verse contained in the Chapter *al-Baqarah* states:

> "He hath only forbidden you dead meat and blood and the flesh of swine and that on which any other name hath been invoked besides that of Allāh but if one is forced by necessity without willful disobedience nor transgressing due limits then is he guiltless. For Allāh is Oft-Forgiving Most Merciful." Qur'ān 2:173

The theme in the verse of *Surah al-Māidah* (5:3) is the same as the above verse quoted, except that it does not contain the different modes of death that negate us from being able to consume the animal. Nevertheless, even if we were to read this verse (2:173) alone, we could understand that the already dead animal would not have had the name of Allāh invoked on it, hence it would not be fit for our consumption. Also a strangled or violently hit animal would cause its blood to coagulate causing us to consume it, which is something we are forbidden from doing. However, as the verse in *Sūrah al-Māidah* has additionally explained this to us, one may have a tendency to state that this is what completed the religion, causing the unbelievers to be left in a state of despair. But, when we think closely in regards to this statement, we should ask ourselves, how is it that by Allāh stating something that has been previously mentioned in other Chapters of the Qur'ān with an additional explanation in regards to the animal's mode of death cause the unbelievers despair? If these words caused despair to the unbelievers then the other verses in regards to the same subject would also have caused the same despair. The subject of forbidden meats could not have been the cause of them being perturbed or anxious.

The aims and ambitions of the unbelievers were to prevent the prevailing of Islām and what we need to focus on is that it must have been something that was an obstacle for them towards their quest in the destruction of Islām. It sounds totally absurd when thinking of such an obstacle as being related to the forbidding of certain meats from human consumption. If we realise this, we can understand that the **middle clause** then separates itself from the rest of the verse and therefore has its own subject and premise.

Despite stating the above, it has been recognised regardless and has been agreed upon by both Sunni and Shī'ah scholars that the **middle clause** indeed holds a different subject matter to the rest of the verse and that the words "this day," found in both sentences is connected to a single day. "This day" is portraying that the disbelievers are in state of despair due to a certain matter that has made the religion complete and perfect, solid in its entirety, which as stated, would be an obstacle for them. The clause has been placed there through the direct instruction of the Prophet (pbuh & hf) who was directed to do so through divine command, the reason behind such a placement being within the knowledge of Allāh. Similar has been stated in regards to verse 5:67, which we have already observed.

What we also find is that there are certain statements that perhaps could be made in regards to which day the clause is speaking of. It would be beneficial to state them before moving onto narrations that have been documented.

It may be stated that "this day" referred to the beginning of the Prophetic mission when the Prophet (pbuh & hf) was initially called to start the propagation of Islām, but this statement would beg the question that all the commands and dictates of the religion had not yet been put in place, and so how was it possible for the religion to have been perfected when many commands were missing? How is it that the disbelievers would have felt despaired at such an early stage of the mission? If the verse was revealed in the early stages of the Prophet's mission, its followers would have been very few and the rejection and animosity at its peak against the Prophet, the feeling of despair would not have taken its toll at such an early stage. When the religion was being accepted by the masses and its domination over the people of Madīnah and surrounding areas was increasing, we can state that the unbelievers were becoming increasingly distressed and unhappy as it was causing a negative impact on their hopes and ambitions to destroy Islām, and the clause being discussed teaches us that:

> This day they have lost all hope, they have become despaired because this day Allāh has perfected the religion.

Then again, the question then comes to mind, but with what has it been perfected, which has caused such despair to the unbelievers who are against all practices that a Muslim is taught to fulfil?

What we may also find is that some people may state that "this day" refers to either the day when the Prophet (pbuh & hf) regained the authority of the Ka'ba, what is known as the Day of Conquest, which occurred in the Islamic year 8 A.H. (A.H. - after *Hijrī*, meaning eight years after the Prophet had migrated to Madīnah) or it refers to the time or period after the revelation of *Surah al-Tawbah*. It is very well known by many, that *Surah al-Tawbah* was revealed at the end of year 9 A.H. The Prophet passed away in the year 11 A.H. and within this year he had received other revelations, *Surah al-Maidah* being the last revealed chapter of the Qur'ān. It is not plausible to state that the middle clause was revealed either in the year 8 A.H. at the conquest of Makkah, or at the end of the year 9 A.H. when all of revelation had not come to completion. The religion could not have reached its perfect state if some of the verses were still to be revealed, and as we can observe, the words "this day I have perfected your religion for you" depict the opposite. On this day the perfection of the religion, its comprehensiveness was made known.

Now, if we were to delve into what we find narrated, we observe on the one hand narrations stating that the perfection of the religion occured on the day of Arafat (10th *Dhu'l- Ḥijjah*) and on the other hand narrations stating that it occured on the day when the Prophet (pbuh & hf) stopped at Ghadir Khumm (18th *Dhu'l- Ḥijjah*).

Jalāl al-Dīn al-Suyūtī a scholar of *Tārikh* and *Ḥadīth*, recognised by many, has quoted both narrations in his book *al-Itqān*, but does not see eye to eye with the tradition that relates the perfection of religion at Ghadir Khumm. It would be beneficial to cite his words when he is explaining that "this day I have perfected your religion for you" was revealed at the time of travel, he states:

> "In an authentic tradition 'Umar was reported as saying that it was sent down in the afternoon of a Friday Arafat in the year of The Farewell Pilgrimage. This tradition has multiple ways of transmission. However, Ibn Mardawayh quoted Abū Sa'īd al-Khudrī as saying: 'It was sent down on the day of Ghadir

> Khumm.' He also quoted Abū Ḥurayra as saying similarly: 'It is the 18th day of *Dhu'l- Ḥijjah*, the day of his return from the Farewell Pilgrimage.' Neither one of them is true.'"[62]

Just to make us aware of which tradition al-Suyūṭī is commenting on, which he is in favour of and considers its conveyance through multiple transmissions:

> Narrated by Tāriq ibn Shihab, a Jew said to 'Umar: "O Chief of the Believers, if this verse: 'This day I have perfected your religion for you, completed My favors upon you, and have chosen for you, Islām as your religion (5.3) had been revealed upon us, we would have taken that day as an 'Id (festival) day.' 'Umar said: 'I know definitely on what day this verse was revealed; it was revealed on the day of Arafat, on a Friday.'"[63]

If al-Suyūṭī states that the above tradition holds multiple transmissions and the traditions which correspond to the revelation of verse 5:3 on the 18th *Dhu'l- Ḥijjah* are untrue. This does not mean that we are obliged to only accept his words; rather, we need to decipher whether or not the tradition bears any credit whatsoever.

Below is the narration quoted by Al-Suyūṭī in regards to the revelation of the verse (5:3) at al-Ghadir:

> Through a weak chain of transmission, Ibn Mardawayh and Ibn 'Asākir quoted Abū Sa'īd al-Khudrī as saying: "When the Messenger of Allāh installed 'Alī as a leader on the day of Ghadir Khumm, Jibrīl (archangel Gabriel) came down to him with this verse: 'Today I have perfected your religion.'"[64]

Scholars of *Ḥadīth* other than al-Suyūṭī have also quoted this tradition through different transmission. One such tradition has already been quoted via Ḥasan ibn Thābit when discussing the proclamation at Ghadir Khumm. We find that this has been expressed again through another chain, which reads as follows:

In his correspondence to me from Hamadān the master of collectors of *Ḥadīth* Abū Mansūr al-Daylāmī Shaḥrdar ibn Shirwayh ibn Shaḥrdar, wrote, Abū al-Fath 'Abdus ibn 'Abdullāh ibn 'Abdus al-Hamadānī wrote to me concerning a tradition he tracked back to Abū Sa'īd al-Khudrī through 'Abdullāh ibn Ishāq al-Baghawī, al-Ḥasan ibn 'Aqil al-Ghanawī, Muḥammad ibn `Abd al-Raḥmān al-Zarra`, Qays ibn Hafs, 'Alī ibn al- Ḥusayn al-'Abdī and Abū al-Ḥasan al-'Abdī, saying: "On the day the Prophet called on people to gather by the Pond of Khumm - it was on Thursday - he ordered for the space under a tree to be cleared of thorns. He then invited people to follow 'Alī and took his arm and lifted it high up so that people were able to see his armpits. They didn't leave each other until the verse 'today I perfected your religion' was sent down. The Messenger of Allāh said then: 'Glory be to Allāh for the perfection of the religion, the completion of the favour, His satisfaction with my mission and for choosing 'Alī as my successor.' He added: 'For whoever I am his master, 'Alī is his master. O' God, love those who love him, be hostile to those who are hostile to him and defend those who defend him.'

Ḥasan ibn Thābit asked for permission to compose a few verses of poetry. The Prophet agreed saying: 'Say with the blessings of Allāh.' Ḥasan started: 'O heads of Quraysh, hear the testimony of Allāh and his Messenger. He continued: 'He calls them, on the day of al-Ghadir, their Prophet in Khumm so hear and heed the Messenger's call.' He said: 'Who is your guide and leader?' They said and there was no apparent blindness (clearly): 'Your God, our guide, and you are our leader and you will not find from among us, in this, any disobedience.' He said to him: 'Stand up O 'Alī, for I am pleased to announce you Imām and guide after me, so whomever I was his leader, then this is his leader, so be to him supporters in truth and followers, there he prayed; Allāh! Be a friend and guide to his follower and be, to the one who is 'Alī's enemy, an enemy.'"[65]

We find that Ibn al-Maghazilī, another *Ḥadīth* scholar recognised by the Sunnis states through another chain:

> Abū Bakr Aḥmad ibn Muḥammad ibn Tawan quoted Ibn Sammak Aḥmad ibn al-Ḥusayn ibn Aḥmad who quoted Ja'far ibn Muḥammad ibn Nasīr al-Khuldī who quoted 'Alī ibn Sa'īd ibn Qutaybah al-Ramlī who quoted Damra ibn Rabī'a al-Qarshi relating from Abū Ḥurayra, through Matar al-Warraq and Shaḥr ibn Hawshab, who said: "The one who fasts the 18th day of the month of *Dhu'l- Ḥijjah*, will get the reward of fasting sixty months. It is the Day of Ghadir Khumm when the Prophet took the hand of 'Alī ibn Abī Tālib and said: 'Do I not have more right over the believers than what they have over themselves?' They said: 'Yes, O Messenger of God.' He said: 'Then, for whomever I am his *mawla*, 'Alī is his *mawla*.' 'Umar said thereafter: 'Well done Ibn Abī Tālib! Today you became the *mawla* of all believing men and women.' Allāh then revealed: 'Today I have perfected your religion.'" (Qur'an 5:3)[66]

Al-Khatīb al-Baghdādī, again recognised by the Sunnis, also refers to a chain leading to Abū Ḥurayra who relates that on the 18th *Dhu'l-Ḥijjah* the Prophet (pbuh & hf) stated the known words: "Do you know that I have greater rights over every believer than he has over his own self?" The companions answered in the affirmative. The Prophet then said: "To whomsoever I am *mawla*, 'Alī is *mawla*" whereupon Hadrat 'Umar congratulated Imām 'Alī and the clause "Today we have perfected for you your religion..." was revealed.[67]

Just to quote the chain:

> 'Abdullāh ibn 'Alī ibn Muḥammad ibn Bashran - from - al-Daraqutnī from Habshun ibn Mūsa ibn Ayyūb - from - 'Alī ibn Sa'īd ibn Qutaybah - from - Damra ibn Rabī'a - from - 'Abdullāh ibn Shawdhab - from - Matr ibn Taḥman - from - Shaḥr ibn Hawshab - from Abū Ḥurayra.

Coming back to al-Suyūtī who although has narrated the tradition, he seems to not recognise that it has been narrated through multiple transmission. Ayatullāh al-Amīnī has commented on al-Suyūtī's attitude towards the tradition in his voluminous book al-Ghadir, which holds numerous traditions touching on the whole subject.

> "If by labelling them both as untrue the author wishes to belittle their chains of transmission, we say that: 'Abū Ḥurayrah's version is considered by the experts of the field (of *Ḥadīth*) to be authentic regarding its chain of transmission and that its relaters are documented. We will detail that when we come to the issue of fasting of al-Ghadir Day, Abū Sa'īd's version has multiple chains of transmission as said earlier in al-Hamawaynī's book 'Farā'id al-Simṭayn'. On the other hand, this version of the tradition is not related exclusively from Abū Sa'īd and Abū Ḥurayrah, but it was also known to have been related by Jābir ibn 'Abdullāh, Mujāhid al-Makkī (the commentator), and by both Imām al-Bāqir and Imām as-Sādiq on whose version the scholars rely. Furthermore, Ibn Marda-wayh was not the only scholar and collector of traditions who related it. Al-Suyūtī himself quoted it in his book *'al-Durr al-Manthūr'* (The version of al-Khatīb and Ibn 'Asākir). Another group of people were also known to have quoted it in their chains of transmission which included people like al-Ḥākim al-Naysābūri, al-Bayhaqī, Ibn Abi Shaybah, al-Darqutnī, al-Daylāmī, al-Haddad and others. Not one of them belittled it! If by judging it to be untrue he meant that it contradicts the story that it was revealed on Arafat Day, he is risking labelling it totally invalid on both sides.'" [68]

He also states:

> "However, the tradition that mentions its revealing on al-Ghadir Day is supported as we mentioned earlier that it was related from al-Rāzī, Abū al-Sa'ūd and others - by the fact that the Prophet did not live for more than eighty-one or eighty-two days after that

> (refer to page 230 for verification). In his judgment, Suyūtī is copying Ibn Kathir who said on page 14 of volume 2 (his *Tafsīr*), after mentioning the two versions of the tradition: 'Neither version is competent'. The one who started it is the worst of the two."[69]

As we read, al-Suyūtī has quoted the tradition in his *al-Durr al-Manthūr* both from al-Khatīb al-Baghdādī and Ibn Asākir in his History of Damascus. Amongst the chains he quotes, we can also find the same chains used by Ibn Kathīr in his *Tafsīr*. Ayatullāh al-Amīnī has noted this and states that Ibn Kathīr regards both these versions from the two companions of the Prophet (pbuh & hf) (meaning Abū Sa'īd al-Khudrī and 'Abū Ḥurayrah) as being incompetent. If one were to think of such a rejection by both al-Suyūtī and Ibn Kathīr, the simple reason would again be its direct contradiction to the Arafat tradition as also pointed out by Ayatullāh al-Amīnī.

Just to add, Ayatullah al-Amīnī in his book al-Ghadir has quoted that al-Juwaynī al-Shāfi'ī observes that the tradition has been received through multiple transmission via Abū Sa'īd al-Khudrī, one such transmission being:

> Abū Mansūr al-Daylāmī - from - al- Ḥasan ibn Aḥmad - from Ibn Nayrī - from Muḥammad ibn Aḥmad ibn 'Alī ibn Mukhallad - from Muḥammad ibn `Uthmān ibn Abī Shaybah - from Yaḥya ibn 'Abd al-Hamīd ibn 'Abdullāh - from - Qays ibn al-Rabī - from - `Umārah ibn Juwayn - from - Abū Sa'īd al-Khudrī.[70]

We could state that a narration, which corresponds to the revelation of a clause in the Qur'ān, is weak on the basis of its singularity, but if we were to find that the narration holds some ground through its transmissions, it is through reason alone that we would make a decision towards its legality.

If we rationally understood both verse 5:67 and 5:3, the narrations that indicate their revelation on the 18th *Dhu'l- Ḥijjah* would then also be understood.

The Historian al-Ya'qūbī states:

> "This verse (5:3), revealed at Ghadir Khumm, was the last verse to be revealed to the Most Noble Messenger.[71]

It is the Shī'ahs who recognise that the religion was perfected after the announcement of the master-ship of Imām 'Alī (AS) and the Ahl al-Bayt, which was after the revelation of verse 5:67. Although this matter has been narrated within the Shī'ah sources, it has also been greatly illuminated within the collections that the Sunnis possess.

Section 7

A Perfected religion allows no room for Deficiency.

> "Today we **have perfected religion** for you, completed our bounty upon you, and satisfied that Islām is your religion." Qur'ān 5:3.

> "...And We have sent down on you a Book explaining all things..." Qur'ān 16:89

Although the above verses signify to us that there is no gap in the religion, it is also very clear that all matters have not been followed, for if they had been, no divisions would have occurred.

The Prophet (pbuh & hf) explained all matters but knew that divisions were inevitable within the Muslims in the same way they had occurred within the Jews and the Christians. He also foretold all of this to his followers.

> Narrated Abū Ḥurayrah: "The Prophet said: 'The Jews were split up into seventy-one or seventy-two sects; and the Christians were split up into seventy one or seventy-two sects; and my community will be split up into seventy-three sects.'"[72]

We Muslims believe that the religious teachings, which came before the final Prophet (pbuh & hf) were not the final word, i.e. they were incomplete. Other prophets/leaders came in the line of authority to continue this teaching, but sadly they were disregarded and rejected causing people to adhere to the religious teachings, which were part of a continuation of the law, without any means of guidance. This caused them to interpret what the previous prophets taught as they deemed fit. This occurred to the Jews and the Christians and the majority of Muslims have also followed suit due to not being able to perceive or understand the reason behind the Imāmate after the Prophet. This Imāmate had nothing to do with the continuation of the law, but it had everything to do with guidance.

As Shī'ahs recognise, the perfection of the religion was related to guidance, in order that the true teachings of the religion would not be lost in a sea of contradiction and misinterpretation by others, in order that the religion would remain as one. They understand that this perfection also put up a barrier in order to prevent division for the Muslims; yet, it is a barrier that is not recognised and has not been adhered to, creating a deficiency that can never be attributed to Allāh. Shī'ahs understand that the **word perfect when used by Allāh, in regards to the religion**, can never incorporate deficiency, and we can only ascribe the word deficiency to peoples actions leading them to become divided.

Allāh teaches:

> "The same religion has He established for you as that which He enjoined on Noah, that which We have sent by inspiration to thee and that which We enjoined on Abraham, Moses and Jesus; namely that ye should remain steadfast in religion and make no divisions therein; to those who worship other things than Allāh hard is the (way) to which thou callest them. **Allāh chooses to Himself those whom He pleases** and guides to Himself those who turn (to Him). **And they became divided only after knowledge reached them through selfish envy as between themselves.** Had it not been for a Word that went forth before from thy Lord (tending) to a term appointed the matter would have been settled between them; but truly those who have inherited the Book after them are in suspicious (disquieting) doubt concerning it." Qur'ān 42:13-14

Allāh warns against such division, He detests that men of faith become disunited and quarrel amongst themselves. Allāh puts forth His choice in order for divisions not to take place, but following this is left to the individual.

> "It is not fitting for a believer man or woman when a matter has been decided by Allāh and His Apostle to have any option about their decision; **if anyone disobeys Allāh and His Apostle he is indeed on a clearly wrong Path**." Qur'ān 33:36

Succession of the Prophet (PBUH)

Despite the fact that we know division has occurred, can we state that the Prophet or more to the point, Allāh, ignored that a pathway was left open for people to divide amongst one another? If we were to believe this, then it is Allāh who provided the route for us to become divided and we are not to blame, it is Allāh who has created an injustice upon His creation because we have been given no clear route to its prevention. Can we truly believe this, when as we know this is against what we attribute to Him? As stated in section two, Allāh provides His faithful servants with all the instructions necessary to prevent them from error, to keep them all on the same path, this is part of His grace, His *lutf*, it is man himself who chooses to ignore it, taking a route other than it, what we would call the wrong path, which would also cause division.

We all know that prophets foretold who was to come after them, but we disregard this when it comes to the final Prophet. It seems incomprehensible by most of us that an instruction related to the issue of succession was given by the Prophet, but why?

We need to contemplate and understand whether or not the Prophet (pbuh & hf) left the people in such a state where there was a possibility of separation.

What is not considered is that the issue of guidance after the Prophet was truly necessary; the protection of the Qur'ān from mis-interpretation was fundamental. No doubt the individual who was to succeed the Prophet would have to enforce laws and give directives through the knowledge of the Qur'ān and not change or misinterpret them. With this in mind we must think, could Allāh have ignored such a necessity? As stated, it is the Shī'ahs who point out that an instruction was given to the people to follow, through which the religion was perfected. Hence through following this perfection, we would be provided with the necessary guidance and security from separation and being lead astray.

> Narrated 'Abdullāh ibn 'Abbās that the Prophet said: "The stars protect the inhabitants of earth against drowning, and my Ahl al-Bayt protect my nation against dissension (in religious matters). If a tribe among the Arabs differs (regarding the command-

> ments of Allāh, the High, the Mighty) from them, they will all then differ and become the party of Satan."

Imām al-Ḥākim who quotes the above tradition in his al-Mustadrak states: "This is an authentic *Ḥadīth* though they (i.e. al-Bukhārī and Muslim) did not include it (in their own books)."[73]

Section 8

The Leader of the Islamic state.

If someone were to carry out a task without having full knowledge of what they were about to do, for example the building of a house, how would they accomplish it? Would the individual be recognised as being capable? It is due to our disposition and qualifications that we are given certain posts because we have the knowledge and capability of carrying out that particular work.

The responsibility of the Islamic state is even greater a task than the building of a house, it cannot be carried out by an individual who does not have the correct disposition and qualifications for that post.

If we think of an individual engaging in an interview for an important responsible position, the interviewer will look for an individual who is of a good nature and whose knowledge fits into the job description. No one wants to employ an individual who is ill mannered and is not acquainted with the necessary skill needed for that role. This would not help the company, and its reputation may be spoiled if employees were of this type and rank. Religion is a matter too important to be spoilt, as the main reason for Allāh to establish it through his chosen prophets was to teach the correct law to the people.

Finality of Prophet-hood came on the demise of Prophet Muhammad (pbuh & hf) but the law still needed implementing after him. This correct law needed to be taught properly through a God fearing-pious individual, one who understood the law.

Allāh states:

> "Verily the God fearing amongst his servants are the ones with knowledge. Verily Allāh is All-Mighty Oft-Forgiving." Qur'ān 35:28

The above verse indicates that the ones with true knowledge are in fact the ones who fear Allāh the most, and this piety along with the knowledge are true requirements of the legislator of the law. Without the fear of Allāh any person in leadership would not implement the law as it should be, but would rather twist it according to his own desires and to suit his own motives. Secondly piety without knowledge is not sufficient, even though the legislator may be God fearing, he would make mistakes through ignorance thus this would consequently lead to misguiding the followers of the law without any bad intentions.

Righteous individuals who do their utmost to adhere to the laws laid down by Allāh would most certainly want their leader of the country to be a man sincere in faith and knowledgeable, who understands the law, whose character reflects righteousness and compassion, who has earned the trust amongst the community he lives in. These qualities within an individual would most certainly qualify them to take lead of affairs of any constitution or organisation. The same can be stated for the type of individual who was to take lead of the Islamic state after the demise of the Prophet (pbuh & hf). An individual who was the strongest in his belief, the most upright in character, bright and knowledgeable was ideal. The leader who was needed to succeed the Prophet most definitely would have to be acquainted with the correct law, such as the laws pertaining to marriage, penal laws and many others required within the Islamic system. If we think of the Prime Minister of a country, although, he has cabinet ministers, it is essential that he is aware of the laws of the land, and protrudes his policies to the people. He certainly has to have knowledge of the laws that pertain to the country, regardless of whether they are concerned with marriage, education, or the health-care system, as he is the pinnacle figure who has to illuminate such issues.

Those who were to become leaders of the Islamic state could never do as they pleased, they were also bound to Allāh's law, and Allāh did not even allow this leniency towards His prophets, they also had to follow the law as it was prescribed. They had no right to say or to do something, which they did not act upon themselves, for this goes against the dictates of the Holy Qur'ān.

> "Why say which you do not do yourselves. It is most hateful in the sight of Allāh if you say that which you do not do yourselves." Qur'ān 61:2-3

The leader of the Islamic state also needed to portray a good spiritual and ethical presence, which would teach the real co-existence of mankind with one another, which is so much lacking within society at this moment in time. The reason why we should take such a dimension into account is because of the role the Prophet (pbuh & hf) played as leader of the Islamic society. The Prophet did not only dictate laws pertaining to various lawful actions and misappropriations but provided the people with many aspects that were necessary towards their spiritual development. Therefore, if we were to think of those who were to succeed the Prophet and take up such an influential position, we could not separate them from this and place them outside of this dimension. It is through such a dimension that the individual would be revered above that of others, as a person who may dictate laws with arrogant or proud disreputable behavior would only irradiate bad thoughts to the one who was placed below him. Many people tend to use the words political and spiritual leadership in order to mark a split, when we understand that such a practice was not dictated to us throughout the Prophet's entire life. For this reason, the Shī'ahs do not recognise such a notion and recognise that a leader in every way is the pinnacle towards, which one is to turn to, be it in regards to the laws of the land, the laws of inheritance, divorce, etc or be it in regards to modes of practice and worship towards the development and uplifting of the inner self, which in turn, would illuminate the true moral behavior that all societies are in need of.

Nonetheless, it is stated by the majority of Muslims, that the individual who best adapted to the criteria of the successor to the Prophet (pbuh & hf), who acted upon and was the most learned regarding the teachings of Islām was Abū Bakr and that the Prophet had also indicated his lead to make him his successor. However, the strange thing in regards to Abū Bakr's position as caliph after the Prophet and the Prophet indicating his succession are reports, which seem to speak against this through the formers attitude. There are no words to the effect that Abū Bakr himself had mentioned his lead as prescribed by the Prophet, rather, his words depict that he advised 'Umar or Abū 'Ubaydah to take up the position.

The very day the Prophet (pbuh & hf) departed, the *Ansār* (helpers, those who were living in Madīnah) had gathered together at the Saqīfah of Banī Saīdah to select a leader themselves. Abū Bakr gave a speech stating that the Quraysh were more deserving of the position of caliphate, but he did not mention anything in regards to his own position as the successor of the Prophet. Abū Bakr stated:

> "...O *Ansār*! You deserve all the qualities that you have attributed to yourselves, but this question (of caliphate) is only for the Quraysh as they are the best of the Arabs as regards descent and home, and I am pleased to suggest that you choose either of these two men, so take the oath of allegiance to either of them as you wish. And then Abū Bakr held my hand ('Umar's) and 'Ubayda ibn 'Abdullāh's hand who was sitting amongst us..."[74]

Abū Bakr never mentioned any words in regards to him being chosen; he never mentioned to the *Ansar* anything along the lines of "why are you all deciding upon a leader when I have been chosen by the Prophet (pbuh & hf)?" Also, many of the Quraysh were not present at this gathering. Sunni traditionists narrate that on the day of Saqīfah:

> 'Umar said: "'Alī ibn Abī Tālib, Zubayr ibn Awwām and those who were with them separated from us (and gathered) in the house of Fāṭimah, the daughter of the Messenger of Allāh."[75]

The Sunni historian Ibn Jarīr al-Ṭabarī reported the following:

> 'Umar came to the door of the Prophet's house but did not enter. He sent a message to Abū Bakr: "'Come immediately; I have urgent business with you.' Abū Bakr sent word to him that he had no time. 'Umar sent another message: 'We are faced with a crisis. Your presence is necessary.' Abū Bakr came out and 'Umar told him about the gathering of the *Ansār* in the Saqīfah and said that they should go there immediately. Both departed, and on the way they met Abū 'Ubaydah and took him with them.[76]

Imām 'Alī (AS) and many of the companions were not informed about the presence at the Saqīfah. The Prophet (pbuh & hf) had only recently departed and his Household members and followers were busy with his burial. If we think deeply about this, when someone whom we love passes away, we feel a deep anxiety in connection with the loved one who has died, our mind is not focused properly on any matter, we do not wish to endeavour anything under these circumstances, our hearts are filled with emotional pain and stress and to even consider carrying out anything, especially something of the nature of selecting a suitable leader would not be our first concern.

The nomination of a leader happened suddenly and irrationally, at a time when grief stricken individuals began mourning the death of the Prophet (pbuh & hf), their hearts filled with emotion and deep sorrow over his passing away. Under these circumstances how could a rational decision have been made? Hastily hurrying to discuss the matter of leadership at such a time when moods were not calm and right proved of no benefit to those who were left grieving for the Prophet.

When news had come to the family of the Prophet and many of the companions about what had happened at the Saqīfah, that the *Ansār* had gathered to choose a leader and Abū Bakr and 'Umar had gone there to deal with the situation, which consequently resulted in Abū Bakr being chosen as the leader, they gathered in the house of Sayyedah Fāṭimah (AS) and opposed the decision, which had been made.

> 'Umar said: "...There was a hue and cry among the gathering and their voices rose so that I was afraid there might be great disagreement, so I said, 'O Abū Bakr! Hold your hand out.' He held his hand out and I pledged allegiance to him, and then all the emigrants gave the pledge of allegiance and so did the *Ansār* afterwards. And so we became victorious over Sa'd ibn 'Ubāda (whom *al-Ansār* wanted to make a ruler)..."[77]

The people who were present at the Saqīfah did not fully represent the Quraysh. All the *Muhājirs* (emigrants, those who migrated to Madīnah) were not present at this gathering, nor was one of the most prominent figures of the Quraysh, Imām 'Alī (AS). Many people comment in regards to this event and mention that a unanimous decision had been made; when yet those who had remained behind were in opposition to this very decision.

> 'Umar said: "'Alī and Zubayr and whoever was with them, opposed us."[78]

We Muslims feel offended when we find that there are people in this day and age who oppose the decision, which had been made at the Saqīfah. We are not aware of those companions who had also opposed it. Al-Ya'qūbī stated the following:

> "A number of the Migrants and the Helpers refused to swear allegiance to Abū Bakr, inclined to favour 'Alī ibn Abī Tālib. Al-'Abbās ibn 'Abd al-Muṭṭālib, al-Fadhl ibn al-'Abbās, az-Zubayr, Khālid ibn Sa'īd, al-Miqdād, Salmān, Abū Dharr, 'Ammār, al-Barā', 'Ubayy ibn Ka'b were part of that group."[79]

If many prominent companions of the Prophet (pbuh & hf) had opposed the decision, how could it have been one of unanimity?

This sudden decision in the appointment of Abū Bakr was a consequence of the *Ansār* meeting to choose a leader. This appointment was given suddenly as 'Umar testifies; his words prove that a rational decision and a fair consultation had not taken place.

> 'Umar said: "...I have been informed that a speaker amongst you says: 'By Allah, if 'Umar should die, I will give the pledge of allegiance to such-and-such person. One should not deceive oneself by saying that the pledge of allegiance given to Abū Bakr was given suddenly and it was successful. No doubt, it was like that, but Allāh saved (the people) from its evil and there is none among you who has the qualities of Abū Bakr. Remember that whoever gives the pledge of allegiance to anybody among you without consulting of the other Muslims, neither that person, nor the person to whom the pledge of allegiance was given, are to be supported, lest they both should be killed. ..."[80]

'Umar's words do not depict to us that what had happened at the Saqīfah was correct. 'Umar stated that should something of this nature ever happen again, without consultation of the Muslims, then both the one nominated and the one who nominated him should be killed.

The historian Ibn Qutaybah in his book *Tārīkh al-Khulafah* (History of the Caliphs) reports the following:

> "Fāṭimah went around the meeting places of the *Ansārs*, asking for support of her husband and cousin and they said to her: 'O daughter of the Messenger of Allāh, we have already acclaimed that man, and if your husband had approached us before him, we would have supported him.' 'Alī said: 'Would I leave the Messenger of Allāh in his house unburied and go to argue with the people about his authority?' Fāṭimah said: 'Abū al-Ḥasan did what was expected of him and for what they did Allāh will hold them responsible and accountable.'"[81]

Why did the family of the Prophet (pbuh & hf) not agree with the decision made at the Saqīfah, they were not interested in the life of this world, there had to have been a very good reason for their disapproval in the nomination of Abū Bakr.

Again, if Abū Bakr was the chosen individual and had been chosen by the Prophet (pbuh & hf), then there most certainly would have been some evidence of him defending this position the Prophet had given him, especially when the *Ansār* were arguing over a position, which the majority of people in this day and age believe was rightly his. Directing the position to someone other than himself does not provide us with any certainty to what many claim.

The only individual who had shown concern for his position was Imām 'Alī (AS) whose words, firm belief, position, truthfulness and knowledge can also be proven through the words of others and through the words of our beloved Prophet (pbuh &hf).

What we observe recorded in regards to Imām 'Alī (AS)

What we observe recorded in regards to Imām 'Alī (AS).

(1) Imām 'Alī's (AS) firm belief.

'Alī said: "I was the first one to accept Islām at the hands of the Holy Prophet."[82]

'Alī said: "I am the servant of Allāh and the brother of his Messenger. I am the strongest in believing in the Prophet. Nobody else can say so except a liar."[83]

Narrated Anas ibn Mālik: "The Messenger was commissioned on Monday and 'Alī believed in him on Tuesday."[84]

Salmān al-Farsī said that the Messenger of God said: "The first one of you to drink from the Basin on the Day of Judgment is your first Muslim, 'Alī, the son of Abī Tālib."[85]

(2) Imām 'Alī's (AS) position.

'Alī said: "By Allāh I am his brother and *walī,* his cousin and the inheritor of his knowledge; who else is more worthy of it than me."[86]

Narrated Abū Ayyūb al-Ansārī, the Prophet addressed Fāṭimah: "O Fāṭimah! Have you not come to know that Allāh, the Dear One, cast a look at the inhabitants of the earth and chose your father from among them and sent him as His Messenger, then he cast a second look and selected your husband and inspired me to marry him to you and appoint him as my successor.[87]

Narration quoted by Ibn 'Abbās quoting the ten merit's of Imām 'Alī mentions one of those merits being: "You are the *walī* of every believer after me."[88]

The Prophet said: "None will repay my debts and discharge my duties except me or 'Alī."[89]

(3) The love of Imām 'Alī (AS) is a mark of sincere faith.

Narrated Zīrr: " 'Alī observed: 'By Him Who split up the seed and created something living, the Apostle gave me a promise that no one but a believer would love me, and none but a hypocrite would nurse grudge against me.'"[90]

Narrated Umm Salama, the Prophet said to 'Alī: "None shall love you except a believer, and none shall hate you except a hypocrite."[91]

Narrated Abū Sa'īd al-Khudrī that Abū Dharr Ghiffārrī said: "We used to recognise the hypocrites by their enmity against 'Alī and in the time of the Holy Prophet we had no other sign of finding out the hypocrites except that they were hostile to 'Alī."[92]

(4) Imām 'Alī's (AS) extensive knowledge.

"Ask me before you lose me. By Allāh if you ask me about anything that could happen up to the Day of Judgement, I will tell you about it. Ask me, for, by Allāh, you will not be able to ask me a question about anything without my informing you. Ask me about the Book of Allāh for by Allāh there is no verse about which I do not know whether it was sent down at night or during the day, or whether it was revealed on a plain or in a mountain."[93]

Sa'īd ibn al-Musaiyyab mentioned that none of the companions except 'Alī ibn Abī Tālib said: "Ask me before you lose me."[94]

The Messenger said to his daughter Fāṭimah: "Would it not please you that I have married you to the first Muslim in my nation, their most knowledge-eable, and their greatest in wisdom."[95]

The Prophet said: "'Among you is one who will fight for its (Qur'ān) interpretation just as I fought for its

> revelation.' The audience was very excited. Among them were Abū Bakr and 'Umar. Abū Bakr asked: 'Am I the one?' The Prophet's answer was negative. 'Umar inquired: 'Is it I?' The Prophet answered: 'No; but it is the one mending the shoes,' meaning thereby 'Alī; therefore we visited 'Alī to convey the good news to him, but he did not even raise his head, as if he had already heard it from the Messenger of Allāh."[96]
>
> Barīda narrated that the Messenger of Allāh said to Fāṭimah that: "I gave you in marriage to the best in my *Ummah*, the most knowledgeable in them, the best in patience in them, and the first Muslim among them."[97]
>
> Narrated Imām 'Alī, the Messenger of Allāh said: "I am the House of Wisdom and 'Alī is its door."[98]

Ibn Jarīr al-Ṭabarī commented on the above tradition and wrote the following:

> "We believe this tradition to be genuine and authentic."

As quoted by al-Muttaqī al-Hindī in his *Kanz al-'Ummāl*.[99]

Imām al-Ḥākim as well as many other scholars of *Ḥadīth* reported the following:

> The Messenger of Allāh said: "I am the city of knowledge, and 'Alī is its gate. So whoever intends to enter the city and the wisdom, he should enter from its gate."

He adds that this tradition is authentic."[100]

(5) Imām 'Alī (AS) is with the truth.

> The Prophet said to him: "You shall inform my nation about the truth and what they dispute after me."

Imām al-Ḥākim quoted in connection with the above *Ḥadīth*, that it is authentic.[101]

> The Prophet also said: "'Alī is with the truth and the truth revolves around 'Alī."[102]

Sibt ibn Jauzī quotes the above *Ḥadīth* in connection with *Ḥadīth* al-Ghadir as the Prophet (pbuh & hf) had also mentioned it on this auspicious occasion.

> Sibt ibn Jauzī states: "This *Ḥadīth* is proof that if there is a difference between 'Alī and any of the companions, the right will certainly be with 'Alī."[103]

> The Prophet said: "'Alī is with the Qur'ān and the Qur'ān is with 'Alī. These two shall not be separated from each other until they reach me at the Pool of Kauthar."[104]

Imām 'Alī (AS) stated many sayings of the Prophet (pbuh & hf), which related to himself. A man of such character, a man whom was brought up by the Prophet himself, who had embraced Islām at the tender age of ten, would not have stated all this to praise himself. His piety, God consciousness, striving in the path of Allāh was known by all and most of all by Allāh and His Apostle.

We could state that Imām 'Alī (AS) provided the masses, the coming generations with a means to understand the words spoken by the Prophet (pbuh & hf) through his speaking out. If he had not done so, no individual then or even now would have greatly understood the position of the Imām, this responsibility, which Allāh had bestowed upon him. If it had been the same case for Abū Bakr and 'Umar, can we positively say without a shadow of doubt, that they would have remained silent in regards to their God given responsibility?

Religious Knowledge is a key requirement for the Leader of the Islamic state.

Imām 'Alī's (AS) knowledge of the Qur'ān is something of which not even the majority of Muslims will deny. The Prophet (pbuh & hf) never would have mentioned Imām 'Alī as being the means to reach the truth if Imām 'Alī did not know of it. After the Prophet's demise, Imām 'Alī remained with the truth making him inseparable from the Qur'ān, a trait, which was most important in an individual who was to be the leader of the Islamic state.

Allāh teaches us:

> "Their Prophet said to them: 'Allāh hath appointed Talūt (Saul) as king over you.' They said: 'How can he exercise authority over us when we are better fitted than he to exercise authority and he is not even gifted with wealth in abundance?' He said: 'Allāh hath chosen him above you and hath gifted him abundantly with knowledge and bodily prowess; Allāh granteth His authority to whom He pleaseth. Allāh careth for all and He knoweth all things.'" Qur'ān 2:247

Talūt (AS) was not a prophet and yet was given the position of authority at the time of a prophet who could have been Samuel (AS). Talūt's position was argued over but Allāh made it clear that it is knowledge and not wealth, which qualifies an individual for a leadership role. No matter what wealth one has, it is the knowledge, which exalts the righteous to a higher rank in the eyes of Allāh. It is this type of individual who has to be preferred above any other, just as Allāh prefers them above any other.

> "Allāh will exalt those who believe and those who have been granted knowledge amongst you." Qur'ān 58:11

Ibrāhīm (AS) said to his stepfather Azar:

> "O my father! I have received such knowledge as has not come to you, so follow me, and I will guide you to the straight path." Qur'ān 19:43

When Abū Bakr was nominated, he is reported to have said:

> "I hold in my hands the reins of your affairs even though I am not the best amongst you. If you see that I am treading the right path, then support me, if you see me embarking on the wrong cause, then guide me back to the right path."[105]

These words are very well known amongst those who have studied the advent of Abū Bakr's caliphate.

Imām 'Alī (AS) asked Abū Bakr in a conversation:

> "'What are the qualities a leader should possess?' He answered: 'A desire for the peoples welfare, faithfulness to his undertakings, justice and equity in his conduct, knowledge of the Qur'ān and the *Sunnah*, and the principles in judgeship – these are among the qualities that are needed. In addition the ruler must refrain from deceit, have no concern for the life of this world, hasten always to aid the oppressed, and regard impartially the rights and claims of all.' Then he fell silent. 'Alī thereupon said: 'Further qualities needed are primacy in embracing Islām and being related to the Messenger of Allāh'. Abū Bakr responded that these two might also be regarded as necessary qualifications. 'Alī then asked Abū Bakr: 'Tell me by God, do you see these qualities in yourself or in me?' He answered: 'All that I have mentioned is to be found in you.'"[106]

If we wished to seek advice in regards to an illness we had, would we turn towards a student doctor or would we feel more secure taking the full advice from a fully qualified one? The student does have a certain amount of capability and knowledge that the doctor has, but the fully qualified doctor is the more capable and the one with the **greater knowledge**. It is more likely that we would take the full advice from the qualified doctor and not fully rely upon the student. It is the doctor who would take the lead and not the student. Our common sense teaches us to follow the one who is more acquainted, this is our understanding, our logic speaking and Allāh's words do not contradict this.

Religious Knowledge is a key requirement for the Leader of the Islamic state

Allāh states:

> "Are those who know and those who know not alike? But only men of understanding will pay heed." Qur'ān 39:9

We all as human beings and the Almighty Allāh favour those individuals who are more capable than ourselves, and we all should understand that it would make sense to follow the righteous individual with the **greater knowledge** of the Qur'ān and to follow his guidance after the Prophet's (pbuh & hf) demise.

If Allāh preferred the righteous individual with the lesser knowledge, He would be going against His own law, His own *Sunnah* (words). And Allāh states:

> "And never will you find a change in the *Sunnah* of Allāh" Qur'ān 33:62.

The words of a human being can never be taken in preference to the words of Allāh, so are we to follow Allāh's *Sunnah,* His teaching, or reject it and take in preference our own and more importantly would the Prophet (pbuh & hf) have ignored these teachings and taken in preference the righteous individual with the lesser knowledge?

Does Allāh's law teach us that the older individual is the wiser individual?

The statement: "Abū Bakr was older, therefore, he was wiser," does not really gain any credit when its words do not make any real sense. If we class Abū Bakr as being a wise man, we should not express it in relation to his age, but rather, in relation to his piety and knowledge.

Imām 'Alī (AS) was a lot younger than Abū Bakr and it is known that he was around thirty years old when the Prophet (pbuh & hf) departed. However, Imām 'Alī had started to experience the religion from childhood, an age far younger than that of Abū Bakr and other companions, but this does not mean that his mind was less dynamic and sharp than the minds of those who had embraced Islām in their later years. At that time, although the Imām was a child, he still was an astounding personality.

It has to be said that we can never rank an individuals wisdom according to the individuals age, because nowhere in the Qur'ān does Allāh teach us that the age of an individual gives us an indication towards how wise one is. If such an idea was the *Sunnah* of Allāh, then Allāh would not have given his prophets wisdom whilst they were young, for example, Yaḥya (AS), He would have waited till they matured.

> "O Yaḥya! Take hold of the Book with might; and We gave him wisdom even as a youth." Qur'ān 19:12

Be it a prophet or a loved one of Allāh, Allāh will give wisdom to whom he pleases and the age of an individual does not serve as any boundary. And Allāh states:

> "He giveth wisdom to who He will and unto whom wisdom is given, he truly has received abundant good. But none remember except the men of understanding." Qur'ān 2:269

Allāh granted knowledge to Imām 'Alī (AS) through his sincere faith in Islām, his age carries no significance hence the reason why the Prophet (pbuh & hf) did not see his age as an obstacle for him to not understand the religion. Imām 'Alī's faith, conduct, sincerity, his acceptance of Islām through understanding the knowledge, which had come to him, was known and acknowledged by the Prophet. This was observed by the Prophet throughout his life and never did the Prophet state: "You do not understand 'Alī, you are not capable of understanding" even when he was a child. It is not a strange thing to believe that a youngster can be extremely sharp and intelligent even in this day and age. There are children within this day and age with astounding capabilities that are extremely intelligent and their abilities far exceed those within the same age group as them and exceed those whom are a lot older than them.

Guidance lies within the hands of the Almighty and Allāh's guidance reaches out to those who sincerely strive onto His path.

Does Allāh's law teach us that the older individual is the wiser individual?

> "And surely as for those who strive hard unto Our ways we will surely guide them." Qur'ān 29:69

If the Qur'ān demonstrates that age is not a criterion for addressing an individual as being wise, then should we? Imām 'Alī's (AS) age can never be used to disregard his position, and the Shī'ahs illuminate his position as the first Imām of the Ahl al-Bayt, regardless of how old he was when the Prophet (pbuh & hf) had proclaimed it.

Imām 'Alī's (AS) capabilities were observed by the Muslims throughout the Prophet's (pbuh & hf) life.

It is the Prophet (pbuh & hf) himself who proved Imām 'Alī's (AS) capabilities in taking charge of many affairs during the course of Prophet-hood. Such examples are when the Prophet left Imām 'Alī in charge of Madīnah whilst he embarked on the expedition to Tabūk, his being placed in charge of the mission to Yemen and the responsibility of reciting *Sūrah al-Tawbah*.

Imām 'Alī (AS) taking charge on the mission to Yemen.

> 'Alī felt some reluctance on his mission to Yemen because of his age and the Prophet said to him: "Certainly Allāh will guide your heart and give you strength."[107]

> Narrated 'Alī ibn Abī Tālib: "The Apostle of Allāh sent me to the Yemen as judge, and I asked: Apostle of Allāh, are you sending me when I am young and have no knowledge of the duties of a judge? He replied: 'Allāh will guide your heart and keep your tongue true. When two litigants sit in front of you, do not decide till you hear what the other has to say as you heard what the first had to say; for it is best that you should have a clear idea of the best decision.' He said: 'I had been a judge (for long); or he said (the narrator is doubtful): 'I have no doubts about a decision afterwards.'" [108]

Succession of the Prophet (PBUH)

There was no doubt in the Prophet's (pbuh & hf) mind in regards to Imān 'Alī's (AS) competency in handling affairs. The Prophet's assurance in him was due to the knowledge which he had in connection to him, that the Imām was guided by Allāh. Clearly such knowledge had come from Allāh; otherwise the Prophet would not have expressed such certainty.

> Narrated by Jābir ibn 'Abdullāh: "On the day Allāh's Messenger sent 'Alī to at-Ta'if, he called him and spoke in private to him." The people said: 'He has had a long private conversation with his cousin,' and Allāh's Messenger replied: 'It was not I but Allāh who had a private conversation with him.'"[109]

Imām 'Alī (AS) being given the responsibility of reciting *Sūrah al-Tawbah*.

The Prophet (pbuh & hf) gave orders to Abū Bakr to proclaim *Sūrah al-Tawbah*. Allāh then through Jibrīl (AS) (Gabriel) informed His Prophet (pbuh & hf) that Imām 'Alī (AS) was to recite it instead. This incident proved that Imām 'Alī's capability was something that was recognised by Allāh, and it was something that was illuminated through such occurrences.

The Sunni scholar Maulana 'Ala Maududī in his *Tafhīm al-Qur'ān*, which has been translated by Zafar Ishāq Ansārī, states in the third Volume of this Book on the section discussing *Sūrah al-Tawbah*:

> "The *Sūrah* comprises three discourses. The first discourse runs from the opening verse to the fifth section of the *Sūrah* (i.e. verses 1-37 –Ed). It was revealed in or around *Dhul- al-Qadah* 9 A.H/631 C.E, soon after the Prophet dispatched Abū Bakr as the leader of the pilgrims to Makkah. After the verses had been revealed, the Prophet instructed 'Alī to follow Abū Bakr and to recite the same verses proclaiming the new directives embodied in them before a representative gathering of Arabs who had gone there for Pilgrimage."

Imām Aḥmad ibn Ḥanbal reported:

Imām 'Alī's (AS) capabilities were observed by the Muslims throughout the Prophet's (pbuh & hf) life

> Narrated Abū Bakr: "'The Prophet of Allāh sent me with *Sūrah al-Tawbah* to the people of Mecca, to proclaim that no polytheist will be permitted to make the pilgrimage after this year, or circum-navigate the Ka'ba in a naked state. No soul shall enter Paradise except a Muslim.'
>
> Abū Bakr travelled on for three days, then the Prophet said to 'Alī: 'Follow him and send Abū Bakr back to me and go and deliver the message yourself.' 'Alī did that and Abū Bakr returned. He wept and said: 'O Prophet of Allāh was there something revealed concerning me?' He said: 'No! But Gabriel came to me and said, one shall do this for you but you or a man related to you.'"[110]

It is not doubted that Allāh instructed His Prophet (pbuh & hf) to direct Abū Bakr to recite the verses of *Sūrah al-Tawbah*, but then instructed him to hand over the responsibility to Imām 'Alī (AS). It is not something out of the ordinary for such an occurrence to happen in relation to God's chosen prophets, and we can understand this through the Qur'ān. The Qur'ān teaches us within the story of Mūsa (AS), that he was instructed to leave his people within the deserts of Sinai whilst he was appointed thirty nights to remain with his Lord. The Qur'ān clearly demonstrates that Allāh further added ten nights to this time period.

> "And when We did appoint for Moses thirty nights (of solitude), and added to them ten, and he completed the whole time appointed by his Lord of forty nights; and Moses said unto his brother: Take my place among the people. Do right, and follow not the way of mischief makers." Qur'ān 7:142

There was a reason for such an occurrence, which was within God's knowledge. Such occurrences manifest the nature of the people whom Musa (AS) had left whilst at Mount Sinai, and it is very well known that they sculpted a calf and fell into idol-worship. Hence, if

Allāh had not added the ten days, then maybe this weak faith in their hearts would not have been revealed.

If we come back to the event, which took place in regards to the reciting of *Sūrah al-Tawbah*, it manifest the calibre of the Imām compared to that of others, and if it had of not taken place in such a way, then maybe we would not have understood the rank of the Imām, which was also manifest to Abū Bakr himself.

We need to comprehend, that throughout the lifetime of the Prophet (pbuh & hf), Imām 'Ali (AS) was never placed under any individual in any battle or expedition, either he would lead it, or, if some other individual was sent, he would remain with the Prophet, close by his side. We will observe such an example in section ten of the book, an expedition, which the Prophet ordered towards the end of his life.

The Prophet wanted to teach others of the importance of the Imām, plus provide the future generations with such knowledge in regards to him, which inshallah will be observed throughout the course of the book.

Imām 'Alī (AS) relationship with the Prophet (pbuh & hf) is the same as the relationship of Hārūn (AS) with his brother Mūsā (AS).

> Related Zayd ibn Abū 'Awfah: "When the Prophet had migrated to Madīnah about five month after the migration, he established brotherhood between the *Muhājir* and *Ansār* where one brother became the brother of another, keeping 'Alī for himself. 'Alī said: 'O Messenger of Allāh! My soul has expired, and my spine has been broken, having seen what you have done for your companions while leaving me alone. If this is a sign of your anger with me, then I complain only to you and beg you pardon.' The Messenger of Allāh said: 'I swear by the one Who sent me to convey the truth about Him, I have not spared you except for my own self. You are to me like Aaron was to Moses except there will be no Prophet after me. You are my brother, heir and companion.' 'Alī asked him: 'What shall I inherit from you?' He answered:

Imām 'Alī (AS) relationship with the Prophet (pbuh & hf) is the same as the relationship of Hārūn (AS) with his brother Mūsā (AS)

> 'Whatever prophet's before me left for those who inherited them, the Book of their Lord, and the *Sunnah* of their prophet. You will be my companion in my house in Paradise together with my daughter Fāṭimah. You are my brother and companion.' Then he recited the verse: 'They are brethren seated conveniently facing each other with sincere compassion..."[111]

The above report speaks of the second brotherhood of Islām, which was established on the migration of the Prophet (pbuh & hf) to Madīnah, the first being established in Makkah before the migration. Scholars such as Ḥalabī in his Sīrah al-Ḥalabīyya,[112] Sibt ibn Jauzī in his Tadhkīra,[113] al-Mas'ūdī in his Murūj al-Dhahab[114] express that the statement: "You are to me like Aaron was to Moses except there will be no Prophet after me," has also been expressed on other occasions by the Prophet. For example it is reported that:

> Abū Bakr, 'Umar, and Abū 'Ubaydah ibn al-Jarrah were in the company of the Prophet who was leaning on 'Alī. The Prophet patted 'Alī's shoulder and said: "O 'Alī! You are the strongest among the believers in faith; the first (man) to embrace Islām, and your status to me is similar to that of Aaron to Moses.[115]

The Prophet (pbuh & hf) also stated the same when he left Imām 'Alī (AS) in charge of Madīnah before his expedition to Tabūk. The hypocrites were conspiring against him because the Prophet had not included him in his expedition to Tabūk. The Prophet silenced them by stating what sort of position and relationship he had with the Imām, his rank in no way was demoted, it remained the same.

> Narrated Sa'd ibn Abī Waqqās: "Allāh's Apostle set out for Tabūk appointing 'Alī as his deputy (in Madīnah). 'Alī said: 'Do you want to leave me with the children and women?' The Prophet said: "Will you not be pleased that you will be to me like Aaron to Moses? But there will be no Prophet after me."[116]

Succession of the Prophet (PBUH)

"We sent Moses, the Book, and appointed his brother Aaron with him as *wazīran* (minister)." Qur'ān 25:35

If we think of the Prime Minister of a country, he always has a deputy, and should he be called away for any reason, his deputy takes over the affairs of the state. If the Prime Minister passes away, this position is automatically taken by his deputy.

We understand that Imām 'Alī (AS) was the Harūn (AS) of the *Ummah*, he was the brother, the deputy minister (*wazīr*) both within the Prophet's (pbuh & hf) lifetime and would also remain so after his demise. The only difference being that Imām 'Alī was not a prophet, unlike Harūn.

We could also state that this close proximity between the Prophet (pbuh & hf) and Imām 'Alī was not something believed to be insignificant, rather, it was a connection established to strengthen the call of Islām as was the connection, which was established between Mūsa (AS) and his brother Hārūn (AS).

It can be rationally understood that the Prophet (pbuh & hf) had publicised to the people from the start of his mission up to the end of his life the Imām's closeness to him, his capabilities, his faith, his knowledge above that of others, so there could be no doubt in the minds of the people about Imām 'Alī (AS) being able to administer the affairs of the *Ummah* after him above anyone else.

Would we associate the matter of accompanying the Prophet (pbuh & hf) on any occasion, to a qualification required for the leader of the Islamic state?

It is well known that Abū Bakr accompanied the Prophet (pbuh & hf) on his migration to Madīnah and was his companion in the cave. A verse was revealed in regards to this event.

> "If you will not aid **him**, Allāh certainly aided **him** when those who disbelieved expelled **him**, **he** being the second of the two, when they both were in the cave, when **he** said to **his** companion: 'Grieve not, surely Allāh is with us.' So Allāh sent down His tranquillity upon **him** and with hosts which you did not see." Qur'ān 9:40

Many Muslims state the above verse in relation to the leadership of Abū Bakr, when yet this verse does not suggest anything in regards to any qualification required in leading the Islamic state. There are many companions who accompanied the Prophet (pbuh & hf) on various occasions within his lifetime; but this does not indicate that they all had acquired a qualification required for the right to the caliphate.

The reality of the verse is that it provides us with a message, a teaching, that there is no need for Allāh's servants to be afraid, when Allāh is always present.

If we look towards the end of the verse closely, we observe:

> "So Allāh sent down His tranquillity upon **him**."

NOT

> "So Allāh sent down His tranquillity upon **them**."

Hence Allāh sent down His tranquillity upon one person and this person, who is mentioned as **him** all the way through the verse is none other than the Prophet (pbuh & hf). The other individual is mentioned as the companion and it is very well known who this companion is through the Prophet's *Ḥadīth*.

We find that when Allāh addresses His tranquillity descending upon others, He distinguishes it separately from the Prophet (pbuh & hf):

> "But Allāh sent down His tranquillity upon His Messenger and **the believers** and sent down forces which you could not see." Qur'ān 9:26

> "Allāh sent down His tranquillity upon His Messenger and **the believers** and adhered them to the word of piety." Qur'ān 48:26

All Muslims are aware that when the verse in regards to the companion in the cave (9:40) is expressed, it is expressed in order to recognise a merit of Abū Bakr, which evidently is due to his accompanying the Prophet (pbuh & hf). If we were informed that such and such an individual accompanied the Prophet, we would automatically think of it as a great privilege. It is observed as exactly this in regards to Abū Bakr. However, we are unmindful of the presence of Imām 'Alī (AS) who took the place of the Prophet when lying in his bed, and are in total ignorance to what is recorded in regards to a verse of the Qur'ān that was revealed solely in total praise of him.

> "When the Prophet left 'Alī sleeping in his bed while the enemies were outside plotting to murder him, Allāh addressed Gabriel and Michael thus: 'I have created brotherhood between both of you and let the life-span of one of you be longer than that of the other. Which one of you wishes the other to have a longer life?' Each held his own life dearer. The Almighty said: 'Why cannot you be like 'Alī ibn Abī Tālib between him and Muḥammad I have created brotherhood, and he has chosen to sleep in Muḥammad's bed, offering to sacrifice his own life for his brother? Go down to earth and protect him from his foes.' They both came down. Gabriel stood at 'Alī's head while Michael stood at his feet. Gabriel cried: 'Congratulations! Congratulations! Who can be

> like you, O son of Abū Tālib? Even Allāh boasts about you to His angels!' Regarding that incident, the verse 'And there are among men those who trade their own lives for the Pleasure of Allāh (Qur'ān 2:207)' was revealed."[117]

Why do we not analyse this through a simple example? Imagine there is a politician residing in a hotel, a fire breaks out. There are two security guards outside the room of the hotel. One guard accompanies the politician out of the hotel while the other tackles the fire and extinguishes it. The local authorities commend the security guard, who extinguished the fire on time, and the second guard is also mentioned as he accompanied the politician out of the building. Both are given a merit but the individual who puts out the fire is commended more so.

Section 9

The Truthfulness of Reports/Statements.

Various reports are brought forward in order to bring into view the position of the first two recognised caliphs of the majority. As mentioned previously, the majority believe that it was Abū Bakr who was best fit for the position of leadership after the Prophet (pbuh & hf).

The Qur'ān provides us with the guidelines to analyse conflicting reports, which are brought forward, hence our acceptance of such reports has to run in accordance with the teachings of the Qur'ān. Separating the truth from the falsehood is a must for us all.

The Prophet (pbuh & hf) would always act and speak in accordance with the teachings of the Qur'ān; we can never believe that he made statements, which did not correlate with the Qur'ān. He and the Imāms of Ahl al-Bayt explain:

> Narrated 'Alī ibn Ibrāhīm from his father from al-Newalla from al-Sauna from Abū 'Abdullāh who has said the following. "The Holy Prophet: 'Over every truth there is a reality and above every valid issue there is light. Whatever agrees with the Holy Qur'ān you must follow it and whatever does not agree disregard it.'"[118]

> Narrated Muḥammad ibn Yaḥyā from Aḥmad ibn Muḥammad ibn Īsa from ibn Fadak from 'Alī ibn 'Unbār from Aye ibn Rushed from Abū 'Abdullāh who has said the following: "Of *Ḥadīth* whatever does not agree with the Holy Qur'ān is a useless statement."[119]

> Narrated Muḥammad ibn Email from al-Fadhl ibn Shīhan from ibn Abū 'Umar from Hishām ibn al-Ḥakam and others from Abū 'Abdullāh who has said the following. "The Holy Prophet once addressed the people in Mīna (a place in Makkah) saying: 'O people, whatever comes to you in the form of my *Ḥadīth* you must see if it agrees with the Holy Book of Allāh then

> know that I have said it but whatever comes to you that does not agree with the Book of Allāh then know that I have not said it."[120]

The statement: "If the *imān* (faith) of Abū Bakr was put in one scale and the *imān* of the whole nation in the other, the *imān* of Abū Bakr would be greater," is one such statement which is brought forward to attest to the leadership of Abū Bakr. This statement is a very heavy statement, which deeply indicates to us that Abū Bakr must have been the most righteous and the highest in rank in the eyes of Allāh to have faith greater than the entire nation. Righteousness, truthfulness and sincere belief are great characteristics of men of faith and are observed the most in prophets and the chosen men of God.

The Qur'ān states:

Righteousness.

> "Surely the most honoured in the sight of Allāh is the most righteous of you, and Allāh has full knowledge and is well acquainted with all things." Qur'ān 49:13

Truthfulness.

> "O ye who believe. Fear Allāh! And be with the truthful." Qur'ān 9:119

Faith and knowledge.

> "Allāh will exalt those who believe amongst you and those who have been granted knowledge and Allāh is well acquainted with all ye do." Qur'ān 58:11

The Verses revealed in connection with the *Mubāhala* (Invoking the curse of Allāh upon the liars).

> "The similitude of Īsā (Jesus) before Allāh is as that of Ādam (Adam); He created him from dust then said to him: 'Be and he was.' The truth (comes) from Allāh alone; so be not of those who doubt, **Say unto him**

> **who disputes with thee after the knowledge has come unto thee therein, say let us summon our sons and your sons, our women and your women, ourselves and yourselves,** and then pray to Allāh to lay the curse on the liars." Qur'ān 3:59-61

Some Christian delegates came from Najrān to see the Prophet (pbuh & hf); they asked him what his thoughts were in regards to Īsa (AS). The Prophet did not give them an answer straight away but waited until he received *Wahi* (revelation) from Allāh as he would only answer when Allāh's words were revealed upon his tongue. The following day a verse was revealed describing the status of Īsa (AS) in the eyes of Allāh, the Christian delegates did not believe this and doubted the Prophet. Allāh revealed to His Prophet to arrange a meeting with the Christian delegates in order that a *Mubāhala* could take place, so that it could be established who the truthful ones as compared to the liars were. They were asked to bring with them those they wished, and the Prophet took with him his chosen ones. Although the verse uses the words our sons, our women, ourselves, the Prophet only took with him, Imām al-Ḥasan (AS) and al-Ḥusayn (AS) as his "sons", Fāṭimah al-Zahra (AS) as his "women" and Imām 'Alī (AS) as those who represented "ourselves". The Christians noticed that the Prophet had confined the *Mubāhala* to only five people, the members of his House. These five truthful people had come to invoke the curse of Allāh upon the liars and the Christians became very much agitated and hesitant, thus even proving the truthfulness of the Ahl al-Bayt to the Christians, so much so that they finally resorted to a peace treaty with the Prophet and the *Mubāhala* did not take place.

> This *Ḥadīth* has been narrated on the authority of Shū'ba with the same chain of transmitters. Amīr ibn Sa'd ibn Abī Waqqās reported on the authority of his father: "...When the (following) verse was revealed, 'let us summon our children and your children.' Allāh's Messenger called 'Alī, Fāṭimah, al-Ḥasan and al-Ḥusayn and said: '*Allāh humma hāūlāi Ahl al-Baytī* (O Allāh! They are my Ahl al-Bayt).'"[121]

If an individual invokes a curse on a liar and is not truthful, then that individual may fall into invoking a curse upon his or herself. When we declare that Abū Bakr's faith was greater than the whole of the nation, there could be no doubt about his truthfulness **above others**, but the Prophet (pbuh & hf) restricted this *Mubāhala* to himself and four other individuals of which Abū Bakr was not included.

Allāh restricted His choice to only five people, had there been other individuals alive at that time, who were **more** truthful than them, the Prophet (pbuh & hf) would never have left them out and taken with him those less deserving.

Allāh teaches in regards to His Prophet:

> "He does not speak from his own desire. It is but a revelation revealed. Taught to him by One Mighty in Power." Qur'ān 53:3-5

It is narrated on the authority of 'Abdullāh ibn 'Umar that:

> The Messenger of Allāh said: "Had there been any soul on the whole earth better than 'Alī, Fātmah, al-Ḥasan and al-Ḥusayn, Allāh would have commanded me to take them along with me to *Mubāhala*. But as they were superior in dignity and respect to all human beings, Allāh confined His choice on them only for participation in *Mubāhala*."[122]

> Narrated Jābir ibn 'Abdullāh al-Ansārī: "The word 'sons' refers to al-Ḥasan and al-Ḥusayn, the word 'women' refers to Fāṭimah, and the word 'our selves' refer to the Prophet and 'Alī. Thus 'Alī is referred as **'the self'** of the Prophet (*nafs*-soul of the Prophet)."[123]

The Prophet (pbuh & hf) many a time addressed Imām 'Alī (AS) in connection with himself.

> Narrated Umm Salama: "Allāh's Messenger said: 'He who reviles 'Alī has reviled me.'"[124]

> Narrated Zayd ibn Arqam: "The Prophet said: 'When I am anyone's patron, 'Alī is his patron also.'"[125]

> Narrated Hubshī ibn Junadah, Allāh's Messenger said: "'Alī pertains to me and I pertain to 'Alī and no one will conclude anything on my behalf but me or 'Alī."[126]

Someone chosen as being the **self** of the Prophet (pbuh & hf) can never be ranked below anyone else and surely the Prophet is the most outstanding and the most exalted in character.

> "And most certainly you are an exalted standard of character." Qur'ān 68:4

The verse (3:61) in question gives us much evidence in connection with the Imām's immense righteousness, faith and upright character above other men.

Righteousness is within us all, many people are pious and righteous but the degree of piety and righteousness differs from one individual to another and Allāh ranks His servants and rewards them accordingly; this is His justice; His *Sunnah*.

Allāh states:

> "And for all are ranks according to their deeds for Thy Lord is not unmindful of what they do." Qur'ān 6:132

Allāh always speaks highly of His righteous and sincere servants, those whose deeds reflect their good morality and faithful nature, ultimately leading them to a life of purity, which they have earned themselves through their righteous actions and good conduct. Purity being a word, which we would use in connection with cleanliness, religiously speaking we would use words such as chaste, modest, upright, honourable and we would never associate the word sin in relation to any part of the word purity. Allāh states:

> "For every man or women who works righteousness and has faith we shall revive a purified life for him. And we will bestow on such their reward according to the best of their actions." Qur'ān 16:97

Āyat al-Tathīr (The Verse of Purification) and *Ḥadīth-e-Kīsa* (Tradition of the Cloak).

> "And stay quietly in your houses, and make not a dazzling display, like that of the former Times of Ignorance; and establish regular Prayer, and give regular Charity; and obey Allāh and His Messenger. Verily Allāh wishes to keep away from you every kind of impurity O People of the House and to make you pure and spotless." Qur'ān 33:33

> Narrated 'Ā'isha: "Allāh's Apostle went out one morning wearing a striped cloak of the black camel's hair that there came al-Ḥasan ibn 'Alī, he wrapped him under it, then came al-Ḥusayn and wrapped him under it along with the other one (al-Ḥasan). Then came Fāṭimah and he took her under it, then came 'Alī and he also took him under it and then said: 'Verily Allāh intends to keep off from you *al-Rijs* (every kind of impurity) O' People of the House (Ahl al-Bayt), and purify you with a perfect purification... Qur'ān 33:33 '"[127]

This tradition is significant proof towards Allāh's favours upon the Ahl al-Bayt.

> Narrated 'Umar ibn Abī Salama, the son of Umm Salama (another wife of Prophet): "'The verse 'Verily Allāh intends to ...' was revealed to the Prophet in the house of Umm Salama. Upon that, the Prophet gathered Fāṭimah, al-Ḥasan, and al-Ḥusayn, and covered them with a cloak, and he also covered 'Alī who was behind him. Then the Prophet said: 'O Allāh! These are the members of my House (Ahl al-Bayt). Keep them away from every impurity and purify them with a perfect purification.' Umm Salama (the wife of Prophet) asked: 'Am I also included among them O Apostle of Allāh?' The Prophet

> replied: 'You remain in your position and you are towards a good ending.'"[128]

If we read the beginning of the verse (33:33), the wives of the Prophet (pbuh & hf) are addressed and Allāh mentions them in the feminine clause. The clause: "Verily Allāh wishes to keep away from you every kind of impurity..." is addressing the Ahl al-Bayt and switches from **feminine to masculine gender**. Those who are familiar with the Arabic language can comprehend that had Allāh continued to address the wives the word *'ankunna* instead of *'ankum* would have been used, as *'ankunna* is the grammatical term expressing the predominantly feminine gender. It is very important to realise that Allāh changes the address when speaking of the Ahl al-Bayt from the **predominantly feminine to the predominantly masculine gender**, Sayyedah Fāṭimah (AS) the only women included, she and Imām 'Alī (AS) being the mother and father of the proceeding Imāms of the Ahl al-Bayt who are all male. We may state that the change of address does not portray the predominantly masculine gender as even if one male was present, Allāh would have changed the address hence still including the females i.e. the Prophet's wives. We have to remember that these comments need to also correspond with the continuous words of the Prophet and we find that traditions in connection with the wives not being included **in reference to this verse (33:33)** are in plenty, and serve to prove who were being projected when addressing these members of the Ahl al-Bayt, leaving no room for personal opinion or contradicting the *Ṣaḥīḥ* that has corroboratory narratives solidifying it i.e. the tradition of 'Ā'isha in *Ṣaḥīḥ* Muslim.

Sunni commentators of the verse of purification mention that:

> 'Verily Allāh intends to ... (the last sentence of the verse 33:33)' was revealed for 'Alī, Fāṭimah, al-Ḥasan, and al-Ḥusayn, because of the **usage of masculine gender** in the word *'Ankum* and after that.'[129]

Various companions of the Prophet (pbuh & hf) also acknowledged whom the Prophet had addressed as his Ahl al-Bayt. This continued custom of addressing them in this way became known amongst them.

Āyat al-Tathīr (The Verse of Purification) and *Ḥadīth-e-Kīsa* (Tradition of the Cloak)

> Narrated Abū Sa'īd al-Khudrī: "I heard the Messenger of Allāh saying: 'This verse has been revealed about five individuals, me, 'Alī, al-Ḥasan, al-Ḥusayn, and Fāṭimah.'"[130]

The following tradition is recorded in al-Tabarī's *Tafsīr al-Kabīr* (the Great Commentary) and Imām Aḥmed's Musnad.

> Narrated Abū 'Ammār: "I was sitting with Wathīlah ibn Asqa' when a discussion took place about 'Alī and the people abused him. When those present rose to leave, he said to me: 'Keep sitting so that I may talk with you about the man whom they have been abusing. I was with the Holy Prophet when 'Alī, Fāṭimah, al-Ḥasan and al-Ḥusayn approached him and the Holy Prophet spread his cloak on them and said, O Allāh! These are the members of my family. Ward off every uncleanness from them and keep them clean and pure.'"[131]

The Prophet (pbuh & hf) never stated or did anything for no reason, he continued to mention this verse for many months in order to demonstrate to the people who the Ahl al-Bayt were and the distinction Allāh had given them. By mentioning them continuously at the door of the House of Sayyedah Sayyedah Fāṭimah (AS), it proved that those who were living in that house were in fact the People of the House (the Ahl al-Bayt).

> Narrated Anas ibn Mālik: "The Messenger of Allāh, from the time the revelation of 'Verily Allāh intends to... the verse in the Qur'ān 33:33' for six months thereafter, stood by the door of the House of Fāṭimah and said: 'Time for prayer Ahl al-Bayt; no doubt! Allāh wishes to keep away all abomination from you and make you pure and spotless.'"[132]

> Narrated Abū 'l-Ḥamrā: "The Messenger of God continued eight months in Madīnah, coming to the door of 'Alī at every morning prayer, putting his two

> hands on the two sides of the door and exclaiming: '*Assalāt! Assalāt!* (Prayer! prayer!) Certainly God ward off all uncleanness from you, O members of the House of Muḥammad, and to make you pure and spotless.'"[133]

These occasions truly mark the fact that the Prophet (pbuh & hf) expressed this verse in connection with his House members many times.

What would be important to address here, is that at the time of the revelation of this verse (33:33), all the members of the Ahl al-Bayt had not been born. It could be stated that how is it possible for the rest of the Imāms (AS) to be included in the Ahl al-Bayt if they did not exist at that time? It would be best if we explained this matter through the teachings of the Qur'ān:

> "And his wife was standing (there) and she laughed; but We gave her glad tidings of Isaac and after him of Jacob. She said: 'Alas for me! Shall I bear a child seeing I am an old woman and my husband here is an old man? That would indeed be a wonderful thing!' They said: 'Dost thou wonder at Allāh's decree? The grace of Allāh and His blessings on you O ye Ahl al-Bayt (People of the House)! For He is indeed worthy of all praise full of all glory!'" Qur'ān 11:71-73

These verses, which speak in regards to Sarah (AS) the wife of Ibrahim (AS) give glad tidings that she would bear a child by the name of Isāc (AS). Isāc had a son called Ya'qūb (AS) whom Allāh also attached to Sarah. What we must realise is that none of these sons existed at that time, but even so, they were classed as the Ahl al-Bayt of Ibrahim as was Sarah who was classed as the mother of both of them. If we think of Sayyedah Fāṭimah (AS), she was included in the Ahl al-Bayt in the same way Sarah was included in the House of Ibrahim, Sayyedah Fāṭimah being the one who bore Imām al-Ḥasan (AS) and then Imām al-Ḥusayn (AS) from whose loins nine Imāms would come into existence to whom she is also mother, Imām Mahdī (AS) being the last one, who is from the Ahl al-Bayt, as various *Aḥadīth* of the Prophet (pbuh & hf) express. We also acknowledge that Imām al-Ḥusayn was present underneath the cloak at the time of the revelation of verse 33:33. Had it been that Sayyedah Fāṭimah, or Imām Ḥusayn, or both of them, had not been placed underneath the cloak, we could have stated that nobody else from their line was included in the Ahl al-Bayt, but this is not the case.

Coming back to the words of Allāh in verse 33:33, Allāh addressed His wish of keeping away all impurity from the Ahl al-Bayt. The Qur'ān is very clear in stating that when Allāh wishes something, it no doubt will occur.

> "Verily, when He wishes a thing, His Command is, 'be', and it is!" Qur'ān 36:82

Allāh rewarded a purified life to the Ahl al-Bayt and we know He gives this distinction to those who work towards righteousness, who are sincere in faith.

We need to contemplate, according to the statement: "If the *imān* of Abū Bakr was put in one scale and the *imān* of the whole nation in the other, the *imān* of Abū Bakr would be greater," Abū Bakr had the greatest faith over all of the nation and yet was not included in *Āyat al-Tathīr*.

The Sunni Scholar Allāmah Shiblī Nu'manī in his book Imām Abū Ḥanīfah, Life and Works comments:

> "Ibn Jauzī in his Fath al-Mughīth mentions that '...If you find a tradition to be contrary to reason or to the principles of transmission, you may dismiss it as a fabrication and need not inquire into the trust-worthiness of its transmitters. Similarly, you may regard as a fabrication any tradition which is falsified by common perception and observation, or which is repugnant to the Qur'ān, to a *Ḥadīth Mutwātir* (i.e. a tradition supported by too many persons to be doubted) or to *ijma' qata'i* (i.e. a conclusive consensus of competent opinion)...'"[134]

> Ibn Khaldūn wrote: "I do not believe any *Ḥadīth* or report of a companion of the Prophet to be true which differs from the common sense meaning of the Qur'ān, no matter how trustworthy the narrators may have been. It is not impossible that a narrator appears to be trustworthy though he may be moved by ulterior motive. If the *Aḥadīth* were criticized for their textual contents as they were for the narrators who transmitted them a great number would have had to be rejected. It is a recognised principle that a *Ḥadīth* could be declared spurious if it departs from the common sense meaning of the Qur'ān from the recognised principles of the *Shārī'ah* (the law of Islām), the rules of logic, the evidence of sense, or any other self-evident truth."[135]

Is it justifiable to refute or over ride those *Aḥadīth,* which are supported by Qur'ānic text, which we can state are a proof of the truthfulness, faith, and righteousness of the Ahl al-Bayt above that of others?

What does one deduce in regards to the statement "If there had been any other prophet after me it would have been 'Umar?"

If we believe that Abū Bakr was the leader chosen by the Prophet (pbuh & hf), then this narration: "If there had been any other prophet after me it would have been 'Umar" should never be expressed towards the caliphate of 'Umar. If there had been a prophet after Muḥammad, he most certainly would have taken the position of leadership after him instead of Abū Bakr. Why should we state this?

Firstly, it is the initial thinking from such a statement. Secondly, we know the Prophet was given the Qur'ān, which contains every matter relating to the religion.

> "...We have sent down to thee the Book explaining all things." Qur'ān 16:89

The Prophet (pbuh & hf) was given the complete Book, which was sent down to guide mankind for all time. If there had been another prophet after Muḥammad, then certainly he would have had extensive knowledge of the Qur'ān above that of others in order to be able to address it to the people. Scholars amongst the Sunni school of thought acknowledge that 'Umar was known to say:

> "If it was not for 'Alī, 'Umar would have perished."[136]

Allāmah Shiblī Nu'manī whom has been referred to previously, mentions in his book entitled Imām Abū Hanīfah, Life and Works:

> "'Alī, having been brought up under the Prophet's tutelage, had more opportunities than anyone else of observing his actions and hearing his utterances. On somebody asking him why he related more traditions than any other companion, he said: 'The Prophet use to tell me things whether I questioned him or not.' Besides he was gifted with intelligence and percipience of an order rare even among the companions and acknowledged by them all. 'Umar is reported to have said: 'God forbid that we should be confronted with a difficulty without 'Alī being there.'"[137]

> Narrated Sa'id ibn al-Musaiyyib: "'Umar ibn al-Khaṭṭāb used to beg God to preserve him from a perplexing case which the father of al-Ḥasan was not present to decide.' Furthermore 'Umar said: 'If there was not 'Alī, 'Umar would have perished.'"[138]

'Umar's own words testify to the fact that he was not as well acquainted with the knowledge of the Qur'ān and the *Sunnah* as was Imām 'Alī (AS).

Thirdly, the prophets of Allāh were of the righteous, and for an individual to fit the criterion of prophet-hood their righteousness and faith had to have excelled above others within their communities. Clearly it is these individuals that Allāh rewards with power and knowledge. Allāh states:

> "When Joseph attained his full manhood we gave him Power (*Hukman*) and Knowledge thus do we reward those who do good." Qur'ān 12:22

For the Prophet (pbuh & hf) to have said: "If there had been any other Prophet it would have been 'Umar," under such a context, 'Umar's *imān* and righteousness must have excelled any other individuals for Allāh to have favoured him to be a prophet amongst the rest, but then where would this leave the statement: "If the *imān* of Abū Bakr was put on a scale, and the *imān* of the nation on the other, the *imān* of Abū Bakr would be heavier?"

We also know that the Prophet (pbuh & hf) stated that Imām 'Alī (AS) was to him as Hārūn (AS) was to Mūsa (AS), except there would be no Prophet after him.[139]

The Prophet would not want to confuse the people by mentioning matters, which all point towards the same thing in order that we quarrel and dispute amongst one another in regards to them. Directing statements to anybody just for pleasure or just to be nice, as one may tend to come up with, is not the role of a prophet, prophets speak words of wisdom and their words are to elucidate matters and teach people in accordance to the truth. If we were to comment on statements in this way, that the Prophet stated something just to be nice, then they really have no meaning and should never be addressed on any issue. The Prophet commenting on such matters just for the pleasure of it or just to be nice within itself is against what Allāh teaches us about him.

> "Surely it is the speech of an honoured messenger. And it is not the speech of a poet; little is it that you believe. Nor is it the speech of a diviner, little is it that you remember. It is a revelation from the Lord of the worlds." Qur'ān 69: 40-43

The Prophet (pbuh & hf) never would have spoken in accordance to his own desire, and neither was he a poet or a fictitious writer, his words were to bring the truth to light, his words were not only for those who were present at that time, but also for the generations to come.

What does one deduce in regards to statement "If there had been any other prophet after me it would have been 'Umar?"

There is no plainness in religion when there are differing calls in regards to one matter; this is what we call confusion. Confusion does not pave a clear route but a route to variance. If variance were benefiting, then we would all be united at this very moment in time.

Section 10

A Deeper Analysis of Statements.

If a statement is heard of, which differs from a set of other statements, it needs to be scrutinised in order to substantiate whether it is true or not.

> "When a statement is formulated, it is checked against the totality of existing statements. If it agrees with them, it is accepted; otherwise, it is marked as not true, there is no other criterion of truth."[140]

Additionally, if a statement is made and its points do not make any sense, then again believing in it is really of no real value to anyone.

> "A statement has a meaning if and only if the fact that it is true makes a verifiable difference."[141]

> Narrated Imām 'Alī: "Do not give two contradictory judgements in one matter, for that will cause discrepancy in your directive and you will deviate from the truth."[142]

> Narrated al-Ḥasan ibn 'Alī: "I have retained in my memory these words of Allāh's Messenger 'Leave what causes you doubt and turn to what does not cause you doubt. Truth is tranquillity, but falsehood is doubt.'"[143]

We find statements being propogated that are not clear-cut and certain steps need to be taken in order to clarify them.

The Subject of the Leading of the Prayers towards the end of the Prophet's (pbuh & hf) life.

It is believed by many people that when the Prophet (pbuh and hf) fell ill towards the end of his life, Abū Bakr led the people in prayer, continued to lead it all the way up until the Prophet's demise, hence through this his succession was illuminated.

The Subject of the Leading of the Prayers towards the end of the Prophet's (pbuh & hf) life

The report of Abū Mūsa.

Narrated Abū Mūsa: "When the Messenger of Allāh became ill and his illness became serious, he ordered Abū Bakr to lead the people in prayer. So Abū Bakr led the prayer (during this period of illness) in the life of the Messenger of Allāh."[144]

The reports of 'Ā'isha.

(1) Narrated 'Ā'isha: "Allāh's Apostle in his illness said: 'Tell Abū Bakr to lead the people in prayer.' I said to him: 'If Abū Bakr stands in your place the people would not hear him owing to his (excessive) weeping. So please order 'Umar to lead the prayer.' 'Ā'isha added, I said to Ḥafsa: 'Say to him if Abū Bakr should lead the people in prayer in your place, the people would not be able to hear him owing to his excessive weeping, so please order 'Umar to lead the prayer.' Ḥafsa did so but Allāh's Apostle said: 'Keep quiet! You are verily the companions of Joseph.' Tell Abū Bakr to lead the people in prayer. Ḥafsa said: 'I never got anything good from you.'"[145]

(2) Narrated 'Ā'isha: "When the health of Allāh's Apostle deteriorated and his condition became serious, he asked the permission of all his wives to allow him to be treated in my house, and they allowed him. He came out, supported by two men and his legs were dragging on the ground between al-'Abbās and another man. (The sub-narrator told Ibn 'Abbās who said: 'Do you know who the other man was, whom 'Ā'isha did not mention?' The sub-narrator said: 'No.' Ibn 'Abbās said: 'It was 'Alī).' Ā'isha added, when the Prophet entered my house and his disease became aggravated, he said: 'Pour on me seven water skins full of water (the tying ribbons of which had not been untied) so that I may give some advice to the people.' So we made him sit in a

> tub belonging to Ḥafsa, the wife of the Prophet and started pouring water on him from those water skins till he waved us to stop. Then he went out to the people and led them in prayer and delivered a speech before them."[146]

> (3) Narrated 'Ubaydullāh ibn 'Abdullāh ibn 'Utba that 'Ā'isha had said: "...Abū Bakr was following the Prophet (in the prayer) and the people were following Abū Bakr. The Prophet (prayed) sitting."

Within the same report Ubaydullāh mentioned that 'Ā'isha said:

> "...When the Prophet felt a bit better he came out for Zuhr prayer with the help of two persons one was al-'Abbās..."

Towards the end of the narration 'Ubaydullāh added:

> "I went to Ibn 'Abbās and asked him: 'Shall I tell you what 'Ā'isha has told me about the fatal illness of the Prophet.' Ibn 'Abbās said: 'Go ahead.' I told him her narration and he did not deny anything of it but asked whether 'Ā'isha had told me the name of the second person (who helped the Prophet) along with al-'Abbās. I said: 'No' He (Ibn 'Abbās) said: 'He was 'Alī (ibn Abī Tālib).'"[147]

Within report (2) 'Ā'isha states that after the Prophet (pbuh & hf) had taken a bath, he went out to deliver a speech and then led the people in prayer. Abū Mūsa's report states: "Abū Bakr led the prayer (during this period of illness) in the life of the Messenger of Allāh," which gives us the sense that Abū Bakr must have led every single prayer up until the Prophet's demise, but we find that this is not the case.

Many reports state that Abū Bakr followed the prayer of the Prophet (pbuh & hf) rather than led it. Due to illness, the Prophet's speech was not reaching the people; hence Abū Bakr repeated his words in order for the prayer to be followed.

The Subject of the Leading of the Prayers towards the end of the Prophet's (pbuh & hf) life

Narrated 'Urwa's father: "... **Abū Bakr was following** the prayer of Allāh's Apostle and the people were following the prayer of Abū Bakr..."[148]

Narrated 'Ā'isha: "... Abū Bakr was praying while standing and Allāh's Apostle was **leading** the prayer while sitting. **Abū Bakr was following** the Prophet and the people were following Abū Bakr (in the prayer)..."[149]

Jābir said: "The Messenger of Allāh **led** the prayer and **Abū Bakr was behind him**. When the Messenger of Allāh recited the *takbir* (saying God is Great), Abū Bakr also recited (it) in order to make it audible to us."[150]

A'mash reported: "When the Messenger of Allāh suffered from illness of which he died, and in the *Ḥadīth* transmitted by Ibn Mushīr, the words are: 'The Messenger of Allāh was brought till he was seated by his (Abū Bakr's) side **and the Apostle led** the people in prayer and Abū Bakr was making *takbir* audible to them, and in the *Ḥadīth* transmitted by Īsa the (words are): 'The Messenger of Allāh sat and led the people in prayer and **Abū Bakr was by his side** and he was making *takbir* audible to the people.'"[151]

The point of 'Ā'isha: "...When the Prophet (pbuh & hf) felt a bit better he came out for Zuhr prayer with the help of two persons one was al-'Abbās..." does not provide us with full assurance that the Prophet was feeling better, in fact it reveals to us that the Prophet was still seriously ill, so much so, that he was still aided by two people on his way to the mosque to lead the people in prayer. Also, the Prophet leaving his residence in this state, with his feet dragging on the earth, being carried by al-'Abbās (his uncle) and Imām 'Alī (AS) to lead the prayers himself provides us with no point of certainty that the Prophet was indicating the leadership of Abū Bakr.

The comments one make in regards to Abū Bakr leading the prayers become blurred and confused when the Prophet's (pbuh & hf) actions do not make the clear point and the real sense to what one expresses. We are not reassured by reading these reports that this is exactly what the Prophet was pointing towards. They do not provide us with clarity of Abū Bakr's leadership or clarity that the Prophet was indicating his leadership.

The Military Expedition led by Usāmah ibn Zayd.

It has also been reported that around the time of the Prophet's (pbuh & hf) illness he ordered his companions to invade a place called 'Ubna and Abū Bakr, 'Umar, Abū 'Ubaydah, Sa'd and many others were placed under the command of young Usāmah ibn Zayd. This has been recorded in the books of history and tradition, two of which are Ibn Sa'd in his Tabaqāt[152] and Imām al-Ḥākim in his al-Mustadrak.[153]

Taken from Abū Bakr Aḥmed ibn 'Abdul-Azīz al-Jawharī in his book al-Saqīfah:

> "Aḥmed ibn Ishāq ibn Sālih has narrated a tradition from Aḥmed ibn Siyār from Sa'd ibn Kathīr al-Ansārī whose men quote 'Abdullāh ibn 'Adul-Raḥmān saying that when the Messenger of Allāh became ill shortly before his death, he appointed Usāmah ibn Zayd ibn Ḥarīthah to take charge in leading an army most of which were men from the *Muhājir* and the *Ansār*. Among them were: Abū Bakr, 'Umar, Abū 'Ubaydah ibn al-Jarrah, 'Abd al-Raḥmān ibn Awf, Talḥa and az-Zubayr, and ordered him to invade Mūta, where his father Zayd had been murdered, and to invade the valley of Palestine. Usāmah slackened, and so did the rest of the army, and the Messenger of Allāh, though ill, kept emphasizing that the army must rush there, till Usāmah said to him: 'O Messenger of Allāh! Would you permit me to stay for a few days till Almighty heals you?' He answered: 'Go and proceed, supported by the blessings of the Allāh.' Usāmah said: 'O Messenger if I proceed while you are sick like that, I will be going with a heart swollen with pain.' He said: 'Proceed towards good victory in good

> health.' Usāmah persisted: 'But I hate to keep asking the traveller's about your condition.' He said: 'Proceed to carry out my orders,' then he fainted. Usāmah left and prepared to proceed. When the Messenger of Allāh regained his consciousness, he immediately inquired about Usāmah, and he was told that he and his men were preparing to proceed, whereupon he kept repeating: 'Carry out Usāmah's mission; the curse of Allāh be upon whoever dodges its draft.' Usāmah finally left the city, the flag above his head, surrounded by the companions, till he reached Jurf. In his company were Abū Bakr, 'Umar, and most of the *Muhājirin* and the *Ansār* such as Asīd ibn Ḥadhr, Bashīr ibn Sa'd and many others. Then Usāmah received a messenger sent by Umm Aymān who informed him to go ahead and enter the city because the Prophet was dying. Usāmah immediately left for Madīnah with the standard still in his hand. Having reached the Prophet's residence, he planted it at the door just when the Prophet had died."

It is also recorded in Ibn Sa'd's Tabaqāt in the Chapter on Usāmah's regiment that two days before the Prophet's (pbuh & hf) demise, he ascended the pulpit with his head bandaged saying:

> "O people! It has come to my knowledge that some of you have felt uneasy about my appointment of Usāmah (as the commander). If you cast doubts about his appointment, you had done so before when I appointed his father who, by Allāh, was worthy of such authority, and so is his son after him."[154]

A similar narration is quoted in *Ṣaḥīḥ al-Bukhārī*.

> Narrated 'Abdullāh ibn 'Umar: "The Prophet sent an army under the command of Usāmah ibn Zayd. When some people criticized his leadership, the Prophet said: 'If you are criticizing Usāmah's leadership, you used to criticize his father's leadership before. By Allāh! He was worthy of leadership and

> was one of the dearest persons to me, and (now) this (i.e. Usāmah) is one of the dearest to me after him (i.e. Zayd).'"[155]

We must contemplate; the Prophet (pbuh & hf) asked Abū Bakr to lead the prayer and then at the same time placed him in an army under the command of Usāmah ibn Zayd. How was it possible for Abū Bakr to have led the people in prayer all the way up until the Prophet's demise, if he had been called on along with others to leave Madīnah in order to take part in an expedition?

Usāmah ibn Zayd was a young man at that time; but the Prophet (pbuh & hf) did not him see him as being incapable to lead the army. Imām 'Alī (AS) was not appointed as the leader on this occasion but rather he remained close to the Prophet's side. This expedition eventually took place after the Prophet's demise, still led by young Usāmah and Abū Bakr did not take part in it as he had taken over the reins of leadership.

It has also been narrated in *Ṣaḥīḥ al-Bukhārī* in a lengthy narration, and also in al-Ṭabarī's *Tārīkh* that Abū Bakr was not in Madīnah at the time of the demise of the Prophet (pbuh & hf).

> Narrated 'Ā'isha: "Allāh's Apostle died while Abū Bakr was at a place called as-Sunah (al-Ālīya)..."[156]

A question needs to be addressed here, when the Prophet (pbuh & hf) passed away, Abū Bakr was at a place called as-Sunah although he had been commanded to leave Madīnah to take part in an expedition under the command of Usāmah, how was it possible for the Prophet to command two contradictory actions at the same time (i.e. go for *Jihād* and stay behind to lead the prayers in Madīnah) when this is clearly against prophetic wisdom?

Additionally, we find a report recorded by Imām Aḥmad ibn Ḥanbal in his Musnad, which indicates that the Prophet (pbuh & hf) had called upon Imām 'Alī (AS):

> "It is written through 'Abdullāh ibn Abbās that during his last illness in which he died, the Prophet was in the house of 'Ā'isha, one day he said send 'Alī to me

> at once. 'Ā'isha said: 'No, we are sending Abū Bakr for you. The Prophet said: 'Very well.' Then Ḥafsa said: 'No, why should we not call for 'Umar.' The Prophet said: 'Very well.' Then Umme Fadhl the wife of Abbās said: 'We will call Abbās for you.' Then the Prophet said: 'Very well.' So when all these persons had congregated, the Prophet raised his head and not finding 'Alī there kept silent. 'Umar understood his object and said: 'Let us move away.' Just then Bilāl came and reminded the Prophet of the prayers. 'Ā'isha said: 'Abū Bakr is a man of emotion and when the people do not see you they will weep, it will be better if you order 'Umar to lead the prayers.' But, Abū Bakr went out to lead the prayers. Then the Prophet finding in himself a slight change for the better, had himself dragged to the mosque with the help of two persons, his legs being trailed on the ground. When the people saw him they informed Abū Bakr of it, Abū Bakr tried to step back but the Prophet asked him to remain where he was. The Prophet was sitting and Abū Bakr was standing at his side. Ibn Abbās says that the Prophet took up the prayers from the stage, which Abū Bakr had reached. The Prophet was leading the prayers with Abū Bakr following him and the people were in turn repeating what Abū Bakr took up from the Prophet."[157]

We may state that Abū Bakr led the prayers hence the Prophet (pbuh & hf) had indicated his leadership, but we find that this is very much so doubted by its projection through the reports we have in regards to it.

Statements, which receive such recognition merely through the word of mouth of others, become fixed in ones mind. Many minds carry this statement with a notion, which when examined does not provide us with the same answer equal to what is claimed.

A Look into Other Statements.

(1) Consider these Statements.

> Narrated 'Abdullāh ibn Abbās: "Allāh's Apostle in his fatal illness came out with a piece of cloth tied round his head and sat on the pulpit. After thanking and praising Allāh he said: 'There is no one who had done more favour to me with life and property than Abū Bakr ibn Abī Quhāfa. If I were to take a *khalīl*, I would certainly have taken Abū Bakr but the Islamic brotherhood is superior. **Close all the small doors in this mosque except that of Abū Bakr**.'"[158]

> Narrated Aiyūb: The Prophet said: "If I were to take a *khalīl*, I would have taken him (i.e. Abū Bakr) as a *khalīl*, but the Islamic brotherhood is better."[159]

Within another narration it is reported:

> Narrated Abū Sa'id al-Khudrī: The Prophet said: "...If I had to take a *khalīl* from my followers, I would certainly have taken Abū Bakr, but the fraternity of Islām is sufficient. **Let no *khūkha* (door) of the mosque remain open, except the door of Abū Bakr**."[160]

(2) Now consider the Contradicting Statements.

> Narrated 'Abdullāh ibn 'Abbās: "The Messenger of Allāh ordered all the doors of his companions closed except that of 'Alī who use to enter even while in a state of *Janāba* (impurity after intimacy with ones wife after which taking a bath is obligatory), having no other way out."[161]

> Narrated Abū Sa'id al-Khudrī, Allāh's Messenger said to 'Alī: "'It is not allowable, 'Alī for anyone but you or me to be in a state of ceremonial impurity in this mosque.' 'Alī ibn al-Mundhīr told that he asked Dirār ibn Surād what was the meaning of this tradition, and

> he replied that the meaning was 'It is not allowable for anyone but you or me to walk through it in a state of ceremonial impurity.'"[162]

Imām Aḥmad ibn Ḥanbal and Imām Tirmidhī were well-respected scholars of *Ḥadīth* and other scholars of *Ḥadīth* have also accepted their narrations. Imām Nasā'ī in his Khasā'is al-'Alawiyya,[163] Sibt ibn Jauzī in his Tadhkirāt,[164] Imām al-Hākim in his al-Mustadrak,[165] have all pointed out the reliability of the *Ḥadīth* in relation to Imām 'Alī (AS) on the basis of the chain of narrators, which have been quoted by Imām Aḥmad ibn Ḥanbal and Imām Tirmidhī.

In the matter of closing all the doors except that of one individual, Imām Tirmidhī reported from Abū Sa'id al-Khudrī and Imām Aḥmad ibn Ḥanbal from 'Abdullāh ibn 'Abbās, that it was the door of Imām 'Alī (AS) (the door to the house of the Ahl al-Bayt), which remained open. These two reports are in variance to the reports mentioned in *Ṣaḥīḥ al-Bukhārī*, however the **same two companions** 'Abdullāh ibn 'Abbās and Abū Sa'id al-Khudrī teach us something very different.

What we also find is that there are other narrations from different companions, who have also expressed that it was the door of Imām 'Alī (AS) that was to remain open.

Imām al-Ḥākim reported on:

> Narrated Sa'id ibn Mālik: "The Messenger of Allāh turned out everyone from the mosque, including his uncle 'Abbās and others. Al-'Abbās asked him: 'Why do you turn us out and keep 'Alī?' He answered: 'It is not I who has turned you out and kept 'Alī. It is Allāh who has turned you out while keeping him.'"[166]
>
> Narrated 'Umar ibn al-Khaṭṭāb: "'Alī ibn Abī Tālib was granted three tokens of prestige; if I had one of them, it would have been dearer to me than all red camels of Arabia, his wife Fāṭimah daughter of the Messenger of Allāh, his residence at the mosque neighbouring the Messenger of Allāh and feeling at

> home therein, and the standard during the Battle of Khaybar."[167]

Imām Aḥmad ibn Ḥanbal reported another narration, but from Zayd ibn Arqam.

> Narrated Zayd ibn Arqam: "A few companions of the Messenger of Allāh used to have the doors of their houses overlooking the mosque. The Messenger of Allāh then said: 'Close down all these doors except 'Alī's'. Some people did not like it, and they talked about it. So, the Messenger of Allāh stood one day praised the Almighty then said: 'I have ordered these doors to be closed save 'Alī's, and some of you have disliked that. I have not closed down a door nor opened it, nor gave any order, except after being commanded by my Lord to do so.'"[168]

Ibn Ḥajar al-'Asqalānī himself being a great *Ḥadīth* scholar and a commentator of *Ṣaḥīḥ al-Bukhārī* has verified the authenticity of the narrations in favour of Imām 'Alī (AS) in his *Fath al-Barī* Vol. 7, p.12-13.

We also observe that he was the only one companion allowed to enter the mosque in a state of *Janāba* and attaching the reference of his house to the mosque portrays the purity in worship of this being and his household no matter what state they were in.

Now, the narrations in *Ṣaḥīḥ al-Bukhārī* portray that the Prophet (pbuh & hf) chose Abū Bakr as a *khalīl* in order to show his proximity with his own self but then his words express that the brotherhood is superior to the friendship. If truly Abū Bakr was the closest companion of the Prophet, then we would have expected this connection at the time of the bondage of brotherhood. Contrary to this view it is observed that the Prophet chose Imām 'Alī (AS) as his brother.

It is reported in Tirmidhi:

> Narrated 'Abdullāh ibn 'Umar: "When Allāh's Messenger arranged brotherhoods among his companions,

> 'Alī came weeping and said: 'You have arranged brotherhoods among your companions, but you have arranged no brotherhood between me and anyone.' He replied: 'You are my brother in this world and the next.'"[169]

The Islamic brotherhood was established twice in the Prophet's (pbuh & hf) lifetime, where one companion was made brother of another companion. As also stated in section eight, the first instance of this took place between the companions in Makkah and second instance between the companions of Makkah and Madīnah, when the migration to Madīnah had occurred:

> The Prophet first created brotherhood between the *Muhājir* before their migration to Madīnah, establishing it between such companions as Abū Bakr and 'Umar, 'Uthmān and 'Abd al-Raḥmān ibn Awf, and creating brotherhood between him and 'Alī. The second instance of when the Prophet established brotherhood was when he and his companions had migrated to Madīnah, creating this time between the *Muhājir* and *Ansār* (which took place after the first few months of the migration in 1 A.H.) again favouring 'Alī for himself, creating brotherhood in this instance between such companions as Abū Bakr and Kharījah ibn Zayd and between 'Umar and 'Atbān ibn Mālik.[170]

From reading the stated report, we understand that Imām 'Alī (AS) was made the brother of the Prophet (pbuh & hf) not once but in both instances of the Islamic brotherhood whilst Abū Bakr was first made brother of 'Umar and then on the second instance was made the brother of Kharījah ibn Zayd. Perhaps we need to ponder over the following questions:

Why did the Prophet (pbuh & hf) select Imām 'Alī (AS) as his brother on both of these occasions of brotherhood while there was a change around amongst his other companions?

Succession of the Prophet (PBUH)

Why did twice the Prophet (pbuh & hf) neglect Abū Bakr when it is recorded in another narration that the Prophet called him his brother?

> "Narrated Ibn 'Abbas, the Prophet said: "If I were to take a *khalīl*, I would have taken Abū Bakr, but he is my brother and my companion (in Islām)."[171]

All the companions were brothers to one another and to the Prophet (pbuh & hf) in a general sense but for the Prophet to select somebody as his own brother on both occasions of the bondage of brotherhood was mainly to show the close proximity of his self to Imām 'Alī (AS) portraying it's specific nature compared to that of the general brotherhood in Islām. We can express the general brotherhood of Islām even in this day and age but when speaking of the event of the two brotherhoods, can we really comprehend why Imām 'Alī was placed nearer to the Prophet? If we observe this verse in the Qur'ān:

> "Verily those of mankind who are **closest to Abraham** are those who **followed him** (*tabaūhū*), and this Prophet and those who believe (with him); and Allāh is the Protecting Friend of the believers." Qur'ān 3:68

We can learn much in regards to what the real reason of such **closeness of Imām 'Alī (AS) to the Prophet** (pbuh & hf) was through the verse quoted. If it had of been that the Imām was not foremost from the rest of the companions in **following the Prophet** and another companion was of a higher rank than him, then he would not have been given this close proximity. The occasion of the two brotherhoods established this closeness for Imām 'Alī and no other companion.

We should also contemplate on this question:

Who was the person who was placed in such a close position with the Prophet (pbuh & hf) that he took him along with the rest of his family members for *Mubāhilah* against the Christians of Najrān, who is mentioned in the verse as the "ourselves" of the Prophet?

A Look into Other Statements

(1) Consider this statement.

Narrated 'Amr ibn al-'Aas: "The Prophet deputed me to lead the Army of Dhat-as-Salasil I came to him and said: 'Who is the most beloved person to you?' He said: 'Ā'isha' I asked: 'Among the men?' He said: 'Her Father.' Who then he said: ''Umar ibn al-Khaṭṭāb.' Then he named other men."[172]

(2) Now consider this statement.

Narrated by Zayd ibn Arqam: "Allāh's Messenger (pbuh) said of 'Alī, Fāṭimah, al-Ḥasan, al-Ḥusayn: 'I am at war to him who makes war on them and at peace to him who makes peace with them.' I went in with my paternal Aunt to visit 'Ā'isha and asked who was dearest to Allāh's Messenger. When she replied that it was Fāṭimah, she was asked who was dearest amongst men and she replied that it was her husband ('Ali ibn Abī Tālib)."[173]

On the subject of the conquest of Khaybar - a very well known narration.

Narrated Sahl ibn Sa'd: "On the day of Khaybar, Allāh's Apostle said: 'Tomorrow I will give this flag to a man through whose hands Allāh will give us victory. He loves Allāh and His Apostle, and he is loved by Allāh and His Apostle.' The people remained that night, wondering as to who would be given it. In the morning the people went to Allāh's Apostle and every one of them was hopeful to receive it (i.e. the flag). The Prophet said: 'Where is Alī ibn Abī Tālib?' It was said: 'He is suffering from eye trouble O Allāh's Apostle.' He said: 'Send for him.' 'Alī was brought and Allāh's Apostle spat in his eye and invoked good upon him. So 'Alī was cured as if he never had any trouble. Then the Prophet gave him the flag. 'Alī said: 'O Allāh's Apostle! I will fight with them till they become like us.' Allāh's Apostle said: 'Proceed and do

> not hurry. When you enter their territory, call them to embrace Islām and inform them of Allāh's rights which they should observe, for by Allāh, even if a single man is led on the right path (of Islām) by Allāh through you, then that will be better for you than the nice red camels.'"[174]

The Prophet (pbuh & hf) expressed that Allāh will give the Muslims victory as he knew that Imām 'Alī (AS) would come back victorious. How could the Prophet have known this if this message had not been conveyed to him from Allāh about his beloved servant 'Alī? Allāh expressed His love towards His devout servant 'Alī, and revealed to His Apostle to give the standard to him above anyone else, his distinction as a beloved of Allāh above others being clearly marked within the details of this event.

Clarifying the most beloved in the sight of Allāh.

The Prophet (pbuh & hf) would never state: "These are the best people or these are the people who I love the most," without him first being informed by Allāh, about who it is He loves the most.

A prophet follows the teachings of his Creator and does not favour one person over another through his own self-interest. Allāh loves those of His servants who are on the right path and whose deeds reflect that which is righteous and good.

Allāh states:

> "**Surely as for those who believe and do good deeds**, upon them Allāh will bestow **love**." Qur'ān 19:96

This is the best reward any human being can achieve, more than any reward given by another human being, any individual who is given this distinction, would be loved by the Prophet (pbuh & hf) and the people who follow him.
The Qur'ān states:

> "That is (the bounty) whereof Allāh gives glad tidings to His servants **who believe and do righteous**

> **deeds.** Say: No ***Ajr*** **(reward)** do I ask of you for this **except the *Mowadda* (love) of *fil qurba* (near of kin)**. And if anyone earns any good We shall give Him an increase of good (in respect thereof)." Qur'ān 42:23

The Shī'ahs state that the above verse was revealed in regards to the love of Ahl al-Bayt due to their sincere faith and righteousness. This can be illuminated through narrations, which are recorded within Sunni sources. Ibn Kathīr in his *Tafsīr* has given a different explanation for this verse using a narration from *Ṣaḥīḥ al-Bukhārī*.

In the book of the Prophetic commentary on the Qur'ān (*Tafsīr* of the Prophet), al-Bukhārī' reports:

> Narrated Ibn 'Abbās: That he was asked (regarding): "Except to be kind to me for my kinship with you. (42.23) Sa'id ibn Zubayr (who was present then) said: 'It means here (to show what is due for) the relatives of Muḥammad.' On that Ibn 'Abbās said: 'You have hurried in giving the answer! There was no branch of the tribe of Quraysh but the Prophet had relatives therein. The Prophet said I do not want anything from (you) except to be kind to me for my kinship with you.'"

Sa'id ibn Zubayr initially states that the verse refers to showing kindness to the relatives of Muḥammad. But then we find that this is refuted by a statement attributed to 'Abdullāh ibn 'Abbās who states that the Prophet was asking for kindness from his relatives.

Ibn Kathīr in his *Tafsīr* states:

> "Say, No reward do I ask of you for this except to be kind to me for my kinship with you) means: 'Say, O Muḥammad, to these idolators among the disbelievers of Quraysh, I do not ask you for anything in return for this message and sincere advice which I bring to you. **All I ask of you is that you withhold your evil from me and let me convey the messages of my**

> **Lord. If you will not help me, then do not disturb me, for the sake of the ties of kinship that exist between you and I.**' Al-Bukhārī' recorded that Ibn 'Abbās, may Allāh be pleased with him, was asked about the Ayah except to be kind to me for my kinship with you. Sa'id ibn Zubayr said: 'To be kind to the family of Muḥammad.' Ibn 'Abbās said: 'No, you have jumped to a hasty conclusion. There was no clan among Quraysh to whom the Prophet did not have some ties of kinship.' Ibn 'Abbās said: 'Except that you uphold the ties of kinship that exist between me and you." This was recorded by al-Bukhārī'. It was also recorded by Imām Ahmed with a different chain of narration."

Ibn Kathīr when quoting the narration from *Ṣaḥīḥ al-Bukhārī* portrayed that the words mentioned in the Qur'ān were in reference to the Prophet (pbuh & hf) asking the Qurayshite unbelievers to whom he had ties of kinship, to withhold their evil and allow him to convey the Message of Islām. Ibn Kathīr further explained that if they did not wish to help the Prophet they should not disturb him from doing his duty because of being related to him. Whether they had ties with the Prophet or not, they would never have been able to withhold their opposition to what was being propagated, even if it was merely speaking against it, because it would not have been acceptable to them. Would we not associate this with evil? The Prophet in a way was causing unrest to them by turning against their beliefs and practices, splitting up the families by bringing in a teaching that would divide them up into Muslims and non-Muslims. It would have angered them and would not their anger have escalated if the Prophet stated to them, which meant something along the lines of: **"By the way, whilst I am carrying my duty of spreading the Message of Islām, unless you wish to help me, do not disturb me please and be kind to me?"** Because this is what can be pictured by the explanation Ibn Kathīr gives, his words revolving around the narration quoted in *Ṣaḥīḥ al-Bukhārī*, which does not make any real sense.

We would be right in stating that this verse is directed to the believers and the beginning of the verse clarifies:

Clarifying the most beloved in the sight of Allāh

> "That is (the bounty) whereof Allāh gives glad tidings to His servants **who believe and do righteous deeds."**

We also read:

> "Say: No ***Ajr*** **(reward)** do I ask of you for this except..."

To claim that the Prophet (pbuh & hf) was directing this to the Qurayshite unbelievers when, as stated, his mission opposed their belief and practices, would be similar to an individual who speaks against a product, which is being marketed by a certain company and then stating to the company, "I do not ask you any reward for this except..." How can we accept such a ridiculous statement?

And the clause:

> "And if anyone earns any good We shall give Him an increase of good (in respect thereof)."

Again, directs us to the believers as we know that the deeds of the unbeliever do not excel them in their ranks, being the rejectors of the message.

This should make us all question the narration in regards to this verse (42:23) in *Ṣaḥīḥ al-Bukhārī* and also question what Ibn Kathīr portrays in regards to it. Are we wrong in stating that both the narration and what Ibn Kathīr portrays is flawed in many ways?

Allāh informed His Prophet (pbuh & hf) to state these words to the believers, and we find narrations directing us to whom this verse referred to.

> Narrated 'Abdullāh ibn 'Abbās: ""When the verse 42:23 was revealed, the companions asked: 'O, The Messenger of Allāh, who are those near kin whose love Allāh has made obligatory for us?' Upon that the Prophet said: 'Alī, Fāṭimah, and their two sons.' He repeated this sentence thrice."[175]

> When the Holy Prophet was asked by his followers as to who were his near of kin whose love God has made obligatory on all Muslims, the Prophet replied: "Fāṭimah, 'Alī, al-Ḥasan and al-Ḥusayn."[176]

Also, the Prophet (pbuh & hf) stated:

> Verily Allāh has dedicated my wage (of prophethood) to love my Ahl al-Bayt, and I shall question you about it on the Day of Judgment." [177]

Imām al-Ḥasan ibn 'Alī (AS) stated the following within a speech, which he delivered when he took over authority after his father Imām 'Alī (AS) was martyred:

> "... I am among the Ahl al-Bayt whom Allāh has made their love obligatory for any Muslim when He revealed to His Prophet: 'Say, I don't ask you any reward except to love my near kin. And if anyone earns any good We shall give Him an increase of good (Qur'ān 42:23).' Thus earn the good deed through loving us Ahl al-Bayt."[178]

If we can understand the sincere faith and righteousness of the Ahl al-Bayt (AS), their love for the truth, their close connection to the Prophet (pbuh & hf), then we would not find it difficult to comprehend why Allāh commanded His Prophet to state this. It was not the Prophet who decided what needed to be addressed to the believers. To notify His Prophet (pbuh & hf) with, Say: "I do not ask..." gives us an indication towards the distinction Allāh has given the Ahl al-Bayt and not His Prophet.

Another point we can address is, although at the time of the revelation of this verse, only Sayyedah Fāṭimah (AS), Imām 'Alī (AS), Imām al-Ḥasan (AS) and Imām al-Ḥusayn (AS) were in existence, the rest of the Imāms of the Ahl al-Bayt (AS) would have been naturalised within the verse. We cannot deny that the Qur'ān can refer to both present and future offspring of the House of prophets, as also explained when discussing the verse of purification (33:33), and we are familiar with the final awaited Imām being part of this offspring.

Nevertheless, the command to love the Ahl al-Bayt is recognised and accepted by many Sunnis and of course the Shiahs, but the Shiahs illuminate that to love them, is also the implication of adherence to them.

The sending of blessings upon the Prophet (pbuh & hf) and his Household.

Allāh revealed:

> "Allāh and his angels send blessings on the Prophet. O ye that believe send blessings on the Prophet and salute him with all respect." Qur'ān 33:56

Verse 33:56 states that Allāh and His angels send blessings on the Prophet (pbuh & hf) and then the believers are informed to salute him, i.e. send blessings upon him.

The following verse needs to be quoted in relation to this salutation, which is regarded by the majority of Muslims.

> They said: "Dost thou wonder at Allāh's decree? The grace of Allāh and His blessings on you O ye People of the House! (*raḥmatullahī* wa *barakatuhū alaykum Ahl al-Bayt(ī)*), for He is indeed worthy of all praise full of all glory!" Qur'ān 11.73

Coming back to the first verse quoted, the companions asked the Prophet (pbuh & hf) in which way were they to salute him.

> "Do not salute for me in short! The companions asked: What is saluting in short?' The Prophet replied: 'Saying that Blessing of Allāh be upon Muḥammad.' They asked: 'What should we say?' The Prophet answered: 'Say, Blessing of Allāh be upon Muḥammad and his Ahl al-Bayt.' In another wording the Prophet replied: 'Say, O Allāh, bless Muḥammad and his Household the same way as you blessed Abraham and his Household. Verily you are worthy of all praise full of all glory!'"[179]

> Narrated Abū Sa'īd al-Khudrī: "We said: 'O Allāh's Apostle! (We know) this greeting (33:56) (to you) but how shall we invoke Allāh for you?' He said: 'Say: O Allāh! Send your greetings on Muḥammad who is Your servant and Your Messenger, the same way as You sent Your greetings on Abraham's family. And send Your blessings on Muḥammad and on Muḥammad's family, the same way as You sent Your blessings on Abraham's family.'"[180]

Majority of Sunnis adhere to these narrations and agree with the words within them as the *Dūrud Sharīf* (*Allāh Humma Salli Alā Muḥammadin wa alā Āl(ī) Muḥammadin kamā sallayta alā Ibrahima wa alā Āl(ī) Ibrahima*...O Allāh shower blessings upon Muḥammad and the Household of Muḥammad as **You** showered blessings upon Ibrahīm and the Household of Ibrahīm). These words correlate with both verses 33:56 and 11:73 of the Qur'ān.

If we state that all the followers, or the companions of the Prophet (pbuh & hf) are also included in this salutation, then verse 11:73 of the Qur'ān is not considered, when in fact the *Dūrud* recited by the Sunnis very much relates to it. Within verse 11:73, the angels stated that Allāh's blessings were upon the members of the House of Ibrahim (AS), the Ahl al-Bayt, which would automatically direct us to the House of Prophet Muḥammad (pbuh & hf) when reciting the same upon him and his *Āl(i)*.

Also it can be noted from this that when the word *Āl* is mentioned in the Qur'ān **in regards to the prophets** we are directed to the Household, the Ahl al-Bayt of that prophet, for e.g *Āl(i)* Imrān.

We observe in the Qur'ān:

> "Allāh did choose Adam and Noah, the *Āl(i)* of Abraham, and the *Āl(i)* of Imran above all people. **Offspring one from the other**; and verily Allāh is all-Hearing, all-Knowing." Qur'ān 3:33

> Narrated Ja'far ibn Abī Tālib: "When the Messenger of Allāh noticed that a blessing from Allāh was to

> descend, he told Safīyya (one of his wives): 'Call for me! Call for me!' Safīyya said: 'Call who, O the Messenger of Allāh?' He said: 'Call for me my Ahl al-Bayt who are 'Alī, Fāṭimah, al-Ḥasan, and al-Ḥusayn.' Thus we sent for them and they came to him. Then the Prophet spread his cloak (upper garment) over them, and raised his hand (toward sky) saying: 'O Allāh! These are my family (*Āli*), so bless Muḥammad and the family (*Āli*) of Muḥammad.' And Allāh, to whom belong Might and Majesty, revealed: 'Verily Allāh intends to keep off from you every kind of uncleanness O' People of the House (Ahl al-Bayt), and purify you a thorough purification (Qur'ān, end of Verse 33:33)'"[181]

The Shī'ah Ithna 'Asheri acknowledge that blessings were sent upon Ibrahīm's (AS) Household through the Qur'ān from the prayer of the angels, but verse 33:56 informed the believers to send separate blessings upon the Prophet and his Household of which *Allāh Humma Salli Alā Muḥammad wa alā Āl(i) Muḥammad* is recited and that this blessed act of salutation is to be carried out in our prayers, and if we fail to recite this, our prayers will become invalid.

> The Messenger of Allāh said: "If one prays, and in it he does not send blessings to me and my family, his prayer will not be accepted."[182]

The well-known saying of Imām Shāfi'ī, the fourth Imām of the Ahl al-Sunnah wa al-Jammāh also supports the words of the Prophet (pbuh & hf):

> "O Ahl al-Bayt of the Messenger of Allāh, your love is a Divine duty on mankind. God revealed it in His Qur'ān. It is enough among your great privileges that whoever does not bless you his prayer is void. If the love of the members of the House of the Prophet is *Rafidhi* (rejection), let mankind and the Jinns testify that I am a *Rafidhi* (rejector)."[183]

This is also the reason why salutations are sent upon the Ahl al-Bayt when they are mentioned individually as Sayyedah Fāṭimah (AS), Imām 'Alī (AS). This is what the Prophet (pbuh & hf) taught us to do, to salute them (Ahl al-Bayt) in the same way as we salute him.

Cursing the Ahl al-Bayt is not an act of sending blessings or showing love towards them.

The act of cursing is something that Allāh sends upon the treacherous, those who reject faith. Cursing is not sent upon those whom He loves.

> "How shall Allāh guide those who reject faith after they accepted it and bore witness that the Apostle was true and that clear signs had come unto them? But Allāh guides not a people unjust." Qur'ān 3:86
>
> "Of such the reward is that on them (rests) the curse of Allāh of His angels and of all mankind." Qur'ān 3:87

Allāh has taught us to express our love towards the Ahl al-Bayt; and it is the love for them that makes many Shī'ahs speak out against the injustices, which they faced and suffered after the Prophet (pbuh & hf) departed.

It would be relevant to mention that after the martyrdom of Imām 'Alī (AS), Mu'āwīya called upon the people to curse him. Mu'āwīya lived at the time of the Prophet (pbuh & hf); his father Abū Sufyān and his mother Hind were deeply opposed to the Prophet up until the conquest of Mecca. When Mecca was conquered Abū Sufyān embraced Islām as did all his family.

Al-Mughīra ibn Shūba was a governor who was placed in charge of Kūfa by Mu'āwiya when the latter was in power. Mu'āwiya stated to him:

> "Now then, indeed a forbearing person has been admonished in the past... The wise might do what you want without instruction. Although I have wanted to advise you about many things, I left them alone, trusting in your discernment of what pleases

me, what helps my regime and what sets my *raiyyah* (subjects) on the right path. I would continue to advise you about a quality of yours, do not refrain from abusing 'Alī and criticizing him, not from asking God's mercy upon 'Uthmān and His forgiveness for him. Continue to shame the companions of 'Alī, keep at a distance, and don't listen to them. Praise the faction of Uthmān, bring them near, and listen to them."[184]

"After the Peace Treaty, Mu'āwiya went to Makkah to perform the Ḥajj. He circumambulated the Kāba. Sa'd ibn Abī Waqqās was with him. When he ended that, he went to the *Dar al-Nadwa* (House of the Council). Mu'āwiya seated Sa'd beside him on his bed and began to curse and defame 'Alī. So Sa'd moved aside, and then he said: 'You have seated me by you on your bed and began cursing 'Alī! By Allāh, if I had a quality of 'Alī's qualities, it would be better for me than what the sun rises over! By Allah, if I was the son-in-law of the Prophet, and had sons as 'Alī had, it would be better for me than what the sun rises over! By Allāh, if the Apostle of Allāh had said to me what he said at the campaign against Khaybar: 'Indeed, tomorrow, I will give the standard to a man whom Allāh and His Apostle love, and who loves Allāh and His Apostle. He does not escape. Allāh will make a conquest through him,' it would have been better for me than what the sun rises over. By Allāh, if the Apostle of Allāh had said to me what he said at the Campaign of Tabūk: 'You are in the same position with respect to me as Harūn was to Mūsa except that there is no prophet after me,' it would have been better for me than what the sun rises over. By Allāh, I will not enter a house belongs to you as long as you are living.'"[185]

Ibn Kathīr in his *al-Bidāyah wa al-Nihāyah* states:

> "Sa'd ibn Abī Waqqās said to Mu'āwiya you have sat me next to you on your throne and begun to curse 'Alī."[186]

Maulana 'Ala Maududī states on p. 174 of his *Khilāfat Mulukīyat*:

> "Ibn Kathīr in al-Bidāyah (Vol. 8 p. 259 and Vol. 9 p.80) records that one unlawful and outrageous practice started by Mu'āwiya was that he and his governors would curse 'Alī during the Friday sermon from the Imām's position. This took such an extreme that this practise even took place in the mosque of the Prophet, in front of the grave of the Prophet, the cursing of the most beloved relative would take place in the presence of 'Alī's family who would hear this abuse with their own ears."

We find recorded in *Ṣaḥīḥ* Muslim:

> Amīr ibn Sa'd ibn Abī Waqqās reported on the authority of his father that Mu'āwīya ibn Abī Sufyān appointed Sa'd as the Governor and said: 'What prevents you from abusing Abū Turāb ('Alī),' whereupon he said: 'It is because of three things which I remember Allāh's Messenger having said about him that I would not abuse him and even if I find one of those three things for me, it would be more dear to me than the red camels...."[187]

> It is narrated on the authority of Abū Hazim that: "The Governor of Madīnah who was one of the members of the house of Marwān called Sahl ibn Sa'd and ordered him to curse 'Alī. But Sahl refused to do so. The governor said: 'If you don't want to curse 'Alī, just say God curse Abū Turāb (the nickname of 'Alī).' Sahl said: "Alī did not like any name for himself better than Abū Turāb, and 'Alī used to become very happy when somebody would call him Abū Turāb.'"[188]

Cursing the Ahl al-Bayt is not an act of sending blessings or showing love towards them

Calling on others to curse Imām 'Alī (AS) portrays no sign of love and compassion towards him. We can never believe that Imām 'Alī was a person that curses were valid upon. Would it not have been an act of injustice to curse the Imām of age? A sincere Muslim would never dislike or worse curse a loved one of Allāh.

The Shī'ahs and some Sunnīs are well acquainted with this, that this practice existed and was called upon to be brought to a halt by 'Umar ibn Abdul Azīz (an Umayyad caliph as mentioned in section four), who showed his sentiments towards the House of the Prophet (pbuh & hf).

Our Stand for the Truth.

A number of scholars in their works have stated that when Mu'āwīya came into authority, he wrote to his governors whom he had appointed and expressed that:

> "As soon as you receive this order of mine you should call upon the people to prepare traditions about the distinctions of the companions and other caliphs also, and take care that if any Muslim relates any tradition about Abū Turāb ('Alī) you should prepare a similar tradition about the companions to contradict it because this gives me great pleasure and cools my eyes, and it weakens the position of Abū Turāb and his party men and is more severe to them than the merits and distinctions of 'Uthmān."[189]

Speaking out to people in regards to the truth and true justice as did many before our time, does not render a human being as being heretical. When one companion Mu'āwīya cursed a member of the Ahl al-Bayt, Imām 'Alī (AS), and is not accused of being heretical, then is it truly fair to accuse those who speak against these actions and wish to establish the truth as heretical?

The third Imām of the Ahl al-Bayt, Imām al-Ḥusayn (AS) himself called out for justice and for the truth against the son of Mu'āwīya (Yazīd) as those who were not practicing it in its pure form were mislaying the true Message of Islām. Imām al-Ḥusayn's martyrdom marks this fact and this fact illuminates as Imām al-Ḥusayn illuminates and his march against falsehood will be never forgotten for all time. We all have to understand the message left by Imām Ḥusayn, his standing forth for the truth so it could never be forgotten in order that the religion would remain in the same beautiful and graceful form that his grandfather, the Prophet (pbuh & hf) had brought it as. Not wanting its foundations, its explicit and implicit teachings to be concealed in a sea of delude and contradiction. Imām al-Ḥusayn words were a stand against the dealings of Yazīd; they were to enlighten everyone in regards to the true teachings of Islām:

> "I am not rising (against Yazīd) as an insolent or an arrogant person, or a mischief-monger or tyrant. I have risen (against Yazīd) as I seek to reform the *Ummah* of my grandfather. I wish to bid the good and forbid the evil."[190]

Imām al-Ḥusayn (AS) did not want the truth to be destroyed by an individual like Yazīd and others who would resemble him in the years to come, in his call, as seen by the Imām, he felt it was his duty to radiate this and he did so, his own martyrdom brought the message of Karbala within the hearts of millions. Following this leading man of Paradise in his stand against falsehood was the call the Imām wanted known, a call, which was left for us individuals to carry on with after his martyrdom.

On the day of Ashūra, (the 10th day in the month Muharram), before the fighting had started, Imām al-Ḥusayn (AS) stated to the army of Yazīd:

> "Trace back my lineage and consider who I am. Then, look back at yourselves and remonstrate with yourselves. Consider whether it is right for you to kill me and desecrate my inviolability. Am I not the son of the daughter of your Prophet, the son of the executor of his will and his cousin, the first of believers in God and the man who first believed in what His Apostle brought from his Lord? Was not Hamzah, the leader of the martyrs, my father's uncle and Ja'far at-Tayyār my own uncle? Have you not heard the Prophet of God saying concerning my

> brother and myself: 'These are the two lords of the youths of the inhabitants of Heaven?' If you believe what I am saying - and it is the truth for, by God, I have never told a lie since I learned that God hated people who told them and that those who opposed Him grieved Him ... If you still regard me as a liar, then there are still to be found people who would tell you the truth if you ask them. Ask Jābir ibn 'Abdullāh al-Ansārī, Abū Sa'īd al-Khudrī, Sahl ibn Sa'd, Zayd ibn Arqam and Anas ibn Mālik to tell you what they have heard from the Apostle of God concerning my brother and myself. Is this not sufficient to prevent your shedding my blood?"[191]

Look at the beautiful words of Imām al-Ḥusayn (AS), his words indeed marked the truth and his stand marked a true fragrance. We know a fragrance lasts when its scent is deep and rich in quality; and due to this, it is adored, we never want it to become worn out or contaminated, as the quality of it will not remain the same, we would lose our attraction towards it, as its distinct aroma would become lost and weak. Islām is the same, we cannot afford to contaminate its teachings with confusion and contradiction, we cannot lose its distinct fragrance which the Prophet (pbuh & hf) brought to us and just as Imām al-Ḥusayn fought for its distinction and its true teachings it is a duty upon every Muslim also to do the same.

Crystal clear waters when polluted look dark and murky and only look beautiful when they become crystal clear again. Our stance is to not let those clear waters become murky, to keep them clear and looking beautiful, not to let the truth drown in falsehood, and every one of us should be aiming towards the same and Allāh has promised that falsehood inevitably will perish.

> And say: "Truth has (now) arrived and Falsehood perished; for Falsehood is (by its nature) bound to perish." Qur'ān 17:81

Section 11

Does one believe that the affairs of the Muslims were administered by the one most capable after the demise of the Prophet (pbuh & hf)?

If we believe that after the Prophet's (pbuh & hf) demise, all affairs had been managed appropriately by the man who was most capable of taking charge of the affairs of the Islamic state, then there should never have been any dispute from the sincere believers. No disagreements should have arisen from them, but we find that this is not the case.

One disagreement, which is very well known amongst Shī'ahs and the Sunni majority, is the case of Sayyedah Fāṭimah (AS) in her protest of her inheritance. This case has been discussed by many. Shī'ahs do bring to light that the Prophet's (pbuh & hf) daughter and Imām 'Alī (AS) could never have asked for something the Prophet had forbidden for them.

> Narrated Zayd ibn Arqam: "The Ahl al-Bayt of the Prophet are his lineage and his descendants (those who come from his blood) for whom the acceptance of *Sadaqah* is prohibited."[192]
>
> Yaḥyā related to me from Mālik that he heard that the Messenger of Allāh, may Allāh bless him and grant him peace, said: "*Sadaqah* to the family of Muḥammad is not *Halal* (permissible). It is only people's impurities."[193]

Abū Bakr had expressed that everything the Prophet (pbuh & hf) had left when he departed, was to be treated as *Sadaqah*, meaning, that all possessions left were only to be utilised and passed on to others in the form of *Sadaqah*.

> Narrated 'Ā'isha: "'Fāṭimah the daughter of the Prophet sent someone to Abū Bakr (when he was a caliph), asking for her inheritance of what Allāh's Apostle had left of the property bestowed on him by Allāh from the *Fai* (i.e. booty gained without fighting)

> in Madīnah, and Fadak, and what remained of the *Khūmus* (a fifth of any booty of war, which is not shared among those of fighting) of the Khaybar booty. On that, Abū Bakr said, Allāh's Apostle said: 'Our property is not inherited. Whatever we leave, is *Sadaqah,*' but the family of (the Prophet) Muḥammad can eat of this property. By Allāh, I will not make any change in the state of the *Sadaqah* of Allāh's Apostle and will leave it as it was during the lifetime of Allāh's Apostle, and will dispose of it as Allāh's Apostle used to do.' So Abū Bakr refused to give anything of that to Fāṭimah…'"[194]

Within the quoted narration, it is 'Ā'isha who calls everything Sayyedah Fāṭimah (AS) came to ask for as everything. However, along with everything else that Sayyedah Fāṭimah (AS) came to ask in regards to in the matter of inheritance was Fadak and Fadak was not part of inheritance. Fadak was a piece of land, which was gifted to her when it was bestowed on the Prophet (pbuh & hf). It was gifted after the Battle of Khaybar, which took place for the reason that the Jews of Khaybar had raised an army against the Prophet to fight him along with the tribe of Ghatafan. Ghatafan had already attacked the Prophet in the Battle of Khandaq (Trench), and because he had defeated both these tribes, we understand that the Jews of Fadak portrayed their withdrawal from them through resorting to reconciliation by giving half of Fadak to him.

It is known that Fadak was given to the Prophet (pbuh & hf) without any battle having taken place, and a verse was revealed informing him to give it to Sayyedah Fāṭimah (AS).

> "And render to the kindred their due rights…" Qur'ān 17:26

Jibra'īl (AS) conveyed to the Prophet (pbuh & hf) to give Fadak to Sayyedah Fāṭimah (AS) and he accordingly did just that.

Sunni commentators of the Qur'ān have also recorded:

> "Who are the Kinsmen and what is their due? The Angel Jibra'īl replied: 'Give Fadak to Fāṭimah for it is her due, and whatever is due to Allāh and the Prophet out of Fadak, that also belongs to her, so entrust it to her also.'"[195]

Fadak was given strictly to Sayyedah Fāṭimah (AS) as a gift and it was in her possession even when the Prophet (pbuh & hf) was present. But Abū Bakr had also perceived Fāṭimah's gift as *Sadaqah,* just as he had perceived everything else left by the Prophet.

We also find the following recorded:

> Narrated Abū Ḥurayra, Allāh's Apostle said: "Not even a single *Dīnar* (Arab currency) of my property should be distributed (after my death) to my inheritors, but whatever I leave excluding the provision for my wives and my servants, should be spent in charity."[196]

The Prophet (pbuh & hf) mentioned that he has inheritors but they were not to inherit anything and then mentioned that everything he left excluding what provisions he would give to his wives and servants was to be spent in charity. Is it that the Book of Allāh ignores those who inherit from their father? Do we believe that the Prophet disregarded the laws of inheritance and decided not to give anything to his next of kin when Allāh teaches otherwise? The rules of inheritance were not only for the people but included the Prophet also. The Qur'ān is not in agreement to the laws of inheritance only corresponding to the people. It does not signify that the family of prophets do not inherit, which shall be addressed further as the section proceeds.

But it will first be appropriate to observe what Sayyedah Fāṭimah (AS) stated in regards to the statement given by Abū Bakr.

> Abū Bakr said: "Allāh's Apostle said, 'We (Prophets), our property is not inherited, and whatever we leave is Sadaqah...'"[197]

Accompanied by women to a mosque, Sayyedah Fāṭimah (AS) delivered a great speech in front of the people; and within this very speech she confronted them about her own right and the specific laws of inheritance, which have been stated in the Qur'ān. Part of this speech is stated here:

> "...O Muslims! Will my inheritance be usurped? O son of Abū Quhāfa! (Abū Bakr), where is it in the Book of Allāh that you inherit your father and I do not inherit mine? Surely you have come up with an unprecedented thing. Do you intentionally abandon the Book of Allāh and cast it behind your back? Do you not read where it says: 'And Sulaymān inherited Dāwūd...(Qur'ān 27:16)?' And when it narrates the story of Zakarīyya and says: 'So give me an heir as from thyself (One that) will inherit ones and inherit the posterity of Ya'qūb...(Qur'ān 19:5-6)' and 'but kindred by blood have prior rights against each other in the Book of Allāh...(Qur'ān 33:6)' and: 'Allāh (thus) directs you as regards your children's (inheritance) to the male, a portion equal to that of two females...(Qur'ān 4:11)' and: '...If he leaves any goods, that he makes a bequest to parents and next of kin, according to reasonable usage; this is due from the pious one. (Qur'ān 2:180). You claim that I have no share! And that I do not inherit my father! What! Did Allāh reveal a (Qur'ānic) verse regarding you from which He excluded my father?' Or do you say: 'These (Fāṭimah and her father) are the people of two faiths; they do not inherit each other?' Are we not, me and my father, a people adhering to one faith? Or is it that you have more knowledge about the specifications and generalisations of the Qur'ān than my father and cousin (Alī)? So, here you are, take it! (Ready with) its nose rope and saddled! But if shall encounter you on the Day of Gathering, (thus) what a wonderful judge is Allāh, a claimant is Muḥammad, and a day is the Day of Rising. At the time of the Hour shall the wrongdoers lose; and it shall not benefit you to regret (your actions) then! For every message, there is a time limit; and soon

> shall ye know who will be inflicted with torture that will humiliate him, and who will be confronted by an everlasting punishment..."[198]

Everyone who was present at this gathering was stunned by Fāṭimah's (AS) words and became silent, as it left them speechless. Although all the speech has not been stated here, it is a lengthy one and has been recorded both by the Sunni and the Shī'ahs and of course widely known amongst the Shī'ah.

Sayyedah Fāṭimah (AS) had nothing against Abū Bakr when the Prophet (pbuh & hf) was alive; she had no qualms against him. After the Prophet passed away she remained unhappy with Abū Bakr to the extent that she refused to speak to him for the rest of her life. But, what we must ask ourselves is, was this action of hers based on her self-desire to gain worldly materialistic possession or was it a protest based on establishing the truth in the matter? Fāṭimah knew that Abū Bakr was a companion of the Prophet but still; this did not prevent her from speaking out. Can we, as rational and intellectual individuals understand why?

Fāṭimah's (AS) disapproval is known by many and has been reported in both Shī'ah and Sunni books.

> Narrated 'Ā'isha: "...**So she became angry with Abū Bakr and kept away from him, and did not speak to him till she died.** She remained alive for six months after the death of the Prophet. When she died 'Alī buried her at night without informing Abū Bakr and he said the funeral prayer by himself. When Fāṭimah was alive the people use to respect 'Alī much, but after her death, 'Alī noticed a change in the peoples attitude towards him. So 'Alī sought reconciliation with Abū Bakr and gave him an oath of allegiance. 'Alī had not given the oath of allegiance during those months (i.e. the period between the Prophet's death and Fāṭimah's death). 'Alī sent someone to Abū Bakr saying: 'Come to us, but let nobody come with you,' as he disliked that 'Umar should come.' 'Umar said: (to Abū Bakr), 'No, by Allah, you shall not enter upon them alone...'"[199]

Does one believe affairs of Muslims were administered by the one most capable after the demise of Prophet (pbuh & hf)?

There are reasons why a human being will take an aversion to another. Nobody begins to avert from another individual for no reason. The reason may be due to jealousy; envy, greed or it may be that the averted individual has performed an action, perhaps without even realising it, which has led to an injustice. An individual who is a victim of this will cry out, regardless of whether it is directed to a minister of the state or the king of a country, because they will want it rectified.

> "Allāh loveth not the utterance of harsh speech, except where injustice hath been done; for Allāh is He who heareth and knoweth all things." Qur'ān 4:148

If the leader of the Islamic state understood the directives of Allāh and His Apostle and was implementing them correctly, there would never be a dispute and disagreement coming from a sincere, true believer and was not Sayyedah Fāṭimah (AS) a sincere, true believer? Were her words not in accordance with the truth?

> "And if any fail to judge by (the light of) what Allāh hath revealed they are (no better than) wrongdoers." Qur'ān 5:45

Can we class Sayyedah Fāṭimah (AS) as a transgressor, a wrongdoer, who is the leading lady of Paradise? We cannot state that Fāṭimah was one of these people and that her calling out and interest in the inheritance was based on her desires for wealth in this material world, this purified leading lady of Paradise can never be accused of being greedy for money or property. Also, even thinking for one minute that Fāṭimah was not thinking straight, was overcome by emotion, was concerned of possessing something of this world, dampens the nobility and distinction Allāh has given her, this gracious lady but only cried out for justice and cried out for the truth.

> Narrated 'Ā'isha that the Prophet said: "O, Fāṭimah! Are you not happy that you are the chief of the believing women?"[200]

> The Messenger of Allāh said: "The most excellent of the women of all worlds whom Allāh chose over all women are, Āsīyah the wife of Pharaoh, Maryam (Mary, Jesus' mother) the daughter of Imrān, Khadīja the daughter of Khūwaylid, and Fāṭimah the daughter of Muḥammad."[201]

We are not here to cause hatred amongst one another, we do not wish to be unjust, what is expressed and stated is but only the daughter of the Prophet's (pbuh & hf) stance, her own actions and her own words. Should we as sincere, just Muslims pay no attention to the words of this leading lady of Paradise?

Sayyedah Fāṭimah (AS) was acquainted with the teachings in regards to inheritance and her words were not contrary to this, if this had been so, would not have Imām 'Alī (AS) corrected his wife? The Imām did no such thing; rather, he further solidified her stand.

> Narrated Ja'far: "Fāṭimah came to Abū Bakr to demand her inheritance. 'Abbās also came to demand his inheritance; 'Alī ibn Abī Tālib also came with him. Abū Bakr said that the Prophet of Allāh had said: 'We do not make any heir to inherit our property, what we leave is charity, and the support that he gave them is now my responsibility.' 'Alī said: 'Prophet Sulaymān was the heir of Prophet Dāwūd. Prophet Zakarīya prayed to Allāh, bestow upon me a son, who is heir to me and the family of Ya'qūb.' Abū Bakr said: 'The matter of the Prophet's legacy is as it is. By Allāh! You know it as I do.' 'Alī said: 'And see what the Book of Allāh is saying.'" [202]

Imām 'Alī (AS) knew the exact meaning of these words of the Qur'ān and that they exclusively referred to the inheritance of the prophets. They never would have been stated by the Ahl al-Bayt if they did not carry this meaning.

Within the above narration, Imām 'Alī (AS) first stated Sulaymān (AS), who was a prophet within his father Dāwūd's (AS) lifetime and was gifted with knowledge and virtue, just as his father was.

Does one believe affairs of Muslims were administered by the one most capable after the demise of Prophet (pbuh & hf)?

> "We gave (in the past) knowledge to David and Solomon, and they both said: 'Praise be to Allāh who has favoured us above many of His servants who believe!'" Qur'ān 27:15

Dāwūd's (AS) wealth was a separate matter and do we not believe that this wealth was given to his righteous son Sulaymān (AS) to manage? Did Sulaymān not inherit anything from his father?

Also, prophet Zakarīyah (AS) prayed to Allāh to grant him a son in order to become his heir:

> "Now I fear (what) my relatives (and colleagues) (will do) after me; but my wife is barren; so give me an heir as from Thyself. (One that) will (truly) represent me and represent the posterity of Jacob; and make him O my Lord! One with whom Thou art well-pleased!" Qur'ān 19:5-6

Many people are prone to saying that prophet Zakarīyah (AS) prayed for a heir to inherit his knowledge because prophets left behind knowledge as inheritance. A statement is quoted, **that is in reality part** of a narration stated in *Usūl al-Kāfī* (Chapter on the reward for the scholars and those who seek knowledge, H57, Ch4, h1) and can also be found in the Sunan of Abū Dāwūd (Book of Knowledge, Book 25, Number 3634) which states:

> "Prophets do not leave dirham or dinar as inheritance but what they leave is knowledge."

If we observe the full narration from *Usūl al-Kāfī*, it states:

> Muḥammad ibn al-Ḥasan and 'Alī ibn Muḥammad has narrated from Saḥl ibn Ziyad and Muḥammad ibn Yaḥya from Aḥmad ibn Muḥammad, all from Ja'far ibn Muḥammad al-Ash'arī from 'Abdullāh ibn Maymun al-Qaddah and 'Alī ibn Ibrahīm from his father from Ḥammad ibn Īsā from al-Qaddah from Aba 'Abdallah who has said the following: "The Holy Prophet has

> said, 'If one sets out on a journey to seek knowledge Allāh will lead him to the way that would take him to paradise. The angels will stretch their wings for the pleasure of the seeker of knowledge and all that is in the heavens and earth even the whales in the oceans will ask forgiveness for him (from Allāh). **The excellence of the scholar over other people is like that of the moon over other stars during a full-moon night. The scholars are the heirs of the prophets, the prophets did not leave any dirham or dinar (wealth) as their legacy but they did leave knowledge as their legacy.** Whoever acquires a share from such legacy has gained a very large share.'"

The whole narration is speaking in context to the excellence of scholars and that a scholar does not inherit the wealth of prophets, but rather, knowledge. Taking part of the narration and relating it with the issue of the wealth of prophets, is not the way to provide a sound understanding of what the Prophet (pbuh & hf) intended when stating such words. It is self evident when reading the whole narration what was intended. The Prophet's words relate to the scholars and depict to us that the **prophets do not leave wealth for the *ulema* (scholars), rather, they leave knowledge.** This does not mean that the prophets had no wealth, on the contrary, we all know that the prophets did have wealth, also this wealth did not solely have to be money, it could have been a house, a camel, or even clothing, nevertheless, whatever form it was in, the fact is that it existed, and it needed to be managed and utilised in the correct way and not fought over after the passing away of any prophet.

We need to ponder and think, Sayyedah Fāṭimah (AS) and Imām 'Alī (AS) **used verses of the Qur'ān to refute** the idea that prophets did not leave dinar or dirham **for their families**. They did not counteract the statement referring to the learned not being given the wealth of the prophets but rather counteracted Abū Bakr's statement, which is in total variance to the Prophet's (pbuh & hf), which as we know, indicates that whatever wealth the prophets had, after their demise, it was left as *Sadaqah*. Sayyedah Fāṭimah (AS) and Imām 'Alī (AS) quoted such a verse (19:5-6) of the Qur'ān because it illustrated to everyone that a heir was needed **who would take responsibility**

of the wealth of his father, keeping the family secure from his relatives and other equals, otherwise, as already stated, it never would have been quoted by them.

Who can state that the prophets had no thought for their families well being? Would not the prophets of Allāh have been concerned of what they were in possession of to be spent accordingly and righteously when they left this world? Whatever the prophets left behind for their families and for the community needed to be appropriately taken care of.

> Narrated Khaula al-Ansārīya I heard Allāh's Apostle saying: "Some people spend Allāh's wealth (i.e. Muslim's wealth) in an unjust manner; such people will be put in the (Hell) Fire on the Day of Resurrection."[203]

Property, assets left by the prophets certainly required heirs to take over the responsibility of maintaining the needs of the family, utilising and administering the assets left, in the righteous and responsible way required for them to do so. The prophets did not have a could not care less attitude towards any matter which was a responsibility upon them, they were moral and good people, they could not have carelessly left their belongings to be fought over, for every responsibility needs to be correctly looked after, requires good management and incorrect management indicates poor conduct, and can poor conduct be ascribed to the prophets?

Some people state that the laws of inheritance were not specific to the Prophet (pbuh & hf) and although other families of the prophets inherited, our Prophet's family could not. There is no foundation in such a statement, as the Qur'ān does not specify as such and neither did the Ahl al-Bayt plus it is known that the Prophet departed leaving possessions and certain wealth (for e.g. *Fai*, *Khūmus*), which we can state his family had right to.

When there is a different ruling for the Prophet (pbuh & hf) to that of the rest of the Muslims, Allāh specifies it in the Qur'ān, for example, the marriage rights of the Prophet were different to that of others and Allāh stated it in the Qur'ān, part of which is quoted here:

> "...and any believing woman who dedicates her soul to the Prophet if the Prophet wishes to wed her this only for thee and not for the believers (at large)..." Qur'ān 33:50

'Abdullāh Yūsuf 'Alī stated in his commentary in regards to the above verse:

> "This introduces no new exemption or privilege. Verses 50-52 merely declare the points in which, on account of the special circumstances, the Prophet's marriages differed from those of ordinary Muslims."

The Prophet (pbuh & hf) married for different reasons than what most people marry for, we all know that he married a lot of widows to give them security, women from other tribes to tie good relationships etc, which is not the topic of discussion here, but what is trying to be revealed is that if the laws of inheritance for the Prophet differed from that of the rest of the Muslims, it would also have been specified through the Qur'ān, but we find that this is not the case.

The same laws of inheritance stood for the Prophet (pbuh & hf) and the Muslims, we also know that previous prophets did inherit and the statement: "We (Prophets), our property is not inherited, and whatever we leave is *Sadaqah*," is in direct disagreement to this.

Do we firmly believe that Abū Bakr could not make any errors in his judgement? We should think back to his words:

> "I hold in my hands the reins of your affairs even though I am not the best amongst you. If you see that I am treading the right path, then support me, if you see me embarking on the wrong cause, then guide me back to the right path."

Could we not state that it was possible for Abū Bakr to have misquoted certain statements of the Prophet (pbuh & hf) or even misunderstood them? Let us look at another statement of Abū Bakr's:

Does one believe affairs of Muslims were administered by the one most capable after the demise of Prophet (pbuh & hf)?

> Abū Tufayl said: "Fāṭimah came to Abū Bakr asking him for the inheritance of the Prophet, Abū Bakr said: 'I heard the Apostle of Allāh say: 'If Allāh, Most High, gives a prophet some means of sustenance, that goes to his successor.'''[204]

This statement uses the words "means of sustenance" rather than "inheritance". We understand that sustenance can come from what an individual is in possession of or from what has been earned. These possessions or earnings, which have provided for the family, are what the next of kin inherit. The narration then depicts that when the Prophet (pbuh & hf) departed, what he was in possession of, his means of sustenance, was to be taken by the successor. This is something that Abū Bakr did not mention in his other statement, when he stated that the Prophet had said:

> "We (Prophets), our property is not inherited, and whatever we leave, is *Sadaqah*."

If all means of sustenance (i.e. possessions, wealth) was to be taken by the successor of the Prophet (pbuh & hf), Abū Bakr is depicting that the Prophet's successor would acquire it, which ultimately means inheritance of it, regardless of how it would be utilized.

We are aware that Abū Bakr had Islamic knowledge; as is the case for many of the Prophet's (pbuh & hf) companions, but do we believe that the formers understanding and knowledge was more extensive and exceeded that of the Ahl al-Bayt? Shī'ahs do not regard Abū Bakr as more acquainted and knowledgeable than the Ahl al-Bayt and adhere to their words above the word of others. The Prophet related in regards to them:

> "Do not go in front of them for you will perish, and do not lag behind them for you will perish, and do not teach them for they are more learned than you."[205]

The Sunni scholar Ibn Ḥajar al-Haythamī comments on this *Ḥadīth* with the words:

> "There is proof that whoever among them is elevated to high offices and religious vocations must be preferred over all others."[206]

When we are not permitted to exceed the Ahl al-Bayt and not permitted to teach them, then regardless of whether an individual is placed above them in some authoritarian position or not, the Ahl al-Bayt remain in their respective position. It is not as Ibn Ḥajar states that if any of them are placed in an elevated position, then they are to be preferred, rather, their position remains unaltered in the eyes of Allah irrespective of whom an individual takes partiality to.

Also, it is legitimate to state, that if an individual is lacking in the knowledge and understanding of the Qur'ān and the *Sunnah*, somewhere along the lines that individual may fall into a wrong judgement without meaning to or without realising it, and no doubt, people will speak against it.

From what we find narrated in the Sunni reference books, we recognise that Abū Bakr wanted to distribute what the Prophet (pbuh & hf) had left in accordance to the statements he gave, which he believed were stated by the Prophet. These statements were not accepted by the Ahl al-Bayt, Sayyedah Fāṭimah (AS) spoke in opposition to them in her own speech. What can be said about what she had brought forth and was she wrong to do so?

We learn that Abū Bakr was generous with his own wealth when he contributed much to the expedition of Tabūk, we learn that he did not have a passion for wealth and he stated he wanted to distribute what the Prophet (pbuh & hf) had left as *Sadaqah* (as this is what he called it) for the people, including the family of the Prophet in this, when, as we know, *Sadaqah* was forbidden for them. This was Abū Bakr's judgement in the matter and from this judgement; it caused the daughter of the Prophet to speak out, clarify and explain the rules of inheritance, to make clear to everyone what the Qur'ān teaches.

It is known that Sayyedah Fāṭimah's (AS) wish was to be buried without anyone knowing. It is because of this reason, which leads one to research into this matter, for one to state, why did she not wish anyone to know, and by saying this, minds open to seek, which then makes one aware of her stand.

Does one believe affairs of Muslims were administered by the one most capable after the demise of Prophet (pbuh & hf)?

This incident will continue to be discussed by many, to enable people to understand the reason behind Fāṭimah's (AS) disapproval and disappointment. It may provide a way for many, to wipe away those cobwebs, which have prevented them from going further into the House. These events left Fāṭimah displeased and saddened when she left this world, her sadness was not based on nothing, her speaking out was not based on nothing either, again why did she do so?

Some people are prone to saying that a Muslim cannot remain annoyed with a person for more than three days, which has been taken from a saying of the Prophet (pbuh & hf), and state that Sayyedah Fāṭimah (AS) remained in this state all the way up until her demise, this portrays that she did not follow this. This comment is far out of the framework of the issue concerned and certainly cannot be used as an argument against Fāṭimah, the leading lady of Paradise.

Sayyedah Fāṭimah (AS) was an individual whose actions illustrated the character of a pure woman, her character did not portray childishness or obstinate behaviour for even in her child-hood years she witnessed the suffering of her father and handled it with maturity. She would aid her father and console him, her sense of direction was not masked by emotion, but was always inline with his (pbuh & hf) teachings and he (pbuh & hf) as well as the companions were known to call her the mother of her father (Umme Abīhah).

When we take into account any issue, where the decision made on it is not in accordance to the law, then the individual to whom this has been perpetrated against will not be pleased with it. Meaning, if the verdict of something, which is based on the *Sharīah* dictates something contrary to it, this verdict will never be accepted by the individual who wishes the correct law to be practiced. To become pleased with the person who has perpetrated this action would mean an acceptance of the verdict given, which can never be accepted if it is against the *Sharīah*. If one was to look into the *Ṣaḥīḥ* of Imām Muslim in "*Kitāb al-Birr was-Salati wal-Adab*, (The Book of Virtue, Good Manners and Joining of the Ties of Relationship) and read the heading for the section under, which the *Ḥadīth* in regards to the Prophet (pbuh & hf) stating that we are not to remain unhappy with someone for more than three days, we will find written:

"It is forbidden for a Muslim to have estranged relations with the other Muslim beyond three days **without any reason of *Sharīah*.**"

We should understand under what condition the *Ḥadīth* is valid. When no reason with respect to *Sharīah* remains then we should mend relations with one another, as clearly there is no reason not to, but if this is not the case, and the matter does not agree with what the *Sharīah* teaches, there can be no reconciliation until the whole issue is resolved in accordance to it. We should ask ourselves, did Sayyedah Fāṭimah (AS) and her husband Imām 'Alī (AS) turn against this?

We are not here to create hatred or disunity amongst one another, we are here to try and make sense of matters relating to capability, to study in order that we recognise the competencies of various individuals after the Prophet.

Section 12

The Reports in al-Bukhārī's *Ṣaḥīḥ* and the Reports of others.

There are many book writers and compilers in this day and age who work for the media, be it for radio or television. Each reporter will at his own discretion record various reports associated with different matters, which they have heard from other people who claim to be witnesses to certain actions or events, which have taken place, or, who have heard a certain matter being stated. These reporters will then decide what to do with the information they have gathered.

Ridiculous reports can be heard of or read in almost any newspaper, which the reader may get puzzled over, or may not even believe in, but at the same time the same paper may report a certain matter, which is both educational and informative. Hence on the one hand we may see or hear a deceptive, unbelieving or ridiculous report and on the other a more reliable, sensible and intellectual one. How would we rank each reporter?

It is very well known that al-Bukhārī has been given the greatest credit towards what he has reported over any other reporter of *Ḥadīth*. It is worth noting that other reporters had also obtained what al-Bukhārī had, their *Aḥadīth* relying on the chain of transmission as quoted by them. It cannot be deduced that al-Bukhārī had a better approach than any other in his method of acceptance of reports, if other scholars had also accepted what he had accepted.

The four Imāms of the Ahl al-Sunnah wa al-Jammāh were born before al-Bukhārī. Imām Aḥmad ibn Ḥanbal was present in his time and was one of his teachers.

Many scholars after al-Bukhārī existed who reported traditions; learnt them and taught them to others, ranking each and every one of them as they deemed it fit.

However, we find that if reports are mentioned, which are not quoted from *Ṣaḥīḥ al-Bukhārī*, comments such as: "Is this in al-Bukhārī's *Ṣaḥīḥ*?" "Such and such *Ḥadīth* is not in *Ṣaḥīḥ al-Bukhārī*, so we do not believe in it," are expressed. If we state that we do not believe in anything, which is not stated in *Ṣaḥīḥ* al-Bukhārī, we need to realise that we are indirectly implying that the work and extensive study of other *Ḥadīth* scholars is insignificant.

It is biased and prejudiced to ignore all other scholars of *Ḥadīth* because a label has been pinned on one (al-Bukhārī) like a highlighted item in a shop window, causing more attraction towards that one object and disregarding the rest. This matter has to be dealt with, as favouritism and self-opinion does not lead to fairness and rationality, it leads to prejudice, hatred and discord. You will love your friend over your neighbour because you know much about your friend and not about your neighbour and many times a human being will not take a matter, which goes against what he or she is attached to.

Imām al-Bukhārī's *Ṣaḥīḥ* does not contain *Ḥadīth al-Thaqalayn* (the Tradition of the Two Weighty Things).

Although many scholars of *Ḥadīth* have narrated the tradition of the two weighty things, we do not find it anywhere in the nine volumes of al-Bukhārī's *Ṣaḥīḥ*. Other scholars of *Ḥadīth* have acknowledged the authenticity of this *Ḥadīth* and recorded it accordingly. Such scholars as Imām Aḥmad ibn Ḥanbal, Imām Hākim, Imām Tirmidhī and Imām Nasā'ī have included it in their works.

Imām Aḥmed has narrated the following tradition:

> Narrated Zayd ibn Thābit: "I am leaving among you two successors, the Book of Allāh a rope extending from Heavens to earth (or between Heavens and earth), and my Household (*Ahl al-Bayt*) from my family (*'itra*); they shall never separate from each other until they reach me by the Pool.[207]

He has also narrated this tradition:

> Narrted Abū Sa'īd al-Khudrī: "I think I am going to be called upon and shall answer that call, and I am leaving among you two weighty things, the Book of Allāh Almighty and my offspring, my Ahl al-Bayt. The Sublime and Omniscient has informed me that they shall never part from each other till they reach me by

> the Pool; so, see how you succeed me in faring with them.[208]

Al-Tirmidhī is reported to have stated in regards to *Ḥadīth al-Thaqalayn*:

> "There are *Ḥadīth* on this subject by Abū Dharr Ghiffārī, Abū Sa'īd al-Khudrī, Zayd ibn Arqam and Ḥudhayfah ibn Usayd."[209]

Imām al-Ḥākim reported the following:

> "Narrated to us Abū Bakr Muḥammad ibn al-Ḥusayn ibn Muslim, the *faqīh* of Ray, from Muḥammad ibn Ayyūb, from Yaḥyā ibn al-Mughīrah al-Sa'dī, from Jarīr ibn 'Abd al-Hamīd, from al-Ḥasan ibn 'Abd Allāh al-Nakha'ī, from Muslim ibn Subayh, from Zayd ibn Arqam, may God be pleased with him, who said: 'The Messenger of Allāh, may Allāh's peace and benedictions be upon him and his progeny, said: 'Verily, I leave behind two weighty things amongst you, the Book of Allāh and my Ahl al-Bayt. Verily, the two will never separate until they come back to me by the side of the Pond.'"

This *Ḥadīth* is *Ṣaḥīḥ al-isnād* according to the conditions laid down by the two Shaykhs (al-Bukhārī and Muslim) though they did not record it. [210]

Imām Muslim has also reported the tradition from Zayd ibn Arqam in his *Ṣaḥīḥ* as quoted in section six of this book. It is mentioning that within this very report Yazīd ibn Hayyān asks Zayd ibn Arqam:

> '...Who are the members of his Household? Aren't his wives the members of his family?' Thereupon Zayd said: 'His wives are the members of his family (but here) the members of his family are those for whom acceptance of Zakāt is forbidden.' And he said: 'Who are they?' Thereupon he said: ' 'Alī and the offspring of 'Alī, Aqīl and the offspring of Aqīl, the offspring of Ja'far and the offspring of 'Abbās.' Ḥusayn said:

> 'These are those for whom the acceptance of Zakāt is forbidden.' Zayd said: 'Yes…'"[211]

We always have to remember the teachings of the Qur'ān and the words of the Prophet (pbuh & hf). Zayd said:

> "'Alī and the offspring of 'Alī, Aqīl and the offspring of Aqīl, the offspring of Ja'far and the offspring of 'Abbās."

We find above that Zayd expressed his own statement when referencing those who were one of the *thaqalayn.*

We find that in another narration, Yazīd ibn Hayyān reported the following:

> '...We said, who are his Ahl al-Bayt (that the Prophet was referring to)? Are they his wives?' Thereupon Zayd said: 'No, by Allāh! A woman lives with a man (as his wife) for a while; he then divorces her and she goes back to her parents and her people. The Ahl al-Bayt of the Prophet are his lineage and his descendants (those who come from his blood) for whom the acceptance of charity *(Sadaqah)* is prohibited.'[212]

Again, we find that Zayd expressed his own statement, but this time in regards to the wives of the Prophet (pbuh & hf), that they are not included in this Ahl al-Bayt that were being addressed here along with the Qur'ān.

If we backtrack our minds towards the Qur'ānic verse 33:33 in reference to the "pure" household (Bayt) of the Prophet (pbuh & hf) we would be able to fathom their placement with the "pure" Qur'ān.

Imām Bukhāri's *Ṣaḥīḥ* does not contain anything in regards to *Ḥadīth al-Ghadīr.*

In section six, glimpses of the tradition from the *khutba* given by the Prophet (pbuh & hf) on the 18th *Dhu'l- Ḥijjah* can be observed, where he declared the authority of Imām 'Alī (AS) and the importance of adherence to the two weighty things. As observed scholars such as Imām Muslim, Imām Aḥmad ibn Ḥanbal, Imām Ḥākim, Imām Nasā'ī and Imām Tirmidhī have quoted narrations in connection with this proclamation.

Additionally, Imām al-Ḥākim has reported:

> "Narrated to us Abū al-Ḥusayn Muḥammad ibn Aḥmad ibn Tamīm al- Ḥanzalī in Baghdad, from Abū Qallabah 'Abd al-Mālik ibn Muḥammad al-Raqqashī, from Yaḥyā ibn Ḥammād; also narrated to me Abū Bakr Muḥammad ibn Balawayh and Abū Bakr Aḥmad ibn Ja'far al-Bazzāz, both of them from 'Abd Allāh ibn Aḥmad ibn Ḥanbal, from his father, from Yaḥyā ibn Hammād; and also narrated to us Abū Nasr Aḥmad ibn Suhayl, the *faqīh* of Bukhāra, from Sālih ibn Muḥammad, the *hāfiz* (one who can recite the Qur'ān by memory) of Baghdad, from Khalaf ibn Salīm al-Makhramī, from Yaḥya ibn Hammād; and Yaḥya ibn Hammād narrated from Abū 'Uwwanah from Sulaymān al-A'māsh, from Habīb ibn Abī Thābit, from Abū al-Tufayl, from Zayd ibn Arqam, may God be pleased with him, who said: 'The Messenger of Allāh, may God's peace and benedictions be upon him and his progeny, while returning from his last *Ḥajj* came down at Ghadir Khumm and ordered (us) towards the big trees, and (the ground) underneath them was swept.' Then he said: 'I am about to answer the call (of death). Verily, I have left behind two weighty things amongst you, one of which is greater than the other. The Book of Allāh, the Exalted, and my *'itrah* (kindred). So watch out how you treat these **two after me, for verily these two (*huma*)** will not separate from each other until they come back to me by the side of the Pond.' Then he said: 'Verily, Allāh,

> the Almighty and the Glorious, is my master (*mawla*) and I am the master of every believer.' Then he took 'Alī, may God be pleased with him, by the hand and said: 'This ('Alī) is the master of whomever I am his master. O God, love whoever loves him and be the enemy of his enemy.'"

Imam al-Ḥākim then adds:

> "This *Ḥadīth* is *Ṣaḥīḥ* in accordance with the conditions to the criterion of the Shaykhs (al-Bukhārī and Muslim), **although they have not recorded it in its full length**."[213]

The fourth Imām of the Sunni school of thought who was alive during al-Bukhārī's time has reported this tradition, and al-Bukhārī's own student Muslim also reported some of it in his *Ṣaḥīḥ*, confirming to us that this tradition had been reported within his time and was also in circulation. Although Imām al-Bukhārī did not report anything in regards to *Ḥadīth* al-Ghadir in his *Ṣaḥīḥ*, he did report some of it in his *Tārīkh al-Kabīr*,[214] confirming to us that al-Bukhārī also knew of the tradition, hence the reason behind why Imām al-Ḥākim is recorded to have stated that both Imām al-Bukhārī and Imām Muslim did not record the tradition in its entirety.

Ibn Ḥajar in his Sawā'iqh al-Muhriqah stated the following:

> "This is a true *Ḥadīth*, its veracity cannot be doubted. Verily Tirmidhī, Nasā'ī and Aḥmad have narrated it, and if studied, its sources are sound enough."[215]

When we block out the sun with our sunglasses, it does not mean that the sun is not there. When we cannot see something in front of our eyes, it does not mean that that particular object or item does not exist. If al-Bukhārī did not report this tradition in his *Ṣaḥīḥ*, it does not mean that the tradition was not known of or did not exist.

> Ibn Kathir writes that many authentic *Aḥadīth* that were left out of *Ṣaḥīḥ* Muslim and al-Bukhārī can be

> found in other *Ḥadīth* books like Tirmidhī, Abū Dāwūd, Al-Nasā'ī.[216]
>
> Ibn Salāh stated that many authentic *Aḥadīth* were left out of *Ṣaḥīḥ* Muslim and al-Bukhārī, he also said that Imām Hākim has collected all the authentic *Aḥadīth*, which met the *Ḥadīth* principles of Muslim and al-Bukhārī, and stated them in a book called "al-Mustadrak."[217]

Imām al-Bukhārī himself stated the following:

> "I have left out many authentic *Ahadīth* because I thought that the book would become too large. This book is the summarisation of the 600,000 *Ahadīth*, which I knew. The book was completed in sixteen years."[218]

Al-Bukhārī did not set out to write his *Ṣaḥīḥ* in order to report every single narration. When we can understand that other authentic *Aḥadīth* can be found in other books, would it be correct to ignore them?

Are not the reports of Imām Aḥmad ibn Ḥanbal, Imām Tirmidhī, Imām Nasā'ī, Imām Ḥākim, and others, worthy of any attention? Can Alexander Fleming's (a microbiologist who discovered penicillin, a fungus growing on his bacteria culture which was killing it) work be refuted over Watson, James D (Ewey) and Sir Francis Cricks, two scientists, who are renowned for their works on the DNA molecule? Both discovered separate issues within the biological world, this does not mean that because one scientist discovered one matter which another scientist did not, it was not true. These discoveries were proven and as of today remain as facts within science and are not looked down upon. Each scientist was rewarded for his work, what can be stated about those scientists who are renowned for their works on *Aḥadīth*, should we only give al-Bukhārī all the credit?

Why not analyse the reports of al-Bukhārī and the reports of others?

Imām Aḥmad ibn Ḥanbal reported the following:

Why not analyse the reports of al-Bukhārī and the reports of others?

> Narrated Buraida: "The Messenger of Allāh sent two armies to Yemen. One of them was led by 'Alī ibn Abī Tālib and the other by Khālid ibn al-Walīd. He instructed them thus: 'When you combine your forces, let 'Ali ibn Abī Tālib be the overall leader. But if you disperse, then each one of you is the leader over his own troops.' We then battled Banū Zubayda and then 'Alī selected one of the captives, a slave-girl, for himself; so, Khālid and I wrote to the Messenger of Allāh to inform him of the incident. When I came to the Messenger of Allah and the letter was read for him I noticed anger in his eyes; therefore, I pleaded to him by saying: 'This is the place for those who seek refuge; you have sent me with a Commander and ordered me to obey him, and I have done just that.' The Messenger of Allāh said: 'Do not plot against 'Alī for he is of me and I am of him, and he is your *walī* after me.'"[219]

Imām Aḥmad ibn Ḥanbal has reported another tradition along with Imām al-Ḥākim in connection with this event.

> Narrated Imrān ibn Ḥusayn: "The Messenger of Allāh deployed an army division under the command of 'Alī ibn Abū Tālib who chose, as his share of the *Khūmus*, a slave-girl for himself, and people criticized him. Four men vowed to complain against him to the Messenger of Allāh. When they came to the Prophet, one of them stood up and said: 'O Messenger of Allāh! Have you seen how 'Alī has done such and such?' The Prophet turned his face away from him. The second stood up and spoke likewise, and the Prophet ignored him, too. The third stood up and repeated what his fellows had previously stated, and he, too, was ignored. The fourth one stood up and stated exactly as had been stated by his fellows. It was then that the Messenger of Allāh turned to them with anger in his eyes and said: 'What do you want of

> 'Alī? 'Alī is of me and I am of him, and only after me is he the *mawla* of all believers.'"[220]

Similarly Tirmidhī reported the following:

> Narrated Imrān ibn Ḥusayn: "Four men came to the Prophet complaining about 'Alī...
>
> The Prophet became angry and said: 'What do you want from 'Alī? What do you want from 'Alī? What do you want from 'Alī? 'Alī is from me and I am from him and he is the *walī* of every believer after me.'"[221]

Al-Tabarani stated the following, which is also quoted in *al-Sawā'iq al-Muhriqah*:

> "Buraida came from Yemen and entered the mosque, he found a crowd standing by the room of the Prophet. Upon seeing him, they stood up to greet him and ask him what news he had brought them. He said: "Good news. Allāh has rendered victory upon the Muslims. They asked him: 'Then what brought you here?' He answered: 'An incident regarding a slave-girl whom 'Alī chose as his share of the *Khūmus*, and I have come here to inform the Prophet about it.' They said: 'Inform him of it, do inform him, so that he may change his heart about 'Alī,' while the Prophet, was standing overhearing their conversation from within. He thereupon came out angrily and said: 'What is the matter with those who bear grudge against 'Alī? Whoever hates 'Alī hates me, too, and whoever abandons 'Alī abandons me. 'Alī is of me and I am of him; he has been created of my own mould, and my own mould is Abraham's and I am even superior to Abraham, one progeny descending from another, and Allāh is all-Hearing, all-Knowing. O Buraida! Have you not come to know that '**Alī's share is a lot more than the slave-girl he took, and that he is your *wali* after me**?'"[222]

Al-Bukhārī reported the following in regards to the incident:

Why not analyse the reports of al-Bukhārī and the reports of others?

> Narrated Buraida: "The Prophet sent 'Alī to Khalid to bring the *Khūmus* (of the booty) and I hated 'Alī, and 'Alī had taken a bath (after a sexual act with a slave-girl from the *Khūmus*). I said to Khālid: 'Do not you see this (i.e. 'Alī)?' When we reached the Prophet I mentioned that to him. He said: 'O Buraida! Do you hate 'Alī?' I said: 'Yes.' He said: 'Do you hate him, **for he deserves more than that from the *Khūmus*.**'[223]

We observe that other scholars have reported something more in relation to the Prophet's (pbuh & hf) words, but does this mean we ignore such words and only pay attention to the report mentioned in al-Bukhārī's *Ṣaḥīḥ*?

As already mentioned in section eight, in 9 A.H. on the occasion of the *Ḥajj*, the Prophet (pbuh & hf) sent Abū Bakr to proclaim the verses of *Sūrah al-Tawbah* and then sent Imām 'Alī (AS) after him in order to recite them instead.

Imām Aḥmad reported the following:

> Narrated Abū Bakr: "The Prophet sent me with the Chapter of *al-Tawbah* to the people of Mecca to proclaim: 'No polytheist should make pilgrimage after this year. No naked shall circum-navigate around the Ka'ba. No one shall enter Paradise except a Muslim soul...' Abū Bakr travelled on for three days, then the Prophet said to 'Alī: 'Follow him and send Abū Bakr back to me, and go on to deliver the message yourself.' 'Alī did that and Abū Bakr came back to the Prophet. He wept and said: 'Messenger of God was there anything revealed concerning me?' The Prophet said: 'No! But Gabriel came to me and said, that none can deliver this for you but yourself or a man from you.'"[224]

Al-Ḥākim in his al-Mustadrak reported the following:

> Narrated 'Abdullāh ibn 'Umar to Jumai'a ibn Umair al-Laithī that: "The Messenger of God sent Abū Bakr and 'Umar with the Chapter of *al-Tawbah* to the people of Mecca. The two men went on and suddenly a man overtook them. They asked: 'Who is this?' He said: 'I am 'Alī. Abū Bakr gives me the written message, which you have. Abū Bakr said: 'What happened concerning me?' 'Alī said: 'By God, I did not know but good.' 'Alī took the written message and went on, and Abū Bakr and 'Umar went back to Madīnah and said: 'Messenger of God, what happened to us?' He said: 'Nothing but good, but I am told; 'No one should deliver for you but you, or a man from you.'"[225]

Al-Tirmidhī reported the following:

> Narrated Anas ibn Mālik that: "The Prophet sent Abū Bakr with Chapter of *al-Tawbah*, then he called him and said: 'No one aught to deliver this except a man from the members of my House,' calling 'Alī and giving him the Chapter."[226]

Al-Nasā'ī reported the following:

> "The Messenger of God sent the Chapter of *al-Tawbah* to Mecca with Abū Bakr. Then he ordered 'Alī to follow him. He told him: 'Take the written message from Abū Bakr and go to the people of Mecca.' 'Alī reached Abū Bakr and took the message from him. Abū Bakr sadly went back and said to the Messenger: 'Did any revelation come down concerning me?' The Prophet said: 'No but I am commanded that either I should deliver it or a man from the members of my House.'"[227]

Al-Bukhārī reported the following:

> Narrated Humaid ibn 'Abdur Raḥmān that Abū Ḥurayra said: "During that *Ḥajj* (in which Abū Bakr was the chief of the pilgrims) Abū Bakr sent me along with announcers on the Day of Nahr (10th of *Dhul-*

> *Hijja*) in Mīna to announce: 'No pagans shall perform, *Ḥajj* after this year, and none shall perform the *Tawāf* (circum-navigate) around the Ka'ba in a naked state.' Humaid ibn 'Abdur Raḥmān added: 'Then Allāh's Apostle sent 'Alī ibn Abī Tālib (after Abū Bakr) and ordered him to recite aloud in public *Sūrah al-Tawbah.*' Abū Ḥurayra added: 'So 'Alī, along with us, recited *Tawbah* (loudly) before the people at Mīna on the Day of Nahr and announced; No pagan shall perform *Ḥajj* after this year and none shall perform the *Tawāf* around the Ka'ba in a naked state.'"[228]

Al-Bukhārī's report states that Abū Bakr gave orders to send Abū Ḥurayra to announce *Sūrah al-Tawbah* along with others, and Imām 'Alī (AS) was sent by the Prophet (pbuh & hf) to proclaim *Sūrah al-Tawbah* with them. In all other reports it has been narrated that it was Imām 'Alī who solely went to proclaim *Sūrah al-Tawbah* himself, taking it from Abū Bakr. Again, other scholars of *Ḥadīth* have reported similarly in context to one another than the report stated in al-Bukhārī's *Ṣaḥīḥ*. Should we ignore every other report and only consider al-Bukhārī's?

Some other reports.

> Narrated 'Alī ibn Abī Tālib: "Ibn 'Abbās said: 'A lunatic woman who had committed adultery was brought to 'Umar. He consulted the people and ordered that she should be stoned.'
>
> 'Alī ibn Abī Tālib passed by and said: 'What is the matter with this (woman)?' They said: 'This is a lunatic woman belonging to a certain family. She has committed adultery. 'Umar has given orders that she should be stoned.' He said: 'Take her back.' He then came to him and said: 'Commander of the Faithful, do you not know that there are three people whose actions are not recorded; a lunatic till he is restored to reason, a sleeper till he awakes, and a boy till he reaches puberty?' He said: 'Yes.' He then asked:

> 'Why is it that this woman is being stoned?' He said: 'There is nothing.' He then said: 'Let her go.' He ('Umar) let her go and began to utter: 'Allāh is most great.'"[229]
>
> It has also been narrated that when 'Umar freed her he said: 'Had it not been for 'Alī, 'Umar would have perished'"[230]

Al-Bukhārī reported the following:

> And 'Alī said to 'Umar: "Don't you know that no deed good or evil are recorded (for the following) and are not responsible for what they do: (1) An insane person till he becomes sane, (2) and a child till he grows to the age of puberty, (3) and a sleeping person till he awakes?'"[231]

We cannot make out from reading only al-Bukhārī's report the actual incident, which led Imām 'Alī (AS) to state what he did. Other narrations, which have been recorded report that 'Umar ordered the lunatic women to be stoned and with Imām 'Alī"s intervention this act was brought to a halt. We can see what led Imām 'Alī to state what he did to 'Umar only when we read the other report. Would only reading al-Bukhārī's report and ignoring the other give us the exact details in regards to this event, which took place within the caliphate of 'Umar, or would we get a clearer picture of the event if we additionally read the reports of the other scholars of *Ḥadīth* along with al-Bukhārī's?

> "'Abd al-Raḥmān ibn 'Abza narrated it on the authority of his father that a man came to 'Umar and said: 'I am (at times) affected by seminal emission but find no water.' He ('Umar) told him not to say prayer.' 'Ammār then said. 'Do you remember, O Commander of the Faithful, when I and you were in a military detachment and we had had a seminal emission and did not find water (for taking bath) and you did not say prayer, but as for myself I rolled in dust and said prayer, and (when it was mentioned before) the Apostle said: 'It was enough for you to

> strike the ground with your hands and then blow (the dust) and then wipe your face and palms.' 'Umar said: 'Ammār, fear Allāh.' He said: 'If you so like, I would not narrate it.' A *Ḥadīth* like this has been transmitted with the same chain of transmitters but for the words, 'Umar said: 'We hold you responsible for what you claim.'"[232]

Al-Bukhārī reported the following:

> 'Abd al-Raḥmān ibn 'Abza: "A man came to 'Umar ibn al-Khaṭṭāb and said: 'I became *Junūb* (in a state of impurity) but no water was available.' 'Ammār ibn Yāsir said to 'Umar: 'Do you remember that you and I (became *Junūb* while both of us) were together on a journey and you didn't pray but I rolled myself on the ground and prayed?' I informed the Prophet about it and he said: 'It would have been sufficient for you to do like this.' The Prophet then stroked lightly the earth with his hands and then blew off the dust and passed his hands over his face and hands."[233]

Muslim in his *Ṣaḥīḥ* narrates that the Commander of the Faithful i.e. 'Umar, informed a man not to perform prayer when he could not find water. 'Ammār then reminded 'Umar that he had practiced *Tayammum* (rubbing ones face and hands with dust) when they were on a military campaign, while 'Umar did not pray, as 'Umar had told the man to practice the same (i.e. not to pray). 'Ammār did not speak against the teachings of the Qur'ān, as we know that *Tayammum* is to be practiced when no water is available. We would not have known the full reason why 'Ammār mentioned what he did, in the way he did, if we had only read the report of al-Bukhārī. Again, reading more than only al-Bukhārī's report would give us more of an insight into the exactness of the event in question.

> Narrated Anas ibn Mālik: "Allāh's Apostle gave a beating with palm branches and shoes, and that Abū Bakr gave forty lashes. When 'Umar (became the Commander of the Faithful) and the people went near

> to pastures and towns, he said (to the companions of the Holy Prophet). What is your opinion about lashing for drinking? Thereupon 'Abd al-Raḥmān ibn Awf said: 'My opinion is that you fix it as the mildest punishment.' Then 'Umar inflicted eighty stripes.'"[234]

Al-Bukhārī reported the following:

> Narrated Anas ibn Mālik: "The Prophet lashed a drunk with date leaf stalks and shoes. And Abū Bakr gave a drunken forty lashes."[235]

Al-Bukhārī's report does not contain a lot of content, but again we can read more in relation to the report stated by his student Muslim. We can understand that when 'Umar became caliph, he asked the opinion of the people as to the prescribed punishment for the lashing of an individual engaged in drinking (intoxicants). He then inflicted eighty lashes on a drunken person.

> This *Ḥadīth* has been narrated on the authority of Shūba with the same chain of transmitters. Amīr ibn Sa'd ibn Abī Waqqās reported on the authority of his father that Mu'āwiya ibn Abī Sufyān appointed Sa'd as the Governor and said: "What prevents you from abusing Abū Turāb ('Alī),' whereupon he said: 'It is because of three things which I remember Allāh's Messenger having said about him that I would not abuse him and even if I find one of those three things for me, it would be more dear to me than the red camels. I heard Allāh's Messenger say about 'Alī as he left him behind in one of his campaigns (that was Tabūk).' 'Alī said to him: 'Allah's Messenger, you leave me behind along with women and children.' Thereupon Allāh's Messenger said to him: 'Aren't you satisfied with being unto me what Aaron was unto Moses but with this exception that there is no Prophet-hood after me. And I (also) heard him say on the Day of Khaybar: 'I would certainly give this standard to a person who loves Allāh and His Messenger and Allāh and His Messenger love him too.' He (the narrator) said that we have been an-

> xiously waiting for it, when he (the Holy Prophet) said: 'Call 'Alī. He was called and his eyes were inflamed. He applied saliva to his eyes and handed over the standard to him, and Allāh gave him victory. (The third occasion is this) when the (following) verse was revealed, 'let us summon our children and your children.' Allāh's Messenger called "Alī, Fāṭimah, al-Ḥasan and al-Ḥusayn and said: 'O Allāh! These are my Ahl al-Bayt.'"[236]

Imām Ḥākim, Imām Tirmidhī, Imām Muslim and Imām Nasā'ī have also recorded this tradition in their books.

Al-Bukhārī reported the following:

> Narrated Sa'd: "Allāh's Apostle set out for Tabūk appointing 'Alī as his deputy (in Madīnah). 'Alī said: 'Do you want to leave me with the children and women?' The Prophet said: 'Will you not be pleased that you will be to me like Aaron to Moses? But there will be no Prophet after me.'"[237]

By being only inclined to al-Bukhārī we would not become acquainted with all that Sa'd had said, but if we had a broader mind we could explore the works of others in addition to his. Needless to say, the report other than the one quoted by al-Bukhāri provides us with a fuller report, which has been narrated by the son of Sa'd ibn Abī Waqqās, which again we would never have come to know of, if we were only inclined to looking at al-Bukhārī's work alone.

We have to be open-minded.

Every book of *Aḥadīth* is not perfect, reading and investigating into all and not only being inclined to one, is what we would call being fair to all of them.

Allāh teaches us that if a human being had written the Qur'ān there would have been many mistakes in it, meaning the Book would not be perfect. Then how can we class any other book, which has been written by a human being as being *Ṣaḥīḥ*? It can never be totally *Ṣaḥīḥ*. Allāh states:

> "Do they not consider the Qur'ān? Had it been from other than Allāh they would surely have found therein much discrepancy." Qur'ān 4:82

If we were to search through the entire volumes of al-Bukhārī's *Ṣaḥīḥ* it would awaken ones mind to the fact that discrepancies can be found in it, and Allāh provides us with this insight if we ponder on His words, which we read in the Qur'ān.

Not only us within this day and age, but also those who came before us, have commented on peculiar reports, which can be found in al-Bukhārī's *Ṣaḥīḥ*, where the content of the reports do not altogether correlate.

Al-Bukhārī reported the following:

> Narrated Sa'īd ibn al-Musaiyyab: "When the first civil strife (in Islām) took place because of the murder of 'Uthmān, it left none of the Badr warriors alive. When the second civil strife, that is the Battle of al-Harra, took place, it left none of the Hudaibīya treaty companions alive. Then the third civil strife took place and it did not subside till it had exhausted all the strength of the people."[238]

Ibn Ḥajar al-'Asqalānī comments in his Fath al-Barī that this report is incorrect because 'Alī, Talḥa, Zubayr, Sa'd and other companions who had participated in Badr were still alive after the death of 'Uthmān.[239]

Al-Bukhāri also reported:

> Narrated Abū Ḥurayra Ad-Dausi: "Once the Prophet went out during the day. Neither did he talk to me nor I to him till he reached the market of Banī Qainuqa and then he sat in the compound of Fāṭimah's house and asked about the small boy (his grandson al-Ḥasan) but Fāṭimah kept the boy in for a while. I thought she was either changing his clothes

> or giving the boy a bath. After a while the boy came out running and the Prophet embraced and kissed him and then said: "O Allāh! Love him, and love whoever loves him."[240]

Ibn Ḥajar al-'Asqalānī has specified that within the above narration, certain words are missing as Fāṭimah's (AS) house was not in Banī Qainuqah, it was in the middle of the houses, which belonged to the wife's of the Prophet (pbuh & hf). He states that the correct narration is the one, which Imām Muslim has recorded[241], which is as follows:

> Abū Ḥurayra reported: "I went along with Allāh's Messenger at a time during the day but he did not talk to me and I did not talk to him until he reached Bazār of Banī Qainuqah. He came back to the tent of Fāṭimah and said: 'Is the little chap (meaning al-Ḥasan) there? We were under the impression that his mother had detained him in order to bathe him and dress him and garland him with a sweet garland. Not much time had passed that he (al-Ḥasan) came running until both of them embraced each other, thereupon Allāh's Messenger said: 'O Allāh, I love him; love him Thou and love one who loves him (al-Ḥasan).'"[242]

As this point can be observed, there is no need to elongate the issue, as those who sincerely wish to research, can scrutinise at their own pace the various *Aḥadīth* , which can be found in al-Bukhārī's *Ṣaḥīḥ* . We do not need to know the reason behind why these discrepancies have occurred by al-Bukhārī in order to know that they have occurred. Is it wrong to enlighten one another about this and to bring to light that it is an injustice to disregard all other scholars of *Ḥadīth* and only consider what is found in al-Bukhāri's *Ṣaḥīḥ*? Allāh states:

> "O ye who believe! Stand out firmly for justice as witnesses to Allāh even as against yourselves or your parents or your kin and whether it be (against) rich or poor; for Allāh can best protect both. Follow not the lusts (of your hearts) lest ye swerve and if ye distort

> (justice) or decline to do justice verily Allāh is well-acquainted with all that ye do." Qur'ān 4:135

> Narrated Abū Dharr: "My friend (meaning the Prophet) ordered me to observe seven things..."He ordered me to speak the truth even when it was bitter; he ordered me not to fear for Allāh's sake reproach anyone may cast on me..."[243]

As stated earlier, a highlighted item in a shop window will draw our attention towards it. Through the highlighted items increased publicity, individuals may be taken to it, making the other items look less appealing. This does not mean that there is nothing else better than that item. There may be many items far better, but we become blinded. There is no total guarantee that only al-Bukhārī's reports are worthy of our attention and everything else that has not been reported by him is not.

Allāmah Shiblī Nu'manī writes in his book entitled Imām Abū Ḥanīfah that:

> "Judging the character of individuals is a matter of opinion in which there can be no definiteness and finality. A man may be regarded by many people as reliable, pious and righteous, and by many others as a poor transmitter, unreliable and untruthful."[244]

He also writes:

> "When a *muḥaddīth* (*Ḥadīth* scholar), no matter what his standing, says that a tradition is *Ṣaḥīḥ* (correct or sound), he implies certain subsidiary statements, to wit, that the tradition is *muttasil* (having an unbroken chain of transmitters), that its transmitters are reliable and possessed of exact minds, that there is no missing part in the transmission and that the tradition is free from all damaging weaknesses. All these are matters of presumption and individual judgement, falling short of certainty. Just as jurist may deduce a point of law from the Qur'ān or *Ḥadīth* and think that he has made a correct deduction of

> which, however, there is no guarantee, since his premises are merely his own suppositions, so may a traditionist. In calling a tradition sound a traditionist relies upon his presumptions and individual judgement. If a traditionist or a number of traditionists claim a tradition to be sound and another traditionist does not recognise it as such, all that the latter is guilty of is being opposed to the other traditionist or traditionists principles of verification, rules of deduction, and chain of transmission, in short, their suppositions and their judgements."[245]

People will continue to refuse to think, even if signs are presented to them from their own back yard. We can take a general lesson from Allāh when He states:

> "Thou canst but admonish **such as fear their Lord** unseen and establish regular prayer and whoever purifies himself does so for the benefit of his own soul; and the destination (of all) is to Allāh." Qur'ān 35:18

Those who sincerely fear their Lord are the ones who take heed from admonition.

Section 13

Whose word is binding?

Analyse the following:

Imagine you and your friend are in a car and you are the driver. Your friend states: "Slow down there is a 30mph speed limit on this road," and you reply: "No, it is okay I am not driving too fast, I am a good driver I know what I am doing," when in fact you are breaking the law. There is a reason behind why that limit has been given; it is for your own benefit and safety as well as for the benefit and safety of others. Not taking into account its importance, you state your own judgement and opinion to justify your actions, despite the fact that your friend is advising you not to speed. We are all judgemental in matters relating to events taking place in everyday life, it is not that we mean to cause harm; but we do make mistakes. It is up to us as individuals to understand and uphold the law as best we can. Although this is a law, which has been passed by politicians to motorists, it is binding and has to be followed.

If a commander in an army informs one of his soldiers to march to the left and instead the soldier marches to the right thinking it is better for him to do so, is he obeying his superior's commands? Would the commander be pleased with this performance of the soldier, who himself thinks that it is more beneficial for him to march the other way? The soldier does not sense the importance of marching towards the left whereas his superior does, as only he has this knowledge. Hence, does or does it not become obligatory for the soldier to obey what his superior has commanded?

Finally, a male customer travels to a goods store in order to buy a particular item of interest to him, he believes the price of the item is too expensive and writes a letter of complaint to the manufacturer in regards to it, the manufacturer then explains to the customer as to why that set price has been given to the item and how that price decision is reached. The customer has to abide by that decision, even if within his heart he may not feel at ease with it. The action to then purchase the product on sale is the free choice of the individual. It is probable that other customers also feel dissatisfied in the same way as the above individual but there may be other customers who are quite content with the price of the item for sale. Either way does the customer pass the final decision or the one in authority over its manufacture?

The words of Allāh and His Apostle can never lead to our destruction, as Allāh wants the best for his righteous servants. The Prophet (pbuh & hf) brought a complete law to guide mankind to the right path, to benefit us in our everyday lives and to reform us as individuals. It is important for us to be aware of this fact as anything, which Allāh and His Prophet commanded, even if it is something we cannot comprehend has to be acknowledged. The Prophet explained and taught everything, which was required to lead an individual towards a purified life, and his words were correct and exalted above anyone else's as he was divinely guided by Allāh. 'Umar himself is reported to have said:

> Narrated 'Umar ibn al-Khaṭṭāb: "'Umar said while he was (sitting) on the pulpit: 'O people, the opinion from the Apostle of Allāh was right, because Allāh showed (i.e. inspired) him; but from us it is sheer conjecture and artifice.'"[246]

If we look into the peace treaty of al-Hudaibīya, which occurred in the year 6 A.H. in the month of *Dhul- al-Qadah*, the following dialogue took place between the Prophet (pbuh & hf) and 'Umar:

> Narrated Abū Wa'īl: "We were in Siffīn and Saḥl ibn Ḥunaif got up and said: 'O people! Blame yourselves! We were with the Prophet on the day of Hudaibīya, and if we had been called to fight, we would have fought. But 'Umar ibn al-Khaṭṭāb came and said: 'O Allāh's Apostle! Aren't we in the right and our opponents in the wrong? Allāh's Apostle said: 'Yes.' 'Umar said: 'Aren't our killed persons in Paradise and theirs in Hell?' He said: 'Yes.' 'Umar said: 'Then why should we accept hard terms in matters concerning our religion? Shall we return before Allāh judges between us and them?' Allāh's Apostle said: 'O Ibn al-Khaṭṭāb! I am the Apostle of Allāh and Allāh will never degrade me.' Then 'Umar went to Abū Bakr

> and told him the same as he had told the Prophet. On that Abū Bakr said (to 'Umar): 'He is the Apostle of Allāh and Allāh will never degrade him.' Then *Sūrah al-Fath* (i.e. Victory) was revealed and Allāh's Apostle recited it to the end in front of 'Umar. On that 'Umar asked: 'O Allāh's Apostle! Was it (i.e. the Hudaibīya Treaty) a victory?' Allāh's Apostle said: 'Yes.'"[247]

'Umar had no knowledge of the reason behind the Prophet (pbuh & hf) **agreeing** on a Peace Treaty with the Quraysh. Only after 'Umar had mentioned his thoughts on the matter, did the Prophet remind him that Allāh would never degrade his Apostle. 'Umar was still very confused and repeated the same to Abū Bakr in which he received the same reply. This matter in respect to 'Umar was perceived as backing down to the Quraysh, his preference being to fight them instead. He felt this was better in bringing victory than the Peace Treaty, with his uneasiness being portrayed through him addressing Abū Bakr in the matter. Nevertheless, at the end of the narration, the Prophet made it clear while 'Umar was present, that the Peace Treaty was a victory and a *Sūrah* was revealed in connection to this event. Allāh and His Apostle knew its importance and what benefits this Peace Treaty would bring whereby its long-term effects would far outweigh the short. Many Muslims embraced Islām through it, which may not have happened if fighting had broken out.

Also, there were people in Makkah who had become Muslim but had been concealing their faith; these people may have also lost their lives if fighting had broken out for the reason that they were not known by the Muslims.

More importantly, it was obligatory upon those who possessed faith to accept this decision of Allāh and His Apostle, even if they did not understand its importance at the time.

As stated previously in section ten, before the Prophet's (pbuh & hf) demise, the Prophet had appointed Usāmah ibn Zayd as the leader of a military detachment, which some people had criticized. If the people had criticized the leadership of Usāmah, they were not at ease with this decision. The Prophet came out during his sickness to make sure that those who had been informed start their movement towards the expedition, that they did not waver in this decision and accept the lead of Usāmah as a similar situation had arisen when the Prophet had appointed his father Zayd (on the expedition of Mūta). It was binding upon every individual who had been commanded to engage in this expedition to follow Usāmah as their commander, even if they did not understand the importance of his leadership and even if their hearts did not feel at ease with this decision.

A Brief Note on Consultation.

> "It was by the mercy of Allāh that thou wast lenient with them (O Muḥammad), for if thou hadst been stern and fierce of heart they would have dispersed from round about thee. So pardon them and ask forgiveness for them and consult with them upon the conduct of affairs. And when thou art resolved, then put thy trust in Allāh. Lo! Allāh loveth those who put their trust (in Him)." Qur'ān 3:159
>
> "Those who hearken to their Lord and establish regular prayer and conduct their affairs by mutual consultation, who spend on what we bestow on them for sustenance." Qur'ān 42:38
>
> Narrated Abū Ḥurayra and Zayd ibn Khālid: "Two men had a dispute in the presence of Allāh's Apostle. One of them said: 'Judge us according to Allāh's Laws.' The other who was wiser said: 'Yes, Allāh's Apostle, judge us according to Allāh's Laws and allow me to speak (first).' The Prophet said to him: 'Speak.' He said: 'My son was a labourer for this man, and he committed illegal sexual intercourse with his wife, and the people told me that my son should be stoned to death, but I have given one-hundred sheep and a slave girl as a ransom (expiation) for my son's sin. Then I asked the religious learned people (about it), and they told me that my son should be flogged one-hundred stripes and should be exiled for one year, and only the wife of this man should be stoned to death.' Allāh's Apostle said: 'By Him in Whose Hand

> my soul is, I will judge you according to Allāh's Laws, O man, as for your sheep and slave girl, they are to be returned to you.' Then the Prophet had the man's son flogged one hundred stripes and exiled for one year, and ordered Unais al-Aslamī to go to the wife of the other man, and if she confessed, stone her to death. She confessed and was stoned to death."[248]

Before the announcement of the religion, the Arabs in Makkah would engage in consultation at a place called *Dar al-Nadwa*. This type of consultation involved making a decision, which agreed with most of those present. It was through such a consultation that a decision was made to boycott connections with the Prophet (pbuh & hf), his family and followers, alienating them in order to weaken the Prophet's mission. It was also this type of consultation that decided upon the assassination of the Prophet, which led to his migration to Madīnah. What we need to understand is that such a consultation was not the same as what Allāh referred His Prophet to undertake with his followers. By no means could the Muslims reach a decision in a matter by leaving out the one in authority i.e. the Prophet. Such matters did not necessarily have to be related to *Ḥajj, Zakāt, Salāt* etc but also social and personal matters.

If we think of this in the sense of a working environment, mutual consultation with colleagues in regards to various matters occurs most frequently. Various matters are always brought forward in meetings to the one in authority, and it is the one in authority who makes the final decision.

The companions could mutually consult (42:38) as Allāh teaches and it is something that the Arabs were accustomed with amongst one another, however, such a consultation did not give them the authority to change or make decisions against the Prophet's (pbuh & hf). It was the Prophet who took the lead and not anyone else.

A note needs to be pointed out here in regards to the issue of leadership after the Prophet (pbuh & hf) because many state that consultation was necessary in order that the Muslims could choose a leader. However, this **type of consultation**, which is addressed, relates to a code of practice, as stated, that resembled something pre-Islāmic and was still existent between the disbelieving Makkāns. The most influential of the Arabs would congregate together and make decisions on matters they felt needed attention. Whereas when the Prophet brought the religion of Islām, it was the Prophet who made decisions upon matters that needed attention, as he was the one in authority regardless of whether consultation took place with those who wished to consult with him or not. Can we state that the matter of leadership was not something that needed attention and so was not addressed by the Prophet?

We could state that the Muslims have been obligated to accept that consultation is the correct pathway chosen to nominate a successor plainly because of the actions and decisions of others, which took place upon the demise of the Prophet (pbuh & hf), which also makes us question whether or not these decisions are truly binding upon us.

The proceeding discussion may provide us with a further understanding of this through giving us an insight into other actions and decisions, which took place after the demise of the Prophet (pbuh & hf).

The importance of Understanding the nature of the Question: "Whose word is binding?"

We should all remember that, it is the words of Allāh and His Apostle, which are always to be followed. We cannot prohibit that, which Allāh has ordained and we cannot allow that, which Allāh has prohibited. This applied throughout the lifetime of the Prophet (pbuh & hf), after he passed away and for all time.

> "O ye who believe! Make not unlawful the good things which Allāh hath made lawful for you but do not transgress: for Allāh loveth not those who transgress." Qur'ān 5:87

> "But say not for any false thing that your tongues may put forth this is lawful and this is forbidden so as to ascribe false things to Allāh. For those who ascribe false things to Allāh will never prosper." Qur'ān 16:116

Succession of the Prophet (PBUH)

(1) *Tarawīh* prayers.

> Narrated 'Ursa: "That he was informed by 'Ā'isha: 'Allāh's Apostle went out in the middle of the night and prayed in the mosque and some men prayed behind him. In the morning, the people spoke about it and then a large number of them gathered and prayed behind him (on the second night). In the next morning the people again talked about it and on the third night the mosque was full with a large number of people. Allāh's Apostle came out and the people prayed behind him. On the fourth night the mosque was overwhelmed with people and could not accommodate them, but the Prophet came out (only) for the Morning Prayer. When the Morning Prayer was finished he recited Tashah-hud and (addressing the people) said: *'Amma ba'du,* your presence was not hidden from me but I was afraid lest the night prayer *(Qiyām)* should be enjoined on you and you might not be able to carry it on.' So, 'Allāh's Apostle died and the situation remained like that (i.e. people prayed individually)."[249]

Al-Bukhārī has quoted another similar report, which has been placed in the Book of the Prayer at Night (*TaḤajjud* – a night prayer performed before Morning Prayer). The Prophet (pbuh & hf) offered prayer in congregation for first three nights and stopped thereafter.

Imām Mālik in his Muwaṭṭā' quotes in connection to the prayer which was enjoined by the Prophet (pbuh & hf) in Ramadhān.

> "Yaḥya related to me from Mālik from Ibn Shihab from 'Urwa ibn az-Zubayr from 'Ā'isha, the wife of the Prophet, may Allāh bless him and grant him peace, that the Messenger of Allāh, may Allāh bless him and grant him peace, prayed in the mosque one night and people prayed behind him. Then he prayed the next night and there were more people. Then they gathered on the third or fourth night and the Messenger of Allāh, may Allāh bless him and grant him peace, did not come out to them. In the morning,

> he said: 'I saw what you were doing and the only thing that prevented me from coming out to you was that I feared that it would become obligatory for you.' This happened in Ramadhān."[250]

This prayer, which the Prophet (pbuh & hf) performed in congregation, is referred to as the *Tarawīh* prayer. This prayer continued to be offered voluntarily (not in congregation) within the caliphate of Abū Bakr and at the beginning of the caliphate of 'Umar.

> "Yaḥya related to me from Mālik from Ibn Shihab from Abū Salama ibn 'Abd al-Rahmān ibn Awf from Abū Ḥurayra that the Messenger of Allāh, may Allāh bless him and grant him peace, used to exhort people to watch the night in prayer in Ramadhān but never ordered it definitely. He used to say: 'Whoever watches the night in prayer in Ramadhān with trust and expectancy, will be forgiven all his previous wrong actions.'"
>
> Ibn Shihab said: "The Messenger of Allāh, may Allāh bless him and grant him peace, died while that was still the custom, and it continued to be the custom in the caliphate of Abū Bakr and at the beginning of the caliphate of 'Umar ibn al-Khaṭṭāb."[251]

Also:

> Narrated Zayd ibn Thābit: "Allāh's Apostle made a small room (with a palm leaf mat). Allāh's Apostle came out (of his house) and prayed in it. Some men came and joined him in his prayer. Then again the next night they came for the prayer, but Allāh's Apostle delayed and did not come out to them. So they raised their voices and knocked the door with small stones (to draw his attention). **He came out to them in a state of anger, saying: 'You are still insisting (on your deed, i.e. *Tarawīh* prayer in the mosque) that I thought that this prayer**

> **(*Tarawīh*) might become obligatory on you. So you people, offer this prayer at your homes, for the best prayer of a person is the one, which he offers at home, except the compulsory (congregational) prayer."**[252]

The above narration quoted, clearly indicates to us that the *Tarawīh* prayer was to be performed individually, after the Prophet (pbuh & hf) had stopped practicing it in congregation.

If the Prophet (pbuh & hf) did carry on practicing the *Tarawīh* prayer in congregation, it would have resulted in its compulsion upon every Muslim. A similar case can be observed below:

> Narrated by 'Ā'isha: "Allāh's Apostle used to give up a good deed, although he loved to do it, for fear that people might act on it and it might be made compulsory for them. The Prophet never prayed the *Duha* prayer, but I offer it."[253]

The Prophet (pbuh & hf) understood the reason behind the *Tarawīh* prayer remaining as non-congregational as Allāh had informed him. The foreknowledge of why it was ordained in this way known to him. Hence, this order was to remain the same at the time of the Prophet (pbuh & hf), after his demise and for all time.

If we have been given a law, a practice, which is to be carried out in a specific way, and we realise that we have not altogether followed it, is it a good thing if we do not change to what is correct, using words such as: "There is nothing wrong with this way, it is not a bad thing; I have *imān*, Allāh will not see it as a bad thing." When in fact in reality this good thing then becomes the self-opinion of the human being and would be seen in the eyes of Allāh and His Apostle as a change.

Also when reading the narrations in regards to this prayer, which was offered by the Prophet (pbuh & hf) for three days in Ramadhān, we notice that the Prophet did not see it as a good thing to continue reading the prayer in congregation, if he had done so, he never would have come out of his house in a state of **anger** informing his companions to offer the prayer at home individually as it provided benefit when read alone. This will be understood why shortly.

The importance of Understanding the nature of the Question: "Whose word is binding?"

Nonetheless, is it right for us to improvise on any matter, which Allāh and His Apostle have already prescribed for us? Would this not amount to violation? We should contemplate, would even considering one practise differently from the practise prescribed, please Allāh?

Performing acts of *Ibādat* (worship) in the way Allāh and his Apostle **have prescribed** them and **not changing** them signifies true devotion, true sincerity, and true faith. This is what we would call truly submitting to the teachings of the beloved, submitting to His will and to His commands. An individual who understands this most certainly would keep the Prophet's (pbuh & hf) *Sunnah* in tact.

We may state the well known saying of the Prophet (pbuh & hf): "The reward for a prayer in congregation is twenty five times greater than that of a prayer read alone" and so reading *Tarawīh* prayer in congregation will give us a greater reward. Although, we believe the statement itself to be correct, what needs to be understood is that this statement is directed towards the prayers practiced in congregation and not the non-congregational, as the latter have to be performed individually, **as prescribed** by the Prophet himself. If we were to start stating in this day and age that we can read any prayer we wish in congregation because it will give us a greater reward than if we read it individually, there is nothing wrong with it if we practice this, again, we are actually **changing the order** of the Prophet and do we have the right to do such a thing? When the Prophet discontinued reading *Tarawīh* prayer in congregation, then it was a duty upon every individual to do the same; but the question is, did everyone understand the reason why? We always have to bear in mind the following Qur'ānic verse:

> "O ye who believe, give your response to Allāh and His Prophet when he calleth you to that which gives you life. And know that Allāh cometh between a man and his heart and it is to He whom ye shall all be gathered." Qur'ān 8:24

Allāh does not wish any hardship on his faithful servants, this matter of *Tarawīh* prayer was left to undertake individually, where it could be read at ones own pace in Ramadhān.

> Narrated 'Ā'isha: "A woman from the tribe of Banī Asad was sitting with me and Allāh's Apostle came to my house and said: 'Who is this?' I said: '(She is) so and so. She does not sleep at night because she is engaged in prayer.' The Prophet said disapprovingly: 'Do (good) deeds which is within your capacity as Allāh never gets tired of giving rewards till you get tired of doing good deeds.'"[254]

Tiredness overtakes every single individual and the Prophet (pbuh & hf) made it clear that we practise what is within our capacity. We need to concentrate and focus in our prayers in order that we do not lose their quality; we are not to fall into the extremes that our bodies cannot cope with. Every individual is different; one individual may become tired more easily while another maybe still full of energy.

Within the five obligatory prayers, which have been ordained to practice everyday, we can perform other non congregational prayers on our own if we wish to do so and that too at our own pace. Within the following narration we read:

> Narrated Anas ibn Mālik: "Once the Prophet entered the mosque and saw a rope hanging in between its two pillars. He said: 'What is this rope?' The people said: 'This rope is for Zaynab who, when she feels tired, holds it (to keep standing for the prayer.)' The Prophet said: 'Don't use it. Remove the rope. You should pray as long as you feel active, and when you get tired, sit down.'"[255]

We can understand that the Prophet (pbuh & hf) was speaking in regards to a prayer, which Zaynab was offering and exerting herself to carry on in a weak state. Within the narration the Prophet addresses her and pronounces: "You should pray as long as you feel active," proving, that she was the one offering the prayer and nobody else. If she had of been performing the prayer behind an Imām, the Prophet would have addressed the Imām. She would not have been the one at fault in standing for such long periods in the prayer, for the reason that when offering prayers behind an Imām, it is the Imām whom we follow and do not complete the prayer until the Imām has.

The importance of Understanding the nature of the Question: "Whose word is binding?"

> Narrated 'Uthmān ibn 'Abul'Ās ath-Thaqafī: "The Apostle of Allāh said to him: 'Lead your people in prayer.' I said: 'Messenger of Allāh, I perceive something (disturbing) in my soul.' He (the Prophet) asked me to draw near him and making me sit down in front of him he placed his hand on my breast between my nipples, and then, telling me to turn round, he placed it on my back between my shoulders. He then said: 'Act as an Imām for your people. He who acts as Imām of the people, he must be brief, for among them are the aged, among them are the sick, among them are the weak and among them are the people who have business to attend. But when any of you prays alone, he may pray as he likes.'"[256]

We know how prolonged the *Tarawīh* prayers can be, we may pray as we like at home, but reading *Tarawīh* prayer behind an Imām means we have to follow him and keep up with him. Individuals cannot stop at differing times amongst one another when they wish to do so if they are tired; this is the choice of the Imām.

If every individual had correctly understood that Allāh and His Apostle finally and strictly **prescribed the *Tarawīh* as a non congregational prayer**, nobody would have performed it in congregation behind an Imām. The Prophet (pbuh & hf) never prescribed a definite number of *rak'āt* (unit of prayer) to be read in the *Tarawīh* prayer, again this matter being left up to the individual, to read however many one could cope with.

(a) The Reason behind the practicing of *Tarawīh* Prayer in Congregation.

> Narrated Abū Ḥurayra: "Allāh's Apostle said: 'Whoever prayed at night the whole month of Ramadhān out of sincere faith and hoping for a reward from Allāh, then all his previous sins will be forgiven.' Ibn Shihab (a sub-narrator) said: '**Allāh's Apostle died and the people continued observing that (i.e. *nawāfil***

> **offered individually, not in congregation), and it remained as it was during the caliphate of Abū Bakr and in the early days of 'Umar's caliphate.'** 'Abd al-Raḥmān ibn 'Abdul Qārī said: 'I went out in the company of 'Umar ibn al-Khaṭṭāb one night in Ramadhan to the mosque and found the people praying in different groups, a man praying alone or a man praying with a little group behind him.' So, 'Umar said: '**In my opinion** I would better collect these (people) under the leadership of one *qā'rī* (reciter) (i.e. let them pray in congregation!).' So, he made up his mind to congregate them behind 'Ubayy ibn Ka'b. Then on another night I went again in his company and the people were praying behind their reciter. On that, 'Umar remarked: '**What an excellent *Bid'a*** (i.e. innovation in religion) this is; but the prayer which they do not perform, but sleep at its time is better than the one they are offering.' He meant the prayer in the last part of the night. (In those days) people used to pray in the early part of the night."[257]
>
> Narrated 'Ubayy ibn Ka'b, al-Ḥasan reported: "'Umar ibn al-Khaṭṭāb gathered the people (in *Tarawīh* prayer) behind 'Ubayy ibn Ka'b (who lead them). He used to lead them for twenty days (during Ramadhān, and would not recite the supplication except in the second half of it (i.e. Ramadhān). When the last ten days remained, he kept away from them, and prayed in his house. They used to say: 'Ubayy ran away."[258]

'Ubayy ibn Ka'b was well versed in the recitation of the Qur'ān; hence the reason 'Umar chose him to lead the people in *Tarawīh* prayer. The above narration does not show any real acceptance by him in taking up the responsibility to act as the Imām in the *Tarawīh* non congregational prayer.

Although 'Umar did what he did, this *Tarawīh* prayer was not even considered by him as a prayer, which was of greater blessing than the one, which is offered later on at night, meaning the *Taḥajjud* prayer (*Salāt al-Layl* – night prayer).

It is the Shī'ahs who offer this prayer at home if they wish to do so, following the words of the Prophet (pbuh & hf): "So you people, offer this prayer at your homes, for the best prayer of a person is the one which he offers at home, except the compulsory (congregational) prayer."

Imām al-Bāqir (AS) and Imām as-Sādiq (AS) have both narrated a tradition where they state:

> "Verily, the offering of *nāfila* prayers in congregation during the nights of Ramadhān is an innovation. O people! Do not say *nāfila* prayers of Ramadhān in congregation. Without doubt, performing a minor act of worship which is according to the *Sunnah* is better than performing a major act of worship, which is an innovation."[259]

(2) Combining the *Hajj* and *Umra*.

We are well acquainted with the fact that *Ḥajj* and *Umra* (lesser pilgrimage) can be combined, as this is known to us through the teachings of the Prophet (pbuh & hf).

> Narrated 'Ā'isha: "We set out with Allāh's Apostle (to Mecca) in the year of the Prophet's last *Ḥajj*. Some of us had assumed *Ihrām* for *Umra* only, some for both *Ḥajj* and *Umra*, and others for *Ḥajj* only. Allāh's Apostle assumed *Ihrām* for *Ḥajj*. So whoever had assumed *Ihrām* for *Ḥajj* or for both *Ḥajj* and *Umra* did not finish the *Ihrām* till the day of sacrifice."[260]

This is a clear matter, which the Prophet (pbuh & hf) had taught.

> Narrated Marwān ibn al-Ḥakam: "I saw 'Uthmān and 'Alī. 'Uthmān used to forbid people to perform *Ḥajj-at-Tamattū'* and *Ḥajj-al-Qiran* (*Ḥajj* and *Umra* together),

> and when 'Alī saw (this act of 'Uthmān), he assumed *Ihrām* for *Ḥajj* and *Umra* together saying: '*Lubbaik* (call) for *Umra* and *Ḥajj*,' and said: **'I will not leave the tradition of the Prophet on the saying of somebody**.'"[261]

> Narrated Sa'īd ibn al-Musaiyyab: "'Alī and 'Uthmān differed regarding *Ḥajj-at-Tamattū'* while they were at Usfan (a familiar place near Mecca). 'Alī said: 'I see you want to forbid people to do a thing that the Prophet did?' When 'Alī saw that, he assumed *Ihrām* for both *Ḥajj* and *Umra*."[262]

We will observe as this section progresses that the practice of *Ḥajj-at-Tamattū'* was first spoken against by 'Umar. Imām 'Alī (AS) never warranted the words of 'Uthmān and did not agree with them. Imām 'Alī understood and explained that we are to follow what the Prophet (pbuh & hf) ordered, i.e. his words were binding, and Imām 'Alī's few words explaining it all: **"I will not leave the tradition of the Prophet on the saying of somebody."**

(3) The two *rak'āt* prayer at Mīna.

> Narrated 'Abdullāh bin 'Umar: "I offered the prayer with the Prophet, Abū Bakr and 'Umar at Mīna and it was of two *rak'āt*. 'Uthmān in the early days of his caliphate did the same, but later on he started praying the full prayer."[263]

'Uthmān began to pray the full prayer instead of the recommended two *rak'āt'* at Mīna, but the question is, did he understand the reason why the prayer was only to be offered as two *rak'āt*?

In times of travel there was a danger of the enemy attacking the Prophet (pbuh & hf) and his followers. However, we read that even when there was no danger, he would still offer the prayer as two *rak'āt*, as it was to be performed only in this way, there most definitely was a reason behind this. Circumstances could easily have changed within time, and the people may have not been able to do justice when offering it as four *rak'āt*, the Prophet never once changed this order, in order for people to be able to fulfil it.

The importance of Understanding the nature of the Question: "Whose word is binding?"

> Narrated Ḥarītha ibn Waḥab al-Khuzā'ī: "The Prophet led us in a two *rak'āt* prayer at Mīna although our number was more than ever and we were in better security than ever.[264]

In the early days of the Prophet's (pbuh & hf) mission, all prayers were performed as two *rakāt*, but when the Prophet migrated to Madīnah, prayers were then performed as four and the prayers when one was travelling remained as two.

> Narrated 'Ā'isha: "Originally, two *rak'āt* were prescribed in every prayer. When the Prophet migrated (to Madīnah) four *rak'āt* were enjoined, **while the journey prayer remained unchanged** (i.e. two *rakāt*)."[265]

Allāh takes into account many matters which His faithful servants face, we know that many people become fatigued in times of travel, taking into account this matter also gives us the understanding of the prayer of the traveller to remain as two *rak'āt* as a mercy from Allāh.

> Narrated 'Abdullah ibn Mas'ūd': "I offered (only a) two *rak'āt* prayer with the Prophet (at Mīna), and similarly with Abū Bakr and with 'Umar, and then you differed in opinions. **Wish that I would be lucky enough to have two of the four *rak'āt* accepted (by Allāh).**"[266]

> Narrated 'Abd al-Raḥmān ibn Yazīd: "We offered a four *rak'āt* prayer at Mīna behind Ibn 'Affan. 'Abdullāh ibn Mas'ūd was informed about it. He said sadly: 'Truly to Allāh we belong and truly to Him we shall return.' And added: 'I prayed two *rak'āt* with Allāh's Apostle at Mīna and similarly with Abū Bakr and with 'Umar (during their caliphates).' He further said: **'May I be lucky enough to have two of the four *rak'āt* accepted (by Allāh)'**"[267]

'Abdullāh ibn Mas'ūd, a devoted companion of the Prophet (pbuh & hf), recognised and understood the prescribed practice of the Prophet, that it was also the same at the time of the caliphate of Abū Bakr and that of 'Umar. He recognised that Allāh may not accept his offering of four *rak'āt,* for this was not the prescribed number of *rak'āt* usual for the prayer at Mīna. He did not put forward an argument in favour of it, he did not state: "It does not matter if we read more, it is not a bad thing, and there is nothing wrong with reading it as a four *rak'āt* prayer because we have *imān.*" His reaction in connection with this matter portrayed greater importance to the prayer being practised as two *rak'āt.* All Muslims in this day and age follow this practice of the two *rak'āt* prayer at Mīna when they are on their pilgrimage.

> Narrated 'Ā'isha: "When the prayers were first enjoined they were of two *rak'āt* each. Later the prayer in a journey was kept as it was but the prayers for non-travellers were completed. Az-Zuhrī said: 'I asked 'Urwa what made 'Ā'isha pray the full prayers (in journey).' He replied: 'She did the same as 'Uthmān did.'"[268]

Everything, which the Prophet (pbuh & hf) has taught is to help mankind, is to save mankind from falling prey to deviation in order to keep us spiritually active. Hence, whatever the Prophet has ordered us to refrain from and whatever he has ordered us to take from is for our own benefit.

> "So take what the Apostle assigns to you and deny yourselves that which he withholds from you." Qur'ān 59:7

> "O ye who believe! Put not yourselves forward before Allāh and His Apostle. But fear Allāh, for Allāh is He who hears and knows all things." Qur'ān 49:1

We are not to think that anything which was taught to us through the Prophet (pbuh & hf) seems strange, as his guidance came from Allāh, we do not have the knowledge Allāh has, and every matter may not be in reach of our comprehension. It is being conscious of this that will also aid in bringing us closer to Him.

The importance of Understanding the nature of the Question: "Whose word is binding?"

(4) The temporary marriage.

Mūt'a (temporary marriage) seems to be one of those matters, which also is misunderstood, and is a matter, which is projected by many in such a bad light, that this very order, which is an ordainment by the Almighty Allāh, is frowned upon.

Mūt'a marriage (temporary) was a type of marriage prescribed by the Prophet (pbuh & hf), and practiced just as the permanent marriage was being practiced all the way up until the Prophet's demise. It continued as a type of marriage within the time of the caliphate of Abū Bakr and 'Umar, which we will observe as the section proceeds.

But firstly, it would be beneficial to quote the verse relating to the *Mūt'a* marriage (temporary). We find that it is separate to the verses relating to permanent marriage and the marriage of the maids.

The verses revealed for the permanent marriage:

> "If ye fear that ye shall not be able to deal justly with the orphans marry women of your choice two or three or four; but if ye fear that ye shall not be able to deal justly (with them) then only one or (a captive) that your right hands possess. That will be more suitable to prevent you from doing injustice. And give the women (on marriage) their dower as a free gift; but if they of their own good pleasure remit any part of it to you take it and enjoy it with right good cheer."
> Qur'ān 4.3-4

The verse revealed for marriage to the maids:

> "If any of you have not the means wherewith to wed free believing women they may wed believing girls from among those whom your right hands possess; and Allāh hath full knowledge about your faith. Ye are one from another; wed them with the leave of their owners and give them their dowers according to what is reasonable; they should be chaste neither

lustful nor taking paramours; when they are taken in wedlock if they fall into shame their punishment is half that for free women. This (permission) is for those among you who fear sin; but it is better for you that ye practice self-restraint and Allāh is Oft-forgiving Most Merciful." Qur'ān 4:25

The verse revealed for the temporary marriage:

"...Except the forbidden women the rest are lawful unto you to seek (them in marriage) with gifts from your property desiring chastity not lust. So for whatever you have had of pleasure (***Istamta'tum***) with them, give them their dowers as a duty. And there is no sin for you in what you both agree after fulfilling the duty. Lo! Allāh is ever Knower, Wise." Qur'ān 4:24

Narrated Mujāhid: "The phrase 'So for whatever you have had of pleasure (***Istamta'tum***) with them (Qur'ān 4:24)' means the *Nikah al-Mūt'a* (temporary marriage)."[269]

The companions of the Prophet (pbuh & hf) all acknowledged the verse of *Mūt'a*; they knew that this was the verse expressing the marriage for a prescribed period of time.

Jābir ibn 'Abdullāh and Salama ibn al-Akwa' said: "There came to us the proclaimer of Allāh's Messenger and said: 'Allāh's Messenger has granted you permission to benefit yourselves, (to have pleasure, ***Istamta'a***), i.e. to contract temporary marriage with women.'" [270]

The word ***Istamta'a***, used in the tradition is the same word Allāh also uses under the same context in the Qur'ān in connection with the verse of the temporary marriage.

Those who fear that they may commit fornication, Allāh ordained *Mūt'a* (temporary marriage) as a mercy in order to protect them from becoming sinners. Again, when a human being fails to understand that everything Allāh ordained was to give us life and was not ordained as a cause to our destruction, then that individual may fall into questioning a command from Allāh and His Apostle.

Some companions use to recite the verse of *Mūt'a* as:

> Narrated Qatadah: "The way that 'Ubayy ibn Ka'b recited the verse was: 'So for those of whom you enjoyed by the contract **to an appointed time** give them their dowries...'"[271]

Ibn Kathīr has quoted the words of 'Ubayy ibn Ka'b where he states in his *Tafsīr* that the companions only by way of *Tafsīr* recited the additional words **to an appointed time**, as we distinguish that this is not part of the Qur'ān.[272]

'Abdullāh ibn 'Abbās also use to recite the verse as that:

> Narrated Abū Nadra: "I asked Ibn 'Abbās about temporary marriage. Ibn Abbās said: 'Do you not read, for whatever you ***Istamta'tum*** of them by the contract **to an appointed time**?' I said: 'If I would have read it this way, I wouldn't ask you (about temporary marriage).' He replied: 'Certainly the verse is about it.'"[273]

The companions recognised the temporary marriage and many contracted the temporary marriage as well as the permanent marriage within their lifetimes, not because they invented it themselves, but because it was a type of marriage recommended to them by the Prophet (pbuh & hf).

Sunni commentators of the Qur'ān have stated the following narration:

> Narrated Imrān ibn Ḥusayn: "The verse of *Mūt'a* was revealed in Allāh's Book, so we did it at the time of Allāh's Apostle, and nothing was revealed in Qur'ān to make it illegal, nor did the Prophet prohibit it till he

> died. But a man (who regarded it illegal) expressed what his own mind suggested."[274]

Although this narration has been stated by Sunni commentators of the Qur'ān in their discussions of the verse of *Mūt'a* (temporary marriage), we find that it has been expressed in al-Bukhārī's *Ṣaḥīḥ* as totally corresponding to the *Ḥajj-at-Tamaṭṭū'* [275].

However, here as some other reports supporting the legality of both:

> Ibn Uraij reported: "'Ata' reported that Jābir ibn 'Abdullāh came to perform *Umra*, and we came to his abode, and the people asked him about different things, and then they made a mention of temporary marriage, whereupon he said: 'Yes, we had been benefiting ourselves by this temporary marriage during the lifetime of the Holy Prophet and during the time of Abū Bakr and 'Umar.'"[276]

> Narrated Abū Jamra: "I heard Ibn 'Abbās (giving a verdict) when he was asked about the Mūt'a with the women, and he permitted it *(Nikah al-Mūt'a)*. On that a freed slave of his said to him: 'That is only when it is very badly needed and (qualified permanent) women are scarce, or similar cases.' On that, Ibn 'Abbās said: 'Yes.'"[277]

> Narrated Jābir ibn 'Abdullāh: "We contracted temporary marriage giving a handful of dates or flour as a dower during the lifetime of Allāh's Messenger and during the time of Abū Bakr until 'Umar forbade it in the case of Amr ibn Ḥuraith."[278]

> Narrated Abū Nadra: "While I was in the company of Jābir ibn Abdullāh, a person came to him and said that Ibn 'Abbās and Ibn Zubayr differed on the two types of *Mūt'as* (*Tamaṭṭū' of Ḥajj* 1846 and *Tamaṭṭū'* with women), whereupon Jābir said: 'We used to do these two during the lifetime of Allāh's Messenger. 'Umar then forbade us to do them, and so we did not revert to them.'"[279]

The importance of Understanding the nature of the Question: "Whose word is binding?"

Yaḥyā related to me from Malik from Ibn Shihab from 'Urwa ibn az-Zubayr that Khawla ibn Hākim came to 'Umar ibn al-Khaṭṭāb and said: "'Rabia ibn 'Umayya practiced *Mūt'a* with a woman and the woman has become pregnant from him.' 'Umar became angry and said: 'About this *Mūt'a*, had I done (the ban) sooner than this, I would have stoned him.'"[280]

'Umar said: "Two types of *Mūt'a* were (legal) during the time of the Prophet and I forbid them both, and I punish those who commit it. They are *Mūt'a* of pilgrimage and *Mūt'a* of women."[281]

Narrated Abū Nadra: "Ibn 'Abbas commanded the performance of *Mūt'a* putting *Ihrām* for *Umra* during the months of *Dhu'l- Ḥijjah* and after completing it, then putting on *Ihrām* for *Ḥajj*, but Ibn Zubayr forbade to do it. I made a mention of it to Jābir ibn 'Abdullāh and he said: 'It is through me that this *Ḥadīth* has been circulated. We entered into the state of *Ihrām* (ritual state ready for the pilgrimage) *at-Tamaṭṭū'* with the Messenger of Allāh. When 'Umar was installed as calīph', he said: 'Verily Allāh made permissible for His Messenger whatever He liked and as He liked. And (every command) of the Holy Qur'ān has been revealed for every occasion. So accomplish *Ḥajj* and *Umra* for Allāh as Allāh has commanded you; and confirm by (proper conditions) the marriage of those women (with whom you have performed *Mūt'a*). And any person would come to me with a marriage of appointed duration *(Mūt'a)*, I would stone him (to death)."

Qatada narrated this *Ḥadīth* with the same chain of transmitters saying: (That 'Umar also said): "Separate your *Ḥajj* from *Umra*, for that is the most complete *Ḥajj*, and complete your *Umra*.'"[282]

What needs to be brought to our attention, is that within these reports we find that both these issues, *Ḥajj-at-Tamattū'* and *Mūt'a al-Nīsa,* were called upon to be discontinued by 'Umar, although they had been practiced at the time of the Prophet (pbuh & hf).

'Umar felt troubled in regards to the two types of *Mūt'a,* but he never signified that both had been forbidden by the Prophet (pbuh & hf).

'Umar preferred the Muslims to be permanently married, declaring that those whom he saw engaged in the *Mūt'a* marriage would be stoned, something, which was never prescribed by the Prophet (pbuh & hf). Whatever opinion 'Umar had on this marriage, it can never alter the fact that its legality came from Allāh and the fact that the Prophet had given permission to his companions to practice it.

> Narrated Imrān ibn Sawadah: "I went to 'Umar's house and told him that I want to give him some advice. His reply was: 'The person giving good advice is welcomed anytime.' I said: 'Your community finds fault with you on four accounts.' 'Umar put the top of his whip in his beard and the lower part on his thigh. Then he said: 'Tell me more.' I continued: 'It has been mentioned that you declared the lesser pilgrimage forbidden during the months of pilgrimage.' He answered: 'It is permitted. (But the reason that I forbade it was that) if they were to perform the lesser pilgrimage during the months of the pilgrimage, they would regard it as being a lieu of the full pilgrimage, and (Mecca) would be celebrated by no one, although it is part of God's greatness. You are right.' I continued: 'It is also said that you have forbidden temporary marriage, although it was a license given by God. We enjoy a temporary marriage for a handful (of dates), and we can separate after three nights.' He replied: 'The Messenger of God permitted it at the time of necessity. Then people regained their life of comfort. I do not know any Muslim who has practiced this or gone back to it (after I forbade). Now, anyone who wishes to can marry for a handful (of dates) and separate after three nights. You are right.' I

> continued: 'You emancipate a slave girl if she gives birth, without her master's (consenting to) the emancipation...'"[283]

When the Prophet (pbuh & hf) was alive, it was the Prophet's duty to clarify what *Ḥajj-at-Tamattū'* and *Mūt'a al-Nīsa* was. This would also have been the duty of the knowledgeable leader of the Islamic state, keeping them educated in regards to the temporary marriage, which the Prophet advised his companions to practice when necessary or in the time of need. Again, the instance when something may become necessary can arise at any time in ones life, we have no knowledge of when circumstances may change, we have no knowledge of the future, expressing something on circumstantial grounds cannot totally eradicate the practicing of a law prescribed by Allāh.

(a) Was the verse of *Mūt'a* canceled by Allāh?

If the verse of *Mūt'a* had been canceled, a verse would have been revealed in the Qur'ān to abrogate it.

> "None of Our revelations do We abrogate or cause to be forgotten but We substitute something better or similar; knowest thou not that Allāh hath power over all things?" Qur'ān 2:106

Allāh had already ordained the permanent marriage and many companions were permanently married when the verse of *Mūt'a* was revealed.

The reasons behind the belief that the temporary marriage has been forbidden are narrations stating its prohibition, which are in variance to one another.

> "Muḥammad ibn 'Alī narrated on the authority of his father 'Alī that Allāh's Apostle on the Day of Khaybar prohibited **forever** the contracting of temporary marriage and eating of the flesh of the domestic asses."[284]

Succession of the Prophet (PBUH)

The quoted tradition speaks of the Prophet (pbuh & hf) prohibiting the *Mūt'a* marriage **forever** when yet in another tradition it seems that the Prophet allowed it again after he had forbidden it **forever** and then forbade it again.

> "Iyās ibn Salama reported on the authority of his father that Allāh's Messenger gave sanction for contracting temporary marriage for three nights in the year of Autas 1847 and then forbade it."[285]

And in another tradition we find the following:

> "'Abd al-Mālik ibn Rabī' ibn Sabrāl-Juhanni reported on the authority of his father who narrated it on the authority of his father (i. e. 'Abd al-Mālik's grandfather, Sabūra al-Juhanni): 'Allāh's Messenger permitted us to contract temporary marriage in the Year of Victory, as we entered Mecca, and we did come out of it but he forbade us to do it.'"[286]

On the one hand the Prophet (pbuh & hf) prohibits the temporary marriage **forever** then on the other hand he again authorises it, allowing his companions to contract temporary marriage in the year of Autas, in fact this was after the Battle of Ḥunayn, which was after the Battle of Khayber, where it had been forbidden **forever** by the Prophet. Then after forbidding it in the Year of Autas, the Prophet again permitted it in the Year of Victory, which was almost towards the end of the Prophet's life. Did not the Apostle of Allāh know the meaning of prohibition **forever**? Or was it that the Prophet was not sure about certain matters when he made decisions about them, when in fact his decisions came from Allāh? If the Prophet had forbidden the temporary marriage **forever**, this means Allāh had forbidden it **forever**, and an abrogation from Allāh is not tantamount to change. Allāh is well acquainted with all things, He does not make mistakes, His decree does not change, He does not eradicate an order **forever** then bring it back after eradication. Also, we must remember that *Aḥadīth* can never cancel verses in the Qur'ān, it is verses in the Qur'ān which abrogate other verses, we do not observe anywhere in the Qur'ān that Allāh abrogated the verse of *Mūt'a* and a verse was revealed in connection with its abrogation.

The importance of Understanding the nature of the Question: "Whose word is binding?"

> Narrated Jābir ibn 'Abdullāh and Salama bin al-Akwa': "While we were in an army, Allāh's Apostle came to us and said: 'You have been allowed to do the *Mūt'a* (marriage), so do it.' Salama bin al-Akwa' said, Allāh's Apostle said: 'If a man and a woman agree (to marry temporarily), their marriage should last for three nights, and if they like to continue, they can do so; and if they want to separate, they can do so.' I do not know whether that was only for us or for all the people in general.'"

Al-Bukhārī cites his own statement after this narration adding:

> "'Alī made it clear that the Prophet said: 'The *Mūt'a* marriage has been cancelled (made unlawful).'"[287]

However we find the contradicting statement:

> 'Alī said: "The *Mūt'a* is a mercy from Allāh to his servants. If it were not for 'Umar forbidding it, no one would commit (the sin) of fornication except the wretched (*Shāqī;* an utmost wrong-doer)."[288]

Also, the rest of the Imāms of the Ahl al-Bayt have taught the same:

> Imām Ja'far as-Sādiq said: "*Mūt'a* was approved by the text of the Qur'ān and became part of the *Sunnah* of the Prophet."[289]
>
> Imām Ja'far as-Sādiq also said: "The verse proves *Mūt'a's* permissibility."[290]

A note needs to be made here, that within the Shī'ah books of fiqh (law) and tradition there is some narrative that contradict the permissibility of the temporary marriage and the Shī'ah *mujtahids* (those who derive rulings through studying and analysing the texts using principles that enable them to ascertain Islamic law) are aware of this. This gives rise to the quoting of these weak opposing narrations in order to prove that this type of marriage was cancelled and to endorse the opposing belief of the mainstream Muslims. What is failed to be realised is that these weak narratives oppose the *Mutwātir Ṣaḥīḥ* narrations in reference to permissibility and are not a *Ḥujjah* (proof) over the *Mutwātir*. Argueing over this, when there is multiple and strong evidences as opposed to the weak, that the *mujtahids* have seen no ambiguity in, is futile. The temporary marriage has indeed been instructed by the Prophet (pbuh & hf) and the Imāms of Ahl al-Bayt (AS) and it needs no elaboration or argueing over from the Shī'ah side. This issue has been dealt with through the Sunni sources purely to bring to light its actual existence and its continuation after the demise of the Prophet (pbuh & hf) with a few accepted Shī'ah narrative just in order for the reader to observe the same.

The companions, who continued to practice both *Mūt'as*, both during the time of the Prophet (pbuh & hf) and after, were acting upon the *Sunnah* of the Prophet, who did not reprimand them for doing so. If the Prophet had forbidden *Mūt'a*, not a single companion would have uttered that someone other than him had forbade it.

(b) The disagreement of 'Abdullāh ibn 'Abbās and 'Abdullāh ibn az-Zubayr on the issue.

> "'Urwa ibn az-Zubayr reported that 'Abdullāh ibn Zubayr stood up (and delivered an address) in Mecca saying: 'Allāh has made blind the hearts of some people as he has deprived them of eyesight that they give religious verdict in favour of temporary marriage,' while he was alluding to a person (Ibn 'Abbās). Ibn 'Abbās called him and said: 'You are a rude person and devoid of sense. By my life, *Mūt'a* was practiced during the lifetime of the leader of pious (he meant Allāh's Messenger),' and Ibn Zubayr said to him: 'Just do it yourself, and by Allāh, if you do that I will stone you with your stones.'"[291]

Ibn Zubayr disputed with the cousin of the Prophet (pbuh & hf), a cousin whom 'Umar himself had spoken highly of, whom 'Umar would pay attention to with interest and allow him to sit with him because of his religious knowledge.

The importance of Understanding the nature of the Question: "Whose word is binding?"

> Narrated Sa'īd ibn Jubair about 'Abdullāh ibn 'Abbās: "'Umar ibn al-Khaṭṭāb used to treat 'Abdullāh ibn 'Abbās very favourably 'Abd al- Raḥmān ibn Awf said to him: 'We also have sons that are equal to him (but you are partial to him.)' 'Umar said: 'It is because of his knowledge.' Then 'Umar asked Ibn 'Abbās about the interpretation of the verse: 'When come the Help of Allāh and the conquest (of Mecca) (Qur'ān 110.1). Ibn 'Abbās said: 'It portended the death of Allāh's Apostle, which Allāh had informed him of.' 'Umar said: 'I do not know from this verse but what you know.'"[292]

'Umar regarded 'Abdullāh ibn 'Abbās as an intelligent youngster and did not regard his religious judgement as being erroneous. 'Umar understood that Ibn 'Abbās was a knowledgeable individual, something of which Ibn Zubayr may not have recognised and acknowledged when arguing with him in connection with the two *Mūt'as*.

> Narrated 'Abdul Warīth: "The Prophet said: 'O Allāh, teach him (Ibn Abbās) the Book (i.e. the understanding of the knowledge of Qur'ān).'"[293]

(c) The recognition of the temporary marriage.

All marriages instituted for Muslims recognise that both the man and woman are husband and wife. We cannot address something as a marriage if there is no recognition of this relationship. Thus, a *Nikah* (words that pertain to the proposal of marriage) is also recited for the temporary marriage specifying a time period and *Maḥr* (a gift specified and agreed upon by the woman to whom marriage is intended). It is essential to recite a *Nikah*, as without it, and just as in the case of the permanent marriage, the marriage will become void.

> "Imām Ja'far as-Sādiq related that he was asked about a man who married a woman for a period of one month, but then found that a love for her was developing in his heart. Before the period expires,

> could he renew the contract and increase the time period and dowry? The Imām answered that it was not permissible so long as the first contract remained. Therefore he had to return to her for the remainder of the days of the contract and then conclude a new contract."[294]

If the marriage is consummated, then after separating, the woman is obliged to practise the *idda* (waiting period before one can re-marry) in the same sense a woman would in the permanent marriage.

> Imām al-Bāqir (the fifth Imām of the Ahl al-Bayt) was asked about a woman's *idda* in the *Mūt'a* marriage, if her husband passed away. He answered: 'For every marriage, if the husband should die, the wife must observe a waiting period of four months and ten days, it makes no difference whether she is free or a servant, and whether the marriage was permanent or temporary. The waiting period of a divorced (free) woman is three months, and that of a divorced servant one-half of what is required of a free woman. What is required of a wife by *Mūt'a* is the same as what is required of a servant.'[295]

Many Muslims have been misled into believing that when a child is born through the temporary marriage, the father has no responsibility towards his child and the woman is left to fend for herself. There is no difference in the law in reference to either the permanent or the temporary marriage on this issue; the maintenance of the child is due from the father in both cases.

> The Imām Ja'far as-Sādiq (AS) was asked: "If the wife becomes pregnant as a result of *Mūt'a*, to whom does the child belong?" He replied: "To the father, i.e. the child is legitimate."[296]

Also, if the man and woman do not wish to remain together at the end of the contract, they leave each other without inheriting anything. However, if they do wish to specify something, they can do so in the contract.

The importance of Understanding the nature of the Question: "Whose word is binding?"

> Imām al-Rida said: "If they should stipulate the condition (of inheritance), it takes place; and if they should not, it does not take place."[297]

The child if born in a temporary marriage is a separate issue, which has already been related.

What also the majority of Muslims are not acquainted with, is that, well-respected Ayatullāhs have stated that the temporary marriage cannot be contracted without the father's or grandfather's permission of the woman to whom marriage is desired, just as in the permanent marriage; there can be no marriage without first asking permission from the father. There are exceptions to this, but they are very strict exceptions, for example, a woman who is a divorcee, whose life experiences differs to the virgin woman, whose maturity is greater. She is not obliged to ask permission from her father, but this does not mean that she cannot seek the aid of her father in this issue if she desires to. There is also the example of when the father has withdrawn from the responsibility of guardian-ship and has no interest in searching for a suitable spouse for his daughter or is not concerned in any way towards her marriage, and clearly this could happen to many converts. What is important to remember is that the *Mūt'a* marriage is not something, which is contracted without any consideration towards the woman to whom marriage is to be undertaken.

Allāh recognises His servants for He created us; He recognises the emotional and physical needs of the human being. Temporary marriage provides protection and helps the emotional and physical needs of those who may lose spiritual concentration if they were to remain in an unstable state. Any faithful servant of Allāh, who has contracted the temporary marriage, should not be insulted. The Prophet (pbuh & hf) also did not insult his companions but recommended them to engage in temporary marriage to avoid any emotional stress or sin.

> 'Abdullāh ibn Mas'ūd reported: "We used to participate in the Holy Battles led by Allāh's Apostle and we had nothing (no wives) with us. So we said:

> 'Shall we get ourselves castrated?' He forbade us that and then allowed us to marry women with a temporary contract and recited to us: 'O you who believe! **Make not unlawful the good things which Allāh has made lawful for you, but commit no transgression**.'" (Qur'ān 5.87).[298]

The temporary marriage has been regarded as one of the lawful and good things prescribed by Allāh as 'Abdullāh ibn Mas'ūd recognised, and these words can also provide the answer towards the reason it remained as **one** of the types of marriages prescribed for the Muslims. Had the bad outweighed the good, the Prophet never would have associated verse 5:87 with this marriage, which also explains the reason why such an ordinance was not abrogated.

If we class *Mūt'a* as disgusting, we forget to realise that this disgusting act was practiced by the companions of the Prophet (pbuh & hf) even after he had passed away. We fail to realise that we are directly insulting and classing the companions as carrying out a disgusting act during his life and also after his demise.

Temporary marriage has no relation to fornication; fornication was practised before the time of the Prophet (pbuh & hf), and the verse of *Mūt'a* was revealed to prevent it. Imām 'Alī (AS) himself stated: "If it were not for 'Umar forbidding it, no one would commit (the sin) of fornication."

Faithful servants acknowledge and respect what Allāh has prescribed, they do not dampen the words of Allāh with abuse and disregard them, because they are sincere, these are the people who also will not abuse or play with the law of Allāh. Those who treat Allāh's s law as a jest are not of the righteous; the righteous will continually uphold the law in the correct and virtuous way.

It was very important for those left in authority to be able to explain the true teachings of the religion and understand that under no circumstance was it deemed acceptable to amend any order prescribed by Allāh and His Messenger, regardless of whether they understood it or not, regardless of whether they liked it or not, because as stated, Allāh has complete knowledge of the reasons behind His ordinances and who are we to change them.

The importance of Understanding the nature of the Question: "Whose word is binding?"

We could state that the issue of Imāmate was also not understood by everyone, its importance of being implemented, the fact that it could not be **rejected, altered or changed** in any way.

Not even the greatest of men can alter the decisions of Allāh.

Allāh guided His prophets, they were men who would always hear the conflicting words of others, but never would they alter the law as prescribed by Him.

> "If the Apostle were to invent any sayings in Our name, We should certainly seize him by his right hand, and We should certainly then cut off the artery of his heart. Nor could any of you withhold him (from Our wrath). But verily this is a Message for the God-fearing." Qur'ān 69:44.
>
> "But when Our Clear Signs are rehearsed unto them those who rest not their hope on their meeting with Us say: 'Bring us a reading other than this (*ghayri hādha*) or **change** (*baddilhū*) this.' Say: 'It is not **for me of my own accord to change it** (*baddilhū*), I follow naught but what is revealed unto me, if I were to disobey my Lord I should myself fear the Penalty of a great day to come.'" Qur'ān 10:15

We men and women of religion as mentioned at the beginning of this section, sometimes carry out certain matters without following what we ought to, we think it is better for us to do so, through our own opinion. This most certainly happened during the Prophet's (pbuh & hf) mission and also after his demise, because not everyone had the deep comprehension of the Qur'ān, which was placed alongside the Ahl al-Bayt.

Succession of the Prophet (PBUH)

Section 14

A Fundamental Instruction left by the Prophet (pbuh & hf).

Let us ponder on the following:

There are a number of students in a classroom, all are being taught by the same teacher, and the teacher's duty is to ensure that whatever is being conveyed does not swerve away from the truth.

It may take some students a lot longer than others to understand what the teacher is conveying. They may understand straight away or have great difficulty and require further help. Also, one student may have a strong understanding of one part of the subject, whilst another, in another part, however, there maybe another student who has astounding capabilities on the subject as a whole. Either way each student cannot be ranked as the same. The merit of each student would depend upon how much understanding and knowledge they have gained.

Competent teachers, who know their subjects well, will have worked at their utmost to teach what they know to their students, in order for them to follow the example of what has been taught to them. Not every student will become capable enough to further teach what he knows to others. If this type of student wished to take over the teachings of his superior, he could end up contradicting him. Would or would not this lead to confusion of the true teachings?

As common sense teaches us, all teachers were also at one time students, and their teachings would have to run in accordance with the teachings of the founder of that subject.

Now, when the Qur'ān was being revealed, the Prophet (pbuh & hf) also had the duty of conveying and explaining the religion to others as was taught to him through Allāh.

The Prophet (pbuh & hf) had many students i.e. the companions, who were constantly learning and understanding the beauty of the new religion, which was taught to them. The Prophet would always explain matters to his companions. This did not mean that from what the Prophet had taught them, they all had the same level of understanding and scope of knowledge as each other and were able to convey all aspects of the religion.

The Prophet (pbuh & hf) at the farewell pilgrimage expressed to these very companions an instruction, which would prevent them from going astray.

Mālik reported in his Muwaṭṭā' that the Prophet (pbuh & hf) said:

> Yaḥyā related to me from Mālik that he heard that the Messenger of Allāh said: "I have left two matters with you. As long as you hold to them, you will not go the wrong way. They are the Book of Allāh and the *Sunnah* of His Prophet."[299]

The above tradition is stated by many Muslims in connection to a sermon spoken by the Prophet (pbuh & hf) at a place called Arafat.

Everyone who had gathered together to hear the Prophet's (pbuh & hf) words did not have the knowledge of the Book and the Prophet's *Sunnah*, and by him stating: "I leave you the Qur'ān and the *Sunnah*" would the people have felt reassured?

For example if a teacher in a classroom was to state to his or her pupils that: "I am on vacation for six or seven weeks and I leave you to study your text book and keep in mind what I have explained to you." Not all students would find it easy to follow the bear text alone and remember everything taught to them. In this situation a replacement teacher who knows the subject would take over. Also, the pupils themselves would expect a stand in teacher to come and help them through what they did not understand and know. This would give them reassurance and stability.

Indeed, the Prophet (pbuh & hf) left for the people the Book of God and the *Sunnah* but who would this teaching have come from? Did the Prophet feel that all the people were competent and able enough to understand it? Imagine us stood amidst the crowd when the Prophet declared follow the Book of God and the *Sunnah*, would we have felt competent enough to interpret the Qur'ān and the words spoken by the Prophet in order to be rightly guided? Or would we have felt reassured if the Prophet had mentioned people who would guide and teach us in regards to this matter after him?

Also, imagine a man who had recently embraced Islām amidst the crowd who did not know anyone, who had little knowledge in regards to the religion. He would want to know from whom he could seek guidance; he would want to know that the information he received and what he was following was correct. From where would he have received this reassurance?

The Qur'ān is a fixed *Kitāb* (Book), but not every human being who reads it understands everything in it. Matters in relation to it were explained in detail by the Prophet (pbuh & hf) but not everyone had the knowledge of it. It was a time when the people were still learning the new religion and needed guidance in many matters. It was most important to have teachers rightly guiding the Muslims.

Would following any Companion provide us with the Security from being led astray?

The majority of Muslims express that it was the companions who were left as the guides and mention that the Prophet (pbuh & hf) stated:

> "Verily, my companions are like the *nujūm* (stars) in the sky; whichever of them you follow, you shall be guided rightly. The disagreement of my companions is a blessing for you."

Firstly, if we read the statement that expresses the Prophet (pbuh & hf) said: "The disagreement of my companions is a blessing for you," we must contemplate, does Allāh teach us this in the Qur'ān? Allāh has never addressed disputation and division in the Qur'ān as a blessing and approves of it amongst the people. When we learn this, then should we contradict Allāh and see it as a blessing?

> "And obey Allāh and His Apostle; and never be drawn into disputes lest you be defeated and your power be scattered to the winds; and be patient and persevering; for Allāh is with those who patiently persevere." Qur'ān 8:46

Secondly, if we only express the first part of the statement, that we can follow any companion for our guidance, we need to understand as stated earlier, that the companions were as the students of the Prophet (pbuh & hf); there were many of them, all learning matters related to the religion from him. This statement declaring that we can follow any companion gives us the notion that everyone was the same. They all had the same intellect, the same understanding and degree of knowledge; hence we could take from any one of them. This statement is against reason and common sense. If this does not agree with our intelligence, and it would be strange if we believe that all companions were the same, the matter is self-evident from reports we find documented. For example:

> Ma'dan ibn Talḥa reported that 'Umar said: "...I do not leave after me anything, which to my mind seems more important than *Kalālah*. I never turned towards the Messenger of Allāh (for guidance) more often than this *Kalālah*, and he (the Holy Prophet) was not annoyed with me on any other (issue) than this. (He was so perturbed) that he struck his fingers on my chest and said: 'Does this verse that is at the end of *Sūrah al-Nīsa* (Chapter of the Woman), which was revealed in the hot season, not suffice you? And if I live longer I would decide this (problem so clearly) that one who reads the Qur'ān, or one who does not read it, would be able to make (correct) decisions (under its light)...'"[300]

If we were alive at the time of 'Umar and were to ask him what *Kalālah* was, he would not have known to explain its exact meaning. Hence would we have been guided in that particular matter, when as stated, taking from any companion would lead to our correct guidance?

We also have observed in section twelve the case where Imām 'Alī (AS) guided 'Umar when he pronounced the stoning of a lunatic woman who had committed adultery. Imām 'Alī explained that there are three types of people whose actions could not be accounted for, one of them being a lunatic woman. If Imām 'Alī had not been present and given this advice, then maybe the woman would have been stoned. Imām 'Alī intervened and explained to 'Umar the necessary route to take in this situation. In this incident, it has to be accepted that 'Umar himself followed the guidance given by Imām 'Alī. If Imām 'Alī had not mentioned this and someone later on had followed 'Umar in this practice, (in the stoning of any other lunatic women) would they have been rightly informed?

Another example:

> Malik related to me that he had heard that 'Uthmān ibn Affan was brought a woman who had given birth after six months and he ordered her to be stoned. 'Ali ibn Abī Tālib said to him: "She does not deserve that. Allāh, the Blessed, the Exalted, says in His Book, 'Their carrying and weaning is thirty months,' (*Sūrah* 46 Āyat 15) and he said: 'Mothers suckle their children for two full years for whoever wishes to complete the suckling. (*Sūrah* 2 Āyat 233) Pregnancy can then be six months, so she does not deserve to be stoned.' 'Uthman ibn Affan sent for her and found that she had already been stoned."[301]

Again, Imām 'Alī (AS) guided another companion of the Prophet (pbuh & hf) and this time it was 'Uthmān. He had ordered a woman believed to have committed adultery, to be stoned. She had given birth to a child after six months and Imām 'Alī explained through the teachings of the Qur'ān that punishment was not due on her as she was entitled to wean her child for a period of two years. 'Uthmān on listening to the advice of the Imām called for her stoning to be stopped but the action had already taken place. If such a case had occurred again and the verdict of 'Uthmān had been followed, would this have been correct? 'Uthmān in this instance followed the guidance given after being corrected.

Moving on to another issue, it is worth stating that Mu'āwīya was also a companion of the Prophet (pbuh & hf) who fought against Imām 'Alī (AS) in the Battle of Siffīn. Many people state that the sole reason for Mu'āwīya's stand in opposition to Imām 'Alī (AS) was the murder of his cousin 'Uthmān, failing to realise who was in the better position to deal with this issue. It is known that Mu'āwīya did not accept and did not abide with the decisions of the caliph. Instead, he waged a war, which was inappropriate towards one whose judgement the Prophet (pbuh & hf) had held in high esteem. What is enlightening is the following narration we find in the *al-Muwaṭṭā'* of Imām Mālik.

> "Malik related to me from Yaḥyā ibn Saīd from Sa'īd ibn al-Musaiyyab that a Syrian man called Ibn Khaybarī found a man with his wife and killed him, or killed them both. Mu'āwīya ibn Abī Sufyān found it difficult to make a decision and he wrote to Abū Mūsa al-Asharī to ask 'Alī ibn Abī Tālib for him about that. So Abū Mūsa asked 'Alī ibn Abī Tālib and 'Alī said to him: 'Is this thing in my land? I adjure you, you must tell me.' Abū Mūsa explained to him how Mu'āwīya ibn Abī Sufyān had written him to ask 'Alī about it. 'Alī said: 'I am Abū Ḥasan. If he does not bring four witnesses, then let him be completely handed over, (to the relatives of the murdered man)."[302]

We read that Mu'āwīya wrote to Abū Mūsa al-Asharī to ask Imām 'Alī (AS) for advice in regards to a situation, which had arisen due to suspected adultery. This portrays that Mu'āwīya recognised the knowledge Imām 'Alī had, and that his words would not be insignificant on the issue of a murder, which had been committed in retaliation to one who had supposedly engaged in adultery. Mu'āwīya would never have asked the Imām if he had doubt in him. When we contemplate on this, what can be stated about the battle at Siffin that the Imām faced from Mu'āwīya? Was it truly due to the murder of 'Uthmān when in such legal issues Mu'āwīya was well aware of the Imām's capabilities? Mu'āwīya was neither the son nor the brother or father of 'Uthmān, he was was not part of his immediate family, and yet wished to retaliate against the Imām and that too through a battle. We must ponder and contemplate, where does it state that a battle is to be fought under such circumstances?

We read in *Nahj al-Balāghah*:

> "You have challenged me to a battle. I accept your challenge. But I have a proposal to make. Why have a war involving murder and bloodshed of thousands of ignorant people? Why be a scourge to mankind?

> Let us have mercy on them, whether they are sincere and God fearing Muslims or ignorant, unenlightened and greedy mercenaries misguided and fooled by you. Let there be peace and tranquillity for all the creatures of Allāh.
>
> Let us, you and I, have a single combat. Let it be a combat unto death. Let the soldiers of both armies stand aside and let two of us alone combat with each other. Let the world see and realise who is the sinner and who has forgotten Allāh and the Day of Judgement. Will you accept this invitation of mine? Have you the courage for it? Are you a man to face death boldly and bravely or are you merely a vampire sucking the blood of others surreptitiously?
>
> Remember Mu'āwīya! Though now old I am still Abū al-Ḥasan, the man who killed your maternal grandfather, your uncle and your brother in single combats in the Battle of Badr. The same sword is still in my hand, the same blood is still flowing in my veins, the same heart is still throbbing in my chest and with the same courage I still face my enemy. Will you come and face me alone?
>
> Remember that I have not introduced any innovation in religion, nor have I insinuated schism. Verily, I sincerely believe in the religion, which you pretended to embrace hypocritically with mental reservations and pretensions, a religion which you in your heart of hearts actually hated and which you gave up quickly and cheerfully.
>
> You pretend that you want to avenge the murder of caliph 'Uthmān. Do you know who actually killed him and who caused his murder? If really you do so, then seek vengeance on them."[303]

What is stated is part of a letter, which was written by Imām 'Alī (AS) to Mu'āwīya. The Imām clearly states that he did not wish to cause war or bloodshed and wanted to avoid it, as Mu'āwīya's army was being misled by him. The Imām wished to face him in single combat but this was not accepted.

Imām 'Alī (AS) addressed those who were with him, under which circumstances it was permissible to strike with the sword.

> "When you face your enemy, stand in the midst of your army, never alone, do not be over anxious to fight and do not behave as if you are craving for a combat or aspiring for an encounter, but at the same time do not try to avoid your enemy or to evade an engagement as if you are afraid or nervous. Keep my orders in mind and act accordingly until you get further instructions. Do not let the hatred and enmity of your opponents force you to a combat, do not begin a battle even if the enemy so desires unless you have explored every avenue of amity and good-will and have exhausted all the chances of a peaceful settlement."[304]

Imām 'Alī (AS) never wished for those who were with him to initiate a battle, but rather taught them to first incline towards peace. Only and only if those who were against them initiated a battle, were they permitted to face them in combat as an act of self-defence.

The following verse of the Quran teaches:

> "If two parties amongst the believers fall into a quarrel, **make ye peace between them but if one of them transgresses beyond bounds against each other, then fight ye (all) against the one that transgresses** until it complies with the command of Allāh and if it complies, then make peace between them with justice and be fair for Allāh loves those who are fair and just." Qur'ān 49:9

The verse clearly signifies that peace is first to be sought amongst the believers and who can utter anything towards the one who understood this verse more than anyone else, suggesting he would have acted contrary to it?

Succession of the Prophet (PBUH)

It is only legitimate for a group of believers to face one another in combat when transgression has become apparent; otherwise it is out of order. The Qur'ān does not teach us that a battle can be sought if the actions of both groups are correct. There is no room for such an opinion from anyone when understanding that such a verse (49.9) is extent in the Qur'ān. The Qur'ān teaches us that a battle can only be sought against the group that has transgressed; otherwise there is no permission for it.

A peaceful approach to matters was the first step Imām 'Alī (AS) took, an approach, which he had also managed to fulfil the moment the Prophet (pbuh & hf) departed.

> Adlai Stevenson (1900-1965) said: "A wise man does not try to hurry history. Many wars have been avoided by patience, and many have been precipitated by reckless haste."[305]

> "...When Fāṭimah was alive, the people used to respect 'Alī much, but after her death, 'Alī noticed a change in the people's attitude towards him. So 'Alī sought reconciliation with Abū Bakr and gave him an oath of allegiance."[306]

If we briefly skip back to the time of Abū Bakr's lead in government, Imām 'Alī (AS) gave his oath of allegiance six months after the demise of his wife Sayyedah Sayyedah Fāṭimah (AS). He noticed that people were beginning to change their attitude towards him and in order to continue to keep his stand of peace in this situation, he adopted such means. Imām 'Alī was the Imām of age and always would remain as this in spite of what had happened, as Allāh's chosen ones always remain as that, whether the people choose to follow them or not. Through this means and through being patient, Imām 'Alī was able to uphold the true teachings of the Qur'ān and the *Sunnah* for those who paid attention to him, and as observed, he became an advisor, correcting whatever he saw as incorrect or as a breach of the law.

The Imām stated:

What was stated on the Day of Arafat?

> "A man is not blamed if he takes his time in obtaining what is his; the blame is on that who takes what does not belong to him."[307]

If an individual's right is taken from him, it takes time to obtain back that right and Imām 'Alī's (AS) primary concern was associated with peace as the Qur'ān teaches us that it is the first point of call. Through peace the prime importance, which was the Message of Islām, could continue. We can also reflect upon what the situation could have been like at that time if the first point of call was over-ridden by the Muslims fighting one another, it being the early days of the Prophet's (pbuh & hf) demise, it being a time that the non-believers were wishing to attack the Arabian Peninsula, it also being something that the hypocrites would have been pleased with. Such an occurrence would have brought an excellent opportunity for the enemies of Islām to annihilate and uproot its teachings, also causing mass carnage and bloodshed. Hence, an act of diplomacy, and that too being what the Qur'ān dictates, enabled Imām 'Alī to prevent such a disaster from occurring. He was also then able to illuminate his teachings, bringing forth awareness for the coming generations.

What also needs to be understood is that a battle had not been set up against the Imām, which allowed him to resort to peaceful measures.

If we speak of the time when Imām 'Alī (AS) was facing opposition from Mu'āwīya, we find that what the Imām had prevented from happening through his patience after the Prophet's (pbuh & hf) demise, had become apparent.

Imām 'Alī (AS) always wanted to prevent bloodshed and dissension, but in his time as leader, Mu'āwīya had set up a league against him in battle, causing mass dissension and due to this very predicament the Imām faced what he faced.

We find that Imām 'Alī (AS) expressed his concerns in a letter he wrote to one of his beloved companions, Mālik ibn Ḥarīth al-Ashtar when he appointed him as the governor of Egypt.

> "The Almighty Allāh, Glory be to Him, entrusted our Holy Prophet with the mission of warning the people

> of the evil effects of their vicious actions and of bearing testimony to the truth actually taught and preached by other prophets. When the Holy Prophet passed away, the Muslims started a tug-of-war for the caliphate. I swear by Allāh that at that juncture it could not even be imagined that the Arabs would snatch the seat of the caliphate from the family and descendants of the Holy Prophet and that they would be swearing the oath of allegiance for the caliphate to a different person.
>
> At every stage I kept myself aloof from that struggle of supremacy and power politics **till I found the heretics had openly taken to heresy and schism and were trying to undermine and ruin the religion preached by our Holy Prophet**. I felt afraid that even after seeing and recognising the evil, **if I did not stand up to help Islām** and the Muslims it would be a worse calamity to me than my losing authority and power over you, which was only a transient and short-lived affair."[308]

Again, Imām 'Alī's (AS) concern was towards Islām and his stand was for it and if we were to hold something against him, it would mean that we were in opposition to someone who was a lover of that very thing as this is what the Imām represented. When he gained back his authority, which he called a "transient and short-lived affair" he fought in the Battle of Siffīn against Mu'āwīya, who no doubt knew what the Imām stood for. Who can state that because of what the Imām was facing, **he was the one who wished to start the battle**? It was only when his opposition had turned to the sword that defensive measures had to be taken and thus instructed!

Now, Allāh has taught us that if peace cannot be achieved between two parties, then fight the party, which has transgressed (Qur'ān 49:9). Imām 'Alī (AS) never would have fought if it was not legitimate for him to do so. Was not the the Qur'ān and the truth with him?

> "'Alī is with the Qur'ān and the Qur'ān is with 'Alī.

> "'Alī is with the truth and the truth revolves around 'Alī."

A certain *Ḥadīth* of the Prophet (pbuh & hf) states:

> This *Ḥadīth* has been transmitted on the authority of Umm Salama that Allāh's Messenger said to 'Ammār: "A group of rebels would kill you."[309]

'Ammār ibn Yāsir who had fought on the side of Imām 'Alī (AS) was killed in this battle and the Prophet (pbuh & hf) had expressed that the aggressors would kill him.

'Ammār ibn Yāsir prior to being martyred in the Battle of Siffīn pointed towards the banner of Mu'āwīya and stated:

> "By God, under the banner of the Messenger, I fought the man of this banner three times, and the man of the banner is not more righteous now than before."[310]

He also stated:

> "By God, if they hit us until they drive us from here to the orchards of Hejar, we will continue to believe that we are the people of truth, and they are people of falsehood."[311]

When battles had been fought prior to the conversion of Mu'āwīya and his family, such personalities like 'Ammār met face to face with falsehood. The Prophet (pbuh & hf) had stated that the aggressors would kill 'Ammār, and the latter knew exactly who these aggressors were.

If we come back to the *Ḥadīth*, my companions are like the stars follow anyone of them and you will be rightly guided, would it have been correct for us to take the side of Mu'āwīya and follow his judgement against the Imām, as we could follow any companion and be rightly guided? Due to many holding this *Ḥadīth* to be true it gives them the leeway to state that both companions were in the right when in fact the Qur'ān does not teach this and even the Prophet (pbuh & hf) gave the guidance that the party who would kill 'Ammār are the rebels.

The Prophet (pbuh & hf) stated to Imām 'Alī (AS) as reported by al-Ḥakim in his al-Mustadrak, who quotes it as being a sound statement:

> Narrated 'Abdullāh ibn 'Abbās: "'The Prophet said to 'Alī: 'In truth, you shall certainly experience great hardship after me.' He asked: 'With my religion safe?' The Prophet said: 'Yes.'"[312]

Any individual who adhered to somebody who did not step outside the boundaries of his religion could not have been marked as following an aggressor and Imām 'Alī (AS) spent most of his caliphate battling against those whom were transgressing against the religion, which in the end led to his martyrdom and consequently the Umayyad dynasty.

The statement itself: "My companions are like the stars follow anyone of them and you will be rightly guided," we find that it has been found to carry weaknesses by many Sunni scholars of *Ḥadīth*. Scholars such as Imām Aḥmad ibn Ḥanbal,[313] al-Dārqutnī,[314] Ibn Hazm,[315] Ibn 'Abd al-Barr,[316] Ibn 'Asākir,[317] al-Dhaḥabi,[318] Ibn Qayyim al-Jawziyyah,[319] Ibn Ḥajar al-'Asqalānī,[320] al-Suyutī,[321] and al-Muttaqī al-Hindī,[322] have considered this narration to be unreliable.

Also, we should compare the statement with another statement of the Prophet (pbuh & hf), which has already previously been stated:

> Narrated 'Abdullāh ibn 'Abbās that the Prophet (pbuh and his family) said: "The stars protect the inhabitants of earth against drowning, and my Ahl al-Bayt protect my nation against dissension (in religious matters). If a tribe among the Arabs differs (regarding the commandments of Allāh, the High, the Mighty) from them, they will all then differ and become the party of Satan."

What was stated on the Day of Arafat?

It already has been stated that on the day of Arafat the Prophet (pbuh & hf) addressed the Muslims to adhere to the Qur'ān and the

Sunnah. But what is not known is that there are other narrations indicating something else.

> On the day of Arafat Jābir ibn 'Abdullāh al-Ansārī reported that the Messenger of Allāh declared: "Jābir saw Allāh's Messenger when performing the *Ḥajj* seated on his she-camel al-Qaswa' on the day of Arafat giving an address, and he heard him saying: 'O people, **I have left among you something of such a nature that if you adhere to it you will not go astray,** Allāh's Book and my close relatives who belong to my Household.'"[323]

It has also been recorded in the *Ṣaḥīḥ* of Muslim, which is a lengthy narration that the same Jābir ibn 'Abdullāh narrated that the Prophet (pbuh & hf) said:

> "The Messenger of Allāh however passed on till he came to 'Arafa and he found that the tent had been pitched for him at Namira. There he got down till the sun had passed the meridian; he commanded that al-Qaswa should be brought and saddled for him....
>
> ...Fear Allāh concerning women! Verily you have taken them on the security of Allāh, and intercourse with them has been made lawful unto you by words of Allāh. You too have right over them, and that they should not allow anyone to sit on your bed whom you do not like. But if they do that, you can chastise them but not severely. Their right upon you is that you should provide them with food and clothing in a fitting manner**. I have left among you the** Book of Allāh, **and if you hold fast to it, you would never go astray**..."[324]

Now if all these statements are taken on board, imagine the Prophet (pbuh & hf) on the day of Arafat conveying to the Muslims: "**I am leaving behind two things which will prevent you from being led astray**, they are the Book of Allāh and my *Sunnah*" but then repeating the first half of the statement with the latter half projecting:

"...they are the Book of Allāh and my Household (Ahl al-Bayt)," and then repeating the same again with the end words as "...the Book of Allāh". It does not sound plausible that the Prophet declared these three different statements on the same day (Day of Arafat).

The Prophet (pbuh & hf) was a messenger, a guide; his whole mission entailed insuring the correct guidance for the Muslims in order to keep them all standing in one direction. The Prophet addressed the Muslims on a very important matter with one statement and he was truly sure of what it was he was conveying. It is for us to decipher, which statement was spoken.

It is not denied that the Prophet (pbuh & hf) wanted his followers to adhere to the Qur'ān and the *Sunnah* and mentioned the word *Sunnah* in his lifetime. However, we can understand that it was essential for this address at Arafat to bring forth exactly from whom the teachings of the Qur'ān and the *Sunnah* could be taken. The Prophet had further proclaimed the authority of his Ahl al-Bayt at Ghadir Khumm, where he stated: "I remind in you in the name of Allāh about my Ahl al-Bayt, I remind you in the name of Allāh about my Ahl al-Bayt, I remind you in the name of Allāh about my Ahl al-Bayt, (three times)," as recorded in the *Ṣaḥīḥ* of Muslim and other books.

Also, it is not denied that the Book of Allāh is required. However, the Prophet's (pbuh & hf) address at Arafat was in terms of not being led astray from it. The Book of Allāh alone would mean that the Prophet left us to fully interpret the verses of the Qur'ān without any means of guidance. This can never be the case as any individual cannot read the Book and understand its wisdom. Its wisdom was taught by the Prophet (pbuh & hf) but as already explained, **not every single individual** during that time and till this very day has been bestowed with it.

Allāh states:

> "We have sent amongst you a Messenger who recites to you our verses and purifies you and teaches you the Book and the Wisdom (of the Book) and teaches you that which you do not know." Qur'ān 2:151

What was stated on the Day of Arafat?

The Qur'ān contains apparent and ambiguous verses, and within the apparent verses we could state that we find a literal aspect to them, which are easy to comprehend. What we must realise is that although verses can be taken in this light, they do have a specific nature to them and it is this that the Prophet (pbuh & hf) would explain. If anyone used his or her own opinion in this, then he or she most definitely would err.

> Narrated Jundub: The Prophet said: "If anyone interprets the Book of Allāh in the light of his opinion even if he is right, he has erred."[325]

> Narrated 'Abdullāh ibn 'Abbās: "Allāh's Messenger said, He who speaks about the Qur'ān on the basis of his personal opinion (only) will find his abode in Hell-Fire. In another version (the words are), He who speaks about the Qur'ān without sound knowledge of it will find his abode in Hell-Fire. [326]

In the Qur'ān the name of Abū Bakr was not mentioned when he accompanied the Prophet (pbuh & hf) in the cave, yet, we acknowledge the companion to be him. When we read the verse (Qur'ān 9:40) in regards to this, we find that its literal aspect serves as a lesson to us all, but its specific aspect could not be attained by reading the Book of Allāh alone. Through this, it should be grasped what is trying to be portrayed here.

We need to contemplate, if the Prophet (pbuh & hf) on the Day of Arafat had stated: "I have left among you the Book of Allāh," it has provided the pathway for the Muslims to pick up the Qur'ān and interpret it in the way they please. We have no right to utter anything against them, even if there is contradiction. How can this be? The Qur'ān is our source of unity; its words can never allow disunity.

> Narrated 'Abdullāh ibn 'Umar: "I went to Allāh's Apostle in the morning and he heard the voice of two persons who had an argument with each other about a verse. Allāh's Apostle came to us (and) the signs of anger could be seen on his face. He said: 'Verily, the

> peoples before you were ruined because of their disputation in the Book.'"[327]

Disputation in regards to the Book does not provide peace and solace, but hostility and divergence, which have been shunned by Allāh and His Prophet (pbuh & hf). Inadequate knowledge of the religion would inevitably cause disputation, and taking from any individual could not have provided protection from disputation.

The Prophet (pbuh & hf) would never have expressed his Ahl al-Bayt alongside the Qur'ān if they did not possess the knowledge of it. Misguidance does not lead to guidance, contradiction does not lead to one answer, irresolute knowledge does not provide security from being led astray, and varying interpretations of the Qur'ān does not lead to unity.

If the Prophet (pbuh & hf) had expressed that we could follow any of his companions for the right guidance, then he most certainly would have expressed it at the farewell pilgrimage, yet there is no mention of this statement expressed by him at that time.

We do not find any tradition directed at Arafat or at Ghadir Khumm, which depict that the Prophet (pbuh & hf) stated: "O people, I have left among you that which if you uphold, you will never go astray. They are the Book of Allāh and my Companions," and in fact it is the companions themselves who have narrated the tradition in regards to the Ahl al-Bayt. A tradition, which has been so widely, transmitted within both the Shī'ah and Sunni sources, moreover those traditions, which indiscriminately oppose it, that those whom adhere to the Imāms cannot be accused of lying or making up stories.

Section 15

The associates of the Prophet (pbuh & hf).

In the Oxford dictionary the meaning of the word companion is "one who associates with or accompanies another". This associate could be your teacher, your work manager, your friend, your husband or your wife. In fact, it could be anyone whom you have associated yourself with for whatever reason or matter throughout the course of your life. These people can vary from one another in character and age, can have varying degrees of knowledge and wisdom and their association can differ from one another. For example you may not know the people you work with very well, as you have not spent that much time with them compared to your close friends who may have accompanied you through your school or college years. The question is would you trust each and every one of these associates or companions to the same degree? Would you know perfectly each individual's inner thoughts and feelings? You may feel close to some and not so close to others but the word companion is incorporated into all these different people you associate with.

Moving on, towards the time of the Prophet (pbuh & hf) anyone who had associated with him was termed a companion and not all the companions had accompanied him at the same time.

Ibn al-Athīr in his Usd al-Ghabah quotes the following words of Imām Aḥmad ibn Ḥanbal:

> "Whoever had accompanied the Prophet for one month, one day, one hour or had only seen the Holy Prophet once is regarded as one of his companions."

Ibn al-Athīr also quotes the words of al-Bukhārī stating:

> "Whoever of the Muslims accompanied the Holy Prophet or even saw him, happens to be one of his companions."[328]

Also, Ibn Ḥajar al-'Asqalānī stated the following:

The associates of the Prophet (pbuh & hf)

> "A companion is the believer who saw and heard God's Messenger at least once and died as a believer."[329]

And Allāh teaches us:

> "*Kuntum khayra* ***Ummatin*** (You are the best nation) raised up for mankind. **Ye enjoin right conduct and forbid indecency**; and ye believe in Allāh and if the people of the Scripture had believed it had been better for them." Qur'ān 3:110

The above verse is signifying that the best nation that has been raised up for mankind enjoin the good and forbid the evil. These people addressed are the adherents of the Prophet (pbuh & hf). Every single individual who states he or she is a Muslim is not part of this *Ummah* for the reason that they may not hold the characteristic that the verse describes i.e. enjoining the good and forbidding the evil.

Another verse in the Qur'ān within the same *Sūrah* can teach us much in regards to this:

> "Let there be **among** you an *Ummah* inviting to all that is good, **enjoining what is right, and forbidding what is wrong**..." Qur'ān 3:104

Allāh clarifies to us the *Ummah*, which is recognised by Him. Merely classing ourselves as Muslims does not mean that we **all** are recognised as great models of the religion and we all will represent it. This is most definitely not the case.

What we find is that some people quote verse 3:110 to legitimise the authority of anyone who associated with the Prophet (pbuh & hf), when the verse portrays no stand on such a notion.

If we also re-iterate what has been stated in section two, that when Allāh uses the word *Ummah*, it does not necessarily mean that it involves every individual. The word *Ummah* could consist of only one individual.

Verses in the Qur'ān also teach us of Allāh's pleasure and also His warnings should one slacken or turn way from Him.

It would be appropriate to observe here a verse of the Qur'ān, which teaches us of a certain action, which pleased Allāh:

> "Allāh's Good Pleasure was on the believers when they swore fealty to thee under the tree; He knew what was in their hearts and He sent down tranquillity to them and He rewarded them with a speedy Victory." Qur'ān 48:18

It would also be appropriate to observe the verse, which was revealed to portray that if the believers were to turn away from this oath, it would only harm their own souls.

> "Verily those who plight their fealty to thee do no less than plight their fealty to Allāh; the Hand of Allāh is over their hands; **then anyone who violates His oath** does so to the harm of his own soul **and anyone who fulfils** what he has covenanted with Allāh, Allāh will soon grant him a great reward." Qur'ān 48:10

If we briefly state something in regards to the revelation of the aforementioned verses, we understand that they were revealed in 6.A.H. when the Prophet (pbuh & hf) led the Muslims on a journey to Mecca in order to perform *'Umra*. The Prophet changed his route to Mecca along with his caravan of people and reached a place called Hudaybīya. The Quraysh were conspiring to intercept and cause interference in order to cause a return of the caravan to Madīnah. The Prophet sent 'Uthmān to Mecca to inform them that he had not come to engage in battle but to perform the pilgrimage. But the Quraysh did not agree to their presence. The Prophet informed his companions to take an oath that they would all join in battle till death overtook them if they were required to do so. This pledge is commonly known as *Bait al-Ridwān*. 'Uthmān returned with a delegate of the Quraysh, a man by the name of Suhail ibn 'Amr, who came to negotiate a peace treaty with the Prophet, what is commonly known as "The Peace Treaty of al-Hudaybīya". The Prophet was then informed to head back to Madīnah and return the following year for *Umrah*.

The pledge, which was taken at that time, received pleasure from Allāh, meaning Allāh became pleased with a **certain action**, which had taken place. Allāh is always pleased with those whose hearts wish to follow His orders and this particular one was to ensure an oath to remain firm in battle, should the circumstance arise. What we need to realise is that when Allāh became pleased with this certain action, all other actions did not automatically become included in this. The verse of the Qur'ān (48:18) very much speaks in regards to the pledge that was taken and not any other action. These glad tidings, which were given by Allāh to the believers, would only remain with them as long as they remained firm in their word and did not violate.

Allāh is never unjust to His faithful servants, those who remain steadfast in their faith and continue to please Allāh in many of their good actions. They are the ones who will attain true salvation.

> "And those who preceded (in belief), **from** the Immigrants and Helpers and those who followed them in what was good, Allāh was satisfied with them; He has prepared for them gardens under which rivers flow to dwell therein for ever. That is the great felicity." Qur'ān 9:100

Take note that not **all** the Immigrants and Helpers are incorporated within the stated verse.

Allāh addresses the issue of becoming insincere or turning back from the faith:

> "O ye who believe! If any from among you turn back from his faith, soon will Allāh produce a people whom He will love as they will love Him, lowly with the believers, Mighty against the rejecters, fighting in the way of Allāh, and never afraid of the reproaches of such as find fault. That is the Grace of Allāh, which He will bestow on whom He pleaseth. And Allāh

> encompasseth all, and He knoweth all things." Qur'ān 5:54

Plus Allāh already had disclosed to His Apostle:

> "Has not the time arrived for the believers that their hearts in all humility should engage in the remembrance of Allāh and of the truth which has been revealed (to them) and that they should not become like those to whom was given the Book aforetime? But long ages passed over them and their hearts grew hard, for many among them are rebellious transgressors." Qur'ān 57:16

If it had of been the case that not even one of the believers were showing any such actions, would Allāh have stated this in regards to them? As observed from the stated verse (57:16), we can comprehend that many followers of the religion were becoming sluggish in their remembrance of Allāh, losing adherence to the true cause. Thus providing us with the insight that not everyone was the same and not **every single action** was pleasing to Him.

It does not mean that just for the reason of associating with the Prophet (pbuh & hf), all of a sudden a person became immune from such verses when in actual fact the verses were revealed to disclose to him the various mentalities of all those present, both good and bad. Many verses in the Qur'ān were revealed as a result of certain actions, which were occurring around that period. If those present had heard the Prophet quote the aforementioned words of the Qur'ān, they would have known themselves that Allāh's warnings were directed to them and would serve as a lesson for future generations.

Many verses of the Qur'ān were sent upon those who were alive at the time of the Prophet (pbuh & hf), praising actions and good works, also warning and informing them of what Allāh knew. Acting upon and surrendering to His will with firm faith, continuing to please Him in good works and deeds and not turning back, is what would earn the pleasure of Allāh. Allāh's glad tidings are conditional on the basis of remaining on this path.

The associates of the Prophet (pbuh & hf)

We should understand that Allāh gives no full proofs guarantee, that **all** those who profess their faith in Islām will remain the same up until the day they die:

If we move on to the *Aḥadīth* of the Prophet (pbuh & hf):

> Narrated Abū Sa'īd al-Khudrī, The Prophet said: "You will follow the ways of those nations who were before you, span by span and cubit by cubit (i.e. inch by inch) so much so that even if they entered a hole of a mastigure (lizard), you would follow them." We said: "O Allāh's Apostle! (Do you mean) the Jews and the Christians?" He said: "Whom else?"[330]

Allāh does not wish His believing servants to become like those who came before them, and wants them to obey the edicts that His Apostle has informed them of. It is self evident in the Qur'ān and *Aḥadīth* that amongst those who had professed their faith in Islām, there would exist certain people who would become like them, meaning they would deviate from the truth and follow other than it.

> Narrated 'Abdullāh, the Prophet said: 'I am your predecessor at the Lake-Fount.' 'Abdullāh added, the Prophet said: 'I am your predecessor at the Lake-Fount, and some of you will be brought in front of me till I will see them and then they will be taken away from me and I will say, O Lord, my companions!' It will be said: 'You do not know what they did after you had left.'"[331]

> Narrated Anas, the Prophet said: "Some of my companions will come to me at my Lake Fount, and after I recognise them, they will then be taken away from me, whereupon I will say, 'My companions!' Then it will be said: 'You do not know what they innovated (new things) in the religion after you.'"[332]

> Narrated Abū Ḥazim from Sahl ibn Sa'd: "The Prophet said: 'I am your predecessor (forerunner) at the Lake-Fount, and whoever will pass by there, he will drink

> from it and whoever will drink from it, he will never be thirsty. There will come to me some people whom I will recognise, and they will recognise me, but a barrier will be placed between me and them.' Abū Ḥazim added, An-Nu'man ibn Abī 'Aiyāsh, on hearing me, said. 'Did you hear this from Sahl?' I said: 'Yes.' He said: 'I bear witness that I heard Abū Sa'īd al-Khudrī saying the same, adding that the Prophet said': 'I will say they are of me (i.e. my followers).' It will be said: 'You do not know what they innovated (new things) in the religion after you left.' I will say (i.e. the Prophet): 'Far removed, far removed (from mercy), those who changed (their religion) after me (*ghayyara ba'dī*).' Abū Ḥurayra narrated that the Prophet said: 'On the Day of Resurrection a group of companions will come to me, but will be driven away from the Lake-Fount, and I will say: 'O Lord (those are) my companions!' It will be said: 'You have no knowledge as to what they innovated after you left; they turned apostate as renegades (reverted from Islām).'"[333]

> Narrated Ibn al-Musaiyyab, the companions of the Prophet said: "Some men from my companions will come to my Lake-Fount and they will be driven away from it, and I will say: 'O Lord, my companions!' It will be said: 'You have no knowledge of what they innovated after you left, they turned apostate as renegades (reverted from Islām).'"[334]

The aforementioned narrations point towards those who associated with the Prophet (pbuh & hf); those who knew the Prophet. These reports beautifully correlate with the teachings of the Qur'ān and shed light about changes being made upon the Prophet's demise.

The Prophet (pbuh & hf) expressed:

> "There will come to me some people, whom I will recognise, and they will recognise me, but a barrier will be placed between me and them."

He also said: "Some men from my companions will come to the Lake Fount and they will be driven away from it..." meaning that some of those the Prophet (pbuh & hf) knew and he associated with, will be drawn away from his Lake and because the Prophet will recognise these companions, he will ask Allāh in order to manifest what happened on his demise. The Prophet had the fore knowledge of the innovations, which took place by those after his demise, but to bring it to light on the Day of Judgement, this process of revealing what took place will occur, just as Īsā (AS) will be asked in regards to those who did not accept him. Although he will know them, as he will witness against them, this process will reveal what took place.

> "And there is none of the People of the Book but must believe in him before his death; and on the Day of Judgment He will be a witness against them." Qur'ān 4:159

This is a topic in itself and is not the topic of our discussion. It can be taken into account by many Shī'ahs and Sunnis and discussed as a separate issue. However if we bring back our attention to the *Aḥadīth* of the Prophet (pbuh & hf), we find that the companions also testify to the fact that matters pertaining to the religion had been changed after his demise.

> Narrated Al-Musaiyyab: "I met al-Barā' ibn Āzib and said (to him): 'May you live prosperously! You enjoyed the company of the Prophet and gave him the Pledge of allegiance (of al-Hudaibīya) under the Tree.' On that, al-Barā' ibn Āzib said: 'O my nephew! You do not know what we have done after him (i.e. his death).'"[335]

Anas ibn Mālik spoke in regards to the prayers:

> Narrated Ghailan, Anas said: "'I do not find (now-a-days) things as they were (practiced) at the time of the Prophet.' Somebody said: 'The prayer (is as it was.)' Anas said: 'Have you not done in the prayer what you have done?'"

> Narrated Az-Zuhrī that he visited Anas ibn Mālik at Damascus and found him weeping and asked him why he was weeping. He replied: "I do not know anything which I used to know during the lifetime of Allāh's Apostle except this prayer which is being lost (not offered as it should be)."[336]
>
> Narrated Abū Sa'īd al-Khudrī: "The Prophet used to proceed to the *Musalla* on the days of Id-al-Fitr and Id-al-Adha; the first thing to begin with was the prayer and after that he would stand in front of the people and the people would keep sitting in their rows. Then he would preach to them, advise them and give them orders, (i.e. *khutba*). And after that if he wished to send an army for an expedition, he would do so, or if he wanted to give an order, he would do so, and then depart. The people followed this tradition till I went out with Marwān, the Governor of Madīnah, for the prayer of Id-al-Adha or Id-al-Fitr.
>
> When we reached the *Musalla*, there was a pulpit made by Kathīr ibn as-Salt. Marwān wanted to get up on that pulpit before the prayer. I got hold of his clothes but he pulled them and ascended the pulpit and delivered the *khutba* before the prayer. I said to him: 'By Allāh, you have changed (the Prophet's tradition).' He replied: 'O Abū Sa'īd! Gone is that which you know.' I said: 'By Allāh! What I know is better than what I do not know.' Marwān said: 'People do not sit to listen to our *khutba* after the prayer, so I delivered the *khutba* before the prayer.'"[337]

It is self evident that these reports were not uttered from people who were strangers to the Prophet (pbuh & hf), but lived amongst him before his demise and were very well known by him.

If companions such as al-Barā' ibn Āzib, Anas ibn Mālik, Abū Sa'īd al-Khudrī, expressed words in such a way as to portray that things had not remained as they should have, then can we truly rely upon each and every individual who was a companion of the Prophet (pbuh & hf) and follow any of them regardless?

Al-Barā' ibn Āzib acknowledged what was stated to him, that an allegiance to stand by the Prophet had occurred at al-Hudaibīya, but sadly after his demise this stand did not altogether remain with everyone.

Anas ibn Mālik's words in regards to the prayer are enough to teach us that not even the prayers were being offered correctly by everyone, his testification to the fact that things were not being practiced as prescribed by the Prophet.

Marwān who was a governor of Muā'wīya was not concerned when Abū Sa'īd al-Khudrī addressed that he was changing i.e. innovating the actual order of the Prophet (pbuh & hf). He continued to offer the *khutbah* before the prayer without any concern. Do we know whose orders this man was following? It would be correct to state that he was not following the Prophet's orders.

> Narrated 'Abdullāh ibn 'Umar: "Allāh's Apostle used to offer the prayer of 'Id-al-Adha and 'Id-ul-Fitr and then deliver the *khutba* after the prayer."[338]

> Narrated by Ibn 'Abbās: "I offered the 'Id prayer with Allāh's Apostle, Abū Bakr, 'Umar and 'Uthmān and all of them offered the prayer before delivering the *khutba.*"[339]

It would be beneficial to just re-iterate a verse, which has been already stated in section five.

> "When the Hypocrites come to thee they say: 'We bear witness that thou art indeed the Apostle of Allāh.' Yea Allāh knoweth that thou art indeed His Apostle and Allāh beareth witness that the hypocrites are indeed liars." Qur'ān 63:1

We need to realise that hypocrites were also counted as amongst those who had professed their faith in Islām and regardless of whether they were known or not, the Prophet (pbuh & hf) addressed them as his companions.

> Narrated Zayd ibn Thābit: "When the Prophet went out for (the battle of) Uhud, some of those who had gone out with him returned. The **companions of the Prophet were divided into two groups**. One group said, we will fight them, the other group said we will not fight them. So, this divine inspiration was revealed: 'Then what is the matter with you that you are divided into two parties **concerning the hypocrites** (4.88).' The Prophet said: 'Madīnah expels the bad persons from it, as fire expels the impurities of silver.'[340]

> Narrated by Jābir ibn 'Abdullāh: "We were in a Ghazwa (Sufyān once said, in an army) and a man from the emigrants kicked an *Ansārī* man (on the buttocks with his foot). The *Ansārī* man said: 'O the *Ansār*! (Help!),' and the emigrant said: 'O the emigrants! (Help!).' Allah's Apostle heard that and said: 'What is this call for, which is characteristic of the period of ignorance?' They said: 'O Allāh's Apostle! A man from the emigrants kicked one of the *Ansār* (on the buttocks with his foot).' Allāh's Apostle said: 'Leave it (that call) as is a detestable thing.' 'Abdullāh ibn Ubai heard that and said: 'Have the (the emigrants) done so? By Allāh, if we return to Madīnah, surely, the more honourable will expel there from the meaner.' When this statement reached the Prophet, 'Umar got up and said: "O Allāh's Apostle! **Let me chop off the head of this hypocrite** ('Abdullāh ibn Ubai)!' The Prophet said: 'Leave him, lest the people say that **Muḥammad kills his companions**." The *Ansār* were then more in number than the emigrants when the latter came to Madīnah, but later on the emigrants increased."[341]

The Prophet (pbuh & hf) did not name all the hypocrites in his lifetime. We observe that although 'Abdullāh ibn Ubai was one of the known hypocrites amongst the Muslims, the Prophet still counted him as one of his companions. Such a companion did not receive the glad tidings from Allāh, which is given to the individual who keeps his oath and keeps his faith in tact.

As already mentioned Allāh always gives glad tidings and is pleased with those who remain steadfast in their good actions and continue to remain like this until the day they die.

Those who remained on the righteous path, remained with what the Prophet conveyed will most certainly be admitted in the garden of Paradise without reckoning and will not serve any term in *Jahannum* (the Hell-Fire). Allāh will not be pleased about those who are against these very people. They are the faithful servants, the loved ones of Allāh, the *Ummah* that upholds the truth, enjoining what is good and forbidding what is not.

> "Let there be **among** you an *Ummah* inviting to all that is good, enjoining what is right, and forbidding what is wrong. They are the ones to attain felicity. Be not like those who are divided amongst themselves and fall into disputations after receiving clear signs, for them is a dreadful chastisement. On the day when some faces will be (lit up with) white, and some faces will be (in the gloom of) black; to those whose faces will be black, (will be said): 'Did ye reject faith after accepting it? Taste then the chastisement for rejecting faith.'" Qur'ān 3:104-106

> Narrated 'Abdullāh ibn Mughaffal: "Allāh's Messenger said: "Fear Allāh regarding my companions, and do not make them a target after I am gone. He who loves them does so from love of me, and he who hates them does so from hatred of me. He who injures them has injured me, he who injures me has injured Allāh, and he who injures Allāh will soon be punished by Him."[342]

The narration stated above would have to be taken in a specific context, in regards to those who remained steadfast, who did not change.

Succession of the Prophet (PBUH)

Faith cannot be measured in an individual, it is known by Allāh, there are differing degrees of faith in us all, and extreme faith lies in total obedience to His law due to the great awareness of His existence. The people who hold such immense faith in their hearts are blessed with the understanding of the religion, they are the great believers whom Allāh favours and loves.

The associates of the Prophet (pbuh & hf) were many; they were from varying backgrounds, some were more learned than others, some had embraced Islām later than others. Would following any one of these people truly provide us with a key of security towards the teachings of the religion? Do the words of Allāh provide us with this notion, words, which can never be changed, which can never be thought of as dubious? Does not Allāh's criterion suffice us? Allāh has expressed that amongst those who had professed their faith in Islām, there were hypocrites and rebellious transgressors hence knowing this does not give us the conviction to follow whom we wish.

Section 16

We have the Criterion.

In our everyday lives we witness various events, whether they are on the TV or Radio, at School or College, or even in our place of work for that matter. These events could be evil and sinful or moral and good.

What we find is that various people will comment on these events taking place around us. Acts, which are immoral and unjust, are usually spoken against and acts, which are moral and good, are usually praised and commended.

If an individual has committed a heinous crime and is detained in prison, we as citizens within a law-abiding community will class the act of the criminal as being morally wrong. Does this mean that we are passing the sentence? Are we committing a sin by classing the criminal act as against the law? The judge is the one who passes the verdict on the offence committed, but due to our understanding of right and wrong we will not approve of the **act**, which has taken place.

All too often when an issue is addressed, we find that the words: "Who am I to judge?" Or, "Who are you to judge?" are spoken.

Allāh has sent upon mankind His law in order for us to distinguish between right and wrong. The Qur'ān sent as a revelation to the Messenger of Allāh (pbuh and his family) is the criterion, the distinguisher between what is right and wrong. If an action is in variance to the Qur'ān, there is no doubt that a just person will disapprove of that particular act.

Allāh states:

> "Those that turn (to Allāh) in repentance; that serve Him and praise Him; that wander in devotion to the Cause of Allāh; that bow down and prostrate themselves in prayer; that **enjoin good and forbid evil**; and observe the limits set by Allāh; (these do rejoice). So proclaim the glad tidings to the believers." Qur'ān 9:112

We have the Criterion

It is odd for the Qur'ān teaches us to **enjoin the good and forbid the evil**, yet the words: "Who am I to judge?" Or, "Who are you to judge?" seem to be spoken by many Muslims. Speaking against an **action**, which is in variance to the teachings of the Qur'ān, does not mean we are passing the sentence or will give verdict on the Day of Judgement, but again, due to our understanding of right and wrong we will not approve of the **act**, which has taken place.

If a young boy was reading about a certain event, which started to trouble him and then enquired about it to an adult, but then the latter replied by stating: "Who am I to judge?" This answer would not only confuse the youngster but he would grow up with a fear of asking about something he wishes to make sense of.

Allāh has given us the ability to acquire knowledge; He has given us intelligence in order to be able to comprehend matters. This has been given to every human being in order that we may be able to distinguish the truth from the falsehood, the right from the wrong. This is not only a teaching for the Jews and the Christians but also for the Muslims. Is it acceptable for us to remain idle and not use the faculties Allāh has given us just for the reason that we have been born into a Muslim family? We also have a duty to understand and acquire religious knowledge. Allāh states:

> "The worst human for Allāh, is the deaf and the dumb, who have no sense (*ya'kilūn*)." Qur'ān 8:22

> "It is He Who brought you forth from the wombs of your mothers when ye knew nothing; and He gave you hearing and sight and intelligence and affections, that ye may give thanks (to Allāh)." Qur'ān 16:78

Allāh addresses every human being in the stated verses, even those who state they believe in Prophet Muḥammad (pbuh & hf). He reminds us that we can hear, we can see, we have been given intelligence, in order that we may understand and give thanks to Him for giving us these capabilities.

If we use the ability, which Allāh has given us, and follow that which is in accordance with His words, we are not sinners; we are in fact obeying Him. Allāh states:

> "O ye who believe, fear Allāh and always say a Word directed to the right i.e. Truth." Qur'ān 33:70

If a person speaks in accordance with the light of the Qur'ān, they are not the wrong doers, as Allāh always welcomes the speaking of words, which are directed towards the truth. Think back to the stand of Fāṭimah (AS). The wrong doers are those who fail to speak in accordance with the light of what has been revealed.

> "And if any fail to judge by (the light of) what Allāh hath revealed they are (no better than) wrongdoers." Qur'ān 5:45

Allāh does not approve of those who speak through conjecture, those who speak contrary to the truth.

> "They have no knowledge therein, they follow nothing but conjecture, and conjecture avails nothing against the truth. Therefore shun those who turn away from our Message and desire nothing but the life of this world." Qur'ān 53:28-29

Imām 'Alī (AS) speaking out.

After the demise of the Prophet (pbuh & hf), Imām 'Alī (AS) spoke of his appointment as the *mawlā* of the Muslims. He spoke against the happenings at the Saqīfah of Banī Saidah, which consequently led to the appointment of Abū Bakr.

The historians Ibn Qutaybah and al-Mas'ūdī have reported that after the events at the Saqīfah Imām 'Alī (AS) stated to Abū Bakr:

> "'You have trampled on my rights, refused to consult with me, and ignored my claims.' Abū Bakr's answered: 'Yes, but I was fearful of chaos and disorder.'"[343]

Imām 'Alī (AS) speaking out

Ibn Qutaybah also reported the following:

> "When the people swore allegiance to Abū Bakr after the death of the Prophet, Abū 'Ubaydah proposed to 'Alī: 'Abandon this *amr* (authority) to Abū Bakr. If you survive him, you are worthier of the office of caliphate than anyone else, for no one can doubt your abundant faith, virtue and intelligence. Furthermore you preceded in your profession of Islām, and you enjoy the additional advantage of being related to the Messenger of God by blood and by marriage.' 'Alī replied: 'O Migrants! I entreat you by God not to remove governance from the Household of the Prophet, and to establish it in your house; do not deprive the People of Muḥammad's House of their station and office.'"[344]

Abū Bakr was a companion and the Imām recognised his connection to the Prophet (pbuh & hf) when he was alive and there was no hostility between any of them. Imām 'Alī (AS) was a man of principles and his words had no bearing towards targeting individuals for no reason. Imām 'Alī spoke out in accordance to the stipulation, which was laid down by the Prophet and would have done so irrespective of who it was, who took the leadership position. The Imām never would have spoken against the subject of leadership, if the leadership was rightfully so. The act, which had occurred was spoken against as his stance was only towards establishing the truth, to speak in accordance with the truth and nothing else.

Imām 'Alī (AS) also spoke out when he was given his right to exercise authority as the *Khalīfah* long after the demise of the Prophet (pbuh & hf), wanting those who had heard the Prophet's proclamation of his leadership to stand forth and testify to what they had heard. He, himself revived the tradition of al-Ghadir; its significance can also be grasped from the words spoken by the Imām.

It is reported:

> "We were in the camp of 'Alī on the day of Battle of Camel, where 'Alī sent for Talha to talk to him (before

> the beginning of war). Talha came forward, and 'Alī told him: 'I adjure you by Allāh! Didn't you hear the Messenger of Allāh when he said, whoever I am his *mawlā*, this 'Alī is his *mawlā*. O God love whoever loves him, and be hostile to whoever is hostile to him?' Talha replied: 'Yes.' 'Alī said: 'Then why do you want to fight me?'"[345]

> 'Abd al-Rahmān ibn Abū Laylah said: "I witnessed 'Alī administering an oath to the people in the plain of Rahbah. 'Alī said: 'I adjure those of you in the name of Allāh who heard the Messenger of Allāh on the day of al-Ghadir saying, 'Alī is the *mawlā* of whom I am *mawlā* to stand up and to testify. He who was not an eyewitness doesn't need to stand up.' Thereupon twelve such companions who had participated in the Battle of Badr stood up. The occasion is still fresh in my memory."[346]

Imām Nasā'ī has narrated similar to the above report on the authority of three other people, Umāyah ibn Sa'd, Zayd ibn Yathigh, and Sa'id ibn Wahab.[347]

> Narrated Abū al-Tufayl: "'Alī gathered the people in the plain of Rahbah in year 35 A.H. and adjured in the name of Allāh every Muslim male present there who had heard the proclamation at al-Ghadir from the Messenger of Allāh to stand up and testify what they had heard from the Messenger on the Day of Ghadīr. Thereupon thirty men stood up and gave evidence that the Prophet grasped 'Alī's hand and said to the audience: 'He, 'Alī has superior authority over those who believe me to have superiority over their lives. O Allāh! Love him who loves him and hate him who hates him.' Abū Ṭufayl says that it was in a state of great mental agitation that he left the plain of Rahbah, for the Muslim masses had not complied with the tradition. He therefore called on Zayd ibn Arqam and told him what he heard from 'Alī. Zayd told him not to entertain any doubt about it for he himself had

> heard the Messenger of Allāh uttering those words."[348]

Imām 'Alī (AS) stated: "I adjure you in the name of Allāh," his statement expressing the importance of the words spoken by the Prophet (pbuh & hf). If the words carried the meaning of a plain friend as stated in section six, was there any need for the Imām to reiterate and call upon people to testify that they had heard the Prophet call Imām 'Alī a friend? A man who had fought alongside them in the Battles of Badr and Uhud, a true friend of the Muslims from the very beginning and defender of the Prophet. The importance of Imām 'Alī's authority can be understood from the words of Abū al-Tufayl as he described that Imām 'Alī "was in a state of great mental agitation that he left the plain of Rahbah, for the Muslim masses had not complied with the tradition."

If we state matters along the same terms as Imām 'Alī (AS) did and the words: "Who are you to judge?" are addressed to us, then these words would also apply to the Imām. If we were alive at the time of Imām 'Alī would we have stood in front of him and said: "Who are you to judge?" when his criterion came from the Qur'ān and his knowledge far exceeded ours? Imām 'Alī revived the words spoken by the Prophet (pbuh & hf) and to this day it is devout Shī'ahs who follow this and continue to revive them, not because of their own opinion but because these words spoken were an actual order from Allāh and His Prophet.

The Companions stand with the Imām.

Many companions who remained with the Imām protested to what had happened on the day of the Saqīfah, companions such as al-'Abbās ibn 'Abd al-Muṭṭālib, al-Fadl ibn al-'Abbās, az-Zubayr, Khālid ibn Sa'īd, al-Miqdād, Salmān, Abū Dharr, 'Ammār, al-Barā', 'Ubayy ibn Ka'b.

> "A man went to the Prophet's mosque and found Miqdād ibn 'Umar kneeling on the ground, the man narrated: 'One day I went to the Prophet's mosque and I saw a man kneeling on the ground.' He was sighing as deeply as if he had lost the whole world

and saying to himself: 'How strange that the Quraysh have taken the caliphate out of the hands of the Prophet's family.'"[349]

"When 'Uthman was elected as caliph 'Ammār ibn Yāsir spoke out: 'It is not the first time you have denied the caliphate to the one most deserving it.'"[350]

We all have the right to speak out when it is in accordance with the Truth.

There is an incident where a woman objected to 'Umar when he wished to stop an increase in the *Mahr*. He had delivered a sermon to the people, which caused her to speak out.

"'If anyone marries and fixes a *mehr* (dowry) for more than 400 dirhams for his wife, I will inflict the prescribed punishment on him and will deposit the excess amount in the *Bait al-Māl* (Public treasury).' A woman from the audience called out: "Umar! Is what you say more acceptable or Allāh's ordinance? Does not Almighty Allāh say: 'And if you wish to have (one) wife in place of another and you have given one of them a heap of gold, then take not back any of it.' Qur'ān 4:20

Having heard this verse and the reply of the woman, 'Umar said: 'You have better knowledge of *fiqh* and problems than 'Umar, all of you, including even the women observing *purdah* (veil) sitting in their homes.'

Then 'Umar again mounted the pulpit and said: 'Although I have forbidden you to give more than 400 dirhams as dowry to your wives. I now permit you to give as much as you like beyond the appointed limit. There is no harm in it.'"[351]

Was this woman's judgement not in accordance with the teachings of the Qur'ān? Was she wrong to object to what 'Umar was saying? Why did the woman not think to herself: "Who am I to judge over what the caliph is going to do because I am only a woman and he is the leader of the state?" The woman recognised that Allāh has not set a limit on the *Mahr*; this is the decision and responsibility of the individual to whom the woman is being wed and therefore spoke out against it. These words were accepted by the caliph and he did not reprimand her. The words: "Who are you to judge?" become meaningless when addressed to the individual who is speaking in accordance to the truth.

If we take another example:

Al-Ḥasan al-Basrī stated in regards to Mu'āwīya:

> "His killing of Ḥujr and his companions. Woe unto him twice for Ḥujr and his companions."[352]

Ḥujr ibn 'Ādī was recognised as a righteous and ascetic man.

> Shurayh ibn Hānī' said: "He was among those who performed the ritual prayers, payed *Zakāt*, performed frequently the lesser and the greater *Ḥajj*, enjoyed (the people) to do good deeds and prevented them from doing evil deeds. It was forbidden to shed his blood and to take his property."[353]

Mu'āwīya performed the *Ḥajj* after the killing of Ḥujr, and on his return visited 'Ā'isha, who stated to him:

> "Did you not fear Allāh when you killed Ḥujr and his companions?"[354]

If Ḥujr and his men were spreading mischief and murder or were misleading others, these are not the words, which would have been used in regards to them. If it was legitimate to have had them killed, no individual at all would have spoken against it and there would have been no reason for anyone to have feared Allāh.

After the death of Mughīra ibn Shu'ba, Ziyād ibn Abih who was given the position of governor over Kūfa by Mu'āwīya, was given orders to capture Ḥujr and his men in order to execute them. When they were about to be executed it was stated to them:

> "We have been ordered that if you show negative feelings towards 'Alī and curse him you shall be free to go, otherwise you shall have to die (shall be killed). Ḥujr answered with: 'I can't utter those words from my tongue that would anger my Lord.'"[355]

This proved that the reason for killing Ḥujr and his men had nothing to do with their disobedience but their love towards Imām 'Alī (AS). Ḥujr ibn 'Ādī was a man who understood the position of the Imām, he and his followers were in no way pleased with the actions of the government. They protested against their actions and the cursing of the Imām, and to be asked to curse the Imām on the point of death, which they rejected, proved that Ḥujr and his men were opposed to this very act and were against this abominable practice. A practice if they had of carried out would have saved them from being executed! Who can state that Ḥujr and his men were of a low rank when opposing such an action and who can state that they followed the wrong path, when their stand was strictly in defence to what Allāh and His Apostle had revealed. Their defence marked their devotion to the truth, such truth as "to whomsoever I am *mawlā* 'Alī is *mawlā*, he who is hostile to 'Alī is hostile to me, he who curses 'Alī curses me, none but a believer loves him, none but a hypocrite hates him," all these sayings and statements of the Prophet (pbuh & hf) were known and followed by those who remained with the truth and fought for it. Ḥujr's love and submission was proven with his martyrdom and his stance against Mu'āwīya can never be dampened by the words: "Who was he to judge?"

Every individual has a right to speak when he or she is speaking in accordance to the truth, as Allāh commands us to enjoin the good and forbid the evil. Nobody has the right to stop this person when Allāh has given them this right and the Prophet (pbuh & hf) himself stated: "Speak the truth even if it is bitter, speak the truth even if it is against yourself," and Imām 'Alī (AS) spoke out as did those righteous beings who remained loyal to him.

Allāh allows us to speak fourth in justice and He allows us to differentiate between right and wrong. The Qur'ān is part of His wisdom revealed to the Prophet (pbuh & hf) who acquainted the Muslims with its knowledge, to remain on the right path, a path if left, would deter us from its great wisdom, leading us to follow self opinion and matters contrary to its teachings. The first to use self opinion was Iblīs (Satan), when he regarded himself as superior to Ādam (AS) as he was created out of fire and Ādam out of clay. His self-opinion and arrogance in not bowing down to Ādam was shunned by Allāh and his one self-opinionated answer earned him the fire of Hell. True words are a safety from the wrath of Allāh, self-opinion and arrogance the traits of the dwellers of the fire of Hell as Iblīs has demonstrated.

Supporting the truth is what every Muslim has been taught to do, not hiding it away to gather cobwebs like an old hat in a cupboard.

> "And he who brings the Truth and he who confirms (and supports) it such are the men who do right." Qur'ān 39:34

> "We sent a foretime Messengers with Clear Signs and sent down with them the Book and the Balance (of right and wrong), that men may stand fourth in justice." Qur'ān 57:25

Section 17

Fulfilment or Negligence?

Contemplate on the following.

Would an owner of a large business leave it unattended if he was called away for a long period of time? If so, this portrays his own negligence and that he has no concern in the way he wishes it to be managed. Leaving such a matter could result in heavy losses. However, if the owner places an individual whom he can trust and is able to ensure correct management of the business, he safeguards it from such destruction. He at the same time ensures the security his family needs. This will give him peace of mind.

Our reasoning mind informs us that the type of individual who leaves things not taken care of, who has no concern for his family or his friends, is an irresponsible, uncaring and neglectful individual. This type of individual is not concerned about his state of affairs or the well being of others. Can we believe that a righteous individual would resemble such characteristics?

Of all characters, the Prophet's (pbuh & hf) was the most exalted, upright and diligent; he could never have been compared to an irresponsible, uncaring and neglectful individual.

The Prophet (pbuh & hf) stated: "He who wakes up without being concerned with the affairs of the *Ummah* is not one of us." He spoke in general under such a context in regards to the concerns of the people. What one must contemplate on is whether or not he had any concern towards the affairs of his *Ummah* towards the end of his life? Did he not have any concern in regards to the correct implementation of the Qur'ān? It is impossible to think that the Prophet had no concern whatsoever. Common sense teaches us that when the time approached for him to leave this world, his concern would have greatly increased.

The Prophet's (pbuh & hf) presence provided the people around him with the security they needed, these good Muslims would have wanted this security to remain, the clarity and preciseness of his words to remain in tact.

Fulfilment or Negligence?

A security guard, guards what is of value, he guards against embezzlement, keeping in tact that which is of importance to the owner, this individual is a protector, and he is serving the interests of the law and abiding by it. In the same way, a guard was required in order to ensure the safety of the Qur'ān, its safety against embezzlement.

History teaches us that towards the end of the Prophet's (pbuh & hf) life, he requested writing materials in order to inscribe something, which would prevent the people from being led astray.

> Narrated 'Abdullāh ibn 'Abbās: "When the time of the death of the Prophet approached while there were some men in the house, and among them was 'Umar ibn al-Khaṭṭṭāb; the Prophet said: 'Come near, let me write for you a writing after which you will never go astray.' 'Umar said: 'The Prophet is seriously ill (*ghalabahū al-wajā'a*), and **you have the Qur'ān, so Allāh's Book is sufficient for us**.' The people in the house differed and disputed. Some of them said: 'Come near so that Allāh's Apostle may write for you a writing, after which you will not go astray,' while some of them said what 'Umar said. When they made much noise and differed greatly before the Prophet, he said to them, 'Go away and leave me.' Ibn 'Abbās used to say: 'It was a great disaster that their difference and noise prevented Allāh's Apostle from writing that writing for them.'"[356]

> Narrated 'Ubaydullāh ibn 'Abdullāh: "Ibn 'Abbās said: 'When Allāh's Apostle was on his deathbed and there were some men in the house,' he said: 'Come near, I will write for you something after which you will not go astray.' Some of them (i.e. his companions) said: 'Allah's Apostle is seriously ill (*ghalabahū al-wajā'a*) and you have the (Holy) Qur'ān. Allāh's Book is sufficient for us.' So the people in the house differed and started disputing. Some of them said: 'Give him writing material so that he may write for you something after which you will not go astray,' while

> the others said the other way round. So when their talk and differences increased, Allāh's Apostle said: 'Get up.' Ibn Abbās used to say: 'No doubt, it was very unfortunate (a great disaster) that Allāh's Apostle was prevented from writing for them that writing because of their differences and noise.'"[357]

Also:

> Narrated Jābir ibn 'Abdullāh: "When the Messenger of God fell sick with the illness that was to end in his death, he asked for paper in order to write down for his *Ummah* instructions that would prevent them from ever going astray or accusing each other of having gone astray. Words were exchanged among those present in the Prophet's house and disagreement resulted in the course of which 'Umar uttered words that caused the Prophet to order him to leave the house."[358]

If our father was seriously ill and asked the family:

> "Please give me some writing materials in order that I can write for you a document that will safeguard you all when I am gone."

We may feel that he is too poorly to write down what he wishes and state this to him. Then suggest to him that we could write for him instead, would this not please him and give peace to his dear soul? Would not his face become bright with the affection and love we are showing towards him? Would he not wish for us to stay with him and help him in his request? Passing ones own directive on the matter, when it is not inline with his yearning would not please him; it would not brighten his dear face and would only distress him. We all have a tendency to jump in on matters without them first fully being stated by the individual who is addressing them to us and we do not think anything of it. We really do not feel that we have done anything wrong, whereas the individual who wishes to address his or her matter will become disappointed with this action.

If we direct our attention towards the Prophet (pbuh & hf), when a request is given from him, that request is never given for the sake of grievance; but for the sake of an advantage to the righteous servants of Allāh. Understanding that our Prophet was concerned for the Muslims even on the brink of death would make us realise that he was in his full senses when he wanted to write that, which would prevent us from being led astray.

> Narrated Sa'īd ibn Jubair: "Ibn 'Abbās said: 'Thursday! What (great thing) took place on Thursday!' Then he started weeping till his tears wetted the gravels of the ground.' Then he said: 'On Thursday the illness of Allāh's Apostle was aggravated and he said: 'Fetch me writing materials so that I may have something written to you after which you will never go astray.' The people (present there) differed in this matter and people should not differ before a Prophet. They said: 'Allāh's Apostle is seriously sick (*hajara RasūlAllāh*).' The Prophet said: 'Let me alone, as the state in which I am now, is better than what you are calling me for.' The Prophet on his death-bed gave three orders saying: 'Expel the pagans from the Arabian Peninsula, respect and give gifts to the foreign delegates as you have seen me dealing with them.' I forgot the third (order)." (Ya'qūb ibn Muḥammad said: "I asked Al-Mughīra ibn 'Abd al-Raḥmān about the Arabian Peninsula and he said: 'It comprises Mecca, Madīnah, al-Yamama and Yemen.'" Ya'qūb added: "And al-Arj, the beginning of Tiḥama.") [359]

> Narrated Ibn 'Abbās: "Thursday! And how great that Thursday was! The ailment of Allāh's Apostle became worse (on Thursday) and he said, fetch me something so that I may write to you something after which you will never go astray. The people (present there) differed in this matter, and it was not right to differ before a Prophet. Some said: 'What is wrong with him? (Do you think) he is delirious (seriously ill)? (*mā Sha'nūhū a'hajara*) Ask him (to understand his state).' So they went to the Prophet and asked him again. The Prophet said: 'Leave me, for my present state is better than what you call me for.'

> Then he ordered them to do three things. He said: 'Turn the pagans out of the 'Arabian Peninsula; respect and give gifts to the foreign delegations as you have seen me dealing with them.' Sa'id ibn Jubair, the sub-narrator said that Ibn 'Abbās kept quiet as regards the third order, or he said, 'I forgot it.'[360]

'Abdullāh ibn 'Abbās called this incident a great disaster, his eyes flooded with tears from recalling this event in his memory. Ibn 'Abbās, whose narrations are mentioned in plenty within the books of both *Ṣaḥīḥs*, had clearly recalled this event, but somehow when mentioning three orders from the Prophet (pbuh & hf); he kept quiet about the very last one because he had forgotten. This indeed is very strange as such a distinguished companion could not remember. Although 'Abdullāh ibn 'Abbās was a youngster, his memory proved no problem in dealing with verses of the Qur'ān, something 'Umar acknowledged, and took an interest in him at the time of his caliphate. Ibn Abbās recalled many words and sayings of the Prophet, and he was much younger in age when the latter was alive.

What we must also contemplate on is, that there was nothing stopping the Prophet (pbuh & hf) from writing what he had been requested to write, he could easily have done so when everyone had left.

If it had been binding on the Prophet (pbuh & hf) to write down what would prevent the people from being led astray, he would never have disobeyed the commands of the Almighty and not written it down, regardless of what had happened on that day. The Prophet's directive to write this matter down, at that time, was therefore cancelled by Allāh and not himself.

We all should realise that Allāh knew what was to happen and through the proceeding of this event, it became apparent that the people were already acquainted with what the Prophet wanted to write; this was clearly revealed through this event. One group of people wanted the request to be executed whilst the other group was stating that the Book of Allāh was sufficient.

Fulfilment or Negligence?

If the people had not have known what it was the Prophet (pbuh & hf) was directing them to, Allāh would never have allowed him to leave this matter unclear to them, as his duty was to convey everything, which Allāh had revealed to him.

> "With clear proofs and writings; and We have revealed unto thee the Remembrance that thou mayst explain to mankind that which hath been revealed for them, and that haply they may reflect."
> Qur'ān 16:44

Hence there was no negligence on behalf of the Prophet (pbuh & hf) on this issue.

Section 18

The word Shī'ah.

The word Shī'ah actually seems to deter people from the followers of the Imāms of Ahl al-Bayt, calling them deviants and those who are astray, hence this word needs to be explained.

All human beings regardless of their descent are devoted to something, be it that, which is based upon religion or not.

Wherever there is good there is also evil, wherever there is justice there is also injustice, wherever there is one who abides by the law, there is always one who disobeys the law. Anyone portraying any one of these actions is a follower of that, which is correct or not. We find that the word Shī'ah has been used in the Qur'ān to portray this in regards to groups of people.

Allāh states:

> "And most surely Abraham was among the ***Shī'ah tīhī*** **(group of followers)** of him (Noah)." Qur'ān 37:83

Ibrāhīm (AS) followed the example of Nūh (AS) and therefore was addressed by Allāh as one who was amongst this group. Obviously these followers were from the **righteous party** of Allāh.

> "And surely the party of Allāh are successful." Qur'ān 58:22

Allāh did not convey the word *Shī'ah tīhī* in the quoted verse (37:83) in relation to a deviant. He addressed his righteous prophet with such words. If we were to hear these words expressed in regards to individuals that are following the righteous group, should we speak against it?

The following verse of the Qur'ān also states:

> "And he Moses went into the city at a time when people (of the city) were not watching, so he found

> therein two men fighting, one being of his ***Shī'ah tīhī*** and the other being his enemy, and the one who was of his ***Shī'ah tīhī*** cried out to him for help against the one who was of his enemy." Qur'ān 28:15

Again, Allāh has the used word *Shī'ah tīhī*, but this time for the individual who was amongst the group who followed the religion of Mūsa (AS), hence, a Shī'ah of Mūsa. Can we address this individual as amongst the group that was on the wrong path?

We also find that Allāh addresses people who are within the same religion but separate amongst one another as ***Shī'ahan***.

> "Those who split up their religion and become ***Shī'ah an* (groups),** each party rejoicing in that which is with itself." Qur'ān 30:32

This could only happen through the following of self-opinion over the prescribed ordinances, causing branching and splitting of the one true religion. When commands are rejected and ignored by people, then these people do not remain on the one true path, but split it apart. Those who understand this and remain with the party that follows the words of Allāh and His Apostle and shun away deviance are the ones who are on the right path. Such people do not belong to those groups who have split away from the truth and rejected it.

Those who adhere to the Ahl al-Bayt of the Prophet (pbuh & hf) do not belong to the other groups, which do not recognise their authority. They are the Shī'ahs of Ahl al-Bayt, and whenever we hear this word in regards to them, we should always remember to translate it.

> "When the verse in the Qur'ān: 'As for those who believe and do good, surely they are the best of creatures, (Qur'ān 98:7)' was revealed, the Prophet said to 'Alī: 'It is for you and your Shī'ah.'
>
> He further said: 'I swear by the one who controls my life that this man ('Alī) and his Shī'ah shall secure deliverance on the Day of Ressurection.'"[361]

Those who sincerely adhere to what the Prophet (pbuh & hf) taught are the true followers; they are best of creatures in the sight of Allāh.

> The Prophet said: "O 'Alī! (On the day of Judgement) you and your Shī'ah will come towards Allāh well-pleased and well-pleasing and there will come to Him your enemies angry and stiff-necked (i.e. their heads forced up)."[362]

> The Prophet also said: "Glad tiding O 'Alī! Verily you and your Shī'ah will be in Paradise."[363]

Individuals who truly follow Imām Ali (AS) are in fact following what the Prophet (pbuh & hf) stated, and Allāh teaches:

> "Say: 'If you love Allāh then follow me and Allāh will love you and forgive you your sins for Allāh is Oft Forgiving Most Merciful.'" Qurān 3:31

Individuals of this calibre will most certainly attain deliverance on the Day of Resurrection.

A narration from Imām Ja'far as-Sādiq (AS) states:

> Narrated 'Alī ibn Maḥzyar from Ja'far ibn Muḥammad, from Ismaīl ibn Abbād, from ('Abdullāh) ibn Bikair, from Abū 'Abdullāh Ja'far ibn Muḥammad who said: "'Surely, we love from amongst our Shī'ahs, one who is wise, understanding, well-versed in religion, tolerant, obliging, patient, truthful and faithful.' Then he said: 'Surely, Allāh has specially blessed His prophet's with the noble virtues of good behaviour. So, whoever has those qualities, should praise and thank Allāh for it, and whoever does not have them, should earnestly entreat and seek from Allāh...'"[364]

Imām Ja'far as-Sādiq (AS) also states:

> "*Shī'ahtū nalladhīna idhā khalow dhikrullāha kathīran,* (Our true Shī'āh are those who, when they are alone, remember Allāh abundantly)."[365]

The word Shī'ah

Such narrations illuminate to us the true nature of the Shī'ahs of Ahl al-Bayt, the true followers the Imams (AS) spoke of. These followers do not have the characteristics of a deviant. They strive to combat their illegitimate self desires, their arrogance, and their jealousy. They will take every step towards the building up of a sincere and good character, and will do their utmost to follow that which is righteous and submit to the divine command of the Almighty.

We must understand, the Prophet's (pbuh & hf) Ahl al-Bayt are not amongst the party of Satan and any individual who strictly adheres to them, is adhering to the Qur'ān and the *Sunnah* of the Prophet as taught by them.

Sunni brothers and sisters have taken their teachings from the Imāms of the Ahl al-Sunnah wa al-Jammāh, Imām Abū Ḥanīfah, Imām Malik, Imām Shāfi'ī and Imām Aḥmad ibn Ḥanbal and are in fact following them.

The word *Rafidī* (rejecter) is directed towards Shī'ahs because they reject the leadership of others except the Ahl al-Bayt. This word is portrayed in a bad light against Shī'ahs, who are in fact **accepters** of a command given by the Prophet (pbuh & hf). We read:

> Imām Muḥammad al-Bāqir (the fifth Imam of the Ahl al-Bayt) said: "When I narrate a *Ḥadīth* without mentioning its chain of narrators, then my link in that is my father (Imām Zayn al-Ābidīn, the fourth Imām) from my grandfather al-Ḥusayn (the third Imām, Imām al-Ḥasan being the second) from his father Imām 'Alī, (the first Imām) from his grandfather, the Messenger of Allāh from Jibra'īl, from Allāh, the Almighty, the Great."[366]

Now, can anybody seriously state that this is a deviant link, a rejecter link? If an individual is sincerely following the teachings of these Imāms, deviant cannot be the word used to describe these individuals and the word Shī'ah in regards to them cannot be used to denote the same.

Succession of the Prophet (PBUH)

Allāh and His Prophet (pbuh & hf) used the word Shī'ah under the context of those who are on the right path. Hence, whenever we come across the word, it is incumbent on us to understand what it relates to, and when it relates to the right cause, we must think twice before asserting evil towards it.

Section 19

Is 'Abdullāh ibn Sa'ba important?

'Abdullāh ibn Sa'ba is a man who many Muslims comment on in relation to the Shī'ahs and mention that he appeared during the caliphate of Uthmān.

This character mentioned in al-Tabarī's works, allegedly spread the doctrine of 'Alī's successorship and executorship.[367]

As known, Shī'ahs illuminate that it was the Prophet (pbuh & hf) who had conveyed the message of the successor-ship of Imām 'Alī (AS) and the Ahl al-Bayt over the people. Many of the companions who had adhered to the Imām did not do so because of 'Abdullāh ibn Sa'ba. He was not present when the Prophet departed. These companions of the Prophet were very much loved by him.

> The Prophet said: "God has enjoined on me to love four people, and informed me that he loves them. When asked who they were, he replied: "Alī (repeating it three times), Abū Dharr, Salmān and al-Miqdād.'"[368]
>
> The Prophet said: "Paradise longs for three men, 'Alī, 'Ammār and Salmān."[369]

If 'Abdullāh ibn Sa'ba appeared at the time of the caliphate of Uthmān, as stated by many, and was the individual who had spread the doctrine of Imām 'Alī's leadership, why were there companions who already acknowledged this before 'Abdullāh ibn Sa'ba appeared on the scene?

> Narrated by Abū Waīl: "When 'Alī sent 'Ammār and al-Ḥasan to (the people of) Kūfa to urge them to fight, 'Ammār addressed them saying: 'I know that she (i.e. 'Ā'īsha) is the wife of the Prophet in this world and in the Hereafter (world to come), but Allāh has put you to test whether you follow Him (i.e. Allāh) or her.'"[370]

Is 'Abdullāh ibn Sa'ba important?

Whose instructions did 'Ammār follow who always remained loyal to Imām 'Alī (AS), who had also fought in the Battle of the Camel and Siffīn alongside the Imām? Could it be stated that because 'Ammār recognised the right of the Imām as the Shī'ahs do and also did so prior to the caliphate of 'Uthmān, he was a follower of 'Abdullāh ibn Sa'ba? Ammār knew of the truth and spoke obediently towards it, even when the nominated council selected by 'Umar were addressing the issue.

> It is reported: "'Abd al-Raḥmān called upon 'Alī. He offered him the caliphate with a new condition: 'Will you pledge to God and covenant him, that you will follow the Book of God and the teachings of the Messenger and the precepts of the two caliphs (Abū Bakr and 'Umar) after him?' 'Alī replied: 'I shall follow the Book of God, the teachings of the Prophet, and I shall follow my knowledge and endeavour to the maximum ability.' As he did not accept the offered condition, 'Abd al-Raḥmān turned to 'Uthmān with the same offer, and 'Uthmān accepted. It is said that 'Abd al-Raḥmān offered it to two men three times and in each time, 'Alī refused the condition and 'Uthmān accepted. 'Abd al-Raḥmān then said: 'God be my witness, I have transferred the responsibility from my neck to the neck of 'Uthmān.' Then he pledged his allegiance to him. 'Alī then said: **'This is not the first day you have collaborated against us (members of the House of the Prophet i.e. Ahl al-Bayt).** By God, you gave him the leadership only to return it to you later. God is able to change the situation.' 'Alī further said turning to 'Uthmān and 'Abd al-Raḥmān: 'May God plight you with a mutual and lasting hostility.' 'Abd al-Raḥmān answered: "Alī, do not incur trouble upon yourself (reminding him that the second caliph ordered them to kill any dissenter.) 'Alī then left giving his pledge to 'Uthmān, saying: 'What is written of timed events will reach maturity.' **'Ammār said to 'Abd al-Raḥmān: 'By God, you have left out the man of truth and correct judgement!' Al-Miqdād ibn al-Aswad**

> **joined in with 'Ammār saying: 'By God, I have never seen anything similar to what has been done to the members of the House of the Prophet after his death.** I am amazed at Quraysh who left out a man unequalled in knowledge, piety, and justice. If I had supporters I will fight the Quraysh now as I fought them in Battles of Badr and Uhud.' 'Abd al-Raḥmān said: 'Miqdād fear God, I am afraid that you will bring divisions amongst the Muslims.' Al-Miqdād retorted angrily, saying: 'The one who creates division is the one who follows his own selfish interest.'[371]

These companions had understood the proclamation by the Prophet (pbuh & hf) regarding Imām 'Alī's (AS) succession at the farewell pilgrimage. They believed this when the Prophet was alive and also believed in it the day he departed. 'Abdullāh ibn Sa'ba was of no significance to them, a man who had supposedly declared his faith in Islām during the time of the caliphate of 'Uthmān proclaiming something that they already knew. Was there any need for anyone to listen to this man, when they were already following the Imām?

It needs to be highlighted that companions such as Abū Dharr Ghiffārī, and Ammār ibn Yāsir[372] have been accused of being influenced by such a person as 'Abdullāh ibn Sa'ba. Can we not comprehend that if any mischief making and lies were being propagated by this converted Jew, then these companions never would have accepted them?

Let us read Abū Dharr's own words, which he stated to another converted Jew called Kāb al-Aḥbar:

> It is reported that Abū Dharr said to 'Uthmān after he came back from Damascus to Madīnah: "'It is not sufficient for a man to pay only Zakāt. He should add to that by helping the needy and feeding the hungry and spending in the way of God.' When Kāb al-Ahbar commented that: 'Whoever fulfils his prescribed duty, does not have to add anything to it.' Abū Dharr became angry and said to Kāb: 'Son of a Jewish lady,

> who are you to say this?' Then he hit him with his rod on his neck."[373]

If Abū Dharr did not accept the words of the above Jewish convert Kāb al-Aḥbar, then how could such an unimportant person by the name of 'Abdullāh ibn Sa'ba who was never heard of until the caliphate of 'Uthmān influence him to such a high degree?

These devoted companions and other faithful followers were not in need of a character called 'Abdullāh ibn Sa'ba to teach them. They did not need to join his throng during the caliphate of 'Uthmān, their lead was Imām 'Alī (AS), the greatest teacher they could ever have, as is the lead of the Shī'ahs of today, 'Abdullāh ibn Sa'ba playing no part in this.

Can we not comprehend that the story of 'Abdullāh ibn Sa'ba provides the means to disguise the true reasons why the Shī'ahs adhere to the twelve Imāms? This is to be deciphered for oneself.

We need to take note that all the reports found in regards to the presence and agitation of 'Abdullāh ibn Sa'ba and his influencing of certain companions have been narrated solely by one person called Saif ibn 'Umar al-Tamīmī, who was not even a witness to such events as he had not even been born. Sunni scholars specialising in the science of *Ḥadīth* have not given any credit to him or his veracity, instead they have commented that he was a weak reporter.

> Ibn Main (died in 277 A.H) said: "Saif is a weak reporter." Al-Nasā'ī (died in 303 A.H) said: "Saif is a weak reporter." Abū Dawūd (died in 317 A.H) said: "Saif is nothing, he was a liar. Some of his *Aḥadīth* were conveyed and the majority of them were denied." al-Ḥākim (died in 405 A.H) said: "Saif is abandoned and accused of being a heretic." Ibn Hibban said (died 354 A.H: "Saif reportedly forged stories and attributed them to reliable reporters, and he was accused of being a heretic." al-Darqūtnī (died in 385 A.H) said: "Saif is a weak reporter and was abandoned." Ibn Ḥajar al-'Asqalānī (died in 850A.H) said: "Saif is a weak reporter."[374]

Saif ibn 'Umar al-Tamīmī's reports are the only ones, which instigate that unrest was caused by 'Abdullāh ibn Sa'ba **in regards to the right of Imām 'Alī (AS)**. Many other reports recorded within the famous history books speak of the unrest being caused by the actions of the government. This shall be observed shortly, however, it is only Saif's remarks, which insinuate the provocation from 'Abdullāh ibn Sa'ba and illuminate that this mans influence in Kūfa, Syria, Basra and Egypt led to the killing of 'Uthmān. These broken and contradictory reports by Saif do not correlate with the many reports, which we find in regards to the uprising of the Muslims against the government of 'Uthmān. Other than the reports of Saif, we do not find any others directing 'Abdullāh ibn Sa'ba's presence as the cause of the rebellion against 'Uthmān.

Many Muslims are aware, this is not only Shī'ahs but also Sunnis, that when 'Uthmān took over the reins of leadership, many of his relatives had been given important governmental positions.

It would be beneficial to cite some actions carried out by 'Uthmān, which may have caused opposition of the masses:

'Uthmān allowed his uncle al-Ḥakam ibn Abī al-Ās back into Madīnah, although the Prophet (pbuh & hf) had banished him, and favoured him with a large sum of money along with his son Marwān ibn al-Ḥakam. This is an action, which had not even been carried out by 'Uthmān's predecessors Abū Bakr and 'Umar, whose precepts he had also accepted to adhere to at the time of his appointment as caliph.

Al-Balathori has stated that 'Uthmān gave his uncle al-Ḥakam ibn Abī al-Ās three hundred thousand dirhams (equivalent to 300,000 dollars) after he allowed him back into Madīnah. Al-Ḥakam ibn al-Ās was exiled by the Prophet (pbuh & hf) due to ridiculing him.[375]

'Uthmān also appointed 'Abdullāh ibn Sa'd ibn Abū Sarh, his foster brother, as governor of Egypt replacing Amr ibn al-Ās.[376]

It is also known that 'Uthmān replaced Sa'd ibn Abī Waqqās with his half-brother Walīd ibn Uqba as the governor of Kūfa in Iraq.

Is 'Abdullāh ibn Sa'ba important?

Walīd ibn Uqba became a Muslim a year after the treaty of Hudaibīyah and is counted amongst the companions of the Prophet. He was the individual to whom the following verse was revealed:

> "O ye who believe! If a wicked person comes to you with any news, ascertain the truth lest ye harm people unwittingly and afterwards become full of repentance for what ye have done." Qur'ān 49:6

This incident, which resulted in the above revelation of verse 49:6 has been documented in Ibn Hishām's, Biography of the Prophet (pbuh & hf) and should be very well known by students of Islamic history.

Walīd ibn Uqba was sent by the Prophet (pbuh & hf) to a tribe called the Banī Mustaliq in order to collect Zakāt funds from them. They awaited the arrival of Walīd and travelled horseback to receive their expected guest. Walīd upon seeing that they were coming towards him became frightened, and suspecting something else, he returned back to the Prophet informing him that Banī Mustaliq wanted to kill him. The Muslims then became ready for reprisal but the Banī Mustaliq had no intention of killing Walīd, they only wanted to greet and honour their guest. The Banī Mustaliq came to the Prophet and informed him of their true intentions, and as a consequence of this event, the above verse was revealed (49:6).[377] This taught the Muslims that if a person of such a character, a wrong doer ever comes to you with any news, it first should be verified before being considered as correct, as undue harm may be caused by it, if it is untrue. This verse also teaches us that this type of person's words cannot be trusted.

Coming back to the time of 'Uthmān, when he had placed Walīd ibn Uqba as the governor of Kūfa, Sa'd ibn Abī Waqqās stated these words:

> "'Have you become wise or have we become fools?' Walīd replied: 'Abū Is-Haq (a name Sa'd was known by), neither of this is the case. It is the royal authority, which some people take as lunch and then others take it as supper.' Sa'd said: 'You (Umayyad) evidently have made the caliphate a kingdom.'

> 'Abdullāh ibn Mas'ūd also said to Walīd: 'I do not know whether you have become good or people have become bad.'"[378]

The Muslims in Kūfa were not happy with such a decision as was not Sa'd and spoke against the appointment of Walīd to 'Uthmān who did not dismiss him. The Muslims spoke against him again when he was found intoxicated through drinking, at a time when he was leading the congregational prayers in a mosque in Kūfa. It was through this that 'Uthmān finally discharged him.[379]

If we read *Nahj al-Balāghah*, we come across letters written by Imām 'Alī (AS) to those whom he had placed in governmental positions. Within these letters we find many guidelines, which are necessary for those taking up such a role. It would be beneficial to quote a few lines of a letter the Imām had written to Mālik al-Ashtar on his appointment as the governor of Egypt.

> "You should not treat good and bad people alike because in this way you will be discouraging good persons and at the same time emboldening the wicked to carry on their wickedness. Everyone should receive the treatment which his deeds make him deserve."

We must understand that should one waver in their duties, then dismissal is necessary in order to keep the sanctity of the religious teachings and as observed, 'Uthmān in this instance acted upon this in the case of Walīd ibn Uqba.

We also find that due to such occurrences Imām 'Alī (AS) acted as a sincere advisor to 'Uthmān. This we will observe as the section proceeds.

Coming back to the actions, which may have caused the unrest of the masses, we find Ibn Jarīr al-Ṭabarī reported:

> "When the people saw what 'Uthmān was doing, the companions of the Prophet in Madīnah wrote to other companions who were scattered throughout the frontier provinces: 'You have gone forth but to

> struggle in the path of Almighty God, for the sake of Muḥammad's religion. In your absence the religion of Muḥammad has been corrupted and forsaken. So come back to re-establish Muḥammad's religion.' Thus, they came from every direction until they killed the caliph (Uthmān)."[380]

We must take note; does such a statement suggest that the companions were following the orders of 'Abdullāh ibn Sa'ba? Obviously the companions were in protest to something, but that something was indicating violation of the religious teachings.

We read that 'Uthmān was placed under house arrest and Talḥa; a known companion of the Prophet (pbuh & hf) had prompted this order. We find instances of such behaviour in Tabarī's *Tarīkh*.

> "'Abdullāh ibn 'Abbās said: 'I entered 'Uthmān's presence (during the agitation against 'Uthmān) and talked with him for an hour.' He said: 'Come Ibn 'Abbās and he took me by the hand and had me listen to what the people were saying at his door. We heard some say, 'what are you waiting for,' while others were saying, 'wait, perhaps he will repent.' While the two of us were standing there (behind the door and listening), Talḥa ibn Ubaydillah passed by and said, 'Where is Ibn Udays?' He was told: 'He is over there.' Ibn Udays came to (Talḥa) and whispered something with him, and then went back to his associates and said: 'Do not let anyone go in (to the house of 'Uthmān) to see this man or leave his house.' 'Uthmān said to me: 'These are the orders of Talḥa.' He continued: 'O God! Protect me from Talḥa for he has provoked all these people against me. By God, I hope nothing will come of it, and that his own blood will be shed. Talḥa has abused me unlawfully. I heard the Messenger of God said: 'The blood of a Muslim is lawful in three cases, apostasy, adultery, and the one who kills except in legitimate retaliation for another. So why should I be killed?' Ibn 'Abbās continued: 'I wanted to leave (the house), but they

> blocked my path until Muḥammad ibn Abī Bakr who was passing by requested them to let me go, and they did so.'"[381]

Were these orders of Talḥa, branching from the orders of 'Abdullah in Sa'ba? Was 'Abdullāh ibn Sa'ba the individual who commanded the above? These companions never indicated that their actions had been caused by the words of 'Abdullāh ibn Sa'ba. There was no indication by them that all the pandemonium was due to the subject of succession in regards to Imām 'Alī (AS).

Also, just to enlighten the reader, a question needs to be addressed here, why is it that companions such as 'Ammār and Abū Dharr are accused of following the words of 'Abdullāh ibn Sa'ba, while other companions who were involved in the house arrest of 'Uthmān are never mentioned? Is it because the stories we hear by the one and only Sayf, which also speak of the influence of 'Abdullāh ibn Sa'ba on such great companions like 'Ammār and Abū Dharr have provided a good deterrent to the actual cause, which of course is then left hidden? Why is it that only those who remained loyal to Imām 'Alī (AS) have been targeted as the ones influenced by 'Abdullāh ibn Sa'ba and nobody else? What is it that is wishing to be dismissed here?

> "'Alī said to Talḥa: 'I ask you by Allāh to send people away from (attacking) 'Uthmān.' Talḥa replied: 'No, by God, not until the Umayyad voluntarily submit to what is right.' ('Uthmān was the head of Umayyad)."[382]

> "Abzay said: 'I witnessed the day they went in against 'Uthmān. They entered the house through an opening in the residence of 'Amr ibn Ḥazm. There was a skirmishing and they got in. By God, I have not forgotten that Sudan ibn Ḥumran came out and I heard him say: 'Where is Talḥa ibn Ubaydillah? We have killed Ibn Affān!'"[383]

Take note, Sudan ibn Ḥumran states:

> 'Where is Talḥa ibn Ubaydillah? We have killed Ibn Affān!'

Is 'Abdullāh ibn Sa'ba important?

Again, where is 'Abdullāh ibn Sa'ba's lead in this? When observing the above and the proceeding reports, one should keep within his or her mind this question.

Before the death of 'Uthmān, Imām 'Alī (AS) reminded him what it was that was causing such unrest, reminded him of his leniency towards those whom were in important governmental positions and those people who were not to be trusted. Imām 'Alī mediated and sincerely advised 'Uthmān, but much to his disappointment after listening to such advice, he, meaning 'Uthmān, continued his own stand.

Below is part of a serious discourse between Imām 'Alī (AS) and 'Uthmān:

> "...'Alī said: 'I would tell you that every one appointed by 'Umar, was kept under close inspection by him, and 'Umar would trample on his ear. If 'Umar would hear a single word concerning him, he would flog him and punish him with the utmost severity. But you do not do that. You have been weak and easygoing with your relatives. 'Uthmān said: 'They are your relatives as well. 'Alī replied: 'By my life, they are closely related to me, but merit is found in other people.' 'Uthmān said: 'Do you know that 'Umar was the one who kept Mua'wīya in the office throughout his entire reign, and I have only done the same.' Then 'Alī said: 'I ask you by Allāh, do you know that Mua'wīya was more afraid of 'Umar than was 'Umar's own slave, Yarfa?' 'Uthmān said: 'Yes.' 'Alī continued: 'Now it has been reached to the point that Mua'wīya makes decisions on the issues without consulting you, and you know it. Mua'wīya says to people: 'This is 'Uthmān's command and you hear of this, but you do not denounce him.' Then 'Alī left 'Uthmān, and 'Uthmān went out on his heels.
>
> Then 'Uthmān ascended the pulpit and said: 'By God, you have surely blamed me for things like those you accepted from 'Umar. But he trampled you

> underfoot, smote you with his hand, and subdued you by his tongue, and thus you submitted to him whether you liked it or not. But I have been lenient with you. I let you step on my shoulders while I restrained my hand and tongue, and therefore you have been rude towards me. By God, I am stronger in the number of relatives, and have allies closer at hand, and possess more supporters. I have appointed your peers over you. But you have attributed to me a nature that I do not possess. Restrain your tongue from slandering your rulers... By God! I have achieved no less than my predecessors or those about whom you have not disagreed. There is a surplus wealth, so why should I not do as I wish with the surplus? Otherwise why did I become leader?'"[384]

The people were not happy with what was happening and we read that a siege against 'Uthmān was carried out. Imām 'Alī (AS) was not an individual who would not explain things properly, he carried forth his duty explaining everything and an Imām appointed by Allāh, would do just that, clarifying the necessary action to take, the following up of such advice being the choice of the individual to whom it was received.

Here is more evidence of Imām 'Alī's (AS) explaining:

> "'Uthmān said: 'You see the trouble caused by this band of dissidents when they came to me today. I know that you enjoy prestige among people and that they will listen to you. I want you to go to them and send them away from me. I do not wish them to come before me, for that would be an insulting act toward me on their part. Let others hear this as well.' 'Alī said: 'On what grounds shall I send them away?' 'Uthmān replied: 'On the grounds that I shall carry out what you have counselled me to do and you thought right, and I will not deviate from your direction.' Then 'Alī said: 'In fact I have spoken to you time after time, and you and I discussed such matters at length. All this is the doing of Marwān ibn

> al-Ḥakam, Sa'īd ibn al-Ās, Ibn Amīr, and Mua'wīya. You have listened to them and defied me.' 'Uthmān said: 'Then I shall defy them and listen to you.'"[385]

Through this explaining, 'Uthmān finally listened to the Imām and addressed the people in regards to his mishaps, but then later succumbed to the words of a person whose credibility could never have been placed above Imām 'Alī.

Imām 'Alī (AS) said:

> "'Make a statement which the people will testify that they have heard from you, and God will be witness as to whether or not you desire to repent in your heart.'
>
> Thus, 'Uthmān went out and preached the sermon in which he laid before the people his heartfelt desire to repent, and said: 'By God, O people, if any one of you has blamed (me), he has not done anything that is unknown to me. I have done nothing unknowingly. But my soul has raised vain hopes within me and lied to me, and my virtue has slipped away from me. ...I ask God's forgiveness for what I have done and I turn to him. A man like me yearns to repent.' Then people had pity on him, and some among them wept. Sa'd ibn Zayd stood up before him ('Uthmān) and said: 'O Commander of Faithful, (from now on) no one comes to you who does not support you. Fear God, in your soul fear God, and fulfil what you have said!'"
>
> When 'Uthmān descended (from the pulpit), he found Marwān ibn al-Ḥakam and Sa'īd ibn al-Ās, and a few other Umayyads at his house. Marwān said: 'Should I speak (to people) or remain silent?' 'Uthmān's wife said: 'Nay! Be silent, for they will kill him of sin. He has made a public statement from which he cannot right-fully withdraw.' Marwān said: 'What does this have to do with you?' Then Marwān said to 'Uthmān: 'To persist in an error for which you must seek God's

forgiveness is better than to repent because you are afraid. If you so will, you may seek repentance without acknowledging error.' 'Uthmān said: 'Go out and speak to them, for I am ashamed to do so.' So Marwān went (to people) and said: 'Why have you gathered here like looters? ... You have come to snatch our power (*Mulk*; kingship) from us. Go! By God, if you mean us (any harm), you will encounter something distasteful from us, and you will not praise the result of your opinions. Return to your homes, for by God we are not men to be robbed of our possessions.' People informed 'Alī of the news. Then 'Alī came to 'Uthmān and said: 'Surely you have satisfied Marwān (again), but he is satisfied with you only if you deviate from your religion and reason like a camel carrying a litter that is led around at will. By God, Marwān is devoid of sense in regard to his religion and his soul. I swear by God, I think he will bring you in and then not send you out again. After this visit, I will not come again to chide you. You have destroyed your own honour and you have been robbed of your authority.'

When 'Alī departed, 'Uthmān's wife told him: 'I have heard that 'Alī said to you that he will never return to you, and that you have obeyed Marwān (again), who leads you wherever he wishes.' 'Uthmān said: 'What shall I do?' She responded: 'You should fear God alone, who has no partner, and you should adhere to the practice of your two predecessors (Abū Bakr and 'Umar), for if you obey Marwān, he will kill you. Marwān enjoys no prestige among the people, and inspires neither awe nor love. People have only abandoned you due to Marwān's position (in your councils). Send to 'Alī then and trust in his honesty and uprightness. He is related to you and he is not a man whom people disobey.' So 'Uthmān sent to 'Alī, but he refused to come, saying: 'I told him I would not return.'"[386]

Is 'Abdullāh ibn Sa'ba important?

Imām 'Alī (AS) had explained all he needed to, he never withheld anything and openly spoke against matters that were causing unrest, but sadly his words were left behind.

Imām 'Alī (AS) stated:

> "By God! I have persisted in defending him ('Uthmān) until I was filled with shame. But Marwān, Mua'wīya, 'Abdullāh ibn 'Amīr, and Sa'īd ibn al-Ās have dealt with him as you witnessed. When I gave him sincere counsel and directed him to send them away, he became suspicious of me, until what you now see has happened."[387]

If we come back to the subject of 'Abdullāh ibn Sa'ba, do the words of Imām 'Alī (AS) depict to us that the reason behind such happenings was the fault of this converted Jew? Do the words of Imām 'Alī depict to us that it was 'Abdullāh ibn Sa'ba and his followers that killed 'Uthmān?

Should we plainly ignore all that has been stated, which only scratches the surface of the issue of the unrest, which has been quoted within our history books? Is it wrong for us to contemplate on what lies and deception have been elevated in order to conceal the truth? Should we divert and pin point the blame upon something, which does not correlate or provide solid evidence of its veracity? Is this not something that we see the west doing in regards to the Muslims? Is not the reason behind such blindness of the following of Ahl al-Bayt, due to the continued publicity of the so-called hypocrite 'Abdullāh ibn Sa'ba? Again, try understanding this with the way the west is publicising Muslims within the media. Can we not see how Shī'ahs are being targeted in order for the masses to turn against them and look at them as an enemy, when in fact they acknowledge the authority of the Ahl al-Bayt through the teachings of our Prophet (pbuh & hf)? Why not realise, that when great companions of the Prophet such as Ammār, al-Miqdād, Abū Dharr themselves spoke boldly in regards to the actions of certain people, then how is it that Shī'ahs are condemned for repeating their very words?

Coming back to 'Abdullāh ibn Sa'ba, we should seriously think, how the rumours of this one irrelevant person could have been the cause of all the unrest amongst the people of Madīnah and the other provinces. Again, was this converted Jew so immensely important and perfect to the people of Madīnah and other regions that everybody would have attentively listened to him, listened to something, which was already an issue, and was acknowledged by many of the companions who had always remained loyal to the Imām? Not forgetting, Imām 'Alī (AS) also proclaimed his right in authority at the time of the demise of the Prophet (pbuh & hf) and when he was given leadership by the people. Did 'Abdullāh ibn Sa'ba also influence the Imām to state words in accordance to his liking? Imām 'Alī was not a liar or a fraud and the truth was with him.

What we must also contemplate on is, after the death of 'Uthmān, Mua'wiya himself never stated that the uprising against his cousin 'Uthmān was due to the mischief of 'Abdullah ibn Sa'ba; he did not illuminate this and did not bring anything in line with its so-called great existence.

As it is believed that the Jewish element killed 'Uthmān,' (the hypocrite Abdullāh ibn Sa'ba and his followers), we must ask ourselves this question, would such hypocrites have allowed his body to be buried in a Jewish cemetery?

Historians have reported that 'Uthmān's body was not buried in a Muslim cemetery.

> "'Uthmān was buried in a Jewish cemetery called 'Ḥahsh Kawkāb,' without his body being washed and without a shroud. When Mu'āwiya came to power he joined the cemetery to al-Baqī by including the land, which was spaced between them and that is why 'Uthmān's grave is on the other side of al-Baqī." [388]

Dr Taha Ḥusayn, a well-known Egyptian Sunni scholar wrote the following:

> "The fact that the historians make no mention of Ibn al-Sawda ('Abdullāh ibn Sa'ba) being present at the Battle of Siffīn together with his followers proves at

> the very least that the whole notion of a group of people led by him is a baseless fabrication. It is one of those inventions that acquired currency when the conflict between the Shī'īs and other Islamic groups intensified. In order to underline their hostility, the enemies of the Shī'ah tried to insert a Jewish element into the origins of their sect. If the story of 'Abdullāh ibn Sa'ba had any historical fact, his cunning and guile could not have failed to show itself at the Battle of Siffīn. I can think of only one reason for his name not occurring in connection with that Battle; that he was an entirely fictitious person, dreamed up by the enemies of the Shī'ah in order to vilify them."[389]

Despite all of this, even if it is still believed that this converted Jewish hypocrite, so called by many, was alive at the time of the caliphate of 'Uthmān, it does not prove that the followers of the progeny of the Prophet (pbuh & hf), his Ahl al-Bayt are from this man. Allāh has given us the greatest matter that is our brain in order for us to understand the reason behind their stand with the Imām from the very beginning.

If 'Abdullāh ibn Sa'ba was the founder of the Shī'ah, the followers of the Ahl al-Bayt, then what can we call those companions who followed the words of the Prophet (pbuh & hf) who had said: "I am leaving behind two weighty things, they are the Book of Allāh and my Ahl al-Bayt?" They were not Jews; they were Muslims, as are the Shī'ahs of today, who follow exactly what those companions followed.

Closing Section

Without Knowledge there is Ignorance.

We are living in an age of ignorance where we do not wish to look into any matter, which seems to direct our minds away from the bliss and comforts of this world, when this world is not our final destination but an intermediate place of residence, a place where we are to take every step possible in working towards the submission of Allāh in every way, on every issue, this being the makings of a sincere believer, a subservient servant of Allāh. We all need to continually remind ourselves of the nature of our existence, that we are living to please the supreme authority, and not those who do not follow Him. We are never to stop referring to Allāh's words and when we are faced with abuse and bad comments from others who confront us because of stating them, it should cause us to become stronger and advance us further towards our Lord.

> Narrated Muḥammad ibn Yaḥyā from Aḥmad ibn Muḥammad ibn Īsa from ibn Faddal from al-Ḥasan ibn al-Jahm who has said the following; I heard Imām al-Rida (A.S) saying: "The friend of a person is his or her intelligence and the enemy of a person is his or her ignorance."[390]

Abusiveness has become a common trait; it is becoming increasingly prominent as the years pass by. It is something of which is not even being distinguished as a terrible thing by those who are spreading it. Allāh teaches:

> "When it is said to them: 'Make not mischief on the earth.' They say: 'Why we only want to make peace!' Of a surety they are the ones who make mischief but they realise (it) not." Qur'ān 2:11-12

If a Shī'ah was abused by a Sunni for stating that the Prophet (pbuh & hf) expressed to the people "to whomsoever I am *mawlā* 'Alī is *mawlā*' and "follow the Qur'ān and my Ahl al-Bayt," who would be the one portraying the bad behavior, the one stating these words or the one hurling the abuse? In the same way if a Sunni stated, for example, that Abū Bakr gave away all his possessions on the expedition of Tabūk, and a Shī'ah began to utter abuse at the individual stating this, then it is the Shī'ah who is portraying the bad behavior not the Sunni. This is neither the way to reason nor the way to discuss. We all have a duty to stop this attitude amongst one another and not to encourage it, be it from a Sunni or Shī'ah it should never be condoned.

The Prophet (pbuh & hf) did not abuse a Jew or a Christian when living in close proximity to them, and yet he knew that these people did not wish to believe in what he came with.

None of us are perfect, we all have much to learn, there are many issues, which we all do not know of, and there is ignorance from all people.

If a Shī'ah is badly behaved, is not following that which is good, this does not mean every other Shī'ah is of the same rank. It does not give one authority to hurl abuse at each and every individual. One individual is not the same as another, there are learned and the not so learned. This can also be stated for the Sunni. It is incorrect to address everyone badly due to the behaviour and ignorance of others; we have no right to brand everyone as the same. Also, if we never acquire knowledge then we are just as terrible as those who hate the Muslims because of their misinformed information and lack of knowledge of the religion. We are taught not to be suspicious, not to speak ill of others behind their backs.

Allāh states:

> "O ye who believe! Avoid suspicion as much (as possible); for suspicion in some cases is a sin; and spy not on each other nor speak ill of each other behind their backs. Would any of you like to eat the flesh of his dead brother? Nay ye would abhor it, but fear Allāh, for Allāh is Oft-Returning Most Merciful." Qur'ān 49:12

How many of us disobey this command of Allāh and suspect our brothers and sisters for something, which they are innocent of?

Succession of the Prophet (PBUH)

Many people brand that the Shī'ah Ithna 'Asherī believe that Imām Ali (AS) was a prophet, this is not true, they believe in his Imāmate and the Imāmate of the Ahl al-Bayt. We can only become acquainted with this if an individual addresses it to us, we do not have access to what is in the hearts of people. Merely pinpointing at individuals and stating: "This is what they believe, they are a deviant, and they are astray" is ignorant and unjust. Our duty is to seek out the truth in the matter, to help towards the establishment of the truth and to implement the teachings of Allāh and His Apostle. If any individual believes this, then they are departing from the teachings of the Qur'ān and the words of the Prophet (pbuh & hf); and it is our duty as Muslims to explain the truth, allow them to then ponder and seek for themselves, in the same way as we speak to a Christian who states Jesus is the son of God.

Those, whom elevate Imām 'Alī (AS) to the status of a prophet or even God, are not those whom the Prophet (pbuh & hf) or the Imāms spoke highly of. There is no other prophet after Muḥammad and no new revelation after him, and this is what we all have to believe in, the true teachings and explain them to one another.

> 'Ali ibn Abī Tālib narrated that the Prophet said: "Allāh's Messenger said to 'Alī: 'You have a resemblance to Jesus whom the Jews hated so much that they slandered his mother and whom the Christians loved so much that they placed him in a position not rightly his.' 'Alī afterwards said: 'Two people will perish on my account, one who loves me so excessively that he praises me for what I do not possess, and one who hates me so much that he will be impelled by his hatred to slander me.'"[391]

It has also been recorded in *Nahj al-Balāghah* that Imām 'Alī (AS) stated:

> "Two categories of persons will face ruin on account of me; he who loves me with exaggeration and he who hates me intensely."[392]

Also, some people have the tendency to state that the Shī'ah in Pakistan do not pay *Zakāt* and disallow the government to take out money from their bank accounts towards it. Any Muslim who does not pay *Zakāt* is not adhering to the law of Allāh. There are many Muslims who do not pay *Zakāt* be they Shī'ah or Sunni and we all know this, but stating this against the Shī'ah in such a way, is to create animosity towards them. Again, this is acting suspiciously and ignorantly of a fellow Muslim. No Imām of the Ahl al-Bayt has taught not to pay *Zakāt*; it is an obligatory command from Allāh and the Shī'ahs acknowledge it. Why do we not ask ourselves the question as to why some individuals do not wish the Pakistani government to take their *Zakāt* money from their bank accounts? This matter is a matter based more towards trust. Who can state that those who previously governed the state of Pakistan earned any trust amongst the people to deal with money in the correct and legislated way of the Prophet? Devout Shī'ahs do pay *Zakāt*, if they wish to know what money they give is properly spent in accordance to the *Shāri'ah* and so they pay it wherever they wish; this does not mean they do not acknowledge payment of *Zakāt.* Can we as honest citizens of society truly believe that previous governments of Pakistan have dealt with transactions and the money of the people money justly? Hoarding of money and corruptness is a huge issue in Pakistan, which has left Pakistan heavily in debt and poverty.

Issues like this are addressed continuously and are causing aggression against those who take from the teachings of the Imāms. Tolerance of this behaviour is something of which every follower of the Imāms has to adopt and try his or her utmost to remain patient over. We should not act unjustly, plainly because of the injustice of others, it is a challenge towards keeping an upright character, and our character should not become like those whom act contrary to the character of our Prophet (pbuh & hf).

Allāh states:

> "O ye who believe! Stand out firmly for Allāh, as witnesses to fair dealing, and let not the hatred of others to you make you swerve to wrong and prevent you from being just. Be just, that is next to piety, and fear Alllāh for Alllāh is well-acquainted with all that ye do." Qurān 5:8

Also, we find that books and articles against Shī'ahs are becoming increasingly apparent and are promoting levels of hatred against righteous individuals who adhere to the Imāms. Much confused, out of context and misleading literature is being tossed around from various sources. The Shī'ah scholars of *Ḥadīth* have not classed their books as totally *Ṣaḥīḥ* as the majority have with their collections. They admit to their books containing weak narrations as well as the correct ones, which not even they follow or believe in, but books published, which have been written by other than the Shī'ah containing such literature, are accepted by people without investigating into it themselves. If I were to take references of absurd narrations, denoting that the Prophet said such and such, which have been stated in various books that the majority of Muslims class as *Ṣaḥīḥ* and state that this is what is believed by them, they would not like it, they would become agitated and angry.

A Sunni cannot represent what the Shī'ahs believe; it is the **knowledgeable and righteous ones** of the Shī'ah community that represent what they believe in. Shī'ah *mujtahids* and *'ulema* (scholars) are the ones who need to be addressed when enquiring, not books written by people who are against those who adhere to the twelve Imāms.

Shī'ah *mujtahids* and scholars and even members of the public are continuously clarifying and correcting misleading information, which is spreading like a wild fire and overshadowing the truth in regards to the authority of the Ahl al-Bayt, deterring people from getting to know about it. Whilst I was becoming aware of the authority of the Ahl al-Bayt, much misleading information was also thrown at me, something, which I have now grown to understand, as its aim is to prevent the acceptance of the Ahl al-Bayt. It did not deter me and never will deter me from following the Ahl al-Bayt, as a command is a command regardless, and this command came from the Prophet (pbuh & hf) and not the people.

When my Prophet (pbuh & hf) has clarified to me, to whom I am to take after him as my guides, then I should not separate from this and follow other than them. When my Prophet has given me the guidance to stay on the one road, then I should not follow another group and take from those who **do not represent the authority of the Ahl**

al-Bayt and will not be recognised as such on the advent of Imām Mahdī (AS).

If we briefly speak of Ayatullāh Khomeinī, many people have also addressed him in a bad light, when in fact they fail to understand that that this man changed Iran, changed it from being a place, which had been drowned by the loss of Islamic awareness and its teachings. It's culture being far away from what the Prophet (pbuh & hf) had brought.

Ayatullāh Khomeinī wrote the following in his last will and testament:

> "...In his most exalted name: I should like to add at the end of this 29-page will and testament with its ending with the following points:
>
> (1) While still here with you, I would like to declare that certain false statements have already been imputed to me and which may increase after I am gone. Therefore, I hereby declare that nothing imputed, ascribed or attributed to me has my confirmation unless it is in my handwriting, has my signature, is in my voice, with the affirmation of the experts, or what I have said on the television of the Islamic Republic.
>
> (2) Some individuals have claimed, even while I am alive, that they have been writing my statements. This is hereby denied. All such statements have been prepared and written by myself only.
>
> (3) Apparently some claim to have arranged my going to Paris, France. This is a lie. After I was turned back from Kuwait, I chose Paris in consultation with Aḥmad for it was probable that Islamic states would decline admission for they were under the Shah's influence but Paris was not...."[393]

Albert Einstein (1879-1955) said: "Great spirits have always encountered violent opposition from mediocre minds."

People cannot understand the depth and context of Ayatullāh Khomeinī's words; his knowledge and wisdom brought forth the duty of the people of Iran to re engage in the fundamentals of the religion, reforming them, changing many, something of which the Shah, his predecessor wished to drown in his lead in government. Knowing the honour and respect he had for the Imāms of the Ahl al-Bayt, his teachings which had come from the study of the knowledge, which these blessed people had, brings out an enlightenment that there was a human being who stood forth for truth and justice, was not afraid to illuminate the nature of the just and the unjust, was not afraid to speak the truth even if it was bitter, was not afraid to drown the falsehood from the truth, a man who excelled the righteous and dispelled the appalling. Pure ignorance, lack of knowledge and false judgement is the grounds of many, in the hatred towards him. No doubt, Ayatullāh Khomeinī was aware of this *fitna* (tribulation) that would arise, and his own words evidently express this awareness.

The Possessors of Great Knowledge.

If people knew of the Ahl al-Bayt and their importance, they would come to know about the possessors of great knowledge, they would come to realise their capabilities and great teaching, about those whom the Prophet (pbuh & hf) spoke highly of, eloquence and etiquette illuminated through them like shining pearls dazzling the beholder, they were from the Prophet's House. Leaving this House behind has caused a curtain to fall in front of the Imāms, their gleam of knowledge losing its recognition and exuberance. If we remain open-minded, it may lead us into becoming acquainted with this House, which has been beautified by hearts of gold and mirrors of piety and wisdom, that its reflection is something, which we would all want to be a part of.

Even if we adhere to another school of thought, it should not stop us from knowing about the People of the House; it should not stop us from benefiting from their knowledge, they are the ones whom the Prophet (pbuh & hf) spoke of as a ship that was safe from drowning its boarders like that of the Ark of Nūh (AS).

The Possessors of Great Knowledge

> The Prophet said: "Behold! My Ahl al-Bayt are like the Ark of Noah. Whoever embarked in it was saved, and whoever turned away from it was perished."[394]

Boarding the Ark of the Ahl al-Bayt, would be boarding that which would remain buoyant and robust and would never capsize, keeping you afloat and secure, never to leave you sinking in confusion and anonymity.

Taking preference to those whom possess great knowledge is a teaching from our Lord, and referring to them would provide us with a path to become united.

The Imāms of the Ahl al-Bayt had a great comprehension of the teachings of the Qur'ān, they were left with it, and their teachings could never have been ignored.

As observed, Imām 'Alī's (AS) guidance in matters pertaining to the religion reached many, his help even reached out to 'Umar to the extent that he would state:

> "If it was not for 'Alī, 'Umar would have perished."

Imām 'Alī (AS) would state:

> "Ask me before you lose me."

Allāmah Shiblī Nu'manī writes in his book Imām Abū Ḥanīfah Life and Works:

> "...He (Imām Abū Ḥanīfah) learnt a great deal from the Imām's (Imām Bāqir) son, Ja'far as-Sādiq also which is in fact mentioned in the history books. Ibn Taymiyyah however denies this on the ground that Abū Ḥanīfah and Ja'far as-Sādiq were contemporaries and equals, which ruled out the former being the latter's pupil. But I consider the sheer impudence and lack of comprehension on Ibn Taymiyyah's part. For all his greatness as an original thinker and master of Fiqh, Abū Ḥanīfah could not compare in learning

> with Imām Ja'far as-Sādiq. The Ahl al-Bayt were the fountainhead of *Ḥadīth* and *Fiqh* and, in fact in all religious learning. 'The master of the house knows best what is in it.'..."[395]

However, Ibn Taymīyyah in his own book quotes the words of Imām Mālik stating that the latter said:

> "No eyes have ever seen, no ears have ever heard, and no heart has ever found anybody greater than Ja'far ibn Muḥammad as-Sādiq in knowledge, piety, and worship."[396]

Although we find such words expressed by those who came before us, we find them being ignored because they seem problematic, when in fact we can rationally understand why they were expressed even by those who held contrary beliefs to the Shī'ahs. It is not a strange thing that the truth can also come out of the mouths of such people, when it is self-evident. Many people do not have a problem if we pick up a book of British history and study it, or further gain an A Level or Degree on the subject, it is not shunned or disallowed and can even be praised.

It is tragic to see that such unreasonable attitudes have emerged amongst our folk, who do not wish for us to read, who find it a problem when matters are brought out into the open, when yet we live in an open world but still stick within the small structure of our houses, only reflecting that which has been cemented in our minds.

It should sink into the hearts that the demise of the Prophet (pbuh & hf) and the topic of succession is a historic episode, which teaches us that although the religion has been firmly established; much struggle has been faced by those whom wished to adhere wholly to it and is still being faced. Even if we have not observed things before our very eyes, it is not that we cannot search matters and decipher them by using our intellect. This should never be shunned and seen as a misgiving when people are studying it.

May Allāh encourage us all to seek for knowledge, to understand the teachings of Islām so that we can unite with one another and bring forth the love and companionship needed amongst our brethren as we Muslims all have one objective, and that is to follow the completed religion as it was taught and conveyed by the Prophet (pbuh & hf) and it is these hearts, the sincere seekers and lovers of the truth, which will unite in the end.

Footnotes

1. **The Rev. Charles Kingsley**, *Alton Locke, Tailor and Poet, An Autobiography.*

2. **Muslim,** *al-Ṣaḥīḥ, Arabic Version, Kitāb al-Imām,* **Vol. 1, p. 90. Ibn Mājah,** *al-Sunan, Kitāb al-Fitan,* **Vol. 2 p. 1320, Number 3988.**

3. **al-Shaykh Muḥammad 'Abdu,** *Sharh Nahj al-Balāghah,* **Vol. 4, p. 673.**

4. **'Allāmah Tabataba'ī,** *An Exegesis of the Holy Qur'ān,* **Tafsīr al-Mizān.**

5. **Ibn Mājah,** *al-Sunan, The Chapter on Tribulations (Kitāb al-Fitan),* **Number 4082 & 4084.**

6. **Muslim,** *al-Ṣaḥīḥ, English Version, The Book on Government (Kitāb al-Imāra),* **Book 020, Number 4477.**

7. **Muslim,** *al-Ṣaḥīḥ, English Version, The Book on Government (Kitāb al-Imāra),* **Book 020, Number 4480.**

8. **al-Ḥākim,** *al-Mustadrak,* **Vol. 3, p. 618.**

9. **al-Qundūzī al-Ḥanafī,** *Yanabī' al-Mawaddah,* **p. 315. Ibn Taymīyyah**, *Maktabah, Second Edition.*

10. **al-Bukhārī,** *al-Ṣaḥīḥ, English Version, Book of Judgements (Aḥkām)* **Vol. 9, Book 89, Number 329.**

11. **Imām Aḥmad ibn Ḥanbal,** *al-Musnad,* **Vol. 4, p241. Nasai,** *Sunan al-Kubra*, **Vol. 3, p.467. Musannaf,** *ibn Abi Shaybah*, **Vol. 6, p. 402.**

12. **al-Ya'qūbī,** *al-Tārīkh,* **Vol. 1, pp. 24-25.**

13. **al-Kulaynī,** *al-Kāfī, English Version, translated by Muḥammad Sarwar. The Book about People with Divine Authority,* **Chapter 16, H 529, Ch. 16, h 5.**

14. **al-Bukhārī,** *al-Ṣaḥīḥ, Pakistan, Sethi Straw Board Mills (Conversion) Ltd, 1971 CE (9 vols),* **Vol. 4, page 437, Number 658.**

15. **al-Qurtubī,** *Tafsīr published by Muāsifah al-Tārīkh al-Arabī 1405*, **Vol. 10, p. 297.**

16. **Ibn Ḥājar al-Haythamī,** *al-Sawā'iq al-Muhriqah, under the commentary of the verse: "And stop them, for they shall be questioned." Qur'ān 37:24.* **Ch. 11, Section 1, p. 231.**

17. **Muslim,** *al-Ṣaḥīḥ, English Version, The Book on Government (Kitāb al-Imāra),* **Book 020, Number 4562.**

18. **al-Bukhārī,** *al-Ṣaḥīḥ, English Version, Afflictions at the end of the world*, **Vol. 9, Book 88, Number 227.**

19. **Lutfu'llah Sāfī Gulpaygānī,** *Muntakhābul Athār*, **Ch. 5, Section 10.**

20. **al-Bukhārī,** *al-Ṣaḥīḥ, English Version, Judgements (Ahkām),* **Vol. 9, Book 89, Number 257.**

21. **al-Juwaynī al-Ḥamawīnī**, *Farā'id al-Simṭayn,* **p. 160.**

22. **al-Dhahabī,** *Tadhkirat al-Huffaz,* **Vol. 4, p. 298.**

23. **Ibn Ḥajar al-'Asqalānī,** *al-Durar al-Kāminah,* **Vol. 1, p. 67.**

24. **al-Juwaynī al-Ḥamawīnī,** *Farā'id al-Simṭayn,* **p. 160.**

25. **al-Juwaynī al-Ḥamawīnī,** *Farā'id al-Simṭayn,* **p. 160.**

26. **al-Qundūzī al-Ḥanafī,** *Yanabī' al-Mawaddah,* **pp. 444-447.**

27. **Imām Ja'far as-Sādiq,** *The Lantern of the Path.*

28. **al-Kulaynī,** *al-Kāfī, English Version, translated by Muḥammad Sarwar. The Book about People with Divine Authority,* **Chapter 8, H443, Ch. 8, h 15.**

29. **Ibn Mājah,** *al-Sunan,* **Vol. 2, Number 4085.**

30. **Abū Dāwūd,** *al-Sunan, English Version, The Promised deliverer (Kitāb al-Mahdī),* **Book 36, Number 4271. Ibn Mājah,** *al-Sunan,* **Vol. 2, Number 4086.**

31. **Imām Aḥmad ibn Ḥanbal,** *al-Musnad,* **Vol. 1, p. 99.**

32. **Abū Dāwūd,** *al-Sunan, English Translation, The Promised deliverer (Kitāb al-Mahdī),* **Book 36, Number 4272.**

33. **Imām Aḥmad ibn Ḥanbal,** *al-Musnad,* **Vol. 1, p. 398.**

34. **Ibn al-Kathīr** *Tārīkh,* **Vol. 6, pp 259-260.**

35. **Ibn Taymīyyah**, *Ra's al-Ḥusayn,* **pp. 200-202.**

36. **al-Radī,** *Nahj al-Balāghah,* **Sermon 142.**

37. **al-Qundūzī al-Ḥanafī,** *Yanabī' al-Mawaddah,* **pp. 446.**

38. **al-Bukhārī,** *al-Ṣaḥīḥ, English Version,* The Book of *Judgements (Akhām),* **Vol. 9, Book 89, Number 251.**

39. **Fakhr al-Dīn al-Rāzī,** *Tafsīr al-Kabīr,* **Vol. 10, p. l44.**

40. **al-Ṭabarī,** *Tārīkh, Arabic Version,* **Vol. 2, p. 84.**

41. **al-Ṭabarī,** *Tārīkh, Arabic Version,* **Vol. 2, p. 319. Imām Aḥmad ibn Ḥanbal,** *al-Musnad, narrated by Ibn 'Abbās on ten merits of the Imām,* **Vol. 1, p. 331. Imām Aḥmad ibn Ḥanbal,** *al-Musnad,* **Vol. 1, p. 111, 159. al-Nasā'ī,** *Khasā'is al-'Alawiyya, narrated by Ibn 'Abbās,* **p. 6. al-Ḥākim,** *al-Mustadrak,* **Vol. 3 p. 132. Nūr al-Dīn al-Shāfi'ī al-Ḥalābī,** *al-Sīrah al-Ḥalabiyyah,* **Vol. 1, p. 311. Ibn al-Athīr,** *al-Kamīl,* **Vol. 2 p. 62. al-Muttaqī al Hindī,** *Kanz al-'Ummāl, quotes from Ibn Jarīr al-Ṭabarī and from Imām Aḥmad ibn Ḥanbal,* **Vol. 6, p. 392, 396, Number 1045 and Number 6008. Also see, Abū Bakr Sirajuddin (Martin Lings),** Muḥammad, his life based on the Earlier Sources, **p. 51.**

42. **al-Ṭabarī**, *at-Ta'wil, Arabic Version,* **Vol. 19, p. 121.**

43. **Fakhr al-Dīn al-Rāzī,** *Tafsīr al-Kabīr, narrated by Ibn 'Abbās, al-Barā' ibn Āzib, and Muḥammad ibn 'Alī,* **Vol. 3, p. 636. al-Hāfiz Jalāl al-Dīn al-Suyūtī,** *al-Durr al-Manthūr,* **Vol. 3 p. 298. Nūr al-Dīn al-Shāfi'ī al-Ḥalābī,** *al-Sīrah al-Ḥalabiyyah,* **Vol. 3, p. 301. Ibn Sabbagh al-Mālikī,** *al-Fusūl al-Muhimmah,* **p. 24. Al-Wāḥidī,** *Asbāb al-Nuzūl narrated by Abū Sa'īd al-Khudrī, and Atiyyah,* **p. 150.**

44. **al-Hāfiz Jalāl al-Dīn al-Suyūti,** *al-Itqān,* **Vol. 1 p. 20.**

45. **Ibn al-Kathīr,** *Tafsīr ibn Kathīr,* **Vol. 2, p. 2, further details can be found in al-Qurtubī,** *Tafsīr,* **Vol. 6, p. 244.**

46. **al-Nasā'ī,** *Khasā'is al-'Alawiyya,* **p. 25.**

47. **Ṭabarānī,** *Mu'jam al-Kabīr,* **Vol. 3.**

48. **al-Nasā'ī,** *Sunan al -Kubra, "Khasā'is 'Ali,"* **p. 96, Number 79. Imām Aḥmad ibn Ḥanbal,** *al-Musnad,* **Vol. 3, p. 17, Vol. 4, p366. al-Ya'qūbī,** *al-Tārīkh,* **Vol. 2, p. 112.**

49. **See Ibn al-Kathīr,** *al-Bidāyah wa al-Nihāyah,* **Vol. 5, p. 209, Vol. 6, p. 199.**

50. **al-Nasā'ī,** *Khasā'is al-'Alawiyya, Wilayat and animosity towards 'Alī,* **p. 25** *and 'Alī's status in the eyes of Allāh,* **p. 281. Imām Aḥmad ibn Ḥanbal,** *al-Musnad,* **Vol. 4, p. 281. al-Tirmidhī,** *Jāmi' Ṣaḥīḥ, English Version,* **Number 6094**.

51. **al-Ḥākim**, *al-Mustadrak, Dar al-Ma'rīfah li al Tiba'ah wa al-Nashr, Beirut,* **Vol. 3, pp. 109-110 also Vol. 2, p129, Vol. 3, pp. 116, 371. al-Tirmidhī,** *Jāmi' Ṣaḥīḥ , Arabic Version,* **Vol. 2, p. 298, Vol. 5, p. 300. Imām Aḥmad ibn Ḥanbal,** *Fadhā'il al-Sahāba,* **Vol. 2, pp. 563, 572. Ibn Mājah,** *al-Sunan,* **Vol. 1, pp. 12, 43. Ibn Ḥajar al-Haythamī,** *Majma' al-Zawā'id,* **Vol. 9, p. 103. Fakhr al-Dīn al-Rāzī,** *Tafsīr al-Kabīr,* **Vol. 12, pp. 49-50. al-Hāfiz Jalāl al-Dīn al- Suyūtī,** *al-Durr al-Manthūr,* **Vol. 3, p. 19. al-Hāfiz Jalāl al-Dīn al- Suyūtī,** *Tārīkh al-Khulāfa,* **pp. 169, 173. Ibn al-Kathīr,** *al-Bidāyah wa al-Nihāyah,* **Vol. 3, p. 213, Vol. 5, p. 208. Ibn al-Athīr,** *Usd al-Ghābah,* **Vol. 4, p. 114. Ibn Ḥajar al-'Asqalānī,** *al-Isabah,* **Vol. 2, p. 509. al-Khatīb al-Baghdādī,** *Tārīkh Baghdād,*

Vol. 8, p. 290. al-Muḥibb al-Ṭabarī, *al-Riyād al-Nadirah* **Vol. 2, p. 172. al-Muḥibb al-Ṭabarī,** *Dhakā'ir al-Uqba,* **p. 68.**

52. Imām Aḥmad ibn Ḥanbal, *al-Musnad,* **Vol. 4 p. 281. Ibn Mājah,** *al-Sunan,* **Vol. 1 p. 45.**

53. Muslim, *al-Ṣaḥīḥ, English Version, The Book Pertaining to the Merits of the Companions (Allah be pleased with them) of the Holy Prophet (pbuh),* **Book 031, Number 5920.**

54. Sibt ibn al-Jauzī, *Tadhkīrat Khwāss al-'Ummah fī ma'rīfat al-A'immah, Najaf, al-Maktabah al-Haydarīyyah, 1964 CE,* **p. 33.**

55. al-Tirmidhī, *Jāmi' al-Ṣaḥīḥ, Arabic Version,* **Vol. 5.**

56. al-Tirmidhī, *Jāmi' al-Ṣaḥīḥ, Arabic Version,* **Vol. 2.**

57. Imām Aḥmad ibn Ḥanbal, *al-Musnad,* **Vol. 1, pp. 84, 118, 119, 152, 330, Vol. 4, pp. 281, 368, 370, 372, 378, Vol. 5, pp. 35, 347, 358, 361, 366, 419.**

58. al-Ḥākim, *al-Mustadrak, Chapter of "Understanding (the virtues) of Companions,"* **Vol. 3, pp. 109, 110, 148, 533.**

59. 'Allāmah Shiblī Nu'manī, *Sīrat-i-Nu'manī, English Translation, Imām Abū Ḥanīfah, Life and Works by Hādī Ḥusayn,* **Chapter 10, Tradition and Principles of Tradition, p. 128.**

60. Nawwāb Siddīq Ḥasan Khan, *Minhāj al-Wusūl,* **p. 13.**

61. al-Hāfiz Jalāl al-Dīn al-Suyūtī, *al-Durr al-Manthūr,* **Vol. 2 p. 259. al-Khatīb al-Baghdādī,** *Tārīkh Baghdād narrated by Abū Hurayra,* **Vol. 8, pp. 290, 596. Ibn Asākir,** *History of Damascus,* **Vol. 2, p. 75. al-Hāfiz Jalāl al-Din al-Suyūtī,** *al-Itqān,* **Vol. 1, p. 31. al-Khātib Khwārazmī al-Ḥanafī,** *Kitāb al-Manāqib,* **p. 80. Ibn al-Kathīr,** *al-Bidāyah wa al-Nihāyah,* **Vol. 2, p. 14. al-Qundūzī al-Ḥanafī,** *Yanābī' al-Mawaddah,* **p. 115.**

62. al-Hāfiz Jalāl al-Din al-Suyūtī, *al-Itqān,* **Vol. 1, p. 31.**

63. al-Bukhārī, *al-Ṣaḥīḥ, English Version, Holding fast to the Qur'ān and Sunnah,* **Vol. 9, Book 92, Number 373.**

64. al-Hāfiz Jalāl al-Dīn al-Suyūtī, *al-Durr al-Manthūr,* **Vol. 2 p. 259.**

65. al-Khātib Khwārazmī al-Ḥanafī, *Kitāb al-Manāqib,* **p. 80.**

66. Ibn al-Maghazilī, *Manāqib 'Alī ibn Abī Tālib,* **pp. 18-19.**

67. Khatīb al-Baghdādī, *Tārīkh Baghdād,* **Vol. 8, pp. 290.**

68. Ayatullāh al-Amīnī, *al-Ghadīr.*

69. Ayatullāh al-Amīnī, *al-Ghadīr.*

70. al-Juwaynī al-Ḥamawīnī, *Farā'id al-Simṭayn,* **Vol.1, p. 74.**

71. al-Ya'qūbī, *al-Tārīkh,* **Vol. 2, p. 36.**

72. Abū Dāwūd, *al-Sunan, Model Behaviour of the Prophet (pbuh),* **Book 40, Number 4579.**

73. al-Ḥākim, *al-Mustadrak,* **Vol. 3, p. 149.**

74. al-Bukhārī, *al-Ṣaḥīḥ, English Version, The Punishment of Disbelievers at War with Allāh and his Apostle,* **Vol. 8, Book 82, Number 817.**

75. Imām Aḥmad ibn Ḥanbal, *al-Musnad,* **Vol. 1, p. 55**. **Nūr al-Dīn al-Shāfi'ī al-Ḥalābī,** *Al-Sīrah al- Ḥalābiyyah,* **Vol. 4, p. 309. al-Ṭabarī,** *Tārīkh, Arabic Version,* **Vol. 1, p. 1822. al-Ṭabarī,** *Tārīkh, English Version,* **Vol. 9, p. 192.**

76. al-Ṭabarī, *Tārīkh, Arabic Version,* **Vol. 2 p. 456.**

77. al-Bukhārī, *al-Ṣaḥīḥ, English Version, Punishment of Disbelievers at War with Allāh and his Apostle,* **Vol. 8, Book 82, Number 817.**

78. al-Bukhārī, *al-Ṣaḥīḥ, English Version, Punishment of Disbelievers at War with Allāh and his Apostle,* **Vol. 8, Book 82, Number 817.**

79. al-Ya'qūbī, *al-Tārīkh,* **Vol. 1 p. 84.**

80. al-Bukhārī, *al-Ṣaḥīḥ, English Version, Punishment of Disbelievers at War with Allāh and his Apostle,* **Vol. 8, Book 82, Number 817.**

81. Ibn Qutaybah, *Tārīkh al-Khulafah,* **Vol. 1, pp. 12-19.**

82. al-Khatīb al-Baghdādī, *Tārīkh Baghdād,* **Vol. 4, p. 333.**

83. Ibn Mājah, *al-Sunan,* **Vol 1 p. 44. al-Ḥākim,** *al-Mustadrak,* **Vol. 3, p. 112.**

84. al-Ḥākim, *al-Mustadrak,* **Vol. 3, p. 112.**

85. al-Ḥākim, *al-Mustadrak,* **Vol. 3, p. 112.**

86. al-Ḥākim, *al-Mustadrak,* **Vol. 3, p. 112. Imām Aḥmad ibn Ḥanbal,** *al-Musnad,* **Vol. 5, p. 40.**

87. al-Muttaqī al Hindī, *Kanz al-'Ummāl,* **Vol. 6, p. 143 Ḥadīth 2541. Imām Aḥmad ibn Ḥanbal,** *al-Musnad,* **Vol. 5, p. 31.**

88. al-Ḥākim, *al-Mustadrak,* **Vol. 3, p. 134. Imām Aḥmad ibn Ḥanbal,** *al-Musnad,* **Vol. 1, p. 331. al-Nasā'ī,** *Khasā'is al-'Alawiyya,* **p. 6.**

89. Imām Aḥmad ibn Ḥanbal, *al-Musnad,* **Vol. 4, p. 174.**

90. Muslim, *al-Ṣaḥīḥ, English Version, The Book of Faith, Kitāb al-Imān,* **Book 001, Number 0141.**

91. al-Tirmidhī, *Jāmi' al-Ṣaḥīḥ, English Version,* **Number 6091. al -Nasā'ī,** *al-Sunan,* **Vol. 8, p. 117. al -Nasā'ī,** *Khasā'is al-'Alawiyya,* **p. 27. al-Hāfiz Jalāl al-Dīn al-Suyūtī,** *Jāmi' al-Kabīr,* **p. 152, 408. Sibt ibn al-Jauzī,** *Tadhkirat Khwāss al-'Ummah,* **p. 15. al-Khatīb al-Baghdādī,** *Tārīkh Baghdād,* **Vol. 14, p. 426.**

92. **al-Hāfiz Jalāl al-Dīn al-Suyūtī,** *Jāmi' al-Kabīr,* **Vol. 6, p. 390. al-Tirmidhī,** *Jāmi' al-Ṣaḥīḥ, Arabic Version,* **Vol 2, p. 299. Abū Nu'aym al-Isbahānī,** *Hilyat al-Awliyā',* **Vol. 6, p. 295.**

93. **al-Muḥibb al-Ṭabarī,** *al-Riyād al-Nadira,* **Vol 2, p. 198. Ibn Sa'd,** *al-Tabaqāt (al-Kabīr),* **Vol 2, p. 101. Ibn Ḥajar al-'Asqalānī,** *al-Isabah,* **Vol 4, p. 568. Ibn Ḥajar al-'Asqalānī,** *Tahdhīb al-Tahdhīb,* **Vol 7, pp. 337-338. Ibn Ḥajar al-'Asqalānī,** *Fath al-Barī,* **Vol. 8, p. 485. al-Hāfiz Jalāl al-Dīn al-Suyūtī,** *Tārīkh al-Khulafa,* **p. 124. al-Hāfiz Jalāl al-Dīn al-Suyūtī,** *al-Itqān,* **Vol. 2, p. 319.**

94. **al-Muḥibb al-Ṭabarī,** *al-Riyād al-Nadira,* **Vol. 2, p. 198. Ibn Ḥājar al-Haythamī,** *al-Sawā'iq al-Muhriqah,* **p.76.**

95. **Imām Aḥmad ibn Ḥanbal,** *al-Musnad,* **Vol. 3, p. 136, Vol. 5, p. 26.**

96. **al-Ḥākim,** *al-Mustadrak, Imām Ḥakim adds that this tradition is authentic according to the endorsement by the two Shaykhs Muslim and Bukhārī who have not included it in their Books,* **Vol. 3 p. 122. Imām Aḥmad ibn Ḥanbal,** *al-Musnad, narrated by Abū Sa'id al-Khudrī,* **Vol. 3 p. 33, 82.**

97. **al-Muttaqī al Hindī,** *Kanz al-'Ummāl,* **Vol. 6, p. 398.**

98. **al-Tirmidhī,** *Arabic Version, Jāmi' al-Ṣaḥīḥ, Kitāb al-Manāqib, Cairo Edition,* **Vol. 5, p. 637, Number 3723. al-Tirmidhī,** *Jāmi' al-Ṣaḥīḥ, English Version,* **Number 6087.**

99. **al-Muttaqī al Hindī,** *Kanz al-'Ummāl,* **Vol. 6, p. 401.**

100. **al-Ḥākim,** *al-Mustadrak, Chapter of the Virtues of 'Alī, narrated by Ibn Abbas, whose report has been transmitted through two different chain of authorities, and Jābir ibn 'Abdullāh al-Ansārī,* **Vol. 3, pp. 126-127, p.226. al-Tirmidhī,** *Arabic Version, Jāmi' al- Ṣaḥīḥ, Kitāb al-Manāqib, Cairo Edition,* **Vol. 5, p. pp. 201, 637. Imām Aḥmad ibn Ḥanbal,** *Fadā'il al-Sahāba,* **Vol. 2, p. 635, Number 1081. al-Hāfiz Jalāl al-Dīn al-Suyūtī,** *Jāmī' al-Saghīr,* **Vol 1, pp. 107, 374. al-Hāfiz Jalāl al-Dīn al-Suyūtī,** *Tārīkh al-Khulafa,* **p.171. Ibn al-Kathīr,** *al-Bidāyah wa al-Nihāyah,* **Vol. 7, p. 358.**

Khatīb al-Baghdādī, *Tārīkh Baghdād,* **Vol. 2, p. 337, Vol. 4, p. 348, Vol. 7, p173, Vol. 11, pp. 48-50, Vol. 13, p. 204. Ibn al-Athīr,** *Usd al-Ghabah,* **Vol. 4, p. 22. Ibn Ḥājar al-Haythamī,** *Majma' al-Zawā'id,* **Vol. 9, p114. al-Muttaqī al Hindī,** *Kanz al-'Ummāl,* **p. 13, 15, Traditions 348-379. Ibn Ḥājar al-Haythamī,** *al-Sawā'iq al-Muhriqah,* **Ch. 9, Section 2, p. 189.**

101. al- Ḥākim, *al-Mustadrak,* **Vol. 3, p.122.**

102. al-Tirmidhī, *Jāmi' al-Ṣaḥīḥ, Arabic Version,* **Vol. 5, p. 297. Khatīb al-Baghdādī,** *Tārīkh Baghdād,* **Vol. 4, p. 321. Fakhr al-Dīn al-Rāzī,** *Tafsīr al-Kabīr,* **Vol. 1, p. 111. Ibn Ḥājar al-Haythamī,** *Jāmī' as-Saghīr,* **Vol. 2, p. 74, 75, 140. Ibn Ḥājar al-Haythamī,** *al-Sawā'iq al-Muhriqah, narrated by Ibn 'Abbās and Umme Salama,* **Ch. 9, p. 11, Number 21. Ibn Qutaybah**, *al-Imāmah wa al-Siyāsah,* **Vol. 1, p. 111.**

103. Sibt ibn al-Jauzī, *Tadhkīrat Khwāss al-'Ummah,* **p. 20.**

104. al-Ḥākim, *al-Mustadrak, narrated by Abū Ḥurayra,* **Vol. 2, p 124**. **al-Ḥākim,** *al-Mustadrak, narrated by Umm Salama,* **Vol. 3, p. 124. Ibn Ḥājar al-Haythamī,** *al-Sawā'iq al-Muhriqah, narrated by Umm Salama,* **Ch. 9, Section 2, pp. 191, 194. al-Hāfiz Jalāl al-Dīn al-Suyūtī,** *Tārīkh al-Khulafa,* **p. 173.**

105. Ibn Sa'd, *al-Tabaqāt (al-Kabīr),* **Vol. 3, p. 151. Ibn al-Kathīr,** *al-Bidāyah wa al-Nihāyah,* **Vol. 6, p. 303. Ibn al-Athīr,** *al-Kamīl,* **Vol. 2, p. 129. al-Ṭabarī,** *Tārīkh, Arabic Version,* **Vol. 2, p. 460.**

106. al-Ṭabarī, *Tārīkh, Arabic Version,* **Vol. 1, p. 159.**

107. al-Nasā'ī, *Khasā'is al-'Alawiyya, (six traditions have been reported relating to this point),* **p14.**

108. Abū Dāwūd, *al-Sunan, The Office of the Judge (Kitāb al-Akdīyah),* **Book 24, Number 3575.**

109. al-Tirmidhī, *Jāmi' al-Ṣaḥīḥ, English Version,* **Number 6088.**

110. Imām Aḥmad ibn Ḥanbal, *al-Musnad,* **Vol. 1, p. 3, 151, Vol. 3, p. 283, Vol. 4, pp. 164-165. al-Ḥākim,** *al-Mustadrak,* **Vol. 3, p. 51. al-Nasā'ī,** *Khasā'is al-'Alawiyya, (The distinctions of 'Alī),* **p.20. al-Tirmidhī,** *Jāmi' al-Ṣaḥīḥ, Arabic Version, narrated by Anas ibn Mālik,* **Vol. 2, p. 183. al-Muḥibb al-Ṭabarī,** *al-Riyād al-Nadira, (in commentary on Sūrah Tawbah)* **p147. al-Hāfiz Jalāl al-Dīn al-Suyūtī,** *al-Durr al-Manthūr,* **Vol. 3, p. 208. al-Muttaqī al Hindī,** *Kanz al-'Ummāl,* **Vol. 1, p. 246-249. Sibt ibn al-Jauzī,** *Tadhkīrat Khwāss al-'Ummah,* **p22. Ibn Kathīr,** *Tafsīr,* **Vol. 2, p. 333. Ibn Ḥājar al-Haythamī,** *Majma' al-Zawā'id,* **Vol. 7, p. 29.**

111. Imām Aḥmad ibn Ḥanbal, *al-Musnad, Manāqib 'Alī,* **Vol. 6 p. 390, Number 4972. al-Muttaqī al Hindī,** *Kanz al-'Ummāl, quotes from Ibn al-Asākir's Tārīkh,* **Vol. 4 p. 40, Number 918.**

112. Nūr al-Dīn al-Shāfi'ī al-Ḥalābī, *al-Sīrah al-Ḥalabīyyah,* **Vol. 2, pp. 26, 120.**

113. Sibt ibn al-Jauzī, *Tadhkīrat Khwāss al-'Ummah,* **p. 13-14.**

114. al-Mas'ūdī, *Murūj al-Dhahab,* **Vol. 2, p. 49.**

115. al-Muttaqī al Hindī, *Kanz al-'Ummāl,* **Vol. 6. p. 395, Number 6029 and Number 6032.**

116. al-Bukhārī, *al-Ṣaḥīḥ, Arabic Version, Book of Ghazawa, Qazwa Tabūk,* **p.54. al-Bukhārī,** *al-Ṣaḥīḥ, English Version, Military Expeditions led by the Prophet, Kitāb al-Maghāzī,* **Volume 5, Book 57, Number 60.**

117. Fakhr al-Dīn al-Rāzī, *Tafsīr al-Kabīr, in the interpretation of the verse of Sūrah Baqarah,* **Vol. 2, p.189. al-Ghazālī,** *Ihya al-Ulūm,* **Vol. 3, p. 223. Ibn al-Athīr,** *Usd al-Ghābah,* **Vol. 4 p. 25. al-Ḥākim,** *al-Mustadrak,* **Vol. 3, p. 4. al-Qurtubī,** *Tafsīr,* **Vol. 3, p. 347.**

118. al-Kulaynī, *al-Kāfī, English Version, translated by Muḥammad Sarwar. The Book on Virtue of Knowledge, Chapter on Following the Sunnah and Evidence of the Book,* **H 197, Ch. 22, h 1.**

119. al-Kulaynī, *al-Kāfī, English Version, translated by Muḥammad Sarwar. The Book on Virtue of Knowledge, Chapter on Following the Sunnah and Evidence of the Book,* **H 200, Ch. 22, h 4.**

120. al-Kulaynī, *al-Kāfī, English Version, translated by Muḥammad Sarwar. The Book on Virtue of Knowledge, Chapter on Following the Sunnah and Evidence of the Book,* **H 201, Ch. 22, h 5.**

121. Muslim, *al-Ṣaḥīḥ, English Version, The Book Pertaining to the Merits of the Companions (May Allah be pleased with them) of the Holy Prophet (pbuh),* **Book 031, Number 5915. Ibn al-Kathīr,** *al-Bidāyah wa al-Nihāyah,* **Vol. 7, p. 341. 163. Ibn Mājah,** *al-Sunan,* **Vol. 1, p. 58. al-Nasā'ī,** *Khasā'is al-'Alawiyya,* **p.50. al-Qundūzī al-Ḥanafī,** *Yanābī' al-Mawaddah,* **p. 51. al-Tirmidhī,** *Jāmi' al-Ṣaḥīḥ, Arabic Version,* **Vol. 5, p654. al-Ḥākim,** *al-Mustadrak, Imām Ḥakim adds that this tradition is authentic based on the criteria of two Shaykhs (al-Bukhārī and Muslim)* **Vol. 3, p. 150. al-Muḥibb al-Ṭabarī,** *Dakā'ir al-Uqba,* **p. 25.**

122. al-Baidhawī, *Tafsīr,* **under the commentary of Verse 3:61.**

123. al-Hāfiz Jalāl al-Dīn al-Suyūtī, *al-Durr al-Manthūr,* **Vol. 2, p. 38.**

124. al-Tirmidhī, *Jāmi' al-Ṣaḥīḥ, English Version,* **Number 6092.**

125. al-Tirmidhī, *Jāmi' al-Ṣaḥīḥ, English Version,* **Number 6082.**

126. al-Tirmidhī, *Jāmi' al-Ṣaḥīḥ, English Version,* **Number 6083. al-Tirmidhī,** *Jāmi' al-Ṣaḥīḥ, Arabic Version,* **Vol. 5 p. 300. Ibn Mājah,** *al-Sunan,* **Vol. 1 p. 44. Imām Aḥmad ibn Ḥanbal,** *al-Musnad,* **Vol. 4 p. 164, 165. al-Nasā'ī,** *Khasā'is al-'Alawiyya,* **p. 20. al-Hāfiz Jalāl al-Dīn al-Suyūtī,** *Jāmī' as-Saghīr,* **Vol. 2, p. 56.**

127. Muslim, *al-Ṣaḥīḥ, English Version, The Book Pertaining to the Merits of the Companions (Allah be pleased with them) of the Holy Prophet (pbuh),* **Book 031, Number 5955.**

128. al-Tirmidhī, *Jāmi' al-Ṣaḥīḥ, Arabic Version,* **Vol. 5, pp. 351, 663.**

129. Ibn Ḥājar al-Haythamī, *al-Sawā'iq al-Muhriqah,* **Ch. 11, Section 1. p. 220. al-Hāfiz Jalāl al-Dīn al-Suyūtī,** *al-Durr al-Manthūr,* **Vol. 5, p. 199. Imām Aḥmad ibn Ḥanbal,** *al-Musnad,* **Vol. 1, p. 331. Fakhr al-Dīn al-Rāzī,** *Tafsīr al-Kabīr,* **Vol. 1 p. 783.**

130. al-Ṭabarī, *Tafsīr al-Kabīr, under the verse 33:33,* **Vol. 22, p. 5. al-Muḥibb al-Ṭabarī,** *Dakā'ir al-Uqba,* **p. 24. Ibn Ḥājar al-Haythamī,** *al-Sawā'iq al-Muhriqah,* **Ch. 11, Section 1, p. 221.**

131. al-Ṭabarī, *Tafsīr al-Kabīr,* **Vol. 22, p. 6. al-Ḥākim,** *al-Mustadrak,* **Vol. 2, p. 416, Vol. 3, p. 417. Imām Aḥmad ibn Ḥanbal,** *al-Musnad,* **Vol. 6, p. 107. Ibn Ḥājar al-Haythamī,** *Majma' al-Zawā'id,* **Vol. 9, p. 167. al-Bayhāqī,** *al-Sunan,* **Vol. 2, p. 152.**

132. al-Tirmidhī, *Jāmi' al-Ṣaḥīḥ, Arabic Version,* **Vol. 12, p. 85. Imām Aḥmad ibn Ḥanbal,** *al-Musnad,* **Vol. 3, p. 258. al- Ḥākim,** *al-Mustadrak, Imām Ḥakim adds that this tradition is authentic based on the criteria of two Shaykhs (al-Bukhārī and Muslim)* **Vol. 3, p. 158.**

133. al-Ṭabarī, *Tafsīr al-Kabīr,* **Vol. 22, p. 6. al-Hāfiz Jalāl al-Dīn al-Suyūtī,** *al-Durr al-Manthūr,* **Vol. 5, pp. 198, 199. al-Muḥibb al-Ṭabarī,** *Dakā'ir al-Uqba, narrated by Anas ibn Mālik,* **p. 24. Ibn al-Athīr,** *Usd al-Ghābah,* **Vol. 5, p. 174. Ibn Ḥājar al-Haythamī,** *Majma' al-Zawā'id,* **Vol. 9, pp. 121, 168. Ibn Kathīr,** *Tafsīr,* **Vol. 3, p. 483.**

134. 'Allāmah Shiblī Nu'manī, *Sīrat-i-Nu'manī, Imām Abū Ḥanīfah, English Translation Imām Abū Ḥanīfah, Life and Works by Hādī Ḥusayn,* **Chapter 10, Tradition and Principles of Tradition, p. 120.**

135. Haykal, *The Life of Muhammad,* **Preface to the Second Edition.**

136. Ibn Ḥajar al-'Asqalānī, *al-Isaba,* **Vol. 2, printed in Egypt, p. 509. Sibt ibn al-Jauzī,** *Tadhkīrat Khwāss al-'Ummah,* **p. 85, 87.**

137. 'Allāmah Shiblī Nu'manī, *Sīrat-i-Nu'manī, Imām Abū Ḥanīfah, English Translation Imām Abū Ḥanīfah, Life and Works by Hādī Ḥusayn,* **Chapter 11, Fiqh, p. 141.**

138. Imām Aḥmad ibn Ḥanbal, *Fadā'il al-Sahāba,* **Vol. 2, p. 647, Number 1100. Ibn Sa'd,** *al-Tabaqāt (al-Kabīr),* **Vol. 2, p. 338. al-Muḥibb al-Ṭabarī,** *al-Riyād al-Nadirah,* **Vol. 2, p. 194. al-Hāfiz Jalāl al-Dīn al-Suyūtī,** *Tārīkh al-Khulāfa,* **p. 171.**

139. al-Bukhārī, *al-Ṣaḥīḥ, Arabic Version, Book of Ghazawa, Qazwa Tabūk,* **p.54. al-Bukhārī,** *al-Ṣaḥīḥ, English Version, Military Expeditions led by the Prophet, Kitāb al-Maghāzī,* **Volume 5, Book 57, Number 60.**

140. Encyclopedia of Philosophy, *'Physikalismus,' in Scientia,* **50, 1931.**

141. M. Schlick, *'Positivismus und Realismus' in Erkenntnis,* **3, 1932.**

142. al-Mufīd, *al-Amālī, English Translation by Mulla Asghar Ali M.M.Jaffer, 'Alī AS writes to people of Kufa,* **p. 247.**

143. al-Tirmidhī, *Jāmi' al-Ṣaḥīḥ, English Version,* **Number 2773.**

144. Muslim, *al-Ṣaḥīḥ, English Version, The Book of Prayers, (Kitāb as-Salāt),* **Book 4, Number 0844.**

145. al-Bukhārī, *al-Ṣaḥīḥ, English Version, Call to Prayers, (Adhān),* **Vol. 1, Book 11, Number 647.**

146. al-Bukhārī, *al-Ṣaḥīḥ, English Version, Medicine,* **Vol. 7, Book 71, Number 612.**

147. al-Bukhārī, *al-Ṣaḥīḥ, English Version, Call to Prayers, (Adhān),* **Vol. 1, Book 11, Number 655.**

148. al-Bukhārī, *al-Ṣaḥīḥ, English Version, Call to Prayers, (Adhān),* **Vol. 1, Book 11, Number 651.**

149. **al-Bukhārī,** *al-Ṣaḥīḥ, English Version, Call to Prayers, (Adhān),* **Vol. 1, Book 11 Number 681. Muslim,** *al-Ṣaḥīḥ, English Version, The Book of Prayers, (Kitāb as-Salāt)* **Book 004 Number 0837.**

150. **Muslim,** *al-Ṣaḥīḥ, English Version, The Book of Prayers, (Kitāb as-Salāt)* **Book 004 Number 0825.**

151. **Muslim,** *al-Ṣaḥīḥ, English Version, The Book of Prayers, (Kitāb as-Salāt)* **Book 004 Number 0838.**

152. **Ibn Sa'd,** *al-Tabaqāt (al-Kabīr),* **Vol. 2, p. 249.**

153. **al-Ḥākim**, *al-Mustadrak,* **Vol. 3, p. 43.**

154. **Ibn Sa'd,** *al-Tabaqāt (al-Kabīr),* **Vol. 2, p. 145, 249.**

155. **al-Bukhārī,** *al-Ṣaḥīḥ, English Version, Book of Companions (May Allah be pleased with them) of the Prophet (pbuh),* **Vol. 5, Book 57, Number 77. al-Bukhārī,** *al-Ṣaḥīḥ, English Version, Book of Judgements,* **Vol. 9, Book 89, Number 297.**

156. **al-Bukhārī,** *al-Ṣaḥīḥ, English Version, Book of Companions (May Allāh be pleased with them) of the Prophet (pbuh),* **Vol. 5, Book 57, Number 19. al-Ṭabarī,** *Tārīkh, Arabic Version,* **Vol. 2, p. 439.**

157. **Imām Aḥmad ibn Ḥanbal,** *al-Musnad,* **Vol. 1, p. 356.**

158. **al-Bukhārī,** *al-Ṣaḥīḥ, English Version, Prayers, (Salāt),* **Vol. 1, Book 8, Number 456.**

159. **al-Bukhārī,** *al-Ṣaḥīḥ, English Version, Book of Companions (May Allah be pleased with them) of the Prophet (pbuh),* **Vol. 5, Book 57, Number 9.**

160. **al-Bukhārī,** *al-Ṣaḥīḥ, English Version, Merits of the Helpers in Madinah,* **Vol. 5, Book 58, Number 244**

161. **Imām Aḥmad ibn Ḥanbal,** *al-Musnad, the ten exclusive merits of 'Alī,* **Vol. 1, p. 175. Imām Aḥmad ibn Ḥanbal,** *al-Musnad,* **Vol. 2 p. 26, Vol. 4, p. 369**. **al-Nasā'ī,** *Khasā'is al-*

'Alawiyya, **p. 13, 14. Sibt ibn al-Jauzī,** *Tadhkīrat Khwāss al-'Ummah,* **p. 24, 25. Ibn al-Kathīr,** *al-Bidāyah wa al-Nihāyah,* **Vol. 7, p. 342. al-Muḥibb al-Ṭabarī,** *al-Riyād al-Nadirah,* **Vol. 2, p. 451. Nūr al-Dīn al-Shāfi'ī al-Ḥalābī,** *al-Sīrah al-Ḥalabiyyah,* **Vol. 3, p. 374.**

162. al-Tirmidhī, *Jāmi' al-Ṣaḥīḥ, English Version,* **Number 6089.**

163. al-Nasā'ī, *Khasā'is al-'Alawiyya,* **pp. 13, 14.**

164. Sibt ibn al-Jauzī, *Tadhkīrat Khwāss al-'Ummah,* **pp. 24-25.**

165. al-Ḥākim, *al-Mustadrak,* **Vol. 3, pp.117-125.**

166. al-Ḥākim, *al-Mustadrak,* **Vol. 3, p. 17.**

167. al-Ḥākim, *al-Mustadrak,* **Vol. 3 p. 125. al-Muḥibb al-Ṭabarī,** *al-Riyād al-Nadirah,* **Vol. 2, p. 192. al-Hāfiz Jalāl al-Dīn al-Suyūtī,** *Tārīkh al-Khulāfa,* **p. 175.**

168. Imām Aḥmad ibn Ḥanbal, *al-Musnad,* **Vol. 4, p. 369.**

169. al-Tirmidhī, *Jāmi' al-Ṣaḥīḥ, English Version,* **Number 6084.**

170. See Nūr al-Dīn al-Shāfi'ī al-Ḥalābī, *al-Sīrah al-Ḥalabīyyah, the first brotherhood,* **Vol. 2 p. 26,** *the second brotherhood,* **Vol. 2, p. 120. Ibn Hishām,** *al-Sīrah al-Nabawīyyah, Biography of the Prophet,* **Vol. 1, p. 505.**

171. al-Bukhārī, *al-Ṣaḥīḥ, English Version, Book of Companions (May Allah be pleased with them) of the Prophet (pbuh),* **Vol. 5, Book 57, Number 8**

172. al-Bukhārī, *al-Ṣaḥīḥ, English Version, Book of Companions (May Allah be pleased with them) of the Prophet (pbuh),* **Vol. 5, Book 57, Number 14.**

173. al-Tirmidhī, *Jāmi' al-Ṣaḥīḥ, English Version,* **Number 6145.**

174. al-Bukhārī, *al-Ṣaḥīḥ, English Version, Military expeditions led by the Prophet (pbuh) (Kitāb al-Maghāzī),* **Vol. 5, Book 59, Number 521.**

175. Fakhr al-Dīn al-Rāzī, *Tafsīr al-Kabīr,* **Vol. 27, pp. 165, 166. Ibn Ḥājar al-Haythamī,** *al-Sawā'iq al-Muhriqah,* **Ch. 11, Section 1, p. 259. al-Ṭabarī,** *Tārīkh, Arabic Version,* **under the commentary of Verse 42:23. al-Qurtubī,** *Tafsīr,* **under commentary of Verse 42:23. al-Baidhawī,** *Tafsīr,* **under the commentary of Verse 42:23.**

176. al-Zamakhsharī, *al-Kashshāf,* **Vol. 4, p. 172. al-Majlisī,** *Bihār al-Anwār,* **Vol. 23, p. 233.**

177. al-Muḥibb al-Ṭabarī, *Dakā'ir al-Uqba,* p.26

178. al-Ḥākim, *al-Mustadrak, "Chapter of understanding the Virtues of the Companions,"* **Vol. 3, p. 172. Ibn Ḥājar al-Haythamī,** *al-Sawā'iq al-Muhriqah,* **Ch. 11, Section 1, p. 259.**

179. Ibn Ḥājar al-Haythamī, *al-Sawā'iq al-Muhriqah,* **Ch. 11, Section 1, p. 225.**

180. al-Bukhārī, *al-Ṣaḥīḥ, English Version, Prophetic Commentary of the Qur'ān, Tafsīr of the Prophet (pbuh),* **Vol. 6, Book 60, Number 321.**

181. al-Ḥākim, *al-Mustadrak, "Chapter of understanding the Virtues of the Companions," Imām al-Ḥākim adds that the tradition is authentic based on the criteria of the two Shaykhs (al-Bukhāri and Muslim).* **Vol. 3, p. 148. al-Dhahabī,** *Talkhīs al-Mustadrak,* **Vol. 3, p. 148. Ibn Athīr,** *Usd al-Ghābah,* **Vol. 3, p. 33.**

182. Ibn Ḥājar al-Haythamī, *al-Sawā'iq al-Muhriqah, quoted from al-Darqutnī and al-Bayhaqī,* **Ch. 11, Section 1, p. 349.**

183. Fakhr al-Dīn al-Rāzī, *Tafsīr al-Kabīr,* **Vol. 27, p. 166 under the commentary of Verse 42:23. Ibn Ḥājar al-Haythamī,** *al-Sawā'iq al-Muhriqah,* **p. 88, in connection with Verse 33:33.**

184. al-Ṭabarī, *Tārīkh, English Version, Events of year 51 A.H, Execution of Ḥujr ibn 'Ādī,* **Vol. 18, pp. 122-123.**

185. al-Mas'ūdī, *Hāmish ibn al-Athīr,* **Vol. 6, pp. 81-82.**

186. Ibn Kathīr, *al-Bidāyah wa al-Nihāyah,* **Vol. 7, p. 341**

187. Muslim, *al-Ṣaḥīḥ, English Version, The Book pertaining to the Merits of the Companions (Allah be pleased with them) of the Holy Prophet (pbuh),* **Book 031, Number 5915.**

188. Muslim, *al-Ṣaḥīḥ, Arabic Version, Chapter of Virtues of Companions, Section of Virtues of 'Alī,* **Vol. 4, p. 1874, Tradition 38.**

189. Ibn Ḥajar al-'Asqalānī, *al-Isabah,* **Vol. 1 p. 154**. **Ibn al-Athīr,** *al-Kāmil,* **Vol. 3 p. 162. Ibn Asākir,** *Tārīkh,* **Vol. 3, p. 222. Ibn Ḥajar al-'Asqalānī,** *Tahdhīb al-Tahdhīb,* **Vol. 1 p. 435. Ibn Abī 'l-Ḥadīd al-Mu'tazilī,** *Sharh Nahj al-Balaghah,* **Vol. 1, p. 116. Ibn 'Abd al-Barr,** *al-Isti'āb,* **Vol. 1, p. 65.**

190. Sayyīd ibn Ta'ūs, *Maqtalu'l Ḥusayn,* **pp. 10-11.**

191. al-Ṭabarī, *Tārīkh, Arabic Version,* **Vol. 2, p. 329.**

192. Muslim, *al-Ṣaḥīḥ, Arabic Version, Chapter of Virtues of the Companions, Section of the virtues of 'Alī, 1980 Edition Pub. in Saudi Arabia,* **Vol. 4, p. 1874, Number 37. Muslim,** *al-Ṣaḥīḥ, English Version, The Book pertaining to the Merits of the Companions (May Allāh be pleased with them) of the Holy Prophet (pbuh),* **Book 031, Number 5923.**

193. Mālik ibn Anas, *al-Muwaṭṭā', English Version, Book on Sadaqah, What is Disliked in Sadaqah,* **Book 58, Number 58.3.13.**

194. al-Bukhārī, *al-Ṣaḥīḥ, English Version, Military Expeditions led by the Prophet (pbuh), Al-Maghaazi,* **Vol. 5, Book 59, Number 546.**

195. al-Ḥāfiz Jalāl al-Dīn al-Suyūtī, *al-Durr al-Manthūr,* **Vol. 4, p. 177. al-Muttaqī al Hindī,** *Kanz al-'Ummāl,* **Vol. 2, p.158. Ibn Ḥājar al-Haythamī,** *al-Sawā'iq al-Muhriqah,* **Ch. 15, p. 21-22.**

196. al-Bukhārī, *al-Ṣaḥīḥ, English Version, Laws of inheritance (Al-Farā'id),* **Vol. 8, Book 80, Number 721.**

197. al-Bukhārī, *al-Ṣaḥīḥ, English Version, Book of Companions (May Allah be pleased with them) of the Prophet (pbuh),* **Vol. 5, Book 57, Number 60.**

198. Nūr al-Dīn al-Shāfī' al-Ḥalābī, *al-Sīrah al-Halabīyyah,* **Vol. 3 p. 391, 400. al-Mas'ūdī,** *Murūj al-Dhahab.*

199. al-Bukhārī, *al-Ṣaḥīḥ, English Version, Military Expeditions led by the Prophet, (Kitāb al Maghāzī),* **Volume 5, Book 59, Number 546.**

200. al-Bukhārī, *al-Ṣaḥīḥ, Arabic Version,* **Vol. 4, p. 64. al-Bukhārī,** *al-Ṣaḥīḥ, English Version, Asking Permission,* **Vol. 8, Book 74, Number 30.**

201. al-Tirmidhī, *Jāmi' al-Ṣaḥīḥ, Arabic Version,* **Vol. 5, p. 702. al-Ḥākim,** *al-Mustadrak, Imām Ḥakim adds that this tradition is authentic based on the criteria of two Shaykhs (al-Bukhārī and Muslim)* **Vol. 3, p. 157. Imām Aḥmad ibn Ḥanbal,** *al-Musnad,* **Vol. 3, p. 135. Imām Aḥmad ibn Ḥanbal,** *Fadā'il al-Sahāba,* **Vol. 2, p. 755, Number 1325. Abū Nu'aym al-Isbahānī,** *Hilyat al-Awliyā',* **Vol. 2, p. 344. Ibn Ḥājar al-Haythamī,** *Majma' al-Zawā'id,* **Vol. 9, p. 223.**

202. Ibn Sa'd, *al-Tabaqāt (al-Kabīr),* **Vol. 4, p. 121, 122.**

203. al-Bukhārī, *al-Ṣaḥīḥ, English Version, One fifth of the Booty to the Cause of Allāh (Khūmus),* **Volume 4, Book 53, Number 347.**

204. Abū Dāwūd, *al-Sunan, Tribute Spoils and Rulership (Kitāb al-Kharaj, Wa al-Fai' Wa al-Imāra),* **Book 19, Number 2967.**

205. Nūr al-Dīn al-Shāfi'ī al-Ḥalābī, *al-Sīrah al-Ḥalabīyyah,* **Vol. 3, p. 273. Ibn Ḥājar al-Haythamī,** *al-Sawā'iq al-Muhriqah,* **Ch. 11, Section 1, p. 230,** *who also quotes from al-Tabarani,* **Section 2, p. 342. Ibn Ḥājar al-Haythamī,** *Majma' al-Zawa'id,* **Vol. 9, p. 163. al-Hāfiz Jalāl al-Dīn al-Suyūtī,** *al-Durr al-Manthūr,* **Vol. 2, p. 60. Ibn al-Athīr,** *Usd al-Ghābah,* **Vol. 3, p137. al-Qundūzī al-**

Ḥanafī, *Yanābī' al-Mawaddah,* **p. 41, 335. al-Muttaqī al Hindī,** *Kanz al-'Ummāl,* **Vol. 1, p. 168. Sibt ibn al-Jauzī,** *Tadhkīrat Khwāss al-'Ummah,* **pp. 28, 33.**

206. Ibn Ḥājar al-Haythamī, *al-Sawā'iq al-Muhriqah, Chapter of The Holy Prophet's Will,* **p. 136.**

207. Imām Aḥmad ibn Ḥanbal, *al-Musnad,* **Vol. 5, p. 182, 189.**

208. Imām Aḥmad ibn Ḥanbal, *al-Musnad,* **Vol. 3 p. 17, 26. al-Muttaqī al Hindī,** *Kanz al-'Ummāl,* **Vol. 1, p. 185, Number 944, 945 and 946.**

209. al-Tirmidhī, *Jāmi' al-Ṣaḥīḥ, Arabic Version,* **Vol. 5, p. 329, Number 387b. al-Tirmidhī,** *Jāmi' al-Ṣaḥīḥ, English Version,* **Number 6144**.

210. al-Ḥākim, *al-Mustadrak,* **Vol. 3, p. 148.**

211. Muslim, *al-Ṣaḥīḥ, English Version, The Book pertaining to the Merits of the Companions (Allah be pleased with them) of the Holy Prophet (pbuh),* **Book 031, Number 5920.**

212. Muslim, *al-Ṣaḥīḥ, English Version, The Book pertaining to the Merits of the Companions (Allah be pleased with them) of the Holy Prophet (pbuh),* **Book 031, Number 5923.**

213. al-Ḥākim, *al-Mustadrak,* **Vol. 3, p. 109.**

214. al-Bukhārī, *Tārikh al-Kabīr,* **Vol. 3, p. 96.**

215. Ibn Ḥajar al-Haythamī, *al-Sawā'iq al-Muhriqah,* **Vol. 1 p. 25.**

216. See Ibn al-Kathīr, *Ikhtaisār al-Ulūm al-Aḥadīth,* **p. 21.**

217. See al-Hāfiz ibn Salāh, *Ulūm al-Aḥadīth, 'Bukhārī and Muslim,'* **p. 17.**

218. See Ibn Ḥajar al-'Asqalānī, *Fath al-Barī, 'Biography of Imām Bukhārī.'*

219. **Imām Aḥmad ibn Ḥanbal,** *al-Musnad,* **Vol. 5, p. 356.**

220. **Imām Aḥmad ibn Ḥanbal,** *al-Musnad,* **Vol. 4, p. 438. al-Ḥākim,** *al-Mustadrak,* **Vol. 3, p. 111.**

221. **al-Tirmidhī,** *Jāmi' al-Ṣaḥīḥ, Arabic Version,* **Vol. 5, p. 296.**

222. **Ibn Ḥajar al-Haythamī,** *al-Sawā'iq al-Muhriqah,* **Ch. 11, p. 103.**

223. **al-Bukhārī,** *al-Ṣaḥīḥ, English Version, Military Expeditions led by the Prophet (pbuh) (al-Maghāzi),* **Vol. 5, Book 59, Number 637.**

224. **Imām Aḥmad ibn Ḥanbal,** *al-Musnad,* **Vol. 1 p. 3.**

225. **al-Ḥākim,** *al-Mustadrak,* **Vol. 3, p. 51.**

226. **al-Tirmidhī,** *Jāmi' al-Ṣaḥīḥ, Arabic Version,* **Vol. 2, p. 183.**

227. **al-Nasā'ī,** *Khasā'is al-'Alawīyya, The distinctions of 'Alī.*

228. **al-Bukhārī,** *al-Ṣaḥīḥ, English Version, Prophetic Commentary of the Qur'ān, Tafsīr of the Prophet (pbuh),* **Vol. 6; Book 60, Number 178.**

229. **Abū Dāwūd,** *al-Sunan, English Translation, Prescribed Punishments (Kitāb al-Hudūd)* **Book 38, Number 4385. Ibn Mājah,** *al-Sunan,* **Vol. 2, p. 227. al-Ḥākim,** *al-Mustadrak,* **Vol. 2, p. 59. al-Bayhaqī,** *al-Sunan al-Kubra,* **Vol. 6, p. 64**.

230. **Sibt ibn al-Jauzī,** *Tadkīrat Khwāss al-'Ummah,* **p.75.**

231. **al-Bukhārī,** *English Version Prescribed Punishments (Kitāb al-Hudūd), Insane male or female should not be stoned to death* (*la yurjam al-majnūn wal-majnūnatu*). Chapter 22. Translated by Muḥammad Muḥsin Khan. **Vol. 8.**

232. **Muslim,** *al-Ṣaḥīḥ, English Version, Book of Menstruation (Kitāb al-Hāidh),* **Book 003, Number 0718**

233. al-Bukhārī, *al-Ṣaḥīḥ, English Version, Rubbing hand and feet with dust (Tayammum),* **Vol. 1, Book 7, Number 334.**

234. Muslim, *al-Ṣaḥīḥ, English Version, The Book Pertaining to Punishments Prescribed by Islām (Kitāb al Hudūd),* **Book 017, Number 4228.**

235. al-Bukhārī, *al-Ṣaḥīḥ, English Version, Limits and Punishments set by Allāh,* **Vol. 8, Book 81, Number 767.**

236. Muslim, *al- al-Ṣaḥīḥ English Version, The Book Pertaining to the Merits of the Companions (May Allah be pleased with them) of the Holy Prophet (pbuh),* **Book 031, Number 5915. Ibn al-Kathīr,** *al-Bidāyah wa al-Nihāyah,* **Vol. 7, p. 341. al-Muttaqī al Hindī,** *Kanz al-'Ummāl,* **Vol. 13, p. 163. Ibn Mājah,** *al-Sunan,* **Vol. 1, p.58. al-Nasā'ī,** *Khasā'is al-'Alawiyya,* **p. 50. al-Qundūzī al-Ḥanafī,** *Yanābī' al-Mawaddah,* **p. 51. al-Tirmidhī,** *Jāmi' al-Ṣaḥīḥ, Arabic Version,* **Vol. 5, p. 654. al-Ḥākim,** *al-Mustadrak, Imām al-Ḥākim adds that the tradition is authentic based on the criteria of the two Shaykhs (al-Bukhāri and Muslim).* **Vol. 3, p. 150. al-Muḥibb al-Ṭabarī,** *Dakā'ir al-Uqba,* **p. 25.**

237. al-Bukhārī, *al-Ṣaḥīḥ, English Version, Military Expeditions led by the Prophet (pbuh) (al-Maghāzi),* **Vol. 5, Book 59, Number 700.**

238. al-Bukhārī, *al-Ṣaḥīḥ, English Version, Military Expedtions led by the Prophet (pbuh) (al-Maghāzi),* **Vol. 5, Book 59, Number 358.**

239. Ibn Ḥajar al-'Asqalānī, Fath al-Bari, **Chapter on Fitan.**

240. al-Bukhārī, *al-Ṣaḥīḥ, English Version, Sales and Trade,* **Vol. 3, Book 34, Number 333.**

241. Ibn Ḥajar al-'Asqalānī, Fath al-Bari**, Chapter on "Fadhā'il Aswaq."**

242. Muslim, *al-Ṣaḥīḥ,* English Version, *The Book Pertaining to the Merits of the Companions (Allah Be Pleased With Them) of the Holy Prophet (May Peace Be Upon Him) (Kitāb Al-Fadā'il Al-Sahābah), The* *merits of* al-Ḥasan and al-Ḥusayn, (Allāh be pleased with them both), **Book 031, Number 5952.**

243. al-Tirmidhī, *Jāmi' al-Ṣaḥīḥ, English Version,* **Number 5259.**

244. 'Allāmah Shiblī Nu'manī, *Sīrat-i-Nu'manī, Imām Abū Ḥanīfah, English Translation Imām Abū Ḥanīfah, Life and Works by Hādī Ḥusayn,* **Chapter 10, Tradition and Principles of Tradition, pp. 133-134.**

245. 'Allāmah Shiblī Nu'manī, *Sīrat-i-Nu'manī, Imām Abū Ḥanīfah, English Translation Imām Abū Ḥanīfah, Life and Works by Hādī Ḥusayn,* **Chapter 10, Tradition and Principles of Tradition, p. 131.**

246. Abū Da'wūd, *al-Sunan, The Office of the Judge (Kitāb al-Aqdīyah),* **Book 24, Number 3564.**

247. al-Bukhārī, *al-Ṣaḥīḥ, English Version, One fifth of Booty to the cause of Allāh (Khumus).* **Vol. 4, Book 53 Number 406.**

248. al-Bukhārī, *al-Ṣaḥīḥ, English Version, Punishment of Disbelievers at War with Allāh and his Apostle,* **Vol. 8, Book 82, Number 826.**

249. al-Bukhārī, *al-Ṣaḥīḥ, English Version, Praying at Night in Ramadhan (Tarawīh),* **Vol. 3, Book 32, Number 229**. **al-Bukhārī,** *al-Ṣaḥīḥ, English Version, Prayer at Night (Tahajud),* **Vol. 2, Book 21, Number 229.**

250. Mālik ibn Anas, *al-Muwaṭṭā', English Version, Stimulation of the Desire for Prayer in Ramadhan,* **Book 6, Number 6.1.1.**

251. Mālik ibn Anas, *al-Muwaṭṭā', English Version, Stimulation of the Desire for Prayer in Ramadhan, Watching the Night in Prayer,* **Book 6, Number 6.1.2.**

252. al-Bukhārī, *al-Ṣaḥīḥ, English Version, Good Manners and Form (al-Adab),* **Vol. 8, Book 73, Number 134. al-Bukhārī,** *al-Ṣaḥīḥ, English Version, Holding Fast to the Qur'ān and the Sunnah,* **Vol. 9, Book 92, Number 393.**

253. al-Bukhārī, *al-Ṣaḥīḥ, English Version, Prayer at Night (Tahajjud),* **Vol. 2, Book 21, Number 228.**

254. al-Bukhārī, *al-Ṣaḥīḥ, English Version, Prayer at Night (Tahajjud),* **Vol. 2, Book 21, Number 251n.**

255. al-Bukhārī, *al-Ṣaḥīḥ, English Version, Prayer at Night (Tahajjud),* **Vol. 2, Book 21, Number 251r.**

256. Muslim, *al-Ṣaḥīḥ, English Version, The Book of Prayers (Kitāb as-Salāt),* **Book 004, Number 0946.**

257. al-Bukhārī, *al-Ṣaḥīḥ, English Version, Praying at Night in Ramadhan (Tarawīh),* **Vol. 3, Book 32, Number 227**. **Mālik ibn Anas,** *al-Muwaṭṭā', English Version, Prayer in Ramadhan*, **Book 6, Number 6.2.3.**

258. Abū Dāwūd, *al-Sunan, English Version, Detailed injunctions about Witr, (Kitāb as-Salāt),* **Book 8, Number 1424.**

259. al-Hūrr al-Amīlī, *Wasā'il al-Shī'ah,* **Vol. 8, p. 45.**

260. al-Bukhārī, *al-Ṣaḥīḥ, English Version, Pilgrimage (Ḥajj),* **Vol. 2, Book 26, Number 633.**

261. al-Bukhārī, *al-Ṣaḥīḥ, English Version, Pilgrimage (Ḥajj),* **Vol. 2, Book 26, Number 634.**

262. al-Bukhārī, *al-Ṣaḥīḥ, English Version, Pilgrimage (Ḥajj),* **Vol. 2, Book 26, Number 640.**

263. al-Bukhārī, *al-Ṣaḥīḥ, English Version, Shortening the Prayers (at-Taqsīr),* **Vol. 2, Book 20, Number 188.**

264. al-Bukhārī, *al-Ṣaḥīḥ, English Version, Shortening the Prayers (At-Taqsīr),* **Vol. 2, Book 20, Number 189.**

265. al-Bukhārī, *al-Ṣaḥīḥ, English Version, Merits of the Helpers in Madīnah,* **Vol. 5, Book 58, Number 272.**

266. al-Bukhārī, *al-Ṣaḥīḥ, English Version, Pilgrimage (Ḥajj),* **Vol. 2, Book 26, Number 719.**

267. al-Bukhārī, *al-Ṣaḥīḥ, English Version, Shortening the Prayers (At-Taqsīr),* **Vol. 2, Book 20, Number 190.**

268. al-Bukhārī, *al-Ṣaḥīḥ, English Version, Shortening the Prayers (At Taqsīr),* **Vol. 2, Book 20, Number 196.**

269. al-Ṭabarī, *Tafsīr al-Kabīr,* **Vol. 8, p176, under the commentary of Verse 4:24, Number 9034.**

270. Muslim, *al-Ṣaḥīḥ, English Version, The Book of Marriage, (Kitāb al-Nikah),* **Book 008, Number 3246 and Number 3247**. **Muslim,** *al-Ṣaḥīḥ, Arabic Version, 1980 Edition Published in Saudi Arabia, Kitāb al-Nikah, Bāb Nikah al-Mut'a,* **Vol. 2, p. 1022, Number 13.**

271. al-Ṭabarī, *Tafsīr al-Kabīr,* **Vol. 8, p. 178, under the commentary of Verse 4:24, Number 9041. Fakhr al-Dīn al-Rāzī,** *Tafsīr al-Kabīr, Mafātiḥ al-Ghayb, Beirut, 1981,* **Vol. 9 p. 53.**

272. Ibn al-Kathīr, *Tafsīr al-Qur'ān al-Azīm, Beirut 1987,* **Vol. 2 p. 244.**

273. al-Ṭabarī, *Tafsīr al-Kabīr,* **Vol. 8, p. 177, under the commentary of verse 4:24, Numbers 9036, 9037.**

274. Fakhr al-Dīn al-Rāzī, *Tafsīr al-Kabīr,* **Vol. 3, pp. 200, 202, under the commentary of Verse 4:24. Imām al-Tha'labī,** *Tafsīr al-Kabīr,* **under commentary of verse 4:24 of Qur'ān. Imām Aḥmad ibn Ḥanbal,** *al-Musnad, narrated by Imrān ibn al-Qasīr,* **Vol. 4, p. 436.**

275. al-Bukhārī, *al-Ṣaḥīḥ, English Version, Prophetic Commentary of the Qur'ān, Tafsīr of the Prophet (pbuh),* **Vol. 6, Book 60, Number 43.**

276. Muslim, *al-Ṣaḥīḥ, Arabic Version, The Book of Marriage, (Kitāb al-Nikah),* **Book 008, Number 3248.**

277. al-Bukhārī, *al-Ṣaḥīḥ, English Version, Prophetic Commentary of the Qur'ān Tafsīr of the Prophet (pbuh), Wedlock, Marriage (Nikah),* **Vol. 7, Book 62, Number 51.**

278. Muslim, *al-Ṣaḥīḥ, English Version, The Book of Marriage, (Kitāb al-Nikah),* **Book 008, Book 008, Number 3249.**

279. Muslim, *al-Ṣaḥīḥ, English Version, The Book of Marriage, (Kitāb al-Nikah),* **Book 008, Book 008, Number 3250.**

280. Mālik ibn Anas, *al-Muwaṭṭā', Temporary marriage, Number 28.42,* **al-Bayhāqī,** *Sunan al-Kubra,* **Vol. 7, p. 206. Imām Shāfī'ī,** *Kitāb al-Am,* **Vol. 7, p. 219.**

281. Imām Aḥmad ibn Ḥanbal, *al-Musnad,* **Vol. 1, p. 52. Fakhr al-Dīn al-Rāzī,** *Tafsīr al-Kabīr,* **Vol. 3, p. 201 under commentary of Verse 4:24.**

282. Muslim, *al-Ṣaḥīḥ, English Version, The Book of Pil-grimage, (Kitāb al-Ḥajj),* **Book 007, Number 2801. Muslim,** *al-Ṣaḥīḥ, Arabic Version, 1980 Edition Published in Saudi Arabia,* **Vol. 2, p. 885, Number 145.**

283. al-Ṭabarī, *Tārīkh, English Version,* **Vol. 14, pp. 139, 140.**

284. Muslim, *al-Ṣaḥīḥ, English Version, The Book of Marriage, (Kitāb al-Nikah),* **Book 008, Book 008, Number 3265.**

285. Muslim, *al-Ṣaḥīḥ, English Version, The Book of Marriage, (Kitāb al-Nikah),* **Book 008, Number 3251.**

286. Muslim, *al-Ṣaḥīḥ, English Version, The Book of Marriage, (Kitāb al-Nikah),* **Book 008, Number 3257.**

287. al-Bukhārī, *al-Ṣaḥīḥ, English Version, Wedlock Marriage, (Nikah),* **Vol. 7, Book 62, Number 52.**

288. al-Ṭabarī, *Tafsīr al-Kabīr,* **Vol. 8, p178, under commentary of Verse 4:24, Number 9042. al-Hāfiz Jalāl al-Dīn al-Suyūtī,** *al-Durr al-Manthūr,* **Vol. 2, p. 140. al-Qurtubī,** *Tafsīr,* **Vol. 5, p. 130, under commentary of Verse 4:24.**

289. al-Hūrr al-Amīlī, *Wasā'il al-Shī'ah,* **Vol. 14, p. 437, Number 5.**

290. al-Hūrr al-Amīlī, *Wasā'il al-Shī'ah,* **Vol. 14, p. 439 Number 19.**

291. Muslim, *al-Ṣaḥīḥ, English Version, The Book of Marriage, (Kitāb al-Nikah),* **Book 008, Number 3261.**

292. al-Bukhārī, *al-Ṣaḥīḥ, English Version, Virtues and Merits of the Prophet (pbuh) and his Companions,* **Vol. 4, Book 56, Number 821. al-Bukhārī,** *al-Ṣaḥīḥ,English Version, Prophetic Commentary of the Qur'ān, Tafsīr of the Prophet (pbuh),* **Vol. 6, Book 60, Number 494.**

293. al-Bukhārī, *al-Ṣaḥīḥ, English Version, Companions of the Prophet (pbuh),* **Vol. 5, Book 57, Number 101r. al-Bukhārī,** *al-Ṣaḥīḥ,English Version, Companions of the Prophet (pbuh),* **Vol. 5 Book 57 Number 100. al- Ḥākim,** *al-Mustadrak,* **Vol. 3, p. 536.**

294. al-Hūrr al-'Amilī, *Wasā'il al-Shī'ah,* **Vol. 14, p. 478, Number 1.**

295. al-Hūrr al-'Amilī, *Wasā'il al-Shī'ah,* **Vol. 14, p. 484, Number 2.**

296. al-Hūrr al-'Amilī, *Wasā'il al-Shī'ah,* **Vol. 14, p. 488.**

297. al-Hūrr al-'Amilī, *Wasā'il al-Shī'ah,* ***Vol.*** **14, p. 485, Number 1.**

298. al-Bukhārī, *al-Ṣaḥīḥ, English Version, Wedlock Marriage, (Nikah),* **Vol. 7, Book 62, Number 13o. al-Bukhārī,** *al-Ṣaḥīḥ,Arabic Version,* **Vol. 6, p. 11, under Tafsir of verse 5:87 of Qur'ān. Muslim,** *al-Ṣaḥīḥ, English Version, The Book of Marriage, (Kitāb al-Nikah),* **Book 008, Number 3243. Muslim,** *al-Ṣaḥīḥ, Arabic Version, 1980 Edition Pub. in Saudi Arabia, Kitāb al-Nikah Bāb Nikah al-Mūt'a,* **Vol. 2, p. 1022, Number 11.**

299. Mālik ibn Anas, *al-Muwaṭṭā', English Version, The Decree,* **Book 46, Number 46.1.3.**

300. Muslim, *al-Ṣaḥīḥ,English Version, The Book of Prayers, (Kitāb as-Salāt),* **Book 004, Number 1151.**

301. Mālik ibn Anas, *al-Muwaṭṭā', English Version, The Mudabbar,* **Book 41, Number 41.1.11.**

302. Mālik ibn Anas, *al-Muwaṭṭā', English Version, On Men Finding Other Men with Their Wives,* **Book 36, Number 36.19.18.**

303. al-Radhī, *Nahj al-Balāghah, To Mu'āwīya,* **Letter 10.**

304. al-Radhī, *Nahj al-Balāghah, When Imām 'Alī (AS) sent an expedition of 3000 soldiers under Ma'qīl ibn Qays Riyāhī against the Syrians,* **Letter 12.**

305. Adlai Ewing Stevenson (II), A*n American politician and statesman, noted for his skill in debate and oratory. He was twice an unsuccessful candidate for President of the United States. (1952 and 1956).* **Princeton University Library.**

306. al-Bukhārī, *al-Ṣaḥīḥ,English Version, Military Expeditions led by the Prophet (pbuh) (Maghāzi),* **Vol. 5, Book 59, Number 546.**

307. Ibn Abi'l-Ḥadīd, *SharhNahj al-Balāghah,* **Vol. 4, p. 324.**

308. al-Radhī, *Nahj al-Balāghah, A letter to the Egyptians which Imām 'Alī (AS) handed over to Mālik bin Hārith Ashtar to take with him when he was appointed as the Governor of that province,* **Letter 62.**

309. Muslim, *al-Ṣaḥīḥ, English Version, The Book Pertaining to the Turmoil and Portents of the Last Hour, (Kitāb al-Fitan wa Ashrat As-Sa'ah),* **Book 041, Number 6968.**

310. Ibn Sa'd, *al-Tabaqāt (al-Kabīr),* **Vol. 3, p. 257.**

311. Ibn Sa'd, *al-Tabaqāt (al-Kabīr),* **Vol. 3, p. 257.**

312. al-Ḥākim, *al-Mustadrak,* **Vol. 3, p.140.**

313. **Imām Aḥmad ibn Ḥanbal,** *as quoted in Taqrīr wa al-Tahbīr,* **Vol. 3, p. 99.**

314. **al-Dārqutnī,** *as quoted in Līsān al-Mīzān,* **Vol. 2, p. 137.**

315. **Ibn Ḥazm,** *as quoted in al-Baḥr al-Muḥit,* **Vol. 5, p. 528.**

316. **Ibn 'Abd al-Barr,** *as quoted in Jamī' Bayān al-ilm,* **Vol. 2, pp. 90-91.**

317. **Ibn 'Asākir,** *as quoted in Fayd al-Qadīr,* **Vol. 4, p. 76.**

318. **al-Dhaḥabī,** *Mizān al-'I'tidāl,* **Vol. 1, p. 413, Vol. 2, p102, 605.**

319. **Ibn Qayyim al-Jawzīyyah,** *I'lām al-Mūqi 'īn,* **Vol. 2, p. 223.**

320. **Ibn Ḥajar al-'Asqalānī,** *Talkhīs al-Khabīr,* **Vol. 4, pp. 190, 191.**

321. **al-Hāfiz Jalāl al-Dīn al-Suyūtī,** *al-Jāmi' as-Saghīr,* **Vol. 4, p. 76.**

322. **al-Muttaqī al Hindī,** *Kanz al-'Ummāl,* **Vol. 6, p. 133.**

323. **al-Tirmidhī,** *Jāmi' al-Ṣaḥīḥ, Arabic Version,* **Vol. 5 p. 328. al-Tirmidhī,** *Jāmi' al-Ṣaḥīḥ, English Version,* **Number 6143. Ibn al-Athīr,** *Jāmi' al-Usūl,* **Vol. 1, p. 277, Number 65. al- Ṭabarānī,** *al-Mu'jām al-Kabīr,* **Vol. 3, p. 63, Number 2679.**

324. **Muslim,** *al-Ṣaḥīḥ,English Version, The Book of Pilgrimage, (Kitāb al-Ḥajj),* **Book 007 Number 2803.1.**

325. **Abū Dāwūd,** *al-Sunan, English Translation, Knowledge (Kitāb al-Ilm)* **Book 25, Number 3644.**

326. **al-Tirmidhī,** *Jāmi' al-Ṣaḥīḥ, English Version,* **Number 234.**

327. **Muslim,** *al-Ṣaḥīḥ, English Version, The Book of Knowledge, (Kitāb al-Ilm),* **Book 034, Number 6443.**

328. Ibn al-Athīr, *Usd al-Ghābah,* **Vol. 1, pp. 11-12.**

329. Ibn Ḥajar al-'Asqalānī, *al-Isabah,* **Vol. 1, p. 7.**

330. al-Bukhārī, *al-Ṣaḥīḥ, English Version, Holding Fast to the Qur'ān and the Sunnah,* **Vol. 9, Book 92, Number 422.**

331. al-Bukhārī, *al-Ṣaḥīḥ, English Version, To Make the Heart Tender, (Ar-Riqāq),* **Vol. 8, Book 76, Number 578.**

332. al-Bukhārī, *al-Ṣaḥīḥ, English Version, To Make the Heart Tender, (Ar-Riqāq),* **Vol. 8, Book 76, Number 584.**

333. al-Bukhārī, *al-Ṣaḥīḥ, English Version, To Make the Heart Tender, (Ar-Riqāq),* **Vol. 8, Book 76, Number 585.**

334. al-Bukhārī, *al-Ṣaḥīḥ, English Version, To Make the Heart Tender, (Ar-Riqāq),* **Vol. 8, Book 76, Number 586.**

335. al-Bukhārī, *al-Ṣaḥīḥ, English Version, Military Expeditions led by the Prophet (pbuh) (Al-Maghāzi),* **Vol. 5, Book 59, Number 488.**

336. al-Bukhārī, *al-Ṣaḥīḥ,English Version, Times of the Prayers,* **Vol. 1, Book 10, Number 507.**

337. al-Bukhārī, *al-Ṣaḥīḥ,English Version, The Two Festival (Eids),* **Vol. 2, Book 15, Number 76.**

338. al-Bukhārī, *al-Ṣaḥīḥ,English Version, The Two Festival (Eids),* **Vol. 2, Book 15, Number**

339. al-Bukhārī, *al-Ṣaḥīḥ,English Version, The Two Festival (Eids),* **Vol. 2, Book 15, Number**

340. al-Bukhārī, *al-Ṣaḥīḥ,English Version, Virtues of Mad-īnah,* **Vol. 3, Book 30, Number 108.**

341. al-Bukhārī, *al-Ṣaḥīḥ,English Version, Prophetic Commentary of the Qur'ān Tafsīr of the Prophet (pbuh),* **Vol. 6, Book 60, Number 428.**

342. al-Tirmidhī, *Jāmi' al-Ṣaḥīḥ, English Version,* **Number 6005.**

343. Ibn Qutaybah, *al-Imāmah wa al-Siyāsah,* **Vol. 1, p. 12, 14. al-Mas'ūdī,** *Murūj al-Dhahab,* **Vol. 1, p. 441.**

344. Ibn Qutaybah, *al-Imāmah wa al-Siyāsah,* **Vol. 1, p. 12.**

345. al-Ḥākim, ***al-Mustadrak,*** **Vol. 3, pp. 169. al-Mas'ūdī,** *Murūj al-Dhahab,* **Vol. 4, p. 321. Ibn Ḥajar al-Haythamī,** *Majma' al-Zawā'id,* **Vol. 9. p. 107.**

346. Imām Aḥmad ibn Ḥanbal, *al-Musnad,* **Vol. 1, p. 119, Vol. 5, p. 366.**

347. al-Nasā'ī, *Khasā'is al-'Alawiyya,* **pp. 21, 103.**

348. Imām Aḥmad ibn Ḥanbal, *al-Musnad,* **Vol. 4, p. 370.**

349. al-Ya'qūbī, *al-Tārīkh,* **Vol. 2, p. 114.**

350. al-Ṭabarī, *Tārīkh, Arabic Version,* **Vol. 2, p. 84.**

351. al-Hāfiz Jalāl al-Dīn al-Suyūtī, *al-Durr al-Manthūr,* **Vol. 2, p. 133. al-Ḥākim,** *al-Mustadrak,* **Vol. 2, p.177. al-Dhaḥabī,** *Takhlīs al-Mustadrak.* **al-Zamakhsharī,** *al-Kashshāf,* **Vol. 1, p. 357. Bayhaqī,** *al-Sunan,* **Vol. 7, p. 233.**

352. Abul 'Ala Maudūdī, *Khilāfat Mulukīyat,* **pp. 165-166. al-Ṭabarī,** *Tārīkh, English Version, The Events of Year 51 AH,* **Vol. 8, p. 154. Ibn al-Athir,** *Tārīkh,* **Vol. 3, p. 242. Ibn al-Kathīr,** *al-Bidāyah wa al-Nihāyah,* **Vol. 3, p. 242, Vol. 8, p. 130 who mentions the first crime as: 'His fighting 'Alī.'**

353. al-Ṭabarī, *Tārīkh, Arabic Version,* **Vol. 6, p. 153.**

354. al-Ṭabarī, *Tārīkh, Arabic Version,* **Vol. 6, p.156.**

355. al-Ṭabarī, *Tārīkh, Arabic Version,* **Vol. 4, pp. 190-206. Ibn al-Kathīr,** *al-Bidāyah wa al-Nihāyah,* **Vol. 3, pp. 234-242, Vol. 8, pp. 50-55.**

356. al-Bukhārī, *al-Ṣaḥīḥ, English Version, Holding Fast to the Qur'ān and the Sunnah,* **Vol. 9, Book 92, Number 468. Imām Aḥmad ibn Ḥanbal,** *al-Musnad,* **Vol. 1, p. 336.**

357. al-Bukhārī, *al-Ṣaḥīḥ, English Version, Military Expeditions led by the Prophet (pbuh), (al-Maghāzi),* **Vol. 5, Book 59, Number 717.**

358. Ibn Sa'd, *al-Tabaqāt (al-Kabīr),* **Vol. 2, p. 243.**

359. al-Bukhārī, *al-Ṣaḥīḥ, English Version, Fighting for the cause of Allāh (Jihād),* **Vol. 4, Book 52, Number 288.**

360. al-Bukhārī, *al-Ṣaḥīḥ, English Version, Military Expeditions led by the Prophet (pbuh) (al-Maghāzi),* **Vol. 5, Book 59, Number 716.**

361. al-Hāfiz Jalāl al-Dīn al-Suyūtī, *al-Durr al-Manthūr, Cairo,* **Vol. 6, p. 379. al-Ṭabarī,** *Tafsīr Jāmi' al-Bayān, Cairo,* **Vol. 33, p.146. Ibn Ḥājar al-Haythamī,** *al-Sawā'iq al-Muhriqah, Cairo,* **Ch. 11, Section 1, pp. 246, 247.**

362. Ibn Ḥājar al-Haythamī, *Majma' al-Zawā'id,* **Vol. 9, Number 14168. Ibn al-Athīr,** *al-Kāmil, al-Nihāya fī ghārib al-Ḥadīth, Beirut, 1399,* **Vol. 4 p.106. al-Ṭabarānī,** *Mu'jām al-Kabīr,* **Vol. 1, p. 319.**

363. Imām Aḥmad ibn Ḥanbal, *Fadā'il al-Sahāba, Beirut,* **Vol. 2, p. 655. al-Khatīb al-Baghdādī,** *Tārīkh Baghdād, Beirut,* **Vol. 12, p. 289. al-Ṭabarānī,** *Mu'jām al-Kabīr,* **Vol. 1 p. 319. Ibn Ḥājar al-Haythamī,** *Majma' al-Zawā'id,* **Vol. 10, pp. 21, 22. Ibn Ḥājar al-Haythamī,** *al-Sawā'iq al-Muhriqah, Cairo,* **Ch. 11, Section 1, p. 247.**

364. al-Mufīd, *al-Amālī, English Translation by Mulla Asgharali M.M.Jaffer, Virtues of a Shī'ah,* **pp.186-187.**

365. Bāqir al-Majlisī, *Biḥār al-Anwār,* **Vol. 93, p. 162.**

366. al-Mufīd, *Kitāb al-Irshād, Tehran, 1377,* **p. 250. Bāqir al-Majlisī,** *Biḥār al-Anwār,* **Vol. 46, p. 288.**

367. See al-Ṭabarī, *Tārīkh, Arabic Version,* **Vol. 4, p. 340.**

368. Ibn Mājah, *al-Sunan,* **Vol. 1, p. 53 Number 149.**

369. al-Tirmidhī, *Jāmi' al-Ṣaḥīḥ, Arabic Version,* **Vol. 5, Number 3884.**

370. al-Bukhārī, *al-Ṣaḥīḥ, English Version, Companions (May Allāh be pleased with them) of the Prophet (pbuh),* **Vol. 5, Book 57, Number 116.**

371. Ibn al-Athīr, *al-Kāmil,* **pp. 32-35. Ibn Abi'l-Ḥadīd,** *Sharḥ Nahj al-Balāghah,* **Vol. 1 p. 63-65, as taken from al-Tabarī's Tārīkh.**

372. See al-Ṭabarī, *Tārīkh, Arabic Version,* **Vol. 4, p. 283, 341.**

373. See al-Ṭabarī, *Tārīkh, Arabic Version,* **Vol. 4, p. 284.**

374. Sayyid Murtada al-'Askarī, *'Abdullāh ibn Sa'ba,* **pp. 27-28.**

375. See al-Balāthorī, *Ansāb al-Ashraf,* **Vol. 4, p. 28, Muḥammad Jawād Chirrī,** *The Brother of the Prophet Muḥammad (The Imām 'Alī)* **Vol. 1, p. 254.**

376. Ibn al-Athīr, *al-Kāmil,* **Vol. 3, p.46**

377. Ibn Hishām, *al-Sīrah al-Nabawīyyah, Biography of the Prophet,* **Vol. 2, p. 296.**

378. Ibn al-Athīr, *al-Kāmil,* **Vol. 3, p. 40.**

379. Ibn al-Athīr, *al-Kāmil,* **Vol. 3, p. 53.**

380. al-Ṭabarī, *Tārīkh, English Version,* **Vol. 15, p. 184.**

381. al-Ṭabarī, *Tārīkh, English Version,* **Vol. 15, pp. 199-200.**

382. al-Ṭabarī, *Tārīkh, English Version,* **Vol. 15, p. 235.**

383. al-Ṭabarī, *Tārīkh, English Version,* **Vol. 15, p. 200.**

384. al-Ṭabarī, *Tārīkh, English Version,* **Vol. 15, pp. 141-144.**

385. al-Ṭabarī, *Tārīkh, English Version,* **Vol. 15, p. 173.**

386. al-Ṭabarī, *Tārīkh, English Version,* **Vol. 15, pp.176-179.**

387. al-Ṭabarī, *Tārīkh, English Version,* **Vol. 15, p. 198.**

388. al-Ṭabarī, *Tārīkh, Arabic Version,* **Vol. 15, pp. 246-250.**

389. Ṭaha Ḥusayn, *al-Fitnat al-Kubrā,* **Vol. 2, p. 90.**

390. al-Kulaynī, *al-Kāfī, English Version, translated by Muḥa-mmad Sarwar. The Book of Intelligence and Ignorance.* **Chapter 1, H 4, Ch. 1, h 4.**

391. al-Tirmidhī, *Jāmi' al-Ṣaḥīḥ, English Version,* **Number 6093.**

392. *Nahj al-Balāghah,* **117, p. 594.**

393. Imām Khomeini, Last will, The most recent edition of the testament has been published by the Institute for Compilation and Publication of the Works of Imām Khomeini, which in addition to complete text of the Will, and complete photocopy of the original Farsi manuscript some explanations about the history of the writing of the Will and a review of its contents, together with topical classification of the contents and guide indices are printed under the title, **A Review of the Political-Divine Testament by subject matters.**

394. al-Ḥākim, *al-Mustadrak, Imām Hakim add that this tradition is authentic, narrated by Abū Dharr,* **Vol. 2, p. 343, Vol. 3, pp. 150, 151**. **Imām Aḥmad ibn Ḥanbal,** *Fadā'il al-Sahāba,* **Vol. 2, p. 786. Fakhr al-Dīn al-Rāzī,** *Tafsīr al-Kabīr,* **Part 27, p167 under the commentary of verse 42:23. al-Ṭabarānī,** *Mu'jām al-Kabīr,* **Vol. 3, pp. 37, 38. al-Ṭabarānī,** *as-Saghīr,* **Vol. 2, p. 22.**

395. 'Allāmah Shiblī Nu'manī, *Sīrat-i-Nu'manī, English Translation, Imām Abū Ḥanīfah, Life and Works by Hādī Ḥusayn.* **Chapter 2, Maturity, Education and Teachers, p. 24.**

396. Ibn Taymīyyah, *The Book of Rawassul wa Wasīlah,* **p. 52.**

Bibliography

'Abdullāh ibn Sa'ba, al-'Allāmah al-Sayyid Murtada, AL-'ASKARĪ.

Ansāb al-Ashraf, Aḥmad b. Yaḥyā b. Jābir, AL-BALĀTHORĪ.

Asbāb al-Nuzūl, Abū al-Ḥasan 'Alī b. Muḥammad al-Shāfi'ī, AL-WĀḤIDĪ

al-Baḥr al-Muḥit, IBN ḤAZM.

al-Bidāyah wa al-Nihāyah, Abū al-Fidā', Ismā'īl b. 'Umar al-Dimashqī al-Shāf'i'ī, IBN KATHĪR.

Biḥār al-Anwār, al-'Allāmah Muḥammad Bāqir, AL-MAJLISĪ.

Dakā'ir al-Uqba, al-Muḥibb al-Dīn, Abū 'l-'Abbās, Aḥmad b. 'Abdillāh al-Shīfi'ī, AL-MUḤIBB AL- ṬABARĪ.

al-Durar al-Kāminah, Shihāb al-Dīn, Abū al-Fadhl, Aḥmad b. 'Alī al-Shafi'ī, IBN ḤAJAR AL-'ASQALĀNĪ.

al-Durr al-Manthūr, Jalāl al-Dīn, 'Abd al-Raḥmān b. Abī Bakr b. Muḥammad al-Shāfi'ī, AL-SUYŪTĪ.

Farā'id al-Simṭayn, Abū Isḥāq, Ibrahīm b. Muḥammad al-Juwaynī, ḤAMAWĪNĪ.

al-Fusūl al-Muhimmah (fī Ma'rifat al-'Aimmah), Nūr al-Dīn al-Mālikī, IBN AL-SABBĀGH.

Fath al-Barī, Shihāb al-Dīn, Abū al-Fadhl, Aḥmad b. 'Alī al-Shafi'ī, IBN ḤAJAR AL-'ASQALĀNĪ.

Fayd al-Qadīr, Abū al-Qāsim, 'Alī b. al-Ḥasan b. Hibatillāh al-Dimashqī, al-Shāfi'ī, Ibn ASĀKIR.

al-Fitnat al-Kubrā, Dr. TAHA ḤUSAYN.

The Life of Muḥammad, HAYKAL.

Hilyat al-Awliyā', Abū Nu'aym, AL-ISFAHĀNĪ.

History of Damascus, Abū al-Qāsim, 'Alī b. al-Ḥasan b Hibatillāh al-Dimashqī, al-Shāfi'ī, Ibn ASĀKIR.

Ihya al-Ulūm, AL-GHAZĀLĪ.

I'lam al-Muqi'īn, Shams al-Dīn Muḥammad b. Abī Bakr ibn Qayyim, AL-JAWZĪYYAH.

al-Imāmah wa al-Siyāsah, Abū Muḥammad, 'Abdullāh b. Muslim al-Dīnwarī, IBN QUTAYBAH.

al-Isabah, Shihāb al-Dīn, Abū al-Fadl, Aḥmad b. 'Alī al-Shafi'ī, IBN ḤAJAR AL-'ASQALĀNĪ.

al-Itqān (fī 'Ulūm al-Qur'ān), Jalāl al-Dīn, 'Abd al-Raḥmān b. Abī Bakr b. Muḥammad al-Shāfi'ī, AL-SUYŪTĪ.

Jamī' Bayān al-ilm, Abū 'Ūmar, Yūsuf b, 'Abdillāh al-Qurtubī al-Mālikī, IBN 'ABD AL-BARR.

Jāmi' al-Kabīr, Jalāl al-Dīn, 'Abd al-Raḥmān b. Abī Bakr b. Muḥammad al-Shāfi'ī, AL-SUYUTĪ.

al-Jāmi' as-Saghīr, Jalāl al-Dīn, 'Abd al-Raḥmān b. Abī Bakr b. Muḥammad al-Shāfi'ī, AL-SUYUTĪ.

Jāmi' al-Ṣaḥīḥ, Abū 'Īsā, Muḥammad b. 'Īsā al-Sulamī, AL-TIRMIDHĪ.

Jāmi' al-Usūl, Abū al-Sa'ādāt Mubārak b. Muḥammad al-Jazarī, IBN Al-ATHĪR.

al-Kāfī, Abū Ja'far, Muḥammad b. Ya'qūb al-Rāzī, AL-KULAYNĪ.

al-Kamīl (fī al-Tārīkh), Abū al- Ḥasan, 'Izz al-Dīn b. Muḥammad al-Jazarī al-Shāfi'ī, IBN Al-ATHĪR.

Kanz al-'Ummal, 'Alā' al-Dīn, 'Alī b. Husām al-Dīn, AL-MUTTAQĪ AL-HINDĪ.

al-Kashshāf, Abū al-Qāsim, Jārullah, Maḥmūd b. 'Umar b. Muḥammad al-Mu'tazilī al- Ḥanafī, AL-ZAMAKHSHARĪ.

Khasā'is al-'Alawiyya, Abū 'Abd al-Raḥmān, Aḥmad b. 'Alī al-Shāfi'ī, AL-NASĀ'Ī.

Khilāfat Mulukīyat, ABUL 'ALA MAUDŪDĪ.

Līsān al-Mīzān, AL-DARQUTNĪ.

Manāqib 'Alī ibn Abī Tālib, Alī b. Muḥammad, Abū al-Ḥasan al-Tayyib al-Jullabi al-Shāfī', IBN MAGHAZILĪ

Majma' al-Zawā'id, Nūr al-Dīn, Abū Bakr, 'Alī b. Abū Bakr b. Sulaymān al-Misrī al-Shāfi'ī, AL-HAYTHAMĪ.

Maqtalu'l Ḥusayn, SAYYID B. ṬA'ŪS.

Manāqib, ('Alī b. Abī Tālib), Abū Mu'ayyad, al-Muwaffaq b. Aḥmad al-Ḥanafī, AL-KHATĪB AL-KHWARAZMĪ.

Minhāj al-Wusūl, NAWWĀB SIDDĪQ ḤASAN KHAN.

Mizān al-'I'tidāl fī Naqad al-Rijāl, Shams al-Dīn, Abū 'Abdillāh, Muḥammad b. Aḥmad b. 'Uthmān al-Dimashq, AL-DHAHABĪ.

al-Mizān fī Tafsīr al-Qur'ān, al-Sayyid Muḥammad Ḥusayn, AL-'ALLĀMAH AL- ṬABAṬABA'Ī

Mu'jām al-Kabīr, al-Hāfiz Abī al-Qāsim Sulaymān ibn Aḥmad, AL-ṬABARĀNĪ.

Muntakhābul Athār, LUTFU'LLAH SĀFĪ GULPAYGĀNĪ.

Murūj al-Dhahab, 'Alī b. al-Ḥusayn, AL-MAS'ŪDĪ.

al-Musnad, Abū 'Abdillāh, Aḥmad b. Muḥammad, IBN ḤANBAL.

al-Mustadrak 'alā as-Ṣaḥīḥayn, Abū 'Abdillāh, Ibn al-Bayyi', Muḥammad b. 'Abdillāh al-Naysābūri al-Shāfi'ī, AL-ḤĀKIM.

al-Muwaṭṭā', Abū 'Abdillāh al-Asbahī al-Madanī, MĀLIK IBN ANAS.

Nahj al-Balāghah, al-Sharīf, Abū al-Ḥasan, Muḥammad b. al-Ḥusayn al-Mūsawī, AL-RADHĪ.

al-Riyād al-Nadira, al-Muḥibb al-Dīn, Abū 'l-'Abbās, Aḥmad b. 'Abdillāh al-Shīfi'ī, AL-MUḤIBB AL-ṬABARĪ.

al-Saghīr, lil-Hāfiz Abī al-Qāsim Sulaymān ibn Aḥmad, AL-ṬABARĀNĪ.

al-Ṣaḥīḥ, Abū 'Abdillāh, Muḥammad b, Ismā'īl, AL-BUKHĀRĪ.

al-Ṣaḥīḥ, Abū al-Ḥusayn, Muslim b. al-Ḥajjāj al-Naysābūrī, MUSLIM.

al-Sawā'iq al-Muhriqah, Abū al-'Abbās, Aḥmad b.Muḥammad al-Makkī al-Shāfi'ī, IBN ḤAJAR Al-HAYTHAMĪ.

Sharh Nahj al-Balāghah, IBN ABĪ AL-HADĪD.

al-Sīrah al-Ḥalabiyyah (Insān al-'Uyūn fī al-Amīn al-Ma'mūn), Nūr al-Dīn al-Shāfi'ī, AL-ḤALABĪ.

al-Sīrah al-Nabawīyyah, Abū Muḥammad, 'Abd al-Mālik b. Hishām al-Bakrī, IBN HISHĀM.

Sīrat-i-Nu'manī, 'ALLĀMAH SHIBLĪ NU'MANĪ.

al-Sunan, Sulaymān b. al-Ash'ath al-Azdī, al-Sijistānī, ABŪ DĀWŪD.

al-Sunan, Abū 'Abdillāh, Muḥammad b. Yazīd al-Qazwīnī, IBN MĀJAH.

al-Sunan al-Kubrā, Abū Bakr, Aḥmad b. Ḥusayn al-Naysābūrī al-Shāfi'ī, AL-BAYHAQĪ.

al-Tabaqāt (al-Kabīr), Abū 'Abdillāh, Muḥammad b. Sa'd al-Baghdādī, IBN SA'D.

Tadhkirat al-Huffaz, Shams al-Dīn, Abū 'Abdillāh, Muḥammad b. Aḥmad b. 'Uthmān al-Dimashq, AL-DHAHABĪ.

Tadhkīrat Khwāss al-'Ummah, Shams al-Dīn Yūsuf b. Qazghalī al-Ḥanafī, SIBT B. AL-JAWZĪ.

al-Tafsīr, AL-BAIDHAWĪ.

al-Tafsīr (al-Kabīr), Abū Isḥāq, Aḥmad b. Muḥammad b. Ibrahīm, AL-THA'LABĪ.

al-Tafsīr (Jāmi' al-Bayān fī Tafsīr al-Qur'ān,), Ibn Jarīr, Muḥammad, AL-ṬABARĪ.

al-Tafsīr al-Kabīr (Mafātih al-Ghayb), Fakhr al-Dīn, Muḥammad b. 'Umar al-Shāfi'ī, AL-RĀZĪ.

Tafsīr ibn Kathīr, Abū al-Fidā', Ismā'īl b. 'Umar al-Dimashqī al-Shāf'i'ī, IBN KATHĪR.

Tahdhīb al-Tahdhīb, IBN ḤAJAR AL-'ASQALĀNĪ.

Talkhīs al-Khabīr, Shihāb al-Dīn, Abū al-Fadhl, Aḥmad b. 'Alī al-Shafi'ī, IBN ḤAJAR AL-'ASQALĀNĪ.

al-Tārīkh, Ibn Wādih, Aḥmad b Ishāq, Al-YA'QŪBĪ.

Tārikh Baghdād, Abū Bakr, Aḥmad b. 'Alī al-Shāfi'ī, AL-KHATĪB AL-BAGHDĀDĪ.

al-Tārīkh al-Kabīr, Abū al-Qāsim, 'Alī b. b. al-Ḥasan b Hibatillāh al-Dimashqī, al-Shāfi'ī, Ibn ASĀKIR.

Tārīkh, (al Umam wa al-Mulūk), Ibn Jarīr Muḥammad, AL-ṬABARĪ.

Tārīkh al-Khulafah, Abū Muḥammad, 'Abdullāh b. Muslim al-Dīnwarī, IBN QUTAYBAH.

Tārīkh al-Khulafah, Jalāl al-Dīn, 'Abd al-Raḥmān b. Abī Bakr b. Muḥammad al-Shāfi'ī, AL-SUYŪTĪ.

Taqrīr wa al-Taḥbīr, Abū 'Abdillāh, Aḥmad b. Muḥammad, IBN ḤANBAL.

The Lantern of the Path, IMĀM JA'FAR AS-SADIQ (AS).

The Book of Rawassul wa Wasīlah, Aḥmad b. 'Abd al-Halīm b 'Abd al-Salām b. Abdullāh b. Abū Qāsim, IBN TAYMĪYYAH.

Ra's al-Ḥusayn, Aḥmad b. 'Abd al-Halīm b 'Abd al-Salām b. Abdullāh b. Abū Qāsim, IBN TAIMĪYYAH.

Usd al-Ghābah, Abū al-Ḥasan, 'Izz al-Dīn b. Muḥammad al-Jazarī al-Shāfi'ī, IBN Al-ATHĪR.

Ulūm al-Aḥadīth , AL-HĀFIDH IBN AL-SALĀH.

Wasā'il al-Shī'ah, AL-HŪRR AL-'AMILĪ.

Yanābī' al-Mawaddah, al-Sayyid Sulaymān b. Ibrahīm b. Muḥammad al-Ḥanafī, AL-QUNDŪZĪ.

Index of Names

Subject Index